QA 76.8 .M67 L48 1978
Leventhal, Lance A., 1945-
6800 assembly language programming

6800
ASSEMBLY LANGUAGE PROGRAMMING

Lance A. Leventhal

Osborne & Associates, Inc.
Berkeley, California

Copyright © 1978 by Adam Osborne & Associates, Incorporated.

All rights reserved. Printed in the United States of America. No part of this publication may be reproduced, stored in any retrieval system, or transmitted in any form or by any means, electronic, mechanical, photocopying, recording or otherwise, without the prior written permission of the publishers.

Published by Adam Osborne & Associates, Incorporated
P.O. Box 2036, Berkeley, California 94702

Portions of Chapter 3 have been reprinted from Adam Osborne & Associates, Incorporated, 6800 Programming for Logic Design with the permission and consent of Adam Osborne & Associates, Incorporated.

ISBN 0-931988-12-8

DISTRIBUTORS OF OSBORNE & ASSOCIATES INC. PUBLICATIONS

For information on translations and book distributors outside of the United States of America, please write:

Adam Osborne & Associates, Inc.
P.O. Box 2036
Berkeley, California 94702
United States of America
(415) 548-2805
TWX 910-366-7277

Cover Design by K.L.T. van Genderen

ACKNOWLEDGMENTS

The author would like to acknowledge the following people:

Mr. William Tester of Grossmont College, who is responsible for the support which made this book possible; Mr. Colin Walsh of Grossmont College, who helped throughout with the design and development of the programming examples; Mr. Curt Ingraham and Mr. Pat McGuire of Osborne & Associates, who made many editorial corrections; Mrs. Teddy Ferguson, who typed the original problem assignments; Mr. Stanley Rogers of the Society for Computer Simulation, who quietly but convincingly suggested many improvements in the author's writing style; his wife Donna, for her patience and understanding throughout the writing of this book; Mr. Victor Wintriss and Ms. Patti Neumann of Electronic Product Associates; faculty members, students, and staff of Southwestern College, including Mr. Tim Mathis, Mr. Joseph Stapczynski, Mr. Bill Sheets, Mr. Charles Matthews, Mr. Robert Schulz, Mr. Buddy Kelley, Mr. Juan Alcalde, Mr. Ray Smith, and Mr. Peter Young.

Others who provided assistance and suggestions were Mr. Jeffrey Haight, Prof. Nicholas Panos, Mr. David Bulman, Mrs. Kati Bulman, Mr. Bernard Laffreniere, Mr. Charles Robe, Mr. Michael Viehman, Mr. Richard Evans, Mr. Frederick Lepow and Mr. William Long. Other students and colleagues also helped to keep the author on the right track.

The author, of course, bears responsibility for any remaining errors, misconceptions and misinterpretations.

This book is dedicated to my wife, Donna, and my daughter, Amanda Catherine.

TABLE OF CONTENTS

CHAPTER		PAGE
1	INTRODUCTION TO ASSEMBLY LANGUAGE PROGRAMMING	1-1
	HOW THIS BOOK HAS BEEN PRINTED	1-1
	THE MEANING OF INSTRUCTIONS	1-1
	A COMPUTER PROGRAM	1-1
	THE PROGRAMMING PROBLEM	1-2
	USING OCTAL OR HEXADECIMAL	1-3
	INSTRUCTION CODE MNEMONICS	1-4
	THE ASSEMBLER PROGRAM	1-5
	ADDITIONAL FEATURES OF ASSEMBLERS	1-6
	DISADVANTAGES OF ASSEMBLY LANGUAGE	1-6
	HIGH-LEVEL LANGUAGES	1-7
	ADVANTAGES OF HIGH-LEVEL LANGUAGES	1-7
	DISADVANTAGES OF HIGH-LEVEL LANGUAGES	1-8
	HIGH-LEVEL LANGUAGES FOR MICROPROCESSORS	1-9
	WHICH LEVEL SHOULD YOU USE?	1-11
	HOW ABOUT THE FUTURE?	1-12
	WHY THIS BOOK?	1-12
2	ASSEMBLERS	2-1
	FEATURES OF ASSEMBLERS	2-1
	ASSEMBLER INSTRUCTIONS	2-1
	LABELS	2-2
	ASSEMBLER MNEMONICS	2-4
	PSEUDO-OPERATIONS	2-4
	THE DATA PSEUDO-OPERATION	2-5
	THE EQUATE (or DEFINE) PSEUDO-OPERATION	2-6
	THE ORIGIN PSEUDO-OPERATION	2-7
	THE RESERVE PSEUDO-OPERATION	2-7
	HOUSEKEEPING PSEUDO-OPERATIONS	2-8
	LABELS WITH PSEUDO-OPERATIONS	2-9
	ADDRESSES AND THE OPERAND FIELD	2-9
	CONDITIONAL ASSEMBLY	2-11
	MACROS	2-11
	COMMENTS	2-13
	TYPES OF ASSEMBLERS	2-14
	ERRORS	2-15
	LOADERS	2-15
3	THE 6800 ASSEMBLY LANGUAGE INSTRUCTION SET	3-1
	CPU REGISTERS AND STATUS FLAGS	3-1
	6800 MEMORY ADDRESSING MODES	3-5
	MEMORY — IMMEDIATE	3-5
	MEMORY — DIRECT	3-7
	MEMORY — INDEXED	3-7
	MEMORY — EXTENDED	3-9
	INHERENT	3-10
	RELATIVE	3-10
	ACCUMULATOR	3-10
	ABBREVIATIONS	3-11
	INSTRUCTION OBJECT CODES	3-12
	INSTRUCTION EXECUTION TIMES AND CODES	3-12

TABLE OF CONTENTS (Continued)

CHAPTER			PAGE
3 (Cont.)	ABA	— ADD ACCUMULATOR B TO ACCUMULATOR A	3-25
	ADC	— ADD MEMORY, WITH CARRY, TO ACCUMULATOR A OR B	3-26
	ADD	— ADD MEMORY TO ACCUMULATOR	3-30
	AND	— AND MEMORY WITH ACCUMULATOR	3-30
	ASL	— SHIFT ACCUMULATOR OR MEMORY BYTE LEFT	3-32
	ASR	— SHIFT ACCUMULATOR OR MEMORY BYTE RIGHT	3-34
	BCC	— BRANCH IF CARRY CLEAR	3-35
	BCS	— BRANCH IF CARRY SET	3-36
	BEQ	— BRANCH IF EQUAL	3-36
	BGE	— BRANCH IF GREATER THAN OR EQUAL TO ZERO	3-36
	BGT	— BRANCH IF GREATER THAN ZERO	3-37
	BHI	— BRANCH IF HIGHER	3-37
	BIT	— BIT TEST	3-38
	BLE	— BRANCH IF LESS THAN OR EQUAL TO ZERO	3-39
	BLS	— BRANCH IF LOWER OR SAME	3-39
	BLT	— BRANCH IF LESS THAN ZERO	3-39
	BMI	— BRANCH IF MINUS	3-40
	BNE	— BRANCH IF NOT EQUAL	3-40
	BPL	— BRANCH IF PLUS	3-41
	BRA	— BRANCH TO THE INSTRUCTION IDENTIFIED IN THE OPERAND	3-41
	BSR	— BRANCH TO THE SUBROUTINE IDENTIFIED IN THE OPERAND	3-42
	BVC	— BRANCH IF OVERFLOW CLEAR	3-42
	BVS	— BRANCH IF OVERFLOW SET	3-43
	CBA	— COMPARE ACCUMULATORS	3-43
	CLC	— CLEAR CARRY	3-44
	CLI	— CLEAR INTERRUPT MASK	3-45
	CLR	— CLEAR ACCUMULATOR OR MEMORY	3-45
	CLV	— CLEAR OVERFLOW	3-46
	CMP	— COMPARE ACCUMULATOR WITH MEMORY	3-47
	COM	— COMPLEMENT ACCUMULATOR WITH MEMORY	3-48
	CPX	— COMPARE INDEX REGISTER	3-49
	DAA	— DECIMAL ADJUST ACCUMULATOR	3-51
	DEC	— DECREMENT ACCUMULATOR OR MEMORY	3-52
	DES	— DECREMENT STACK POINTER	3-54
	DEX	— DECREMENT INDEX REGISTER	3-54
	EOR	— EXCLUSIVE-OR ACCUMULATOR WITH MEMORY	3-55
	INC	— INCREMENT ACCUMULATOR OR MEMORY	3-56
	INS	— INCREMENT STACK POINTER	3-57
	INX	— INCREMENT INDEX REGISTER	3-58
	JMP	— JUMP VIA INDEXED OR EXTENDED ADDRESSING	3-59
	JSR	— JUMP TO SUBROUTINE USING INDEXED OR EXTENDED ADDRESSING	3-60
	LDA	— LOAD ACCUMULATOR FROM MEMORY	3-61
	LDS	— LOAD STACK POINTER	3-62
	LDX	— LOAD INDEX REGISTER	3-63
	LSR	— LOGICAL RIGHT SHIFT OF ACCUMULATOR OR MEMORY	3-64
	NEG	— NEGATE ACCUMULATOR OR MEMORY	3-66
	NOP	— NO OPERATION	3-67

TABLE OF CONTENTS

CHAPTER			PAGE
3 (Cont.)	ORA	— OR ACCUMULATOR WITH MEMORY	3-68
	PSH	— PUSH ACCUMULATOR ONTO STACK	3-69
	PUL	— PULL DATA FROM STACK	3-70
	ROL	— ROTATE ACCUMULATOR OR MEMORY LEFT THROUGH CARRY	3-71
	ROR	— ROTATE ACCUMULATOR OR MEMORY RIGHT THROUGH CARRY	3-73
	RTI	— RETURN FROM INTERRUPT	3-75
	RTS	— RETURN FROM SUBROUTINE	3-76
	SBA	— SUBTRACT ACCUMULATORS	3-76
	SBC	— SUBTRACT MEMORY FROM ACCUMULATOR WITH BORROW	3-77
	SEC	— SET CARRY	3-78
	SEI	— SET INTERRUPT MASK	3-79
	SEV	— SET OVERFLOW STATUS	3-79
	STA	— STORE ACCUMULATOR IN MEMORY	3-80
	STS	— STORE STACK POINTER	3-81
	STX	— STORE INDEX REGISTER	3-82
	SUB	— SUBTRACT MEMORY FROM ACCUMULATOR	3-83
	SWI	— SOFTWARE INTERRUPT	3-84
	TAB	— MOVE FROM ACCUMULATOR A TO ACCUMULATOR B	3-85
	TAP	— MOVE FROM ACCUMULATOR A TO CCR	3-85
	TBA	— MOVE FROM ACCUMULATOR B TO ACCUMULATOR A	3-86
	TPA	— MOVE CCR TO ACCUMULATOR A	3-87
	TST	— TEST THE CONTENTS OF ACCUMULATOR OR MEMORY	3-88
	TSX	— MOVE FROM STACK POINTER TO INDEX REGISTER	3-89
	TXS	— MOVE FROM INDEX REGISTER TO STACK POINTER	3-90
	WAI	— WAIT FOR INTERRUPT	3-91
	MOTOROLA 6800 ASSEMBLER CONVENTIONS		3-92
	ASSEMBLER FIELD STRUCTURE		3-92
	LABELS		3-92
	PSEUDO-OPERATIONS		3-92
	LABELS WITH PSEUDO-OPERATIONS		3-93
	ADDRESSES		3-94
	OTHER ASSEMBLER FEATURES		3-94
4	SIMPLE PROGRAMS		4-1
	GENERAL FORMAT OF EXAMPLES		4-1
	PROGRAM EXAMPLES		4-2
	ONES COMPLEMENT		4-2
	8-BIT ADDITION		4-3
	SHIFT LEFT ONE BIT		4-4
	MASK OFF MOST SIGNIFICANT FOUR BITS		4-4
	CLEAR A MEMORY LOCATION		4-5
	WORD DISASSEMBLY		4-5
	FIND THE LARGER OF TWO NUMBERS		4-6

TABLE OF CONTENTS (Continued)

CHAPTER			PAGE
4 (Cont.)		16-BIT ADDITION	4-7
		TABLE OF SQUARES	4-8
		16-BIT ONES COMPLEMENT	4-10
	PROBLEMS		
	1)	TWOS COMPLEMENT	4-11
	2)	8-BIT SUBTRACTION	4-11
	3)	SHIFT LEFT TWO BITS	4-11
	4)	MASK OFF LEAST SIGNIFICANT FOUR BITS	4-11
	5)	SET A MEMORY LOCATION TO ALL ONES	4-11
	6)	WORD ASSEMBLY	4-11
	7)	FIND SMALLER OF TWO NUMBERS	4-12
	8)	24-BIT ADDITION	4-12
	9)	SUM OF SQUARES	4-12
	10)	16-BIT TWOS COMPLEMENT	4-13
5		SIMPLE PROGRAM LOOPS	5-1
	EXAMPLES		5-3
		SUM OF DATA	5-3
		16-BIT SUM OF DATA	5-6
		NUMBER OF NEGATIVE ELEMENTS	5-8
		FIND MAXIMUM	5-10
		JUSTIFY A BINARY FRACTION	5-13
	PROBLEMS		5-15
	1)	CHECKSUM OF DATA	5-15
	2)	SUM OF 16-BIT DATA	5-15
	3)	NUMBER OF ZERO, POSITIVE, AND NEGATIVE NUMBERS	5-16
	4)	FIND MINIMUM	5-16
	5)	COUNT 1 BITS	5-16
6		CHARACTER-CODED DATA	6-1
	EXAMPLES		6-2
		LENGTH OF A STRING OF CHARACTERS	6-2
		FIND FIRST NON-BLANK CHARACTER	6-5
		REPLACE LEADING ZEROS WITH BLANKS	6-8
		ADD EVEN PARITY TO ASCII CHARACTERS	6-10
		PATTERN MATCH	6-13
	PROBLEMS		6-15
	1)	LENGTH OF A TELETYPEWRITER MESSAGE	6-15
	2)	FIND LAST NON-BLANK CHARACTER	6-16
	3)	TRUNCATE DECIMAL STRING TO INTEGER FORM	6-16
	4)	CHECK EVEN PARITY IN ASCII CHARACTERS	6-17
	5)	STRING COMPARISON	6-17
7		CODE CONVERSION	7-1
	EXAMPLES		7-1
		HEX TO ASCII	7-1
		DECIMAL TO SEVEN-SEGMENT	7-3
		ASCII TO DECIMAL	7-5
		BCD TO BINARY	7-7
		CONVERT BINARY NUMBER TO ASCII STRING	7-8

TABLE OF CONTENTS (Continued)

CHAPTER		PAGE
7 (Cont.)	PROBLEMS	7-10
	1) ASCII TO HEX	7-10
	2) SEVEN-SEGMENT TO DECIMAL	7-10
	3) DECIMAL TO ASCII	7-11
	4) BINARY TO BCD	7-11
	5) BINARY NUMBER TO ASCII STRING	7-11
	REFERENCES	7-12
8	ARITHMETIC PROBLEMS	8-1
	EXAMPLES	8-1
	MULTIPLE-PRECISION ADDITION	8-1
	DECIMAL ADDITION	8-4
	8-BIT BINARY MULTIPLICATION	8-6
	8-BIT BINARY DIVISION	8-10
	SELF-CHECKING NUMBERS, DOUBLE ADD DOUBLE MOD 10	8-15
	PROBLEMS	8-19
	1) MULTIPLE-PRECISION SUBTRACTION	8-19
	2) DECIMAL SUBTRACTION	8-19
	3) 8-BIT BY 16-BIT BINARY MULTIPLICATION	8-20
	4) SIGNED BINARY DIVISION	8-20
	5) SELF-CHECKING NUMBERS ALIGNED 1, 3, 7 MOD 10	8-21
9	TABLES AND LISTS	9-1
	EXAMPLES	9-1
	ADD ENTRY TO LIST	9-1
	CHECK AN ORDERED LIST	9-4
	REMOVE ELEMENT FROM QUEUE	9-6
	8-BIT SORT	9-8
	USING AN ORDERED JUMP TABLE	9-12
	PROBLEMS	9-14
	1) REMOVE AN ENTRY FROM A LIST	9-14
	2) ADD AN ENTRY TO AN ORDERED LIST	9-14
	3) ADD AN ELEMENT TO A QUEUE	9-15
	4) 16-BIT SORT	9-15
	5) USING A JUMP TABLE WITH A KEY	9-16
10	SUBROUTINES	10-1
	SUBROUTINE DOCUMENTATION	10-2
	EXAMPLES	10-2
	HEX TO ASCII	10-2
	LENGTH OF A STRING OF CHARACTERS	10-6
	ADD EVEN PARITY TO ASCII CHARACTERS	10-9
	PATTERN MATCH	10-12
	MULTIPLE-PRECISION ADDITION	10-16
	PROBLEMS	10-21
	1) ASCII TO HEX	10-21
	2) LENGTH OF A TELETYPEWRITER MESSAGE	10-21
	3) CHECK EVEN PARITY IN ASCII CHARACTERS	10-21
	4) STRING COMPARISON	10-22
	5) DECIMAL SUBTRACTION	10-23

TABLE OF CONTENTS (Continued)

CHAPTER		PAGE
11	INPUT/OUTPUT	11-1
	TIMING INTERVALS (DELAYS)	11-8
	DELAY ROUTINES	11-8
	EXAMPLES	11-9
	DELAY PROGRAM USING ACCUMULATORS	11-9
	DELAY PROGRAM USING INDEX REGISTER	11-11
	THE 6820 PERIPHERAL INTERFACE ADAPTER (PIA)	11-12
	PIA CONTROL REGISTER	11-15
	CONFIGURING THE PIA	11-16
	EXAMPLES OF PIA CONFIGURATION	11-18
	USING THE PIA TO TRANSFER DATA	11-20
	EXAMPLES	11-21
	A PUSHBUTTON SWITCH	11-21
	A TOGGLE SWITCH	11-26
	A MULTIPLE-POSITION (ROTARY, SELECTOR, OR THUMBWHEEL) SWITCH	11-30
	ASSEMBLY LANGUAGE PROGRAMS	11-31
	EXAMPLES	11-31
	DETERMINE SWITCH POSITION	11-31
	WAIT FOR SWITCH POSITION TO CHANGE	11-34
	A SINGLE LED	11-37
	TURN THE LIGHT ON OR OFF	11-38
	SEVEN-SEGMENT LED DISPLAY	11-39
	PROBLEMS	11-48
	1) AN ON-OFF PUSHBUTTON	11-48
	2) DEBOUNCING A SWITCH IN SOFTWARE	11-48
	3) CONTROL FOR A ROTARY SWITCH	11-48
	4) RECORD SWITCH POSITIONS ON LIGHTS	11-49
	5) COUNT ON A SEVEN-SEGMENT DISPLAY	11-49
	MORE COMPLEX I/O DEVICES	11-49
	EXAMPLES	11-52
	AN UNENCODED KEYBOARD	11-52
	AN ENCODED KEYBOARD	11-59
	A DIGITAL-TO-ANALOG CONVERTER	11-62
	ANALOG-TO-DIGITAL CONVERTER	11-65
	A TELETYPEWRITER (TTY)	11-69
	THE 6850 ASYNCHRONOUS COMMUNICATIONS INTERFACE ADAPTER (ACIA)	11-75
	STANDARD INTERFACES	11-80
	PROBLEMS	11-80
	1) SEPARATING CLOSURES FROM AN UNENCODED KEYBOARD	11-80
	2) READ A SENTENCE FROM AN ENCODED KEYBOARD	11-81
	3) A VARIABLE AMPLITUDE SQUARE WAVE GENERATOR	11-81
	4) AVERAGING ANALOG READINGS	11-82
	5) A 30 CHARACTER-PER-SECOND TERMINAL	11-82
	REFERENCES	11-83

TABLE OF CONTENTS (Continued)

CHAPTER		PAGE
12	INTERRUPTS	12-1
	6800 INTERRUPT SYSTEM	12-2
	PIA INTERRUPTS	12-5
	ACIA INTERRUPTS	12-6
	6800 POLLING INTERRUPT SYSTEMS	12-6
	6800 VECTORED INTERRUPT SYSTEMS	12-7
	EXAMPLES	12-7
	A STARTUP INTERRUPT	12-7
	A KEYBOARD INTERRUPT	12-9
	A PRINTER INTERRUPT	12-14
	A REAL-TIME CLOCK INTERRUPT	12-16
	A TELETYPEWRITER INTERRUPT	12-21
	MORE GENERAL SERVICE ROUTINES	12-24
	PROBLEMS	12-25
	1) A TEST INTERRUPT	12-25
	2) A KEYBOARD INTERRUPT	12-25
	3) A PRINTER INTERRUPT	12-25
	4) A REAL-TIME CLOCK INTERRUPT	12-25
	5) A TELETYPEWRITER INTERRUPT	12-25
13	PROBLEM DEFINITION AND PROGRAM DESIGN	13-1
	THE TASKS OF SOFTWARE DEVELOPMENT	13-1
	DEFINITION OF THE STAGES	13-3
	PROBLEM DEFINITION	13-3
	DEFINING THE INPUTS	13-3
	DEFINING THE OUTPUTS	13-4
	PROCESSING SECTION	13-4
	ERROR HANDLING	13-5
	HUMAN FACTORS	13-5
	EXAMPLES	13-6
	RESPONSE TO A SWITCH	13-6
	A SWITCH-BASED MEMORY LOADER	13-7
	A VERIFICATION TERMINAL	13-10
	REVIEW OF PROBLEM DEFINITION	13-13
	PROGRAM DESIGN	13-14
	FLOWCHARTING	13-15
	EXAMPLES	13-16
	RESPONSE TO A SWITCH	13-16
	THE SWITCH-BASED MEMORY LOADER	13-17
	THE CREDIT-VERIFICATION TERMINAL	13-19
	MODULAR PROGRAMMING	13-23
	EXAMPLES	13-24
	RESPONSE TO A SWITCH	13-24
	THE SWITCH-BASED MEMORY LOADER	13-24
	THE VERIFICATION TERMINAL	13-24
	REVIEW OF MODULAR PROGRAMMING	13-25
	STRUCTURED PROGRAMMING	13-25
	EXAMPLES	13-29
	RESPONSE TO A SWITCH	13-29
	THE SWITCH-BASED MEMORY LOADER	13-30
	THE CREDIT-VERIFICATION TERMINAL	13-31

TABLE OF CONTENTS (Continued)

CHAPTER		PAGE
13 (Cont.)	REVIEW OF STRUCTURED PROGRAMMING	13-25
	TOP-DOWN DESIGN	13-36
	EXAMPLES	13-37
	RESPONSE TO A SWITCH	13-37
	THE SWITCH-BASED MEMORY LOADER	13-38
	THE TRANSACTION TERMINAL	13-39
	REVIEW OF TOP-DOWN DESIGN	13-41
	REVIEW OF PROBLEM DEFINITION AND PROGRAM DESIGN	13-41
	REFERENCES	13-42
14	DEBUGGING AND TESTING	14-1
	SIMPLE DEBUGGING TOOLS	14-1
	MORE ADVANCED DEBUGGING TOOLS	14-6
	DEBUGGING WITH CHECKLISTS	14-8
	LOOKING FOR ERRORS	14-9
	DEBUGGING EXAMPLE 1: DECIMAL TO SEVEN-SEGMENT CONVERSION	14-11
	DEBUGGING EXAMPLE 2: SORT INTO DECREASING ORDER	14-15
	INTRODUCTION TO TESTING	14-20
	SELECTING TEST DATA	14-21
	TESTING EXAMPLE 1: SORT PROGRAM	14-22
	TESTING EXAMPLE 2: SELF-CHECKING NUMBERS	14-22
	TESTING PRECAUTIONS	14-22
	CONCLUSIONS	14-23
15	DOCUMENTATION AND REDESIGN	15-1
	SELF-DOCUMENTING PROGRAMS	15-1
	COMMENTS	15-2
	COMMENTING EXAMPLE 1: MULTIPLE-PRECISION ADDITION	15-3
	COMMENTING EXAMPLE 2: TELETYPEWRITER OUTPUT	15-5
	FLOWCHARTS AS DOCUMENTATION	15-6
	STRUCTURED PROGRAMS AS DOCUMENTATION	15-6
	MEMORY MAPS	15-6
	PARAMETER AND DEFINITION LISTS	15-7
	LIBRARY ROUTINES	15-8
	LIBRARY EXAMPLE 1: SUM OF DATA	15-9
	LIBRARY EXAMPLE 2: DECIMAL-TO-SEVEN-SEGMENT CONVERSION	15-9
	LIBRARY EXAMPLE 3: DECIMAL SUM	15-10
	TOTAL DOCUMENTATION	15-11
	REDESIGN	15-11
	REORGANIZING TO USE LESS MEMORY	15-12
	MAJOR REORGANIZATIONS	15-14
	REFERENCES	15-15
16	SAMPLE PROJECTS	16-1
	PROJECT #1: A DIGITAL STOPWATCH	16-1
	PROJECT #2: A DIGITAL THERMOMETER	16-8
	REFERENCES	16-26

LIST OF FIGURES

FIGURE		PAGE
5-1	Flowchart of a Program Loop	5-2
5-2	A Program Loop That Allows Zero Iterations	5-3
7-1	Seven-Segment Arrangement	7-3
11-1	An Output Demultiplexer Controlled by a Counter	11-3
11-2	An Output Demultiplexer Controlled by a Port	11-3
11-3	An Input Multiplexer Controlled by a Counter	11-4
11-4	An Input Multiplexer Controlled by a Port	11-4
11-5	An Input Handshake	11-6
11-6	An Output Handshake	11-7
11-7	Block Diagram of the 6820 Peripheral Adapter (Courtesy of Motorola)	11-14
11-8	A Pushbutton Circuit	11-22
11-9	A Toggle Switch Circuit	11-27
11-10	A Debounce Circuit Based on Cross-Coupled NAND Gates	11-27
11-11	A Multiple-Position Switch	11-31
11-12	A Multiple-Position Switch with an Encoder	11-32
11-13	Interfacing an LED	11-37
11-14	Interfacing a Seven-Segment Display	11-39
11-15	Seven-Segment Display Organization	11-40
11-16	Seven-Segment Representations of Decimal Digits	11-41
11-17	Multiplexed Seven-Segment Displays	11-47
11-18	A Small Keyboard	11-53
11-19	A Keyboard Matrix	11-53
11-20	I/O Arrangement for a Keyboard Scan	11-55
11-21	I/O Interface for an Encoded Keyboard	11-61
11-22	Signetics NE5018 D/A Converter	11-63
11-23	Interface for an 8-bit Digital-to-Analog Converter	11-64
11-24	Teledyne 8703 A/D Converter	11-66
11-25	Interface for an 8-bit Analog-to-Digital Converter	11-67
11-26	Teletypewriter Data Format	11-69
11-27	Flowchart for Receive Procedure	11-70
11-28	Flowchart for Transmit Procedure	11-72
11-29	Block Diagram of the 6850 ACIA (Courtesy of Motorola)	11-78
12-1	6800 State Transition Flowchart (Courtesy of Motorola)	12-3
12-2	Saving the Status of the Microprocessor in the Stack (Courtesy of Motorola)	12-5
13-1	Flowchart of Software Development	13-2
13-2	The Switch and Light System	13-6
13-3	The Switch-Based Memory Loader	13-8
13-4	Block Diagram of a Verification Terminal	13-10
13-5	Verification Terminal Keyboard	13-11
13-6	Verification Terminal Display	13-11

LIST OF FIGURES (Continued)

FIGURE		PAGE
13-7	Standard Flow Diagram Symbols	13-15
13-8	Flowchart of One-Second Response to a Switch	13-17
13-9	Flowchart of Switch-Based Memory Loader	13-18
13-10	Flowchart of Keyboard Entry Process	13-19
13-11	Flowchart of Keyboard Entry Process with Send Key	13-20
13-12	Flowchart of Keyboard Entry Process with Function Keys	13-21
13-13	Flowchart of Receive Routine	13-22
13-14	Flowchart of an Unstructured Program	13-26
13-15	Flowchart of the If-Then-Else Structure	13-27
13-16	Flowchart of the Do-While Structure	13-27
13-17	Initial Flowchart for Transaction Terminal	13-39
13-18	Flowchart for Expanded KEYBOARD Routine	13-40
14-1	A Simple Breakpoint Routine	14-3
14-2	Flowchart of Register Dump Program	14-4
14-3	Results of a Typical Register Dump (6800)	14-4
14-4	Results of a Typical Memory Dump	14-5
14-5	Flowchart of Decimal to Seven-Segment Conversion	14-12
14-6	Flowchart of Sort Program	14-15
16-1	I/O Configuration	16-2
16-2	I/O Configuration	16-9
16-3	Analog Hardware	16-10
16-4	Thermistor Characteristics (Fenwal GA51J1 Bead)	16-11
16-5	Typical E-1 Curve for Thermistor (25° C)	16-11
16-6	Generating an Internal Clock Frequency	16-12

LIST OF TABLES

TABLE		PAGE
1-1	Hexadecimal Conversion Table	1-4
2-1	The Fields of an Assembly Language Instruction	2-1
2-2	Standard 6800 Assembler Delimiters	2-2
2-3	Assigning and Using a Label	2-3
3-1	Frequently Used Instructions of the 6800	3-3
3-2	Occasionally Used Instructions of the 6800	3-4
3-3	Seldom Used Instructions of the 6800	3-4
3-4	A Summary of the 6800 Instruction Set	3-13
3-5	6800 Instruction Set Object Codes	3-22
6-1	Hex-ASCII Table	6-2
11-1	Addressing 6820 Internal Registers	11-13
11-2	Organization of the PIA Control Registers (Courtesy of Motorola)	11-13
11-3	Control of Interrupt Inputs CA1 and CB1	11-15
11-4	Control of CA2 and CB2 as Interrupt Inputs (CRA5 (CRB5) is low)	11-16
11-5	Control of CB2 as an Output (CRB5 is high)	11-17
11-6	Control of CA2 as an Output (CRA5 is high)	11-17
11-7	Data Input vs. Switch Position	11-31
11-8	Seven-Segment Representations of Decimal Numbers	11-42
11-9	Seven-Segment Representations of Letters and Symbols	11-43
11-10	Comparison Between Independent Connections and Matrix Connections for Keyboards	11-54
11-11	Definition of ACIA Register Contents	11-76
11-12	Meaning of the ACIA Control Register Bits	11-77
12-1	Memory Maps for 6800 Addresses Used in Response to Interrupts and Reset	12-4
14-1	6800 Interrupt Vectors	14-2
16-1	Input Connections for Timer Keyboard	16-2
16-2	Output Connections for Timer Keyboard	16-2

QUICK INDEX

INDEX		PAGE
A	ACCUMULATORS, USING THE	4-2
	ACIA CONFIGURATION, EXAMPLE OF	11-77
	ACIA INTERRUPT ROUTINE	12-21
	ACIA REGISTERS	11-75
	ACIA, SPECIAL FEATURES OF	11-75
	ADDRESSING AN ACIA	11-79
	ADDRESSING MODES	3-94
	ALGEBRAIC NOTATION	1-8
	ALLOCATING RAM	2-7
	ARITHMETIC AND LOGICAL EXPRESSIONS	2-10
	ASCII, HANDLING DATA IN	6-1
	ASCII CHARACTERS	2-10
	ASSEMBLER	1-5
	ASSEMBLER, CHOOSING AN	1-6
	ASSEMBLER ARITHMETIC EXPRESSIONS	3-94
	ASSEMBLER DIRECTIVE	2-4
	ASSEMBLY LANGUAGE, APPLICATIONS FOR	1-11
	ASSEMBLY LANGUAGE FIELDS	2-1
	ASSEMBLY LANGUAGE PROGRAM	1-5
B	BASIC SOFTWARE DELAY	11-8
	BETTER ALGORITHMS	15-14
	BINARY INSTRUCTIONS	1-1
	BINARY ROUNDING	8-18
	BLANKING A LEADING ZERO	16-15
	BOOTSTRAP LOADER	2-15
	BOTTOM-UP DESIGN	13-36
	BREAKPOINT	14-2
C	CHANGING REGISTER VALUES IN STACK	12-21
	CHARACTER FORMAT	11-69
	CHECKLIST, WHAT TO INCLUDE IN	14-8
	CHOOSING LABELS	2-3
	CHOOSING A TIMING METHOD	11-8
	CHOOSING USEFUL NAMES	15-2
	CODING	13-3
	CODING, RELATIVE IMPORTANCE OF	13-1
	COMBINING CONTROL INFORMATION	11-51
	COMMENTING EXAMPLES	15-3
	COMMENTING GUIDELINES	15-2
	COMMENTING TECHNIQUES	2-13
	COMMON-ANODE OR COMMON-CATHODE DISPLAYS	11-39
	COMMON ERRORS	14-9
	COMPILERS	1-7
	COMPILERS, COST OF	1-8
	COMPUTER PROGRAM	1-2
	CONTROL AND STATUS INFORMATION	11-50
	CROSS-ASSEMBLER	2-14
D	DATA, FORMING CLASSES OF	14-22
	DEBOUNCING IN SOFTWARE	11-24
	DEBOUNCING WITH CROSS-COUPLED NAND GATES	11-26
	DEBUGGING	13-3

QUICK INDEX (Continued)

INDEX		PAGE
	DEBUGGING, USING TEST CASES FROM	14-20
	DEBUGGING A CODE CONVERSION PROGRAM	14-11
	DEBUGGING A SORT PROGRAM	14-15
	DEBUGGING INTERRUPT-DRIVEN PROGRAMS	14-11
	DECIDING ON A MAJOR CHANGE	15-14
	DECIMAL ACCURACY IN BINARY	8-3
	DECIMAL ADJUST	8-5
	DECIMAL DATA OR ADDRESSES	2-9
	DECIMAL ROUNDING	8-18
	DEFAULT VALUE	2-7
	DEFINING NAMES	2-6
	DEFINITION LISTS, RULES FOR	15-7
	DEFINITION, PLACEMENT OF	2-6
	DELIMITER	2-2
	DIRECT ADDRESSING, USING	4-2
	DIRECT MEMORY ACCESS	11-5
	DISABLING INTERRUPTS	12-20
	DIVISION ALGORITHM	8-10
	DOCUMENTATION	13-3
	DOCUMENTATION PACKAGE	15-11
	DOCUMENTING STATUS AND CONTROL TRANSFERS	11-52
	DOCUMENTING SUBROUTINES	10-2
	DOUBLE BUFFERING	12-13
	DOUBLING AND HALVING BINARY NUMBERS	8-18
E	8-BIT SUMMATION	5-3
	EMPTYING A BUFFER WITH INTERRUPTS	12-15
	ENABLING AND DISABLING INTERRUPTS	12-2
	ERROR CONSIDERATIONS	13-5
	EXAMPLE FORMAT	4-1
F	FCB, FCC, FDB PSEUDO-OPERATIONS	3-92
	FILLING A BUFFER VIA INTERRUPTS	12-12
	FLOWCHARTING, ADVANTAGES OF	13-15
	FLOWCHARTING, DISADVANTAGES OF	13-16
	FLOWCHARTING SECTIONS	13-19
	FLOWCHARTING SWITCH AND LIGHT SYSTEM	13-16
	FLOWCHARTING THE CREDIT VERIFICATION	13-19
	FLOWCHARTING THE SWITCH-BASED MEMORY LOADER	13-17
	FLOWCHARTS, HINTS FOR USING	15-6
	FORMAT	2-2
	FORTRAN	1-7
G	GENERAL SERVICE ROUTINES, TASKS FOR	12-24
	GUIDELINES FOR EXAMPLES	4-1
H	HAND ASSEMBLY	1-5
	HAND CHECKING QUESTIONS	14-8
	HANDSHAKE	11-2
	HASHING	9-3
	HEXADECIMAL LOADER	1-3
	HIGH-LEVEL LANGUAGES, ADVANTAGES OF	1-9
	HIGH-LEVEL LANGUAGES, APPLICATIONS FOR	1-11

QUICK INDEX (Continued)

INDEX		PAGE
	HIGH-LEVEL LANGUAGES, DISADVANTAGES OF	1-9
	HIGH-LEVEL LANGUAGES, INEFFICIENCY OF	1-9
	HIGH-LEVEL LANGUAGES, MACHINE INDEPENDENCE OF	1-8
	HIGH-LEVEL LANGUAGES, OVERHEAD FOR	1-10
	HIGH-LEVEL LANGUAGES, PORTABILITY OF	1-8
	HIGH-LEVEL LANGUAGES, SYNTAX OF	1-8
	HIGH-LEVEL LANGUAGES, UNSUITABILITY OF	1-10
I	INFORMATION-HIDING PRINCIPLE	13-25
	INITIALIZING RAM	2-8
	INPUT, FACTORS IN	13-4
	INSTRUCTIONS, DEFINING A SEQUENCE OF	2-11
	INTERFACING SLOW DEVICES	11-2
	INTERRUPT HANDLING BY MONITORS	12-8
	INTERRUPT SYSTEMS, CHARACTERISTICS OF	12-1
	INTERRUPTS, DISADVANTAGES OF	12-2
	INTERRUPTS ON PARTICULAR MICROCOMPUTERS	12-8
	I/O AND MEMORY	11-1
	I/O CATEGORIES	11-1
K	KEY TABLE	16-6
	KEYBOARD ERRORS, CORRECTING	13-13
	KEYBOARD INTERRUPT	12-9
	KEYBOARD ROUTINE, EXPANDING THE	13-40
	KEYBOARD SCAN	11-54
L	LABEL FIELD	2-2
	LABELING, RULES OF	2-3
	LABELS IN JUMP INSTRUCTIONS	2-2
	LANGUAGE LEVELS, APPLICATION AREAS FOR	1-10
	LANGUAGE LEVELS, FUTURE TRENDS IN	1-12
	LED CONTROL	11-37
	LINKING LOADERS	2-15
	LOCAL OR GLOBAL VARIABLES	2-13
	LOCATION COUNTER	2-7
	LOGIC ANALYZER	14-7
	LOGIC ANALYZERS, IMPORTANT FEATURES OF	14-7
M	MACHINE LANGUAGE, APPLICATIONS FOR	1-11
	MACHINE LANGUAGE PROGRAM	1-2
	MACRO-ASSEMBLER	2-14
	MACROS, ADVANTAGES OF	2-12
	MACROS, DISADVANTAGES OF	2-13
	MAINTAINING REAL TIME	12-19
	MAINTENANCE AND REDESIGN	13-3
	MAJOR OR MINOR REORGANIZATION	15-12
	MATRIX KEYBOARD	11-52
	MEASURING PROGRESS IN STAGES	13-1
	MEMORY DUMP	14-5
	MEMORY LOADER, OPERATOR ERROR CORRECTION IN	13-9
	MEMORY LOADER ERROR HANDLING	13-9
	META-ASSEMBLER	2-14
	MICRO-ASSEMBLER	2-14

QUICK INDEX (Continued)

INDEX		PAGE
	MNEMONICS, PROBLEM WITH	1-4
	MODULAR PROGRAMMING, ADVANTAGES OF	13-23
	MODULAR PROGRAMMING, DISADVANTAGES OF	13-23
	MODULAR PROGRAMMING, RULES FOR	13-25
	MODULARIZING THE SWITCH AND LIGHT SYSTEM	13-24
	MODULARIZING THE SWITCH-BASED MEMORY LOADER	13-24
	MODULARIZING THE VERIFICATION TERMINAL	13-24
	MULTIPLICATION, REFERENCES ON	8-10
	MULTIPLICATION ALGORITHM	8-6
N	NAMES, CHOICE OF	2-6
	NAMES, USE OF	2-6
	NON-MASKABLE INTERRUPT	12-2, 12-5
	NUMBERS AND CHARACTERS IN ADDRESS FIELD	3-94
O	OBJECT PROGRAM	1-2, 1-5
	OCTAL OR HEXADECIMAL	1-3
	ONE-PASS ASSEMBLER	2-14
	OPERATOR INTERACTION	13-5
	OPTIMIZING COMPILER	1-9
	ORG PSEUDO-OPERATION	3-93
	OTHER MAJOR CHANGES	15-14
	OTHER NUMBER SYSTEMS	2-9
	OTHER SORTING METHODS	9-11
P	PASSING PARAMETERS	10-1
	PIA ADDRESSES	11-12
	PIA CONFIGURATION EXAMPLES	11-18
	PIA CONTROL REGISTER BITS	11-15
	PIA INPUT/OUTPUT	11-20
	PIA REGISTERS AND CONTROL LINES	11-12
	PIA STATUS BITS	11-21
	POLLING	12-2
	POLLING INTERRUPTS	12-6
	POLLING INTERRUPTS, DISADVANTAGES OF	12-6
	PORTABILITY	1-7
	PRIORITY	12-2
	PROBLEM DEFINITION	13-3
	PROCESSING, FACTORS IN	13-4
	PROGRAM DESIGN	13-3
	PROGRAM DESIGN, BASIC PRINCIPLES OF	13-14
	PROGRAM STUBS	13-36
	PROGRAM STUBS, EXPANDING	13-36
	PROGRAMMING GUIDELINES	4-2
	PSEUDO-OPERATIONS	2-4
Q	QUESTIONS FOR COMMENTING	15-4
R	REAL-TIME CLOCK	12-16
	REAL-TIME CLOCK, FREQUENCY OF	12-16
	REAL-TIME CLOCK, PRIORITY OF	12-17
	REAL-TIME CLOCK, SYNCHRONIZATION WITH	12-17
	REASONING BEHIND INTERRUPTS	12-1
	REDESIGN, COST OF	15-11

QUICK INDEX (Continued)

INDEX   **PAGE**

REDUCING TRANSMISSION ERRORS	11-5
RE-ENTRANT SUBROUTINE	10-2
REGISTER DUMP	14-3
RELOCATING LOADER	2-15
RELOCATION	10-2
RELOCATION CONSTANT	2-3
RESIDENT ASSEMBLER	2-14
RULES FOR TESTING	14-22

S

SAVING EXECUTION TIME	15-13
SAVING MEMORY	15-12
SEARCHING METHODS	9-5
SELECTING DATA FROM CLASSES	14-22
SELF-CHECKING NUMBERS	8-15
SELF-DOCUMENTING PROGRAMS, RULES FOR	15-1
SEPARATING STATUS INFORMATION	11-51
SEVEN-SEGMENT REPRESENTATIONS	11-40
SIMPLE SORTING ALGORITHM	9-9
SINGLE-STEP	14-1
SINGLE-STEP MODE, LIMITATIONS OF	14-2
6800 ACIA INTERRUPTS	12-6
6800 DELAY LOOP CONSTANT	11-11
6800 INTERRUPT INPUTS	12-2
6800 INTERRUPT SYSTEM, SPECIAL FEATURES OF	12-4
6800 VECTORED INTERRUPTS	12-7
6820 PIA INTERRUPTS	12-5
SOFTWARE DEVELOPMENT, STAGES OF	13-1
SOFTWARE SIMULATOR	14-6
SOURCE PROGRAM	1-5
STANDARD INTERFACES	11-80
STANDARD PROGRAM LIBRARY FORMS	15-8
STANDARD TTY	11-69
START BIT INTERRUPT	12-22
STATUS CHANGES WITH INSTRUCTION EXECUTION	3-12
STEPS IN CONFIGURING A PIA	11-16
STOPWATCH INPUT PROCEDURE	16-1
STROBE	11-5
STRUCTURED KEYBOARD ROUTINE	13-31
STRUCTURED PROGRAM FOR THE CREDIT-VERIFICATION TERMINAL	13-31
STRUCTURED PROGRAMMING, ADVANTAGES OF	13-28
STRUCTURED PROGRAMMING, BASIC STRUCTURES OF	13-26
STRUCTURED PROGRAMMING, DISADVANTAGES OF	13-29
STRUCTURED PROGRAMMING, RULES FOR	13-36
STRUCTURED PROGRAMMING, WHEN TO USE	13-29
STRUCTURED PROGRAMMING FOR THE SWITCH-BASED MEMORY LOADER	13-30
STRUCTURED PROGRAMMING IN THE SWITCH AND LIGHT SYSTEM	13-29
STRUCTURED RECEIVE ROUTINE	13-33
STRUCTURED TESTING	14-21
STRUCTURES, EXAMPLES OF	13-28

QUICK INDEX (Continued)

INDEX		PAGE
	SUBROUTINE INSTRUCTIONS	10-1
	SUBROUTINE LIBRARY	10-1
	SWI AS A BREAKPOINT	14-2
	SWITCH AND LIGHT ERROR HANDLING	13-7
	SWITCH AND LIGHT INPUT	13-6
	SWITCH AND LIGHT OUTPUTS	13-6
	SWITCH AND LIGHT SYSTEM, DEFINING	13-6
	SWITCH-BASED MEMORY LOADER, DEFINING A	13-7
	SWITCH BOUNCE	11-24
	SYMBOL TABLE	2-6
	SYNCHRONIZING WITH I/O DEVICES	11-50
T	TERMINATORS FOR STRUCTURES	13-35
	TESTING	13-3
	TESTING AIDS	14-20
	TESTING AN ARITHMETIC PROGRAM	14-22
	TESTING A SORT PROGRAM	14-22
	TESTING SPECIAL CASES	14-21
	THERMOMETER ANALOG HARDWARE	16-8
	TIMING INTERVALS, METHODS FOR PRODUCING	11-8
	TIMING INTERVALS, USES OF	11-8
	TOP-DOWN DESIGN, ADVANTAGES OF	13-36
	TOP-DOWN DESIGN, DISADVANTAGES OF	13-36
	TOP-DOWN DESIGN, FORMAT FOR	13-41
	TOP-DOWN DESIGN METHODS	13-36
	TOP-DOWN DESIGN OF SWITCH AND LIGHT SYSTEM	13-37
	TOP-DOWN DESIGN OF SWITCH-BASED MEMORY LOADER	13-38
	TOP-DOWN DESIGN OF VERIFICATION TERMINAL	13-39
	TRANSMISSION ERRORS, CORRECTING	13-13
	TRANSPARENT DELAY ROUTINE	11-8
	TTY INTERFACE	11-69
	TTY RECEIVE MODE	11-69
	TTY RECEIVE PROGRAM	11-71
	TTY TRANSMIT MODE	11-72
	TTY TRANSMIT PROGRAM	11-73
	TWO-PASS ASSEMBLER	2-14
	TYPICAL DEFINITION LIST	15-7
	TYPICAL MEMORY MAP	15-6
U	UART	11-74
	USING A CALIBRATION TABLE	16-13
	USING A TTL ENCODER	11-31
V	VECTORING	12-2
	VERIFICATION TERMINAL, DEFINING A	13-10
	VERIFICATION TERMINAL ERROR HANDLING	13-12
	VERIFICATION TERMINAL INPUTS	13-11
	VERIFICATION TERMINAL OUTPUTS	13-12
W	WAITING FOR A KEY CLOSURE	11-54

Chapter 1
INTRODUCTION TO ASSEMBLY LANGUAGE PROGRAMMING

This book describes assembly language programming. It assumes that you are familiar with <u>An Introduction to Microcomputers: Volume I — Basic Concepts</u> (particularly Chapters 6 and 7). This book does not discuss the general features of computers, microcomputers, addressing methods, or instruction sets; you should refer to <u>An Introduction to Microcomputers: Volume I</u> for that information.

HOW THIS BOOK HAS BEEN PRINTED

Notice that text in this book has been printed in **boldface type** and lightface type. This has been done to help you skip those parts of the book that cover subject matter with which you are familiar. You can be sure that lightface type only expands on information presented in the previous boldface type. Therefore, only read boldface type until you reach a subject about which you want to know more, at which point start reading the lightface type.

THE MEANING OF INSTRUCTIONS

The instruction set of a microprocessor is the set of binary inputs that produce defined actions during an instruction cycle. An instruction set is to a microprocessor what a function table is to a logic device, such as a gate, adder, or shift register. Of course, the actions that the microprocessor performs in response to its instruction inputs are far more complex than the actions that logic devices perform in response to their inputs.

An instruction is a binary bit pattern — it must be available at the data inputs to the microprocessor at the proper time in order to be interpreted as an instruction. For example, when the 6800 microprocessor receives the 8-bit binary pattern 01001111 as the input during an instruction fetch, the pattern means:

BINARY INSTRUCTIONS

"Clear (put zero in) Accumulator A"

Similarly, the pattern 10000110 means:

"Load Accumulator A with the contents of the next word of program memory"

The microprocessor (like any other computer) only recognizes binary patterns as instructions or data; it does not recognize words or octal, decimal, or hexadecimal numbers.

A COMPUTER PROGRAM

A program is a series of instructions that cause a computer to perform a particular task.

Actually, a computer program includes more than instructions; it also contains the data and memory addresses that the microprocessor needs to accomplish the tasks defined by the instructions. Clearly, if the microprocessor is to perform an addition, it must have two numbers to add and a place to put the result. The computer program must determine the sources of the data and the destination of the result as well as the operation to be performed.

COMPUTER PROGRAM

Most microprocessors execute instructions sequentially unless one of the instructions changes the execution sequence or halts the computer; i.e., the processor gets the next instruction from the next higher memory address unless the current instruction specifically directs it to do otherwise.

Ultimately, every program is transformed into a set of binary numbers. For example, this is the 6800 program which adds the contents of memory locations 60_{16} and 61_{16} and places the result in memory location 62_{16}:

```
10010110
01100000
10011011
01100001
10010111
01100010
```

This is a machine language, or object, program. If this program were entered into the memory of a 6800-based microcomputer, the microcomputer would be able to execute it directly.

OBJECT PROGRAM

MACHINE LANGUAGE PROGRAM

THE PROGRAMMING PROBLEM

There are many difficulties associated with creating programs as object, or binary machine language, programs. These are some of the problems:

1) The programs are difficult to understand or debug (binary numbers all look the same, particularly after you have looked at them for a few hours).
2) The programs are slow to enter, since you must determine each bit individually.
3) The programs do not describe the task which you want the computer to perform in anything resembling a human-readable format.
4) The programs are long and tiresome to write.
5) The programmer often makes careless errors that are very difficult to find.

For example, **the following version of the addition object program contains a single bit error. Try to find it:**

```
10010110
01100000
10011011
01110001
10010111
01100010
```

Although the computer handles binary numbers with ease, people do not. People find binary programs long, tiresome, confusing, and meaningless. A programmer may eventually start remembering some of the binary codes, but such effort should be spent more productively.

USING OCTAL OR HEXADECIMAL

We can improve the situation somewhat by writing instructions as octal or hexadecimal, rather than binary, numbers. We will use hexadecimal numbers in this book because they are shorter, and because they are the standard for the microprocessor industry. Table 1-1 defines the hexadecimal digits and their binary equivalents. **The 6800 program to add two numbers now becomes:**

> OCTAL OR HEXADECIMAL

```
96
60
9B
61
97
62
```

At the very least, the hexadecimal version is shorter to write and not quite so tiring to examine.

Errors are somewhat easier to find in a sequence of hexadecimal digits. The erroneous version of the addition program, in hexadecimal form, becomes:

```
96
60
9B
71
97
62
```

The mistake is easier to spot.

What do we do with this hexadecimal program? The microprocessor only understands binary instruction codes. The answer is that we must convert the hexadecimal numbers to binary numbers. This conversion is a repetitive, tiresome task. People who attempt it make all sorts of petty mistakes, such as looking at the wrong line, dropping a bit, or transposing a bit or a digit.

This repetitive, grueling task is, however, a perfect job for a computer. The computer never gets tired or bored and never makes silly mistakes. The idea, then, is to write **a program which takes hexadecimal numbers, converts them into binary numbers, and places the binary numbers into the microcomputer memory. This is a standard** program provided with many microprocessors; it is called a **hexadecimal loader.**

> HEXADECIMAL LOADER

Is a hexadecimal loader worth having? If you are willing to write a program using binary numbers and are prepared to enter the program in its binary form into the computer, then you will not need the hexadecimal loader.

If you choose the hexadecimal loader, you will have to pay a price for it. The hexadecimal loader is itself a program that you must load into memory. Furthermore, the hexadecimal loader will occupy memory — memory that you may want to use in some other way.

The basic tradeoff, therefore, is the cost and memory requirements of the hexadecimal loader versus the savings in programmer time.

A hexadecimal loader is well worth its small cost.

A hexadecimal loader certainly does not solve every programming problem. The hexadecimal version of the program is still difficult to read or understand; for example, it does not distinguish instructions from data or addresses, nor does the program listing provide any suggestion as to what the program does. What does 86 or 3F mean? Memorizing a card full of codes is hardly an appetizing proposition. Furthermore, the codes will be entirely different for a different microprocessor, and the program will require a large amount of documentation.

Table 1-1. Hexadecimal Conversion Table

Hexadecimal Digit	Binary Equivalent	Decimal Equivalent
0	0000	0
1	0001	1
2	0010	2
3	0011	3
4	0100	4
5	0101	5
6	0110	6
7	0111	7
8	1000	8
9	1001	9
A	1010	10
B	1011	11
C	1100	12
D	1101	13
E	1110	14
F	1111	15

INSTRUCTION CODE MNEMONICS

An obvious programming improvement is to assign a name to each instruction code. The instruction code name is called a mnemonic, or memory aid. The instruction mnemonic should describe in some way what the instruction does.

In fact, every microprocessor manufacturer (they cannot remember hexadecimal codes either) provides a set of mnemonics for the microprocessor instruction set. **You do not have to abide by the manufacturer's mnemonics;** there is nothing sacred about them.

PROBLEM WITH MNEMONICS

However, they are standard for a given microprocessor, and therefore understood by all users. These are the instruction names that you will find in manuals, cards, books, articles, and programs. The problem with selecting instruction mnemonics is that not all instructions have "obvious" names. Some instructions do (e.g., ADD, AND, OR), others have obvious contractions (e.g., SUB for subtraction, XOR for exclusive-OR), while still others have neither. The result is such mnemonics as WMP, PCHL, and even SOB (try to guess what that means!). Most manufacturers come up with some reasonable names and some hopeless ones. However, users who devise their own mnemonics rarely seem to do much better than the manufacturer.

Along with the instruction mnemonics, the manufacturer will usually assign names to the CPU's registers. As with the instruction names, some register names are obvious (e.g., A for Accumulator) while others may have only historical significance. Again, we will use the manufacturer's suggestions simply to promote standardization.

If we use standard 6800 instruction and register mnemonics, as defined by Motorola, our 6800 addition program becomes:

ASSEMBLY LANGUAGE PROGRAM

        LDAA
        60
        ADDA
        61
        STAA
        62

The program is still far from obvious, but at least some parts of it are comprehensible. ADDA is a considerable improvement over 9B; LDAA and STAA do suggest loading and storing, respectively. We now know which lines are instructions and which are data or addresses. **Such a program is an assembly language program.**

THE ASSEMBLER PROGRAM

How do we get the assembly language program into the computer? We have to translate it, either into hexadecimal or into binary numbers. **You can translate an assembly language program by hand,** instruction by instruction. This is called hand assembly.

HAND ASSEMBLY

Hand assembly of a three-instruction sequence may be illustrated as follows:

Instruction Name	Addressing Method	Hexadecimal Equivalent
LDAA direct	direct	96
ADDA direct	direct	9B
STAA direct	direct	97

As in the case of hexadecimal to binary conversion, hand assembly is a rote task which is uninteresting, repetitive, and subject to numerous minor errors. Picking the wrong line, transposing digits, omitting instructions, and misreading the codes are only a few of the mistakes that you may make. Most microprocessors complicate the task even further by having instructions with different word lengths. Some instructions are one word long, while others are two or three words long. Some instructions require data in the second and third words; others require memory addresses, register numbers, or other information.

Assembly is another rote task that we can assign to the microcomputer. The microcomputer never makes any mistakes when translating codes; it always knows how many words and what format each instruction requires. The program that does this job is an Assembler. The Assembler program translates a user program, or <u>source</u> program written with mnemonics, into a machine language program, or <u>object</u> program, which the microcomputer can execute. The Assembler's input is a source program, and its output is an object program.

ASSEMBLER

SOURCE PROGRAM

OBJECT PROGRAM

The tradeoffs that we discussed in connection with the hexadecimal loader are magnified in the case of the Assembler. Assemblers are more expensive, occupy more memory, and require more peripherals and execution time than do hexadecimal loaders. While users may (and often do) write their own loaders, few care to write their own assemblers.

Assemblers have their own rules that you must learn to abide by. These include the use of certain markers (such as spaces, commas, semi-colons, or colons) in appropriate places, correct spelling, the proper control information, and perhaps even the correct placement of names and numbers. These rules typically are a minor hindrance that can be quickly overcome.

ADDITIONAL FEATURES OF ASSEMBLERS

Early assembler programs did little more than translate the mnemonic names of instructions and registers into their binary equivalents. However, most assemblers now provide such additional features as:

1) Allowing the user to assign names to memory locations, input and output devices, and even sequences of instructions.
2) Converting data or addresses from various number systems (e.g., decimal or hexadecimal) to binary and converting characters into their ASCII or EBCDIC binary codes.
3) Performing some arithmetic as part of the assembly process.
4) Telling the loader program where in memory parts of the program or data should be placed.
5) Allowing the user to assign areas of memory as temporary data storage and to place fixed data in areas of program memory.
6) Providing the information required to include standard programs from program libraries, or programs written at some other time, in the current program.
7) Allowing the user to control the format of the program listing and the input and output devices employed.

All of these features, of course, involve additional cost and memory. Microcomputers generally have much simpler assemblers than do larger computers, but the tendency always is for the size of assemblers to increase. You will often have a choice of assemblers. The important criterion is not how many off-beat features the Assembler has, but rather how convenient it is to use in normal practice.

CHOOSING AN ASSEMBLER

DISADVANTAGES OF ASSEMBLY LANGUAGE

The Assembler, like the hexadecimal loader, does not solve all the problems of programming. One problem is the tremendous gap between the microcomputer instruction set and the tasks which the microcomputer is to perform. Computer instructions tend to do things like add the contents of two registers, shift the contents of the Accumulator one bit, or place a new value in the Program Counter. On the other hand, a user generally wants a microcomputer to do something like check if an analog reading has exceeded a threshold, look for and react to a particular command from a teletypewriter, or activate a relay at the proper time. An assembly language programmer must translate such tasks into a sequence of simple computer instructions. The translation can be a difficult, time-consuming job.

Furthermore, **if you are programming in assembly language, you must have detailed knowledge of the particular microcomputer that you are using.** You must know what registers and instructions the microcomputer has, precisely how the instructions affect the various registers, what addressing methods the computer uses, and a myriad of other information. None of this information is relevant to the task which the microcomputer must ultimately perform.

In addition, **assembly language programs are not portable.** Each microcomputer has its own assembly language, which reflects its own architecture. An assembly language program written for the 6800 will not run on the 8080, the F8, or the PACE. For example, the addition program written for the 8080 would be:

LDA	60H
MOV	B,A
LDA	61H
ADD	B
STA	62H

`PORTABILITY`

The lack of portability not only means that you will not be able to use your assembly language program on another microcomputer; it also means that you will not be able to use any programs that were not specifically written for the microcomputer you are using. This is a particular drawback for microcomputers, since these devices are new and few assembly language programs exist for them. The result, too frequently, is that you are on your own. If you need a program to perform a particular task, you are not likely to find it in the small program libraries that most manufacturers provide. Nor are you likely to find it in an archive, journal article, or someone's old program file. You will probably have to write it yourself.

HIGH-LEVEL LANGUAGES

The solution to many of the difficulties associated with assembly language programs is to use, instead, "high-level" or "procedure-oriented" languages. Such languages allow you to describe tasks in forms that are problem-oriented rather than computer-oriented. Each statement in a high-level language performs a recognizable function; it will generally correspond to many assembly language instructions. A program called a Compiler translates the high-level language source program into object-code or machine-language instructions.

`COMPILER`

Many different high-level languages exist for different types of tasks. If, for example, you can express what you want the computer to do in algebraic notation, you can write your program in FORTRAN (FORmula TRANslation language), the oldest and most widely used of the high-level languages. Now, if you want to add two numbers, you just tell the computer:

`FORTRAN`

$$SUM = NUMB1 + NUMB2$$

That is a lot simpler (and a lot shorter) than either the equivalent machine language program or the equivalent assembly language program. Other high-level languages include COBOL (for business applications), ALGOL and PASCAL (other algebraic languages), PL/1 (a combination of FORTRAN, ALGOL and COBOL), and APL and BASIC (languages that are popular for time-sharing systems).

ADVANTAGES OF HIGH-LEVEL LANGUAGES

Clearly, high-level languages make programs easier and faster to write. A common estimate is that a programmer can write a program about ten times as fast in a high-level language as compared to assembly language. That is just writing the program; it does not include problem definition, program design, debugging, testing, or documentation, all of which become simpler and faster. The high-level language program is, for instance, partly self-documenting. Even if you do not know FORTRAN, you probably could tell what the statement illustrated above does.

High-level languages solve many other problems associated with assembly language programming. The high-level language has its own syntax (usually defined by a national or international standard). The language does not mention the instruction set, registers, or other features of a particular computer. The compiler takes care of all such details. Programmers can concentrate on their own tasks; they do not need a detailed understanding of the underlying CPU architecture -- for that matter, they do not need to know anything about the computer they are programming.

MACHINE INDEPENDENCE OF HIGH-LEVEL LANGUAGES

Programs written in a high-level language are portable -- at least, in theory. They will run on any computer that has a standard compiler for that language.

PORTABILITY OF HIGH-LEVEL LANGUAGES

At the same time, all previous programs written in a high-level language for prior computers are available to you when programming a new computer. This can mean thousands of programs in the case of a common language like FORTRAN or BASIC.

DISADVANTAGES OF HIGH-LEVEL LANGUAGES

Well, if all the good things we have said about high-level languages are true, if you can write programs faster and make them portable besides, why bother with assembly languages? Who wants to worry about registers, instruction codes, mnemonics, and all that garbage! As usual, there are disadvantages that balance the advantages.

One obvious problem is that **you have to learn the "rules" or "syntax" of any high-level language** you want to use. A high-level language has a fairly complicated set of rules. You will find that it takes a lot of time just to get a program that is syntactically correct (and even then it probably will not do what you want). A high-level computer language is like a foreign language. If you have a little talent, you will get used to the rules and be able to turn out programs that the compiler will accept. Still, learning the rules and trying to get the program accepted by the compiler do not contribute directly to doing your job.

SYNTAX OF HIGH-LEVEL LANGUAGES

Here, for example, are some FORTRAN rules:

- Labels must consist entirely of numbers and must be placed in the first five card columns
- Statements must start in column seven
- Integer variables must start with the letters I, J, K, L, M or N

Another obvious problem is that **you need a compiler to translate programs written in a high-level language to machine language.** Compilers are expensive and use a large amount of memory. While most assemblers occupy 2K to 16K bytes of memory (1K = 1024), compilers usually occupy much more memory. So, the amount of overhead involved in using the compiler is rather large.

COST OF COMPILERS

Furthermore, **only some compilers will make the implementation of your task simpler.** FORTRAN, for example, is well-suited to problems that can be expressed as algebraic formulas. If, however, your problem is controlling a printer, editing a string of characters, or monitoring an alarm system, your problem cannot be easily expressed in algebraic notation. In fact, formulating the solution in algebraic notation may be more awkward and more difficult than formulating it in assembly language. The answer is, of course, to use a more suitable high-level language. Some such languages exist, but they are far less

ALGEBRAIC NOTATION

widely used and standardized than FORTRAN. You will not get many of the advantages of high-level languages if you use these so-called system implementation languages.

High-level languages often do not produce very efficient machine language programs. The basic reason for this is that compilation is an automatic process which is riddled with compromises to allow for many possibilities. The compiler works much like a computerized language translator -- sometimes the words are right, but the sounds and sentence structures are awkward. A simple compiler cannot know when a variable is no longer being used and can be discarded, when a register should be used rather than a memory location, or when variables have simple relationships. The experienced programmer can take advantage of shortcuts to shorten execution time or reduce memory usage. A few compilers (known as optimizing compilers) can also do this, but such compilers are much larger and slower than regular compilers.

| INEFFICIENCY OF HIGH-LEVEL LANGUAGES |
| OPTIMIZING COMPILER |

The general advantages and disadvantages of high-level languages are:

Advantages:

- More convenient descriptions of tasks
- Greater programmer productivity
- Easier documentation
- Standard syntax
- Independence of the structure of a particular computer
- Portability
- Availability of library and other programs

| ADVANTAGES OF HIGH-LEVEL LANGUAGES |

Disadvantages:

- Special rules
- Extensive hardware and software support required
- Orientation of common languages to algebraic or business problems
- Inefficient programs
- Difficulty of optimizing code to meet time and memory requirements
- Inability to use special features of a computer conveniently

| DISADVANTAGES OF HIGH-LEVEL LANGUAGES |

HIGH-LEVEL LANGUAGES FOR MICROPROCESSORS

Microprocessor users will encounter several special difficulties when using high-level languages. Among these are:

- **Few high-level languages exist for microprocessors**
- **No standard languages are widely available**
- **Few compilers actually run on microcomputers. Those that do often require very large amounts of memory**
- **Most microprocessor applications are not well-suited to high-level languages**
- **Memory costs are often critical in microprocessor applications**

The lack of high-level languages is partly a result of the fact that microprocessors are quite new and are the products of semiconductor manufacturers rather than computer manufacturers. Very few high-level languages exist for microprocessors. The most common are the PL/1-type languages such as Intel's PL/M, Motorola's MPL, and Signetics' PLμS.

Even the few high-level languages that exist do not conform to recognized standards, so the microprocessor user cannot expect to gain much program portability, access to program libraries, or use of previous experience or programs. The main advantages remaining are the reduction in programming effort and the smaller amount of detailed understanding of the computer architecture that is necessary.

The overhead involved in using a high-level language with microprocessors is considerable. Microprocessors themselves are better suited to control and slow interactive applications than they are to the character manipulation and language analysis involved in compilation. Therefore, most compilers for microprocessors will not run on a microprocessor-based system. Instead, they require a much larger computer; i.e., they are cross-compilers rather than self-compilers. A user must not only bear the expense of the larger computer, he must also physically transfer the program from the larger computer to the microprocessor-based computer.

OVERHEAD FOR HIGH-LEVEL LANGUAGES

A few self-compilers are available. These compilers run on the microcomputer for which they produce object code. Unfortunately, they require large amounts of memory (16K or more), plus special supporting hardware and software.

High-level languages also are not generally well-suited to microprocessor applications. Most of the common languages were devised either to help solve scientific problems or to handle large-scale business data processing. Few microprocessor applications fall in either of these areas. Most microprocessor applications involve sending data and control information to output devices and receiving data and status information from input devices. Often the control and status information consists of a few binary digits with very precise hardware-related meanings. If you try to write a typical control program in a high-level language, you often feel like someone who is trying to eat soup with chopsticks. For tasks in such areas as test equipment, terminals, navigation systems, and business equipment, the high-level languages work much better than they do in instrumentation, communications, peripherals, and automotive applications.

UNSUITABILITY OF HIGH-LEVEL LANGUAGES

Applications better suited to high-level languages are those which require large memories. If the cost of a single memory chip is important, as in a valve controller, electronic game, appliance controller, or small instrument, then the inefficiency of high-level languages is intolerable. If, on the other hand, the system has many thousands of bytes of memory anyway, as in a terminal or test equipment, the inefficiency of high-level languages is not as important. Clearly, the size of the program and the volume of the product are important factors as well. A large program will greatly increase the advantages of high-level languages. On the other hand, a high-volume application will mean that fixed software development costs are not as important as memory costs that are part of each system.

APPLICATION AREAS FOR LANGUAGE LEVELS

WHICH LEVEL SHOULD YOU USE?

That depends on your particular application. Let us briefly note some of the factors which may favor particular levels:

Machine Language

- Virtually no one programs in machine language. Its use cannot be justified considering the low cost of an assembler.

> **APPLICATIONS FOR MACHINE LANGUAGE**

Assembly Language

- Small to moderate-sized programs
- Applications where memory cost is a factor
- Real-time control applications
- Limited data processing
- High-volume applications

> **APPLICATIONS FOR ASSEMBLY LANGUAGE**

High-Level Languages

- Large programs
- Low-volume applications requiring long programs
- Applications requiring large memories
- More computation than input/output or control
- Compatibility with similar applications using larger computers
- Availability of specific programs in a high-level language which can be used in the application

> **APPLICATIONS FOR HIGH-LEVEL LANGUAGE**

Many other factors are also important, such as the availability of a large computer for use in development, experience with particular languages, and compatibility with other applications.

If hardware will ultimately be the largest cost in your application or if speed is critical, you should favor assembly language. But be prepared to spend extra time in software development in exchange for lower memory costs and higher execution speeds. If software will be the largest cost in your application, you should favor a high-level language. But be prepared to spend the extra money required for the supporting hardware and software.

Of course, no one except some theorists will object if you use both assembly and high-level languages. You can write the program originally in a high-level language and then patch some sections in assembly language. However, most users prefer not to do this because of the havoc it creates in debugging, testing and documentation.

HOW ABOUT THE FUTURE?

We expect that the future will tend to favor high-level languages, for the following reasons:

> FUTURE TRENDS IN LANGUAGE LEVELS

- Programs always seem to accumulate extra features and grow larger
- Hardware and memory are becoming less expensive
- Software and programmers are becoming more expensive
- Memory chips are becoming available in larger sizes at lower "per bit" cost, so actual savings in memory cost are less likely
- More suitable and more efficient high-level languages are being developed
- More standardization of high-level languages will occur

Assembly language programming of microprocessors will not be a dying art any more than it is now for large computers. But longer programs, cheaper memory, and more expensive programmers will make software costs a larger part of most applications. The edge in many applications will therefore go to high-level languages.

WHY THIS BOOK?

If the future would seem to favor high-level languages, why have a book on assembly language programming? The reasons are:

1) Most current microcomputer users program in assembly language (almost 2/3, according to one recent survey).
2) Many microcomputer users will continue to program in assembly language, since they need the detailed control that it provides.
3) No suitable high-level language has yet become widely available or standardized.
4) Many applications require the efficiency of assembly language.
5) An understanding of assembly language can help in evaluating high-level languages.

The rest of this book will deal exclusively with assemblers and assembly language programming. However, we do want readers to know that assembly language is not the only alternative. You should watch for new developments that may significantly reduce programming costs, if such costs are a major factor in your application.

Chapter 2
ASSEMBLERS

This chapter discusses the functions performed by assemblers, beginning with features common to most assemblers and proceeding through more elaborate capabilities such as macros and conditional assembly. **You may wish to skim this chapter for the present and return to it when you feel more comfortable with the material.**

FEATURES OF ASSEMBLERS

As we mentioned previously, today's assemblers do much more than translate assembly language mnemonics into binary codes. We will describe how an assembler handles the translation of mnemonics before describing additional assembler features. Finally, we will explain how assemblers are used.

ASSEMBLER INSTRUCTIONS

Assembly language instructions (or "statements") are divided into a number of fields, as shown in Table 2-1.

ASSEMBLY LANGUAGE FIELDS

The operation code field is the only field which can never be empty; it always contains either an instruction mnemonic or a directive to the Assembler, called a pseudo-instruction, pseudo-operation, or pseudo-op.

The address field may contain an address or data, or it may be blank.

Table 2-1. The Fields of an Assembly Language Instruction

Label Field	Operation Code or Mnemonic Field	Operand or Address Field	Comment Field
START	LDAA	VAL1	LOAD FIRST NUMBER INTO A
	ADDA	VAL2	ADD SECOND NUMBER TO A
	STAA	SUM	STORE SUM
NEXT	?	?	NEXT INSTRUCTION
VAL1	RMB	1	
VAL2	RMB	1	
SUM	RMB	1	

The comment and label fields are optional. A programmer will assign a label to a statement or add a comment as a personal convenience; e.g., to make the program easier to use and read.

Of course, the Assembler must have some way of telling where one field ends and another begins. Assemblers which use punched card input often require that each field start in a specific card column. This is a fixed format. However, fixed formats are inconvenient and a nuisance to programmers. The alternative is a free format where the fields may appear anywhere on the line.

`FORMAT`

If the Assembler cannot use the position on the line to tell the fields apart, it must use something else. **Most assemblers use a special symbol or delimiter at the beginning or end of each field.** The most common delimiter is the space character. Commas, periods, semi-colons, slashes, question marks and other characters which would not otherwise be used in assembly language programs also may serve as delimiters. Table 2-2 lists standard Motorola 6800 Assembler delimiters.

`DELIMITER`

You will have to exercise a little care with delimiters. Some assemblers are fussy about extra spaces or the appearance of delimiters in comments or labels. A well-written assembler will handle these minor problems, but many assemblers are not well-written. Our recommendation is simple: avoid potential problems if you can. The following rules will help:

1) Do not use extra spaces, particularly after commas that separate operands.
2) Do not use delimiter characters in names or labels.
3) Include standard delimiters even if your Assembler does not require them. Your programs will then be acceptable to any assembler.

Table 2-2. Standard 6800 Assembler Delimiters

'space'	between label and operation code, between operation code and address, and before an entry in the comment field.
,	between operands in the address field
*	before an entire line of comments

LABELS

The label field is the first field of an assembly language instruction; it may be blank. If a label is present, the Assembler assigns to the label the value of the address of the memory location into which the first byte of the object program resulting from that instruction will be loaded. You may subsequently use the label as an address or as data in another instruction's address field. The Assembler will replace the label with the assigned value when creating an object program.

`LABEL FIELD`

Labels are most frequently used by Jump, Call, or Branch instructions. These instructions place a new value in the Program Counter, and so alter the normal sequential execution of instructions. JUMP $1E50_{16}$ means "place the value $1E50_{16}$ in the Program Counter". The next instruction to be executed will be the one in memory location $1E50_{16}$. The instruction JUMP START means "place the value assigned to the label START in the Program Counter". The next instruction to be executed will be the one in the memory location which corresponds to the label START. Table 2-3 contains an example.

`LABELS IN JUMP INSTRUCTIONS`

Table 2-3. Assigning and Using a Label

```
              ASSEMBLY LANGUAGE PROGRAM
     START        LOAD ACCUMULATOR 100
                       .
                       .
                       .
                    MAIN PROGRAM
                       .
                       .
                       .
                    JUMP START
```

When the machine language version of this program is executed, the instruction JUMP START causes the address of the instruction labeled START to be placed in the Program Counter. That instruction will then be executed.

Why use a label? Here are some reasons:

1) A label makes a program location easier to find and remember.

2) The label can be moved to correct a program. You do not have to change any subsequent instructions that use the label; the Assembler will make all the necessary changes.

3) The Assembler or Loader can relocate the whole program by adding a constant (a relocation constant) to each address to which a label was assigned. Thus, we can move the program to allow for the insertion of other programs or simply to rearrange memory.   **RELOCATION CONSTANT**

4) The program is easier to use as a library program; i.e., it is easier for someone else to take your program and add it to some totally different program.

5) You do not have to figure out memory addresses. Figuring out memory addresses is particularly difficult with microprocessors which have instructions that vary in length.

It makes sense to assign a label to any instruction that you might want to use as a destination or otherwise identify.

The next question is what label to use. The Assembler often places some restrictions on the number of characters (usually 5 or 6), the leading character (often must be a letter), and the trailing characters (often must be letters, numbers, or one of a few special characters). Beyond these restrictions, the choice is up to you.   **CHOOSING LABELS**

Our own preference is to use labels that suggest their purpose; i.e., mnemonic labels. Typical examples are ADDW in a routine that adds one word into a sum, SRETX in a routine that searches for the ASCII character ETX, or NKEYS for a location in data memory that contains the number of key entries. Meaningful labels are easier to remember, and contribute to program documentation. Some programmers prefer to use a standard format for labels, such as starting with L0000. These labels are self-sequencing (you can skip a few numbers to permit insertions), but they do not help document the program.

Some label selection rules will keep you out of trouble. We recommend the following: **RULES OF LABELING**

1) Do not use labels that are the same as operation codes or other mnemonics. Most assemblers will not allow this usage; others will, but it is very confusing.

2) Do not use labels that are longer than the Assembler permits. Assemblers have various truncation rules.

3) Avoid special characters (non-alphabetic and non-numeric). Some assemblers will not permit them; others only allow certain ones. The simplest practice is to stick to letters and numbers.

4) Start each label with a letter. Such labels are always acceptable.

5) Do not use labels that could be confused with each other. Avoid the letters I, O, Z and the numbers 0, 1 and 2. Also avoid things like XXXX and XXXXX, as these are not easily distinguishable.

6) When you are not sure if a label is allowed, do not use it. You will not get any real benefit from discovering exactly what the Assembler will accept.

These are recommendations, not rules. You do not have to follow them, but do not blame us if you waste time on silly problems.

ASSEMBLER MNEMONICS

The main task of the Assembler is the translation of mnemonics into their binary operation code equivalents. The Assembler performs this task using a fixed table, much as you would if you were doing the assembly by hand.

The Assembler must, however, do more than just translate the operation codes. It **must also somehow determine how many operands the instruction requires and what type they are.** This may be rather complex — some instructions (like a Wait for Interrupt instruction) have no operands, others (like a Jump instruction) have one, while still others require two. Some instructions may even allow alternatives, e.g., some computers have instructions (like Shift or Clear) which can either apply to the Accumulator or to a memory location. We will not discuss how the Assembler makes these distinctions; we will just note that it must do so.

PSEUDO-OPERATIONS

Some assembly language instructions are not directly translated into machine language instructions. These instructions are directives to the Assembler; they assign the program to certain areas in memory, define symbols, designate areas of RAM for temporary data storage, place tables or other fixed data in memory, and perform other housekeeping functions.

| PSEUDO-OPERATIONS |
| ASSEMBLER DIRECTIVE |

To use these directives or pseudo-operations, a programmer places the pseudo-operation's mnemonic in the operation code field and an address or data in the address field, if the specified pseudo-operation requires it.

The most common pseudo-operations are:

      DATA
      EQUATE or DEFINE
      ORIGIN
      RESERVE

Different assemblers use different names for these operations, but their functions are the same. Housekeeping pseudo-operations include:

      END
      LIST
      NAME
      PAGE
      SPACE
      TITLE

We will discuss these pseudo-operations briefly, although their functions are usually obvious.

THE DATA PSEUDO-OPERATION

The Data pseudo-operation allows the programmer to enter fixed data into program memory. This data may include:

- Lookup tables
- Code conversion tables
- Messages
- Synchronization patterns
- Thresholds
- Names
- Coefficients for equations
- Commands
- Conversion factors
- Weighting factors
- Characteristic times or frequencies
- Subroutine addresses
- Key identifications
- Test patterns
- Character generation patterns
- Identification patterns
- Tax tables
- Standard forms
- Masking patterns
- State transition tables

The Data pseudo-operation treats the data as a permanent part of the program.

The format of a Data pseudo-operation is usually quite simple. An instruction like

```
      DZCON    DATA  12
```

will place the number 12 in the next available memory location and assign that location the name DZCON. Usually every Data pseudo-operation has a label, unless it is one of a series of Data pseudo-operations. The data and label may take any form that the Assembler permits.

Most assemblers allow more elaborate Data instructions that handle a large amount of data at one time, e.g.:

```
      EMESS    DATA  'ERROR'
      SQRS     DATA  1,4,9,16,25
```

A single instruction may fill many words of program memory, limited only by the length of a line. Note that if you cannot get all the data on one line, you can always follow one Data instruction with another, e.g.,

```
  MESSG    DATA    'NOW IS THE '
           DATA    'TIME FOR ALL '
           DATA    'GOOD MEN '
           DATA    'TO COME TO THE '
           DATA    'AID OF THEIR '
           DATA    'COUNTRY.'
```

Microprocessor assemblers typically have some variations of standard Data pseudo-operations. DEFINE BYTE or FORM CONSTANT BYTE handles 8-bit numbers; DEFINE WORD or FORM CONSTANT WORD handles 16-bit numbers or addresses. Other special pseudo-operations may handle character-coded data.

THE EQUATE (or DEFINE) PSEUDO-OPERATION

The Equate pseudo-operation allows the programmer to equate names with addresses or data. This pseudo-operation is almost always given the mnemonic EQU. The names may refer to device addresses, numeric data, starting addresses, fixed addresses, etc.

DEFINING NAMES

The Equate pseudo-operation assigns the numeric value in its operand field to the name in its label field. Here are two examples:

```
    TTY     EQU     5
    LAST    EQU     5000
```

Most assemblers will allow you to define one label in terms of another, e.g.:

```
    LAST    EQU     FINAL
    ST1     EQU     START+1
```

The label in the operand field must, of course, have been previously defined. Often, the operand field may contain more complex expressions, as we shall see later. Double name assignments (two names for the same data or address) may be useful in patching together programs that use different names for the same variable (or different spellings of what was supposed to be the same name).

Note that an EQU pseudo-operation does not cause the Assembler to place anything in program memory. The Assembler simply places an additional name in a table (called a symbol table). This table, unlike the mnemonic table, must be in RAM since it varies with each program. The Assembler program will always need some RAM to hold the symbol table; the more RAM it has, the more symbols it can accept. This RAM is in addition to any that the Assembler needs as temporary storage.

SYMBOL TABLE

When do you use a name? The answer is whenever you have a parameter that you might want to change or that has some meaning besides its ordinary numeric value. We typically assign names to time constants, device addresses, masking patterns, conversion factors, and the like. A name like DELAY, TTY, KBD, KROW or OPEN not only makes the parameter easier to change, it also adds to program documentation. We also assign names to memory locations that have special purposes; they may hold data, mark the start of the program, or be available for intermediate storage.

USE OF NAMES

What name do you use? The best rules are much the same as in the case of labels, except that here meaningful names really count. Why not call the teletypewriter TTY instead of X15, a bit time delay BTIME or BTDLY rather than WW, the number of the "GO" key on a keyboard GOKEY rather than HORSE? This advice seems straightforward, but a surprising number of programmers do not follow it.

CHOICE OF NAMES

Where do you place the Equate pseudo-operations? The best place is at the start of the program, under appropriate comment headings such as I/O Addresses, Temporary Storage, Time Constants, or Program Locations. This makes the definitions easy to find if you want to change them. Furthermore, another user will be able to look up all the definitions in one centralized place. Clearly this practice improves documentation and makes the program easier to use.

PLACEMENT OF DEFINITIONS

Definitions used only in a specific subroutine should appear at the start of the subroutine.

THE ORIGIN PSEUDO-OPERATION

The Origin pseudo-operation (almost always abbreviated ORG) allows the programmer to assemble programs, subroutines or data anywhere in memory. Programs and data may be located in different areas of memory depending on the memory configuration. Startup routines, interrupt service routines, and other required programs may be scattered around memory at fixed or convenient addresses.

The Assembler maintains a Location Counter (comparable to the computer's Program Counter) which contains the location in memory of the next instruction or data item being processed. An ORG pseudo-operation causes the Assembler to place a new value in the Location Counter, much as a Jump instruction causes the CPU to place a new value in the Program Counter. The output from the Assembler must not only contain instructions and data, but must also indicate to the loader program where in memory it should place the instructions and data.

> LOCATION COUNTER

Microprocessor programs often contain several Origin statements for the following purposes:

> Reset (startup) address
> Interrupt service addresses
> Trap addresses
> RAM storage
> Memory stack
> Main program
> Subroutines
> Memory addresses reserved for input/output devices or special functions

Still other Origin statements may allow room for later insertions, place tables or data in memory, or assign vacant RAM space for data buffers. Program and data memory in microcomputers may occupy widely scattered addresses in order to simplify the hardware design.

Typical Origin statements are:

```
ORG     RESET
ORG     1000
ORG     INT3
```

Some assemblers default to (assume) an origin of zero if the programmer does not put an ORG statement at the start of the program. The convenience is slight; we recommend the inclusion of an ORG statement to avoid confusion.

> DEFAULT VALUE

THE RESERVE PSEUDO-OPERATION

The Reserve pseudo-operation allows the programmer to allocate RAM for various purposes such as data tables, temporary storage, indirect addresses, a stack, etc.

> ALLOCATING RAM

Using the Reserve pseudo-operation, you assign a name to the memory area and declare the number of locations to be assigned. Here are some examples:

NOKEY	RESERVE	1
TEMP	RESERVE	50
VOLTG	RESERVE	80
BUFR	RESERVE	100

You can use the Reserve pseudo-operation to reserve memory locations in program memory or in data memory; however, the Reserve pseudo-operation is more meaningful when applied to data memory.

In reality, all the Reserve pseudo-operation does is increase the Assembler's Location Counter by the amount declared in the operand field. The Assembler does not actually produce any object code at all.

Note the following features of Reserve:

1) The label of the Reserve pseudo-operation is assigned to the value of the first address reserved. For example, the sequence:

    TEMP   RESERVE   20

    reserves 20 bytes of RAM and assigns the name TEMP to the address of the first byte.

2) You must specify the number of locations to be reserved. There is no default case.

3) No data is placed in the reserved locations. Any data that, by chance, may be in these locations will be left there.

Some assemblers allow the programmer to place initial values in RAM. We strongly recommend that you do not use this feature -- it assumes that the program (along with the initial values) will be loaded from an external device (e.g., paper tape or floppy disk) each time it is run. Most microprocessor programs, on the other hand, reside in non-volatile ROM and start when power comes on. The RAM in such situations does not retain its contents, nor is it reloaded. Always include instructions to initialize the RAM in your program.

INITIALIZING RAM

HOUSEKEEPING PSEUDO-OPERATIONS

There are various housekeeping pseudo-operations that affect the operation of the Assembler and its program listing rather than the output program itself. Common housekeeping pseudo-operations include:

> End, which marks the end of the assembly language source program.
>
> List, which tells the Assembler to print the source program. Some assemblers allow such variations as No List or List.
>
> Symbol Table, to avoid long, repetitive listings.
>
> Name or Title, which prints a name at the top of each page of the listing.
>
> Page or Space, which skips to the next page or next line, respectively, and improves the appearance of the listing, making it easier to read.
>
> Punch, which transfers subsequent object code to the paper tape punch. This pseudo-operation may in some cases be the default option, and therefore unnecessary.

LABELS WITH PSEUDO-OPERATIONS

Users often wonder if or when they can assign a label to a pseudo-operation. These are our recommendations:

1) All Equate pseudo-operations must have labels; they do not make any sense otherwise since their purpose is to define the meaning of the labels.
2) Data and Reserve pseudo-operations usually have labels. The label identifies the first memory location used or assigned.
3) Other pseudo-operations should not have labels. Some Assemblers allow other pseudo-operations to have labels, but the meaning of the labels varies. We recommend that you avoid this practice.

ADDRESSES AND THE OPERAND FIELD

Most assemblers allow the programmer a lot of freedom in describing the contents of the Operand Address field. But remember that the Assembler has built-in names for registers and instructions, and may have other built-in names.

Some common options for the operand field are:

1) **Decimal numbers** | **DECIMAL DATA OR ADDRESSES**

   Most assemblers assume all numbers to be decimal unless they are marked otherwise. So:

        ADD   100

   means "add the contents of memory location 100 (decimal) to the contents of the Accumulator".

2) **Other number systems** | **OTHER NUMBER SYSTEMS**

   Most assemblers will also accept binary, octal or hexadecimal entries. But you must identify these number systems in some way, e.g., by preceding or following the number with an identifying character or letter. Here are some common identifiers:

   B or % for binary

   O, @, Q, or C for octal (we usually avoid the letter O because of the confusion with zero).

   H or $ for hexadecimal (or standard BCD)

   D for decimal. D may be omitted; it is the default case.

   Assemblers sometimes require hexadecimal numbers to start with a digit (e.g., 0A36 instead of A36) in order to distinguish between numbers and names or labels. It is good practice to enter numbers in the base in which their meaning is the clearest; i.e., decimal constants in decimal; addresses and BCD numbers in hexadecimal; masking patterns or bit outputs in binary if they are short, and in hexadecimal if they are long.

3) **Names**

Names can appear in the operand field; they will be treated as the data that they represent. But remember, there is a difference between data and addresses. The sequence

      FIVE   EQU   5
                    ADDA   FIVE

will add the contents of memory location 5 (not necessarily the number 5) to the contents of Accumulator A.

4) **The current value of the Location Counter (usually referred to as * or $).**

This is useful mainly in Jump instructions; for example

      JUMP   * + 6

causes a jump to the memory location six words beyond the word which contains the first byte of the Jump instruction:

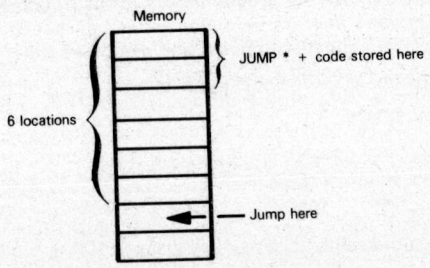

Most microprocessors have many two and three-word instructions. Thus, you will have difficulty determining exactly how far apart two assembly language statements are. Using offsets from the Location Counter, therefore, frequently results in errors that you can avoid if you use labels instead.

5) **Character codes**   `ASCII CHARACTERS`

Most assemblers allow text to be entered as ASCII strings. Such strings may be surrounded either with single or double quotation marks; strings may also use a beginning or ending symbol such as A or C. A few assemblers also permit EBCDIC strings.

We recommend that you use character strings for all text. It improves the clarity and readability of the program.

6) **Combination of 1) through 5) with arithmetic, logical, or special operators.**   `ARITHMETIC AND LOGICAL EXPRESSIONS`

Almost all assemblers allow simple arithmetic combinations such as START+1. Some assemblers also permit multiplication, division, logical functions, shifts, etc. These are referred to as expressions. Note that the Assembler evaluates expressions at assembly time. Even though an expression in the operand field may involve multiplications, you may not be able to use multiplication in the logic of your own program - unless you write a subroutine for that specific purpose.

Assemblers vary in what expressions they accept and how they interpret them. Complex expressions make a program difficult to read and understand.

We have made some recommendations during this section, but will repeat them and add others here. In general, you should emphasizeze clarity and simplicity. There is no payoff for being an expert in the intricacies of the assemblers or in using very complex expressions when not necessary. We suggest the following approach:

- Use the clearest number system or character code for data.
- Masks and BCD numbers in decimal, ASCII characters in octal, or ordinary numerical constants in hexadecimal serve no purpose and therefore should not be used.
- Remember to distinguish data and addresses.
- Do not use offsets from the Location Counter.
- Keep expressions simple and obvious. Do not rely on obscure features of the Assembler.

CONDITIONAL ASSEMBLY

Some assemblers allow you to include or exclude parts of source programs, depending on conditions existing at assembly time. This is called conditional assembly; it gives the Assembler some of the flexibility of a compiler. **Most microcomputer assemblers have limited capabilities for conditional assembly.**

```
    IF    COND

    .    CONDITIONAL PROGRAM
    .
    .
    ENDIF
```

If the expression COND is true at assembly time, the instructions between IF and ENDIF (two pseudo-operations) are included in the program.

Typical uses of conditional assembly are:

1) To include or exclude extra variables.
2) To place diagnostics in test runs.
3) To allow data of various bit lengths.

Unfortunately, conditional assembly tends to clutter programs and make them difficult to read. Use conditional assembly only if it is necessary.

MACROS

You will often find that particular sequences of instructions occur many times in a source program. Repeated instruction sequences may reflect the needs of your program logic, or they may be compensating for deficiencies in your microprocessor's instruction set. You can avoid repeatedly writing out the same instruction sequence by using a macro.

> **DEFINING A SEQUENCE OF INSTRUCTIONS**

Macros allow you to assign a name to an instruction sequence. You then use the macro name in your source program instead of the repeated instruction sequence. The Assembler will replace the macro name with the appropriate sequence of instructions. This may be illustrated as follows:

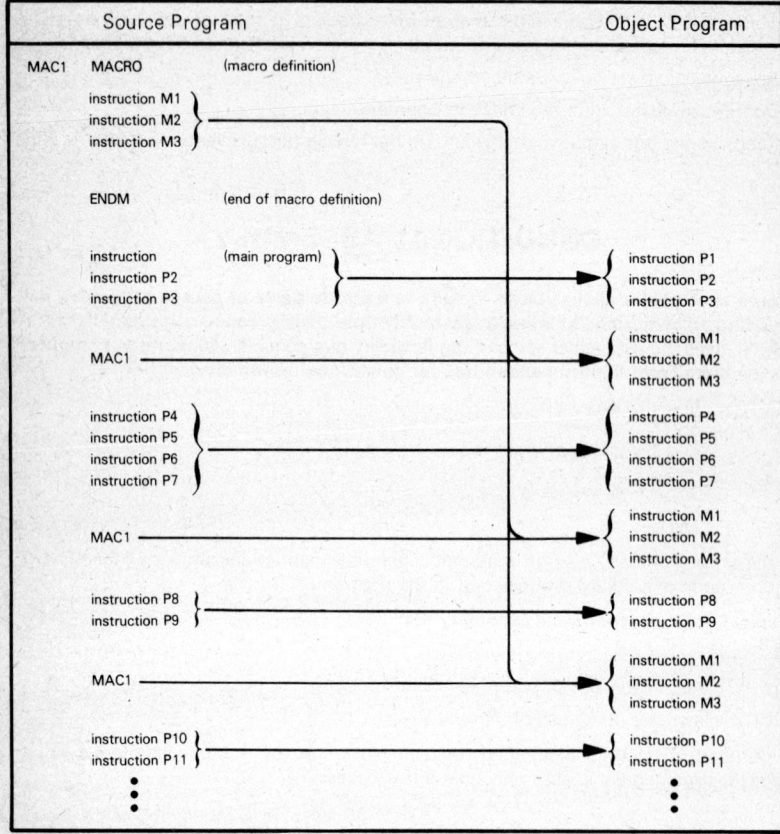

Macros are not the same as subroutines. A subroutine occurs once in a program, and program execution branches to the subroutine. A macro is expanded to an actual instruction sequence each time the macro occurs; thus a macro does not cause any branching.

Macros have the following advantages:

> **ADVANTAGES OF MACROS**

1) Shorter source programs.
2) Better program documentation.
3) Use of debugged instruction sequences — once the macro has been debugged, you are sure of an error-free instruction sequence every time you use the macro.
4) Easier changes. Change the macro definition and the Assembler makes the change for you every time the macro is used.
5) Inclusion of commands, key words, or other computer instructions in the basic instruction set. You use macros to extend or clarify the instruction set.

The disadvantages of macros are: **DISADVANTAGES OF MACROS**
1) Repetition of the same instruction sequences.
2) A single macro may create a lot of instructions.
3) Lack of standardization.
4) Possible effects on registers and flags that may not be clearly stated.

One problem is that variables used in a macro are only known within it (i.e., they are local rather than global). This can often create a great deal of confusion, without any gain in return. You should be aware of this problem when using macros. A complete monograph on macros is M. Campbell-Kelly, <u>An Introduction to Macros</u>, American Elsevier, New York, 1973. **LOCAL OR GLOBAL VARIABLES**

COMMENTS

All assemblers allow you to place comments in a source program. Comments have no effect on the object code, but they help you to read, understand, and document the program. Good commenting is an essential part of writing assembly language diagrams; without comments programs are very difficult to understand.

We will discuss commenting along with documentation in a later chapter, but here are some guidelines: **COMMENTING TECHNIQUES**

1) Use comments to tell what application task the program is doing, not how the microcomputer executes the instructions.

   Comments should say things like "IS TEMPERATURE ABOVE LIMIT?", "LINE FEED TO TTY" or "EXAMINE LOAD SWITCH".

   Comments should not say things like "ADD 1 TO ACCUMULATOR", "JUMP TO START" or "LOOK AT CARRY". You should describe how the program is affecting the system; internal effects on the CPU are seldom of any interest.

2) Keep comments brief and to the point. Details should be available elsewhere in the documentation.
3) Comment all key points.
4) Do not comment standard instructions or sequences which change counters and pointers; pay special attention to instructions that may not have an obvious meaning.
5) Do not use obscure abbreviations.
6) Make the comments neat and readable.
7) Comment all definitions, describing their purposes. Also mark all tables and data storage areas.
8) Comment sections of the program as well as individual instructions.
9) Be consistent in your terminology. You can (should) be repetitive; you do not need to consult a thesaurus.
10) Leave yourself notes at points which you find confusing, e.g., "REMEMBER CARRY WAS SET BY LAST INSTRUCTION". You may drop these in the final documentation.

A well-commented program is easy to work with. You will recover the time spent in commenting many times over. We will try to show good commenting style in the programming examples, although we often over-comment for instructional purposes.

TYPES OF ASSEMBLERS

Although all assemblers perform the same tasks, their implementations vary greatly. We will not try to describe all the existing types of assemblers; we will merely define the terms and indicate some of the choices.

A cross-assembler is an assembler that runs on a computer other than the one for which it assembles programs. `CROSS-ASSEMBLER`

The computer on which the cross-assembler runs is typically a large computer with extensive software support and fast peripherals -- such as an IBM 360 or 370, a Univac 1108, or a Burroughs 6700. The computer for which the cross-assembler assembles programs is typically a microprocessor such as the Intel 8080 or Motorola 6800. Most cross-assemblers are written in FORTRAN so that they are portable.

A self-assembler or resident assembler is an assembler that runs on the computer for which it assembles programs. The self-assembler will require some memory and peripherals, and it may run quite slowly. `RESIDENT ASSEMBLER`

A macro-assembler is an assembler that allows you to define sequences of instructions as macros. `MACRO-ASSEMBLER`

A micro-assembler or microprogram assembler is an assembler used to write the microprograms which define the instruction set of a computer. Microprogramming has nothing specifically to do with microcomputers. Microprogramming is described conceptually in An Introduction to Microcomputers: Volume I — Basic Concepts, Chapter 4. A more complete description is in A.K. Agrawala and T.G. Rauscher, Foundations of Microprogramming, Academic Press, New York, 1976. `MICRO-ASSEMBLER`

A meta-assembler is an assembler that can handle many different instruction sets. The user must define the particular instruction set being used. `META-ASSEMBLER`

A one-pass assembler is an assembler that only goes through the assembly language program once. The major difficulty that a one-pass assembler faces is the presence of an instruction which references a label that appears further on in the source program. In the example `ONE-PASS ASSEMBLER`

```
        JMP     THERE


THERE   ADDA
```

the instruction JMP THERE references a label, THERE, which the Assembler has not yet processed. A one-pass assembler must have some way of resolving these forward references.

A two-pass assembler is an assembler that goes through the assembly language source program twice. The first time the Assembler simply collects and defines all the symbols; the second time it replaces the references with the actual definitions. A two-pass assembler has no problems with forward references, but may be quite slow if no fast mass storage (like a floppy disk) is available; then the Assembler must physically read the program twice from a slow input medium (like a teletypewriter paper tape reader). Most microprocessor-based assemblers require two passes. `TWO-PASS ASSEMBLER`

ERRORS

Assemblers normally provide error messages, often consisting of a single coded letter. Some typical errors are:

1) Undefined name (often a misspelling or an omitted definition).
2) Invalid character (e.g., a 2 in a binary number).
3) Invalid format (wrong delimiter or incorrect operands).
4) Invalid expression (e.g., two operators in a row).
5) Invalid value (usually too large).
6) Missing operand.
7) Double definition (i.e., two different values assigned to one name).
8) Invalid label (e.g., a label on a pseudo-operation that cannot have one).
9) Missing label.
10) Undefined mnemonic.

In interpreting Assembler errors, you must remember that the Assembler may get on the wrong track if it finds a stray letter, an extra space, or incorrect punctuation. Many assemblers will then proceed to misinterpret the following instructions and produce meaningless error messages. Always look at the first error very carefully; subsequent ones may depend on it. Caution and consistent adherence to standard formats will eliminate many annoying mistakes.

LOADERS

The Loader is the program which actually takes the output (object code) from the Assembler and places it in memory. Loaders range from the very simple to the very complex. We will describe a few different types.

A bootstrap loader is a program that uses its own first few instructions to load the rest of itself or another loader program into memory. The bootstrap loader may be in ROM, or you may have to enter it into the computer memory by using front panel switches. The Assembler may place a bootstrap loader at the start of the object program that it produces.

> BOOTSTRAP LOADER

A relocating loader can load programs anywhere in memory. It typically loads each program into the memory space immediately following that used by the previous program. The programs, however, must themselves be capable of being moved around in this way; i.e., they must be relocatable. An absolute loader, in contrast, will always place the programs in the same area of memory.

> RELOCATING LOADER

A linking loader loads programs and subroutines separately; it resolves cross-references -- that is, an instruction in one program or subroutine which refers to a label in another. Object programs loaded by a linking loader must be created by an assembler which permits and marks cross-references.

> LINKING LOADERS

You can find more detailed descriptions of assemblers and loaders in D.W. Barron, <u>Assemblers and Loaders</u>, American Elsevier, New York, 1972, and in C.W. Gear, <u>Computer Organization and Programming</u>, McGraw-Hill, New York, 1974.

Chapter 3
THE 6800 ASSEMBLY LANGUAGE INSTRUCTION SET

We are now ready to start creating assembly language programs. We begin in this chapter by defining the individual instructions of the 6800 assembly language instruction set, plus the syntax rules of the Motorola assemblers.

We do not discuss any aspects of microcomputer hardware, signals, interfaces, or CPU architecture in this book. This information is described in detail in An Introduction to Microcomputers: Volume II — Some Real Products, while 6800 Programming for Logic Design discusses assembly language as an extension of digital logic. In this book, we look at programming techniques from the assembly language programmer's viewpoint, where pins and signals are irrelevant and there are no important differences between a minicomputer and a microcomputer.

Interrupts, Direct Memory Access, and the Stack architecture for the 6800 will be described in later chapters of this book, in conjunction with assembly language programming discussions of the same subjects.

This chapter contains a detailed definition of each assembly language instruction. These definitions are identical to Chapter 6 of 6800 Programming for Logic Design.

The detailed description of individual instructions is preceded by a general discussion of the 6800 instruction set that divides instructions into those which are commonly used, infrequently used, and rarely used. If you are an experienced assembly language programmer, this categorization is not particularly important — and, depending on your own programming prejudices, it may not even be accurate. If you are a novice assembly language programmer, we recommend that you begin by writing programs using only instructions in the "commonly used" category. Once you have mastered the concepts of assembly language programming, you may examine other instructions and use them where appropriate.

CPU REGISTERS AND STATUS FLAGS

The 6800 has two Accumulators, a Status register, an Index register, a Stack Pointer and a Program Counter. These may be illustrated as follows:

8 bits	Accumulator A
8 bits	Accumulator B
16 bits	Index Register X
16 bits	Program Counter PC
16 bits	Stack Pointer SP
8 bits	Status Register

The two Accumulators, A and B, are both primary Accumulators. The only instructions which apply to one Accumulator but not the other are the instructions which move statuses between Accumulator A and the Status register.

The Index register is a typical microcomputer Index register, as described in <u>An Introduction to Microcomputers: Volume I</u>.

The 6800 has a Stack implemented in memory and indexed by the Stack Pointer, as described in Volume I. Because of the nature of the 6800 instruction set, it is more realistic to look upon the 6800 Stack Pointer as a cross between a Stack Pointer and a Data Counter. Memory reference instructions make it very easy to store the contents of either the Stack Pointer or the Index register in read/write memory; by maintaining a number of base page memory locations as storage for these two Address registers, each can be put to multiple use.

The Program Counter is a typical Program Counter, as described in Volume I.

The 6800 has a Status register which maintains five status flags and an interrupt control bit. These are the five status flags:

      Carry (C)
      Overflow (O)
      Sign (S)
      Zero (Z)
      Auxiliary Carry (A_C)

Statuses are assigned bit positions within the Status register as follows:

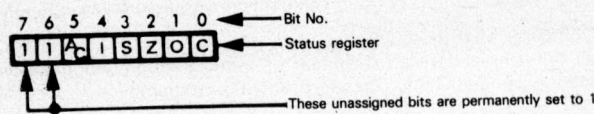

I is the external interrupt enable/disable flag. When it is 1, interrupts via IRQ are disabled; when it is 0, interrupts via IRQ are enabled.

6800 literature refers to the Sign bit as a negative bit, given the symbol N; the Overflow bit is given the symbol V. The Intermediate Carry bit represents the standard carry out of bit 3 and is referred to as the Half Carry bit, given the symbol H. Statuses are nevertheless set and reset as described for our hypothetical microcomputer in <u>An Introduction to Microcomputers: Volume I</u>.

Table 3-1. Frequently Used Instructions of the 6800

Instruction Code	Meaning
ADC	ADD WITH CARRY
ADD, ABA	ADD
AND	LOGICAL AND
ASL	ARITHMETIC SHIFT LEFT
BCC	BRANCH IF CARRY CLEAR
BCS	BRANCH IF CARRY SET
BEQ	BRANCH IF = ZERO
BHI	BRANCH IF HIGHER
BLS	BRANCH IF LOWER OR SAME
BMI	BRANCH IF NEGATIVE SET
BNE	BRANCH IF NOT EQUAL ZERO
BPL	BRANCH IF NEGATIVE CLEAR
BRA	BRANCH ALWAYS
BSR	BRANCH TO SUBROUTINE
CLR	CLEAR
CMP, CBA	COMPARE
DEC	DECREMENT
DEX	DECREMENT INDEX REGISTER
INC	INCREMENT
INX	INCREMENT INDEX REGISTER
JSR	JUMP TO SUBROUTINE
LDA	LOAD ACCUMULATOR
LDX	LOAD INDEX REGISTER
LSR	LOGICAL SHIFT RIGHT
PSH	PUSH DATA ONTO STACK
PUL	PULL DATA FROM STACK
ROL	ROTATE LEFT
ROR	ROTATE RIGHT
RTS	RETURN FROM SUBROUTINE
STA	STORE ACCUMULATOR
STX	STORE INDEX REGISTER
SUB, SBA	SUBTRACT

Table 3-2. Occasionally Used Instructions of the 6800

Instruction Code	Meaning
ASR	ARITHMETIC SHIFT RIGHT
BGE	BRANCH IF > ZERO
BGT	BRANCH IF GREATER THAN ZERO
BIT	BIT TEST
BLE	BRANCH IF < ZERO
BLT	BRANCH IF LESS THAN ZERO
CLC	CLEAR CARRY
CLI	CLEAR (ENABLE) INTERRUPT
COM	ONES COMPLEMENT
CPX	COMPARE INDEX REGISTER
DAA	DECIMAL ADJUST A
EOR	EXCLUSIVE OR
JMP	JUMP
LDS	LOAD STACK POINTER
NEG	TWOS COMPLEMENT
NOP	NO OPERATION
ORA	LOGICAL (INCLUSIVE) OR
RTI	RETURN FROM INTERRUPT
SEC	SET CARRY
SEI	SET (DISABLE) INTERRUPT
STS	STORE STACK POINTER
SWI	SOFTWARE INTERRUPT
TAB	TRANSFER A TO B
TBA	TRANSFER B TO A
TST	TEST

Table 3-3. Seldom Used Instructions of the 6800

Instruction Code	Meaning
BVC	BRANCH IF OVERFLOW CLEAR
BVS	BRANCH IF OVERFLOW SET
CLV	CLEAR OVERFLOW
DES	DECREMENT STACK POINTER
INS	INCREMENT STACK POINTER
SBC	SUBTRACT WITH CARRY (BORROW)
SEV	SET OVERFLOW
TAP	TRANSFER A TO CONDITION CODE REGISTER
TPA	TRANSFER CONDITION CODE REGISTER TO A
TSX	TRANSFER STACK POINTER TO INDEX REGISTER
TXS	TRANSFER INDEX REGISTER TO STACK POINTER
WAI	WAIT FOR INTERRUPT

6800 MEMORY ADDRESSING MODES

The Motorola 6800 offers seven basic addressing methods:

1) Memory - Immediate
2) Memory - Direct
3) Memory - Indexed
4) Memory - Extended
5) Inherent
6) Relative
7) Accumulator

6800 instructions allow various combinations of these addressing modes to address the operands required for the instruction. See Table 3-5 for the addressing options available with each instruction.

MEMORY — IMMEDIATE

In this form of addressing, one of the operands is present in the byte(s) immediately following the first byte of object code. An immediate operand is specified by prefacing the operand with the # symbol. For example:

    ADDA   #$30

requests the Assembler to generate an ADD instruction which will add the value 30_{16} to Accumulator A.

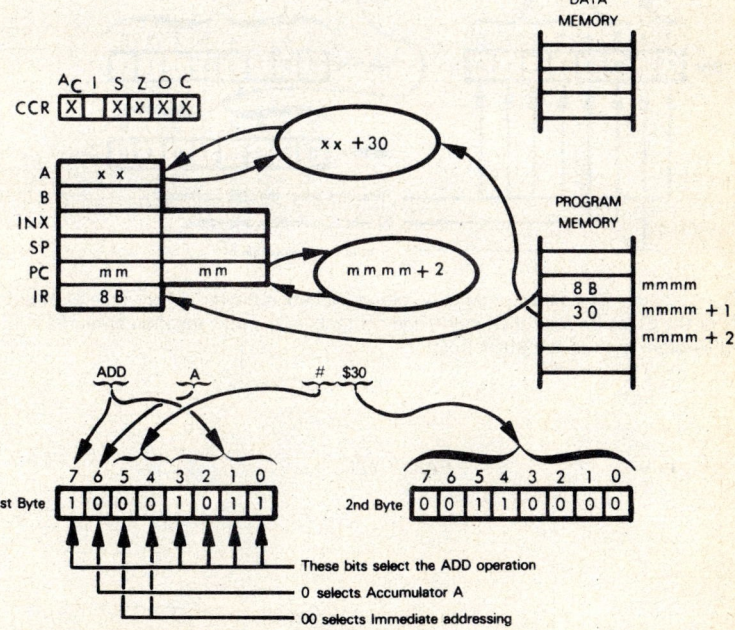

This example demonstrates a single byte immediate operand. Instructions such as AND, BIT, EOR and SBC use this form.

Double-byte immediate operands are employed by the CPX, LDS and LDX instructions. The LDS instruction, for example, may load the Stack Pointer with the two bytes following the first object code byte. The instruction:

LDS   #$3F2A

is illustrated in the following diagram:

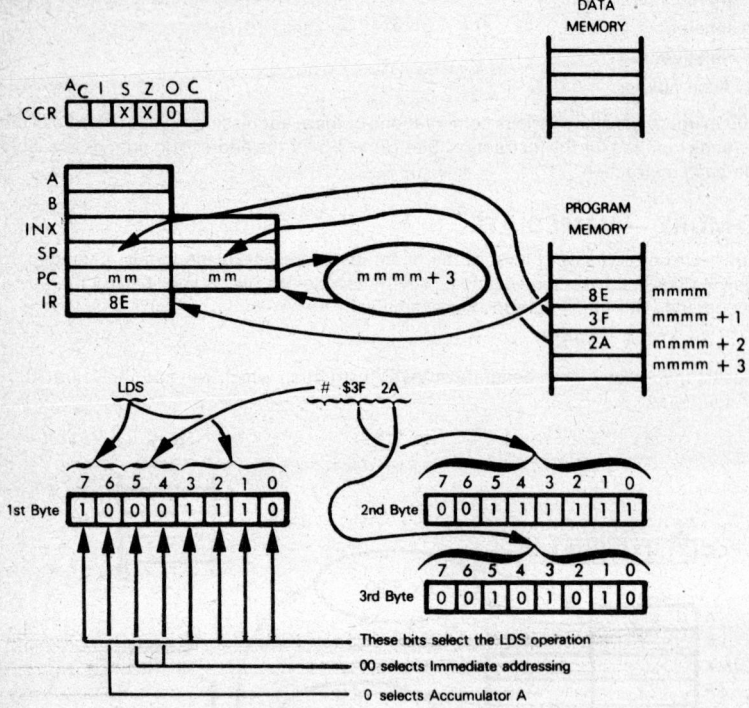

This instruction stores the contents of memory location mmmm+1 into the high-order byte of the Stack Pointer, then stores the contents of memory location mmmm+2 into the low-order byte of the Stack Pointer.

MEMORY — DIRECT

This form of addressing uses the second byte of the instruction to identify an operand present in the low 256_{10} words of memory. This form of addressing is specified when the expression used as the operand reduces to a value between 00_{16} and FF_{16}. For example:

    ADDA $30

requests the Assembler to generate an ADD instruction which will add the value present at memory location 0030_{16} to Accumulator A.

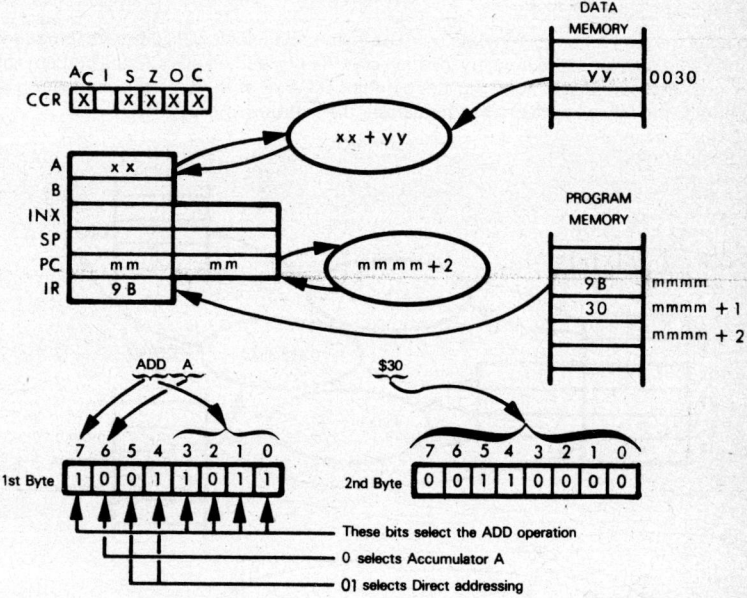

MEMORY — INDEXED

This form of addressing combines the second byte of the instruction with the contents of the Index register to produce the memory address of the data to be used as an operand. Indexed addressing on the 6800 differs from indexed addressing as described in <u>An Introduction to Microcomputers: Volume I</u>, in that the one-byte displacement provided by the memory reference instruction is added to the Index register as an unsigned 8-bit value. The contents of the Index register are not changed.

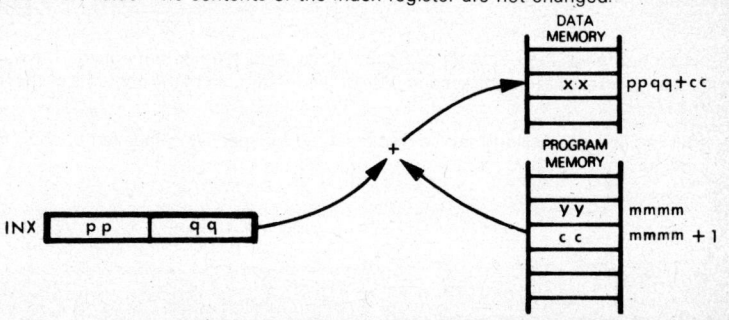

If instruction yy specifies indexed addressing, then the effective address of one operand will be ppqq+cc. Therefore xx will be one of the operands used by the instruction.

Indexed addressing is specified by including:

> X
> ,X
> expr,X

in the operand field of the instruction. For example:

> ADDA $30,X

requests the Assembler to generate an ADD instruction which will add to Accumulator A the value present at the memory location specified by adding 30_{16} to the contents of the Index register. If the Index register contains 0316_{16} at the time this instruction is executed, the following diagram summarizes the instruction execution:

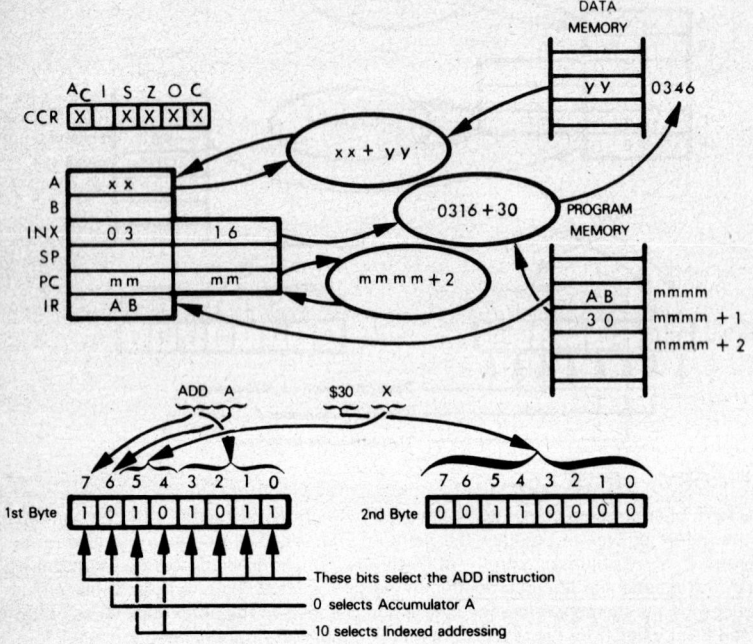

This instruction adds the contents of Accumulator A to the contents of the memory location specified by adding the second byte of the instruction to the contents of the Index register.

Note that implied addressing may be implemented by specifying indexed addressing with a displacement of 0.

MEMORY — EXTENDED

This form of addressing combines the second and third bytes of object code to form the address of the data to be used as an operand. Motorola extended addressing is identical to the direct addressing mode described in <u>An Introduction to Microcomputers: Volume I</u>. Extended addressing is specified in the same way as direct addressing, i.e., an expression is given as the operand. If the expression evaluates to a number in the range 256 < expression < 65,535, then extended addressing is used. For example:

    ADDA $31F6

requests the Assembler to generate an ADD instruction which will add the value present at memory location $31F6_{16}$ to the contents of Accumulator A.

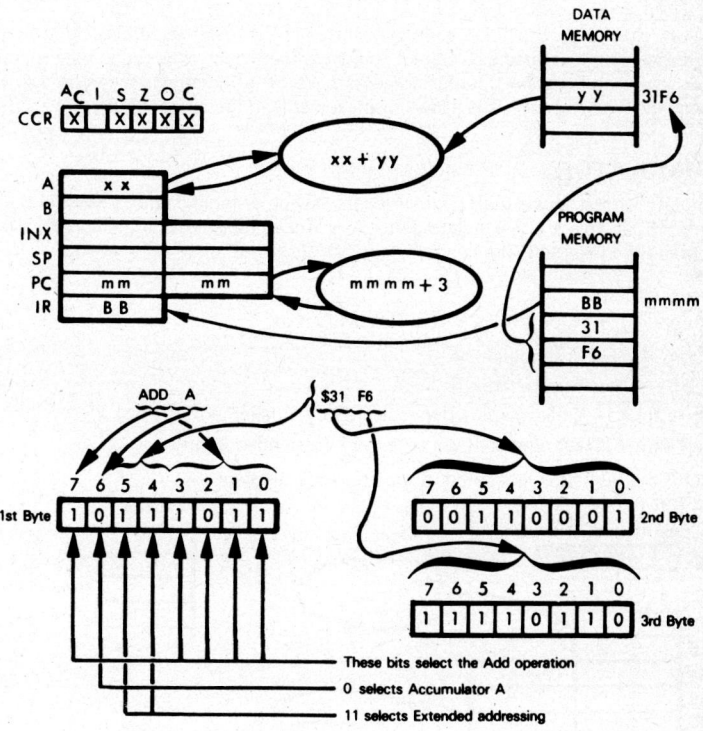

In addition, there are several instructions which do not provide a direct addressing option (0 ≤ expr ≤ 255), e.g., CLR, DEC, ROR. For those instructions, extended addressing is used whenever a memory location is to be directly accessed.

INHERENT

Inherent addressing is specified when it is obvious by the nature of the instruction mnemonic which registers, statuses or memory locations are to be used as operands. For example, ABA, the Add Accumulator B to Accumulator A instruction, specifies what registers are to be the operands. CLI, the Clear Interrupt Mask instruction, specifies what status is to be affected by the instruction, and RTS, the Return-from-Subroutine instruction, specifies that a return is to be executed; this will access the Stack to determine the new value of the Program Counter.

RELATIVE

Branch and Branch-on-Condition instructions use program relative addressing; a single byte displacement is treated as a signed binary number which is added to the Program Counter, after the Program Counter contents have been incremented to address the next sequential instruction. This allows displacements in the range $+129_{10}$ to -126_{10} bytes.

ACCUMULATOR

Accumulator addressing is used by instructions having a single operand. Most of these instructions can select either Accumulator A or Accumulator B or a memory byte via the operand. For example, the

    CLRA

instruction is one of four forms of the CLR instruction:

1) CLRA — Clear Accumulator A
2) CLRB — Clear Accumulator B
3) CLR expr,X — Clear memory byte selected by indexed addressing.
4) CLR expr — Clear memory byte selected by extended addressing.

The CLRA instruction is illustrated in the following diagram:

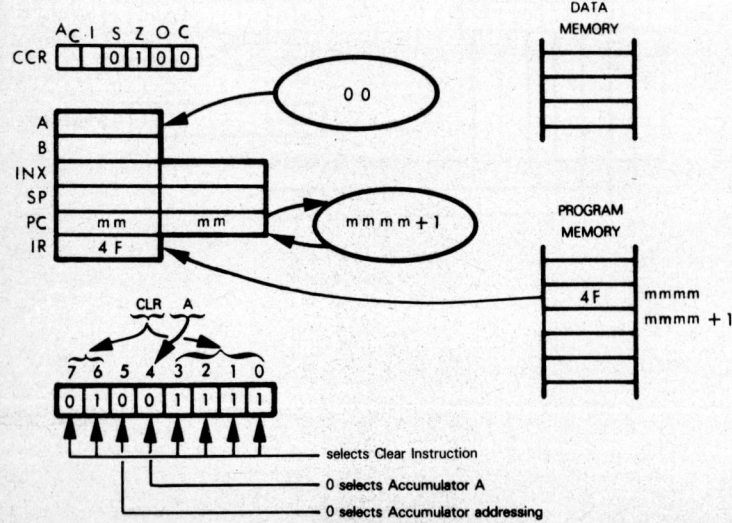

Instructions falsely frighten microcomputer users who are new to programming. Taken as an isolated event, operations associated with the execution of a single instruction are easy enough to follow — and that is the purpose of this chapter.

Why are the instructions of a microcomputer referred to as an instruction "set"? Because the instructions selected by the designers of any microcomputer are selected with great care; it must be easy to execute complex operations as a sequence of simple events — each of which is represented by one instruction from a well designed instruction "set".

Remaining consistent with An Introduction to Microcomputers: Volume II, Table 3-4 summarizes the 6800 microcomputer instruction set, with similar instructions grouped together.

Individual instructions are described next in alphabetical order of instruction mnemonic.

In addition to simply stating what each instruction does, the purpose of the instruction within normal programming logic is identified.

ABBREVIATIONS

These are the abbreviations used in this chapter:

ACX   Either Accumulator A or Accumulator B

The registers:

    A,B Accumulator
    X   Index register
    PC   Program Counter
    SP   Stack Pointer
    SR   Status register

Statuses shown:

    C   Carry status
    Z   Zero status
    S   Sign status
    O   Overflow status
    I   Interrupt Mask status
    A_C Auxiliary Carry status

Symbols in the STATUSES column:

    (blank) operation does not affect status
    X   operation affects status
    0   flag is cleared by the operation
    1   flag is set by the operation

ADR8   An 8-bit (1-byte) quantity which may be used to directly address the first 256 locations in memory, or may be an 8-bit unsigned displacement to be added to the Index register.

ADR16   A 16-bit memory address

B2   Instruction Byte 2

B3   Instruction Byte 3

DATA   An 8-bit binary data unit

DATA16 A 16-bit binary data unit

DISP   An 8-bit signed binary address displacement

xx(HI)   The high-order 8 bits of the 16-bit quantity xx; for example, SP(HI) means bits 15 - 8 of the Stack Pointer

xx(LO)	The low-order 8 bits of the 16-bit quantity xx; for example, PC(LO) means bits 7 - 0 of the Program Counter
[ ]	Contents of location enclosed with brackets
[[ ]]	Implied memory addressing; the contents of the memory location designated by the contents of a register.

[MEM]	Symbol for memory location indicated by base page direct, extended direct, or indexed addressing. That is:
	    [MEM] = [ADR8]
	or
	    [ADR16]
	or
	    [[X] + ADR8]

[M]	Symbol for memory location indicated by extended direct or indexed addressing. That is:
	    [M] = [ADR16]
	or
	    [[X] + ADR8]

$\wedge$	Logical AND
V	Logical OR
$\veebar$	Logical Exclusive-OR
$\leftarrow$	Data is transferred in the direction of the arrow

The effect of instruction execution on status is illustrated in the following way:

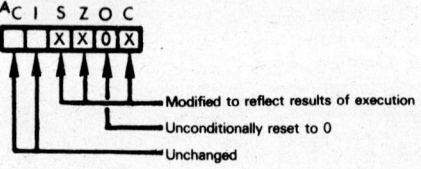

Within instruction execution illustrations, an X identifies a status that is set or reset. A 0 identifies a status that is always cleared. A blank means the status does not change.

STATUS CHANGES WITH INSTRUCTION EXECUTION

INSTRUCTION OBJECT CODES

Instruction object codes are represented as 2 hexadecimal digits for instructions without variations.

Instruction object codes are represented as 8 binary digits for instructions with variations; the binary digit representation of variations is then identifiable.

INSTRUCTION EXECUTION TIMES AND CODES

Table 3-5 lists instructions in alphabetical order, showing object codes and execution times, expressed as machine cycles.

Table 3-4. A Summary of the 6800 Instruction Set

TYPE	MNEMONIC	OPERAND(S)	BYTES	C	Z	S	O	A_C	I	OPERATION PERFORMED
PRIMARY MEMORY REFERENCE AND I/O	LDA	ACX,ADR8	2		X	X	0			[ACX]←[MEM]
		ACX,ADR16	3							Load A or B using base page direct, extended direct, or indexed addressing.
	STA	ACX,ADR8	2		X	X	0			[MEM]←[ACX]
		ACX,ADR16	3							Store A or B using direct, extended, or indexed addressing.
	LDX	ADR8	2		X	X	0			[X(HI)]←[MEM], [X(LO)]←[MEM + 1]
		ADR16	3							Load Index register using direct, extended, or indexed addressing. Sign status reflects Index register bit 15.
	STX	ADR8	2		X	X	0			[MEM]←[X(HI)], [MEM + 1]←[X(LO)]
		ADR16	3							Store contents of Index register using direct, extended, or indexed addressing. Sign status reflects Index register bit 15.
	LDS	ADR8	2		X	X	0			[SP(HI)]←[MEM], [SP(LO)]←[MEM + 1]
		ADR16	3							Load Stack Pointer using direct, extended, or indexed addressing. Sign status reflects Stack Pointer bit 15.
	STS	ADR8	2		X	X	0			[MEM]←[SP(HI)], [MEM + 1]←[SP(LO)]
		ADR16	3							Store contents of Stack Pointer using direct, extended, or indexed addressing. Sign status reflects Stack Pointer bit 15.
SECONDARY MEMORY REFERENCE (MEMORY OPERATE)	ADD	ACX,ADR8	2	X	X	X	X	X		[ACX]←[ACX] + [MEM]
		ACX,ADR16	3							Add to Accumulator A or B using base page direct, extended direct, or indexed addressing.
	ADC	ACX,ADR8	2	X	X	X	X	X		[ACX]←[ACX] + [MEM] + C
		ACX,ADR16	3							Add with carry to Accumulator A or B using direct, extended, or indexed addressing.
	AND	ACX,ADR8	2		X	X	0			[ACX]←[ACX] ∧ [MEM]
		ACX,ADR16	3							AND with Accumulator A or B using direct, extended, or indexed addressing.
	BIT	ACX,ADR8	2		X	X	0			[ACX] ∧ [MEM]
		ACX,ADR16	3							AND with Accumulator A or B, but only Status register is affected.
	CMP	ACX,ADR8	2	X	X	X	X			[ACX] - [MEM]
		ACX,ADR16	3							Compare with Accumulator A or B (only Status register is affected).
	EOR	ACX,ADR8	2		X	X	0			[ACX]←[ACX] ⊻ [MEM]
		ACX,ADR16	3							Exclusive-OR with Accumulator A or B using direct, extended, or indexed addressing.
	ORA	ACX,ADR8	2		X	X	0			[ACX]←[ACX] ∨ [MEM]
		ACX,ADR16	3							OR with Accumulator A or B using direct, extended, or indexed addressing.

Table 3-4. A Summary of the 6800 Instruction Set (Continued)

TYPE	MNEMONIC	OPERAND(S)	BYTES	STATUSES C Z S O A_C I	OPERATION PERFORMED
SECONDARY MEMORY REFERENCE (MEMORY OPERATE) CONTINUED	SUB	ACX,ADR8 ACX,ADR16	2 3	x x x x	[ACX]←[ACX] - [MEM]. Subtract from Accumulator A or B using direct, extended, or indexed addressing.
	SBC	ACX,ADR8 ACX,ADR16	2 3	x x x x	[ACX]←[ACX] - [MEM] - C Subtract with carry from Accumulator A or B using direct, extended, or indexed addressing.
	CPX	ADR8 ADR16	2 3	x x x	[X(HI)] ← [MEM], [X(LO)] ← [MEM + 1] Compare with contents of Index register (only Status register is affected). Sign and Overflow statuses reflect result on most significant byte.
	CLR	ADR8 ADR16	2 3	0 1 0 0	[M] ← 00_{16} Clear memory location using extended or indexed addressing.
	COM	ADR8 ADR16	2 3	1 x x 0	[M]←[$\overline{M}$] Complement contents of memory location (ones complement).
	NEG	ADR8 ADR16	2 3	x x x x	[M] ← 00_{16} - [M] Negate contents of memory location (twos complement). Carry status is set if result is 00_{16} and reset otherwise. Overflow status is set if result is 80_{16} and reset otherwise.
	DEC	ADR8 ADR16	2 3	x x x	[M]←[M] - 1 Decrement contents of memory location, using extended or indexed addressing. Overflow status is set if operand was 80_{16} before execution, and cleared otherwise.
	INC	ADR8 ADR16	2 3	x x x	[M]←[M] + 1 Increment contents of memory location, using extended or indexed addressing. Overflow status is set if operand was $7F_{16}$ before execution, and cleared otherwise.
	ROL	ADR8 ADR16	2 3	x x x x	$C \leftarrow [7 \cdots 0] \leftarrow , . 0 \leftarrow S \leftarrow C$ [M] Rotate contents of memory location left through carry.
	ROR	ADR8 ADR16	2 3	x x x x	$C \rightarrow [7 \cdots 0] \rightarrow , . 0 \leftarrow S \leftarrow C$ [M] Rotate contents of memory location right through carry.

3-14

Table 3-4. A Summary of the 6800 Instruction Set (Continued)

TYPE	MNEMONIC	OPERAND(S)	BYTES	STATUSES C Z S O A$_C$ I	OPERATION PERFORMED
SECONDARY MEMORY REFERENCE (MEMORY OPERATE) CONTINUED	ASL	ADR8 ADR16	2 3	x x x x	Arithmetic shift left. Bit 0 is set to 0.
	ASR	ADR8 ADR16	2 3	x x x x	Arithmetic shift right. Bit 7 stays the same.
	LSR	ADR8 ADR16	2 3	x x x 0 x	Logical shift right. Bit 7 is set to 0.
	TST	ADR8 ADR16	2 3	0 x x x 0	[M] - 00$_{16}$ Test contents of memory location for zero or negative value.
IMMEDIATE	LDA	ACX,DATA	2	x x x 0	[ACX] ← DATA Load A or B immediate.
	LDX	DATA16	3	x x x 0	[X(HI)] ← [B2], [X(LO)] ← [B3] Load Index register immediate. Sign status reflects Index register bit 15.
	LDS	DATA16	3	x x x 0	[SP(HI)] ← [B2], [X(LO)] ← [B3] Load Stack Pointer immediate. Sign status reflects Stack Pointer bit 15.
IMMEDIATE OPERATE	ADD	ACX,DATA	2	x x x x x x	[ACX] ← [ACX] + DATA Add immediate to Accumulator A or B.
	ADC	ACX,DATA	2	x x x x x x	[ACX] ← [ACX] + DATA + C Add immediate with carry to Accumulator A or B.
	AND	ACX,DATA	2	x x x 0	[ACX] ← [ACX] ∧ DATA AND immediate with Accumulator A or B.
	BIT	ACX,DATA	2	x x x 0	[ACX] ∧ DATA AND immediate with Accumulator A or B, but only the Status register is affected.

Table 3-4. A Summary of the 6800 Instruction Set (Continued)

TYPE	MNEMONIC	OPERAND(S)	BYTES	STATUSES C	Z	S	O	A_C	I	OPERATION PERFORMED
IMMEDIATE OPERATE (CONTINUED)	CMP	ACX,DATA	2	X	X	X	X			[ACX] - DATA Compare immediate with Accumulator A or B (only the Status register is affected).
	EOR	ACX,DATA	2		X	X	0			[ACX]←[ACX]⊕DATA Exclusive-OR immediate with Accumulator A or B.
	ORA	ACX,DATA	2		X	X	0			[ACX]←[ACX] V DATA OR immediate with Accumulator A or B.
	SUB	ACX,DATA	2	X	X	X	X			[ACX]←[ACX] - DATA Subtract immediate from Accumulator A or B.
	SBC	ACX,DATA	2	X	X	X	X			[ACX]←[ACX] - DATA - C Subtract immediate with carry from Accumulator A or B.
	CPX	DATA16	3		X	X	X			[X(HI)] - [B2], [X(LO)] - [B3] Compare immediate with contents of Index register (only the Status register is affected). Sign and Overflow status reflect result on most significant byte.
JUMP	JMP	ADR8 ADR16	2 3							[PC] ← [X] + ADR8 or [PC(HI)]←[B2], [PC(LO)]←[B3] Jump to indexed or extended address.
	JSR	ADR8 ADR16	2 3							[[SP]]←[PC(LO)], [[SP]-1]←[PC(HI)], [SP]←[SP]-2 [PC]←[X] + ADR8 or [PC(HI)]←[B2], [PC(LO)]←[B3] Jump to subroutine (indexed or extended addressing).
	BRA	DISP	2							[PC]←[PC] + DISP + 2 Unconditional branch relative to present Program Counter contents.
	BSR	DISP	2							[[SP]]←[PC(LO)], [[SP]-1]←[PC(HI)], [SP]←[SP]-2, [PC]←[PC] + DISP + 2 Unconditional branch to subroutine located relative to present Program Counter contents.

Table 3-4. A Summary of the 6800 Instruction Set (Continued)

TYPE	MNEMONIC	OPERAND(S)	BYTES	C	Z	S	O	Ac	I	OPERATION PERFORMED
BRANCH ON CONDITION	BCC	DISP	2							[PC]←[PC]+DISP+2 if the given condition is true:
	BCS	DISP	2							C = 0 (Branch if carry clear)
	BEQ	DISP	2							C = 1 (Branch if carry set)
	BGE	DISP	2							Z = 1 (Branch if equal to zero)
	BGT	DISP	2							S∀O = 0 (Branch if greater than or equal to zero)
	BHI	DISP	2							Z∨(S∀O) = 0 (Branch if greater than zero)
	BLE	DISP	2							C∨Z = 0 (Branch if Accumulator contents higher than comparand)
	BLS	DISP	2							Z∨(S∀O) = 1 (Branch if less than or equal to zero)
	BLT	DISP	2							C∨Z = 1 (Branch if Accumulator contents less than or same as comparand)
	BMI	DISP	2							S∀O = 1 (Branch if less than zero)
	BNE	DISP	2							S = 1 (Branch if minus)
	BVC	DISP	2							Z = 0 (Branch if not equal to zero)
	BVS	DISP	2							O = 0 (Branch if overflow clear)
	BPL	DISP	2							O = 1 (Branch if overflow set)
										S = 0 (Branch if plus)
REGISTER-REGISTER MOVE	TAB		1		x	x	0			[B]←[A] Move Accumulator A contents to Accumulator B.
	TBA		1		x	x	0			[A]←[B] Move Accumulator B contents to Accumulator A.
	TXS		1							[SP]←[X]-1 Move Index register contents to Stack Pointer and decrement.
	TSX		1							[X]←[SP]+1 Move Stack Pointer contents to Index register and increment.
REGISTER OPERATE	ABA		1	x	x	x	x	x		[A]←[A]+[B] Add contents of Accumulators A and B.
	CBA		1	x	x	x	x			[A]-[B] Compare contents of Accumulators A and B. Only the Status register is affected.
	SBA		1	x	x	x	x			[A]←[A]-[B] Subtract contents of Accumulator B from those of Accumulator A.

Table 3-4. A Summary of the 6800 Instruction Set (Continued)

TYPE	MNEMONIC	OPERAND(S)	BYTES	STATUSES C Z S O A_C I	OPERATION PERFORMED
REGISTER OPERATE	CLR	ACX	1	0 1 0 0	$[ACX] \leftarrow 00_{16}$ Clear Accumulator A or B.
	COM	ACX	1	1 x x 0	$[ACX] \leftarrow \overline{[ACX]}$ Complement contents of Accumulator A or B (ones complement).
	NEG	ACX	1	x x x x	$[ACX] \leftarrow 00_{16} - [ACX]$ Negate contents of Accumulator A or B (twos complement). Carry status is set if result is 00_{16} and reset otherwise. Overflow status is set if result is 80_{16} and reset otherwise.
	DAA		1	x x x x	Decimal adjust A. Convert contents of A (the binary sum of BCD operands) to BCD format. Carry status is set if value of upper four bits is greater than 9, but not cleared if previously set.
	DEC	ACX	1	x x x	$[ACX] \leftarrow [ACX] - 1$ Decrement contents of Accumulator A or B. Overflow status is set if operand was 80_{16} before execution, and cleared otherwise.
	DEX		1	x	$[X] \leftarrow [X] - 1$ Decrement contents of Index register.
	DES		1		$[SP] \leftarrow [SP] - 1$ Decrement contents of Stack Pointer.
	INC	ACX	1	x x x	$[ACX] \leftarrow [ACX] + 1$ Increment contents of Accumulator A or B. Overflow status is set if operand was $7F_{16}$ before execution, and cleared otherwise.
	INX		1	x	$[X] \leftarrow [X] + 1$ Increment contents of Index register.
	INS		1		$[SP] \leftarrow [SP] + 1$ Increment contents of Stack Pointer.
	ROL	ACX	1	x x x x	$\boxed{C} \leftarrow \boxed{7 \leftarrow 0} \leftarrow , 0 \rightarrow S \forall C$ $[ACX]$ Rotate Accumulator A or B left through carry.

Table 3-4. A Summary of the 6800 Instruction Set (Continued)

TYPE	MNEMONIC	OPERAND(S)	BYTES	STATUSES C Z S O A_C I	OPERATION PERFORMED
REGISTER OPERATE (CONTINUED)	ROR	ACX	1	X X X X	Rotate Accumulator A or B right through carry. [ACX], $0 \to S \leftarrow C$
	ASL	ACX	1	X X X X	Arithmetic shift left. Bit 0 is set to 0. [ACX], $0 \to S \leftarrow C$
	ASR	ACX	1	X X X X	Arithmetic shift right. Bit 7 stays the same. [ACX], $0 \to S \leftarrow C$
	LSR	ACX	1	X X X 0 X	Logical shift right. Bit 7 is set to 0. $0 \to S \leftarrow C$
	TST	ACX	1	0 X X 0	$[ACX] - 00_{16}$. Test contents of Accumulator A or B for zero or negative value.
STACK	PSH	ACX	1		$[[SP]] \leftarrow [ACX]$, $[SP] \leftarrow [SP] - 1$. Push contents of Accumulator A or B onto top of Stack and decrement Stack Pointer.
	PUL	ACX	1		$[SP] \leftarrow [SP] + 1$, $[ACX] \leftarrow [[SP]]$. Increment Stack Pointer and pull Accumulator A or B from top of Stack.
	RTS		1		$[PC(HI)] \leftarrow [[SP] + 1]$, $[PC(LO)] \leftarrow [[SP] + 2]$, $[SP] \leftarrow [SP] + 2$. Return from subroutine. Pull PC from top of Stack and increment Stack Pointer.

Table 3-4. A Summary of the 6800 Instruction Set (Continued)

TYPE	MNEMONIC	OPERAND(S)	BYTES	STATUSES C Z S O A$_C$ I	OPERATION PERFORMED
INTERRUPT	CLI		1	0	I→0 Clear interrupt mask to enable interrupts.
	SEI		1	1	I→1 Set interrupt mask to disable interrupts.
	RTI		1	X X X X X X	[SR]→[[SP]+1], [B]→[[SP]+2], [A]→[[SP]+3], [X(HI)]→[[SP]+4], [X(LO)]→[[SP]+5], [PC(HI)]→[[SP]+6], [PC(LO)]→[[SP]+7], [SP]→[SP]+7 Return from interrupt. Pull registers from Stack and increment Stack Pointer.
	SWI		1	1	[[SP]]→[PC(LO)], [[SP]-1]→[PC(HI)], [[SP]-2]→[X(LO)], [[SP]-3]→[X(HI)], [[SP]-4]→[A], [[SP]-5]→[B], [[SP]-6]→[SR], [SP]→[SP]-7, [PC(HI)]→[FFFA$_{16}$] [PC(LO)]→[FFFB$_{16}$] Software Interrupt: push registers onto Stack, decrement Stack Pointer, and jump to interrupt subroutine.

Table 3-4. A Summary of the 6800 Instruction Set (Continued)

TYPE	MNEMONIC	OPERAND(S)	BYTES	STATUSES C Z S O Ac I	OPERATION PERFORMED
INTERRUPT (CONTINUED)	WAI		1	1	[[SP]]←[PC(LO)], [[SP]-1]←[PC(HI)], [[SP]-2]←[X(LO)], [[SP]-3]←[X(HI)], [[SP]-4]←[A], [[SP]-5]←[B], [[SP]-6]←[SR], [SP]←[SP]-7 Push registers onto Stack, decrement Stack Pointer, and wait for interrupt. If [I]=1 when WAI is executed, a non-maskable interrupt is required to exit the Wait state. Otherwise, [I]←1 when the interrupt occurs.
STATUS	CLC		1	0	C←0 Clear carry
	SEC		1	1	C←1 Set carry
	CLV		1	0	O←0 Clear overflow status bit
	SEV		1	1	O←1 Set overflow status bit
	TAP		1	X X X X X X	[SR]←[A] Transfer contents of Accumulator A to Status register.
	TPA		1		[A]←[SR] Transfer contents of Status register to Accumulator A.
	NOP		1		No Operation

The following codes are used in Table 3-5:

data8	8-bit immediate data
data16	16-bit immediate data
addr8	8-bit direct address
addr16	16-bit extended address
disp	8-bit signed address displacement
index	8-bit unsigned address index

Table 3-5. 6800 Instruction Set Object Codes

MNEMONIC	OPERAND	ADDRESS MODE	OBJECT CODE	BYTES	MACHINE CYCLES
ABA		Inher	1B	1	2
ADCA/ADCB	data8	Immed	89/C9	2	2
	addr8	Direct	99/D9	2	3
	index	Index	A9/E9	2	5
	addr16	Extend	B9/F9	3	4
ADDA/ADDB	data8	Immed	8B/CB	2	2
	addr8	Direct	9B/DB	2	3
	index	Index	AB/EB	2	5
	addr16	Extend	BB/FB	3	4
ANDA/ANDB	data8	Immed	84/C4	2	2
	addr8	Direct	94/D4	2	3
	index	Index	A4/E4	2	5
	addr16	Extend	B4/F4	3	4
ASL	index	Index	68	2	7
	addr16	Extend	78	3	6
ASLA/ASLB		Accum	48/58	1	2
ASR	index	Index	67	2	7
	addr16	Extend	77	3	6
ASRA/ASRB		Accum	47/57	1	2
BCC	disp	Rel	24	2	4
BCS	disp	Rel	25	2	4
BEQ	disp	Rel	27	2	4
BGE	disp	Rel	2C	2	4
BGT	disp	Rel	2E	2	4
BHI	disp	Rel	22	2	4
BITA/BITB	data8	Immed	85/C5	2	2
	addr8	Direct	95/D5	2	3
	index	Index	A5/E5	2	5
	addr16	Extend	B5/F5	3	4
BLE	disp	Rel	2F	2	4
BLS	disp	Rel	23	2	4
BLT	disp	Rel	2D	2	4
BMI	disp	Rel	2B	2	4
BNE	disp	Rel	26	2	4
BPL	disp	Rel	2A	2	4
BRA	disp	Rel	20	2	4
BSR	disp	Rel	8D	2	8
BVC	disp	Rel	28	2	4
BVS	disp	Rel	29	2	4
CBA		Inher	11	1	2

Table 3-5. 6800 Instruction Set Object Codes (Continued)

MNEMONIC	OPERAND	ADDRESS MODE	OBJECT CODE	BYTES	MACHINE CYCLES
CLC		Inher	0C	1	2
CLI		Inher	0E	1	2
CLR	index	Index	6F	2	7
	addr16	Extend	7F	3	6
CLRA/CLRB		Accum	4F/5F	1	2
CLV		Inher	0A	1	2
CMPA/CMPB	data8	Immed	81/C1	2	2
	addr8	Direct	91/D1	2	3
	index	Index	A1/E1	2	5
	addr16	Extend	B1/F1	3	4
COM	index	Index	63	2	7
	addr16	Extend	73	3	6
COMA/COMB		Accum	43/53	1	2
CPX	data16	Immed	8C	3	3
	addr8	Direct	9C	2	4
	index	Index	AC	2	6
	addr16	Extend	BC	3	5
DAA		Inher	19	1	2
DEC	index	Index	6A	2	7
	addr16	Extend	7A	3	6
DECA/DECB		Accum	4A/5A	1	2
DES		Inher	34	1	4
DEX		Inher	09	1	4
EORA/EORB	data8	Immed	88/C8	2	2
	addr8	Direct	98/D8	2	3
	index	Index	A8/E8	2	5
	addr16	Extend	B8/F8	3	4
INC	index	Index	6C	2	7
	addr16	Extend	7C	3	6
INCA/INCB		Accum	4C/5C	1	2
INS		Inher	31	1	4
INX		Inher	08	1	4
JMP	index	Index	6E	2	4
	addr16	Extend	7E	3	3
JSR	index	Index	AD	2	8
	addr16	Extend	BD	3	9
LDAA/LDAB	data8	Immed	86/C6	2	2
	addr8	Direct	96/D6	2	3
	index	Index	A6/E6	2	5
	addr16	Extend	B6/F6	3	4
LDS	data16	Immed	8E	3	3
	addr8	Direct	9E	2	4
	index	Index	AE	2	6
	addr16	Extend	BE	3	5
LDX	data16	Immed	CE	3	3
	addr8	Direct	DE	2	4
	index	Index	EE	2	6
	addr16	Extend	FE	3	5
LSR	index	Index	64	2	7
	addr16	Extend	74	3	6

Table 3-5. 6800 Instruction Set Object Codes (Continued)

MNEMONIC	OPERAND	ADDRESS MODE	OBJECT CODE	BYTES	MACHINE CYCLES
LSRA/LSRB		Accum	44/54	1	2
NEG	index	Index	60	2	7
	addr16	Extend	70	3	6
NEGA/NEGB		Accum	40/50	1	2
NOP		Inher	01	1	2
ORAA/ORAB	data8	Immed	8A/CA	2	2
	addr8	Direct	9A/DA	2	3
	index	Index	AA/EA	2	5
	addr16	Extend	BA/FA	3	4
PSHA/PSHB		Accum	36/37	1	4
PULA/PULB		Accum	32/33	1	4
ROL	index	Index	69	2	7
	addr16	Extend	79	3	6
ROLA/ROLB		Accum	49/59	1	2
ROR	index	Index	66	2	7
	addr16	Extend	76	3	6
RORA/RORB		Accum	46/56	1	2
RTI		Inher	3B	1	10
RTS		Inher	39	1	5
SBA		Inher	10	1	2
SBCA/SBCB	data8	Immed	82/C2	2	2
	addr8	Direct	92/D2	2	3
	index	Index	A2/E2	2	5
	addr16	Extend	B2/F2	3	4
SEC		Inher	0D	1	2
SEI		Inher	0F	1	2
SEV		Inher	0B	1	2
STAA/STAB	addr8	Direct	97/D7	2	4
	index	Index	A7/E7	2	6
	addr16	Extend	B7/F7	3	5
STS	addr8	Direct	9F	2	5
	index	Index	AF	2	7
	addr16	Extend	BF	3	6
STX	addr8	Direct	DF	2	5
	index	Index	EF	2	7
	addr16	Extend	FF	3	6
SUBA/SUBB	data8	Immed	80/C0	2	2
	addr8	Direct	90/D0	2	3
	index	Index	A0/E0	2	5
	addr16	Extend	B0/F0	3	4
SWI		Inher	3F	1	12
TAB		Inher	16	1	2
TAP		Inher	06	1	2
TBA		Inher	17	1	2
TPA		Inher	07	1	2
TST	index	Index	6D	2	7
	addr16	Extend	7D	3	6
TSTA/TSTB		Accum	4D/5D	1	2
TSX		Inher	30	1	4
TXS		Inher	35	1	4
WAI		Inher	3E	1	9

ABA — ADD ACCUMULATOR B TO ACCUMULATOR A

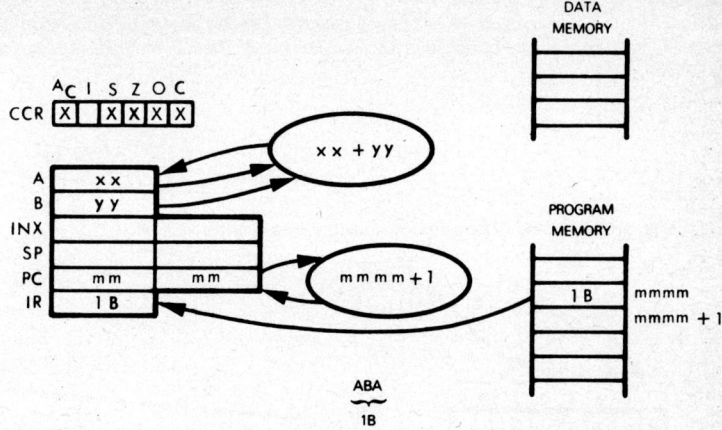

Add the contents of Accumulator B to the contents of Accumulator A. Store the result in Accumulator A. If xx = $B4_{16}$ and yy = $2D_{16}$, then after the instruction:

    ABA

has executed, Accumulator A will contain $E1_{16}$.

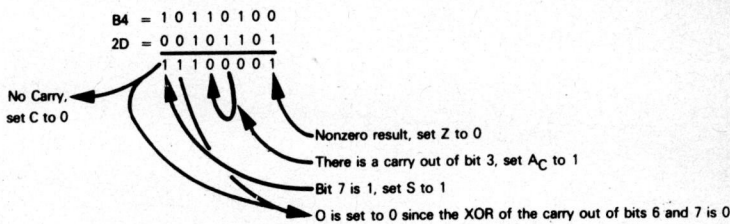

This is a routine data manipulation instruction.

ADC — ADD MEMORY, WITH CARRY, TO ACCUMULATOR A OR B

This instruction uses four methods of addressing data memory and allows the contents of data memory and the carry status to be added to Accumulator A or B. The four methods of addressing memory are:

1) Immediate
2) Direct
3) Extended
4) Indexed

The first byte of object code determines which addressing options are selected:

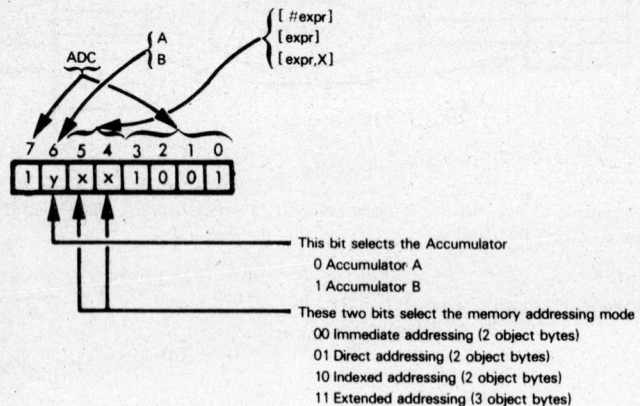

This bit selects the Accumulator
 0 Accumulator A
 1 Accumulator B

These two bits select the memory addressing mode
 00 Immediate addressing (2 object bytes)
 01 Direct addressing (2 object bytes)
 10 Indexed addressing (2 object bytes)
 11 Extended addressing (3 object bytes)

First, consider performing an addition with carry using immediate data.

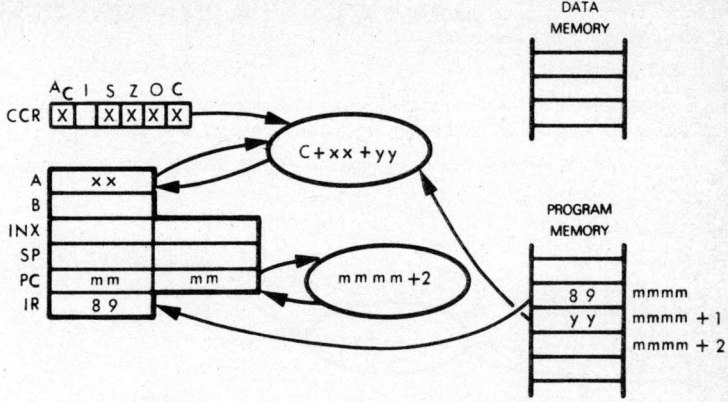

To Accumulator A, (selected by bit 6 of the byte in the Instruction register), add the contents of the next program memory byte, (addressing mode selected by bits 5 and 4 of the byte in the Instruction register) and the Carry status. Suppose xx = $3A_{16}$, yy = $7C_{16}$, C = 1. After the instruction:

    ADC A   #$7C

has executed, the Accumulator will contain $B7_{16}$:

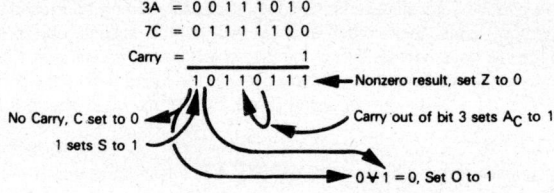

Consider adding using direct memory addressing:

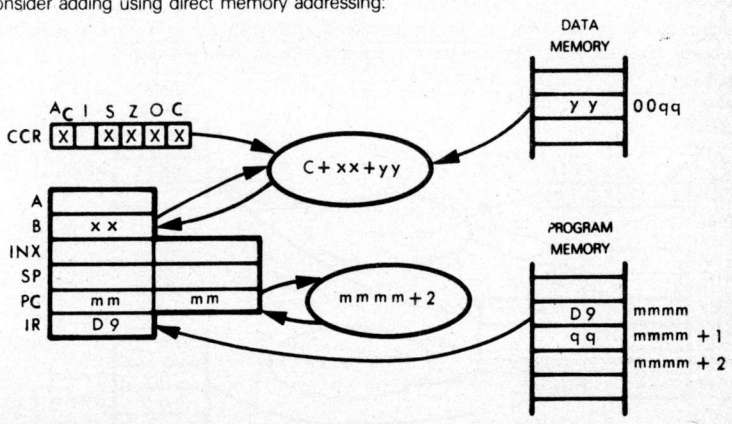

3-27

To Accumulator B add the Carry status and the contents of the data memory addressed by the next program memory byte (mmmm + 1). Note that the next program memory byte will address data memory bytes in the range $0_{10} \leq qq \leq 255_{10}$. If $xx = 3A_{16}$, $qq = 1F_{16}$, $yy = 7C_{16}$ and $C = 1$, then execution of the instruction:

    ADC B $1F

generates the same result as execution of the previously described ADC A   #$7C instruction, with the exception that the result is stored in Accumulator B instead of Accumulator A.

Addition with carry using extended addressing works in a similar manner to direct addressing:

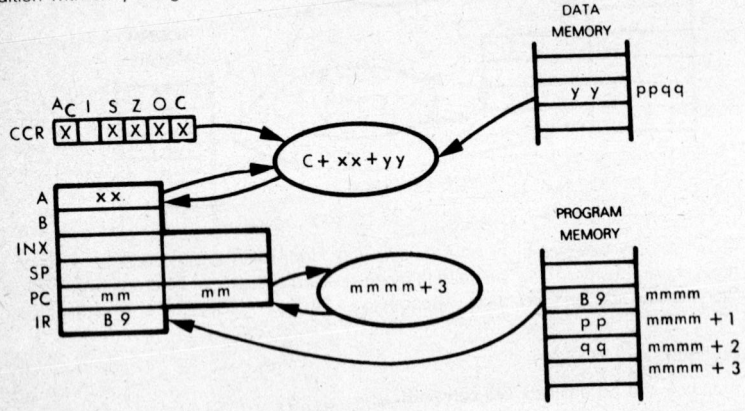

To Accumulator A, add the Carry status and the contents of data memory addressed by the next two program memory bytes, (high order address byte in the second object code byte, mmmm + 1, and the low order address byte in the third object code byte, mmmm + 2). Note that the two program bytes can address data memory bytes in the range $0 \leq ppqq \leq 65,355_{10}$. If $xx = 3A_{16}$, $pp = 50_{16}$, $qq = 23_{16}$, $yy = 7C_{16}$ and $C = 1$, then execution of the instruction:

    ADC A $5023

produces the same result as execution of the ADC A   #$7C instruction which was described above.

Indexed addressing takes two different forms. Indexed addressing with no displacement, similar to implied addressing described in <u>An Introduction To Microcomputers: Volume I</u> uses the contents of the Index register to ascertain the memory address to be referenced.

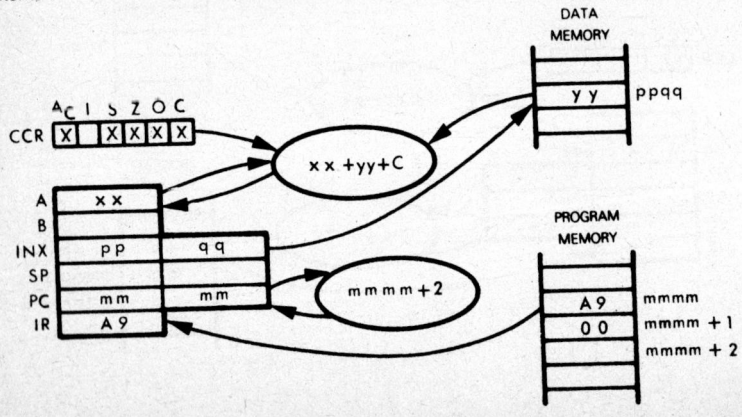

3-28

To Accumulator A, add the Carry status and the contents of data memory addressed by the Index register. Note that the Index register can address data memory bytes in the range $0 \leq ppqq \leq 65{,}355$. If $xx = 3A_{16}$, $ppqq$ (the contents of INX) $= 5023_{16}$, $yy = 76_{16}$ and $C = 1$, then execution of the instruction:

    ADC A   X

produces the same result as ADC A $5023 which has been described above.

Indexed addressing with displacement allows a displacement in the byte following the instruction to be added to the contents of the Index register.

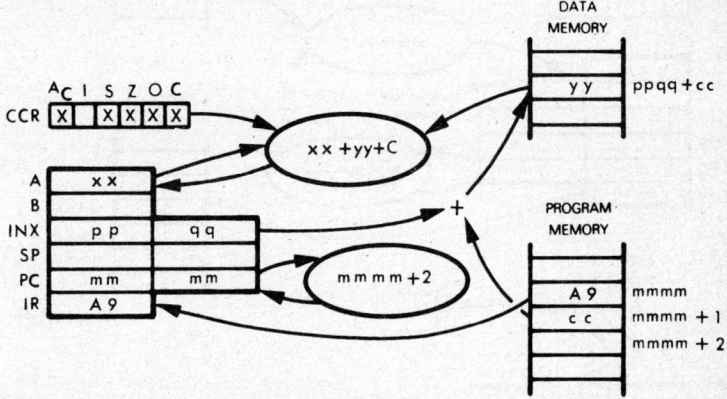

To Accumulator A, add the contents of memory addressed by the sum of the Index register and the program memory byte following the instruction code. (Note that in the previous example $mmmm + 1$ was 0), and the Carry status. The value in $mmmm + 1$ is treated as an 8-bit unsigned integer when the addition with the Index register is performed. If $xx = 3A_{16}$, $ppqq = 500D_{16}$, $cc = 16_{16}$, $yy = 76_{16}$ and $C = 1$, then the instruction:

    ADC A $16,X

generates the same result as the ADC A $5023 instruction discussed previously.

The ADC instruction is most frequently used in multibyte additions, to include the carry in the addition of the second and subsequent bytes.

ADD — ADD MEMORY TO ACCUMULATOR

This instruction ADDs the contents of a memory location to Accumulator A or B. This instruction offers the same memory addressing options as the ADC instruction, and will be illustrated using direct addressing; consult the ADC instruction for the other available modes.

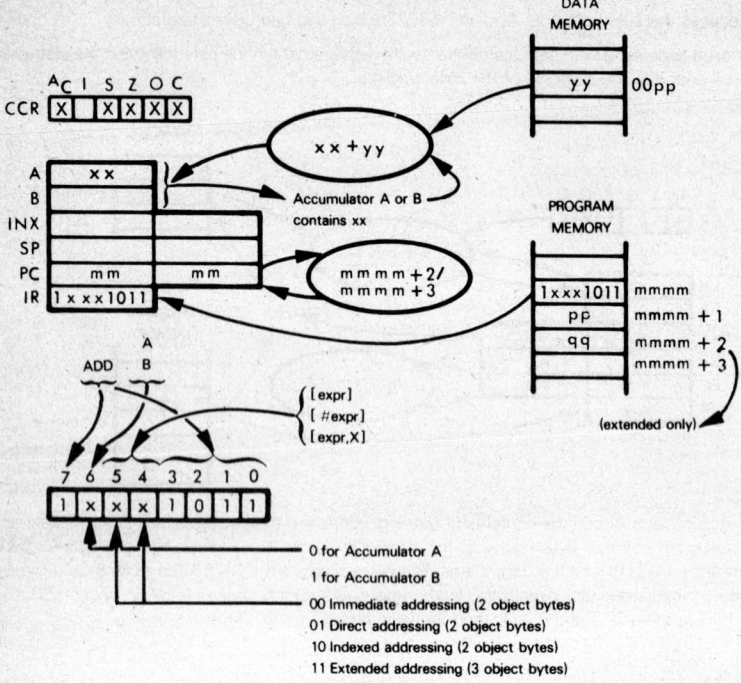

To the selected Accumulator, add the contents of the selected memory byte. Suppose $xx = 24_{16}$, $yy = 8B_{16}$, $pp = 43_{16}$ and $C = 1$. After the instruction:

    ADD A $43

has executed, Accumulator A will contain AF_{16}:

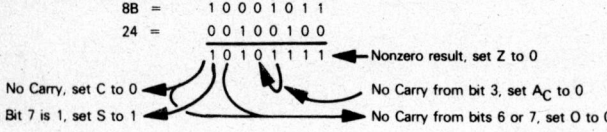

ADD is the binary addition instruction used in normal, single-byte operations; it is also the instruction used to add the low order bytes of two multibyte numbers.

AND — AND MEMORY WITH ACCUMULATOR

This instruction ANDs the contents of a memory location with the contents of Accumulator A or B. This instruction offers the same memory addressing options as the ADC instruction, and will be illustrated using immediate addressing; consult the description of the ADC instruction for the other addressing modes.

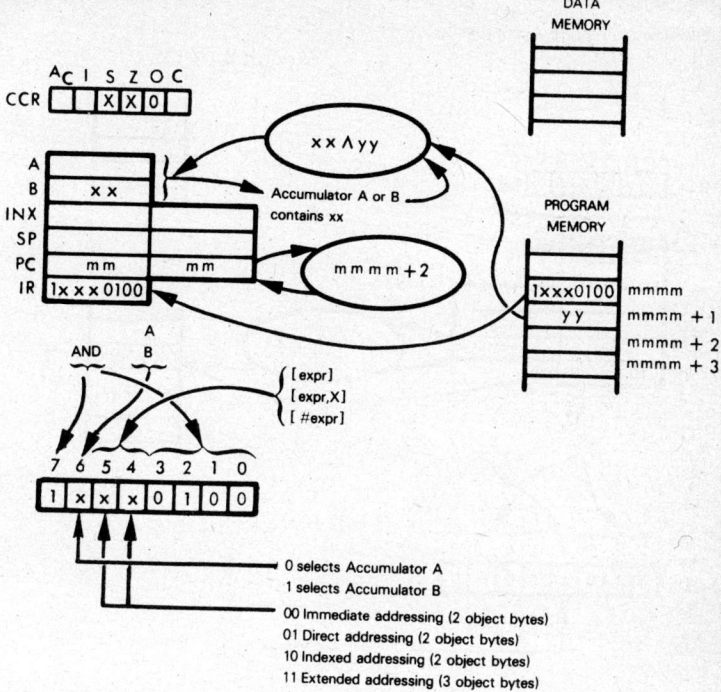

AND the contents of the selected memory byte with the selected Accumulator and store the result in the selected Accumulator. Suppose $xx = FC_{16}$ and $yy = 13_{16}$. After the instruction:

    AND B   #$13

has executed, Accumulator B will contain 10_{16}:

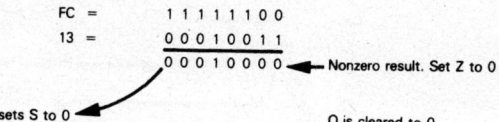

AND is a frequently used logical instruction.

ASL — SHIFT ACCUMULATOR OR MEMORY BYTE LEFT

Perform a one-bit arithmetic left shift of the contents of Accumulator A or B or the contents of the selected memory byte.

First, consider shifting an Accumulator:

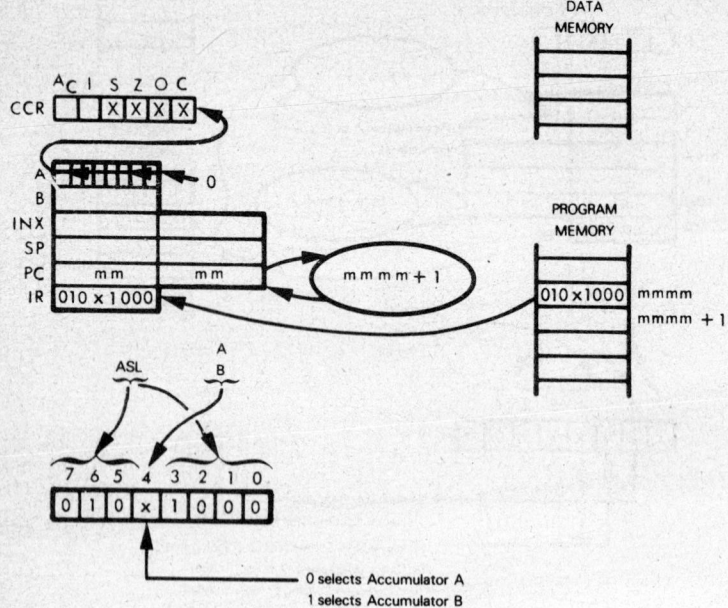

Suppose Accumulator A contains $7A_{16}$. Performing an:

ASL A

instruction will set the Carry status to 0, the Sign status to 1, the Overflow status to 1, the Zero status to 0 and store $F4_{16}$ in Accumulator A.

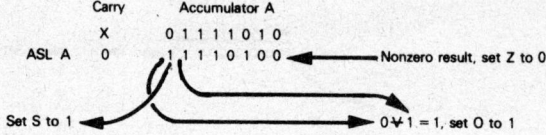

The ASL instruction uses two data memory addressing options:

1) Extended
2) Indexed

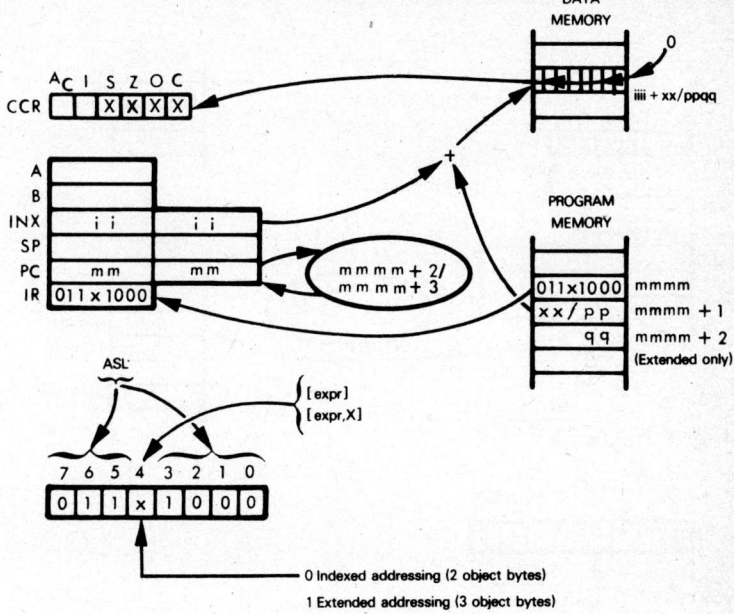

Suppose indexed addressing is used, iiii = 3F3C$_{16}$, xx = 4A$_{16}$, ppqq = 3F86$_{16}$ and the contents of ppqq are CB$_{16}$. After executing an:

    ASL $4A,X

instruction, the contents of ppqq will be altered to 96$_{16}$ and Carry will be set to l:

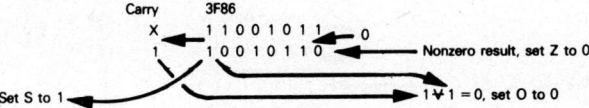

The ASL instruction is often used in multiplication routines and as a standard logical instruction. Note that a single ASL instruction multiplies its operand by 2.

ASR — SHIFT ACCUMULATOR OR MEMORY BYTE RIGHT

Perform a one-bit arithmetic right shift of the contents of Accumulator A or B or the contents of a selected memory byte.

First, consider right shifting an Accumulator:

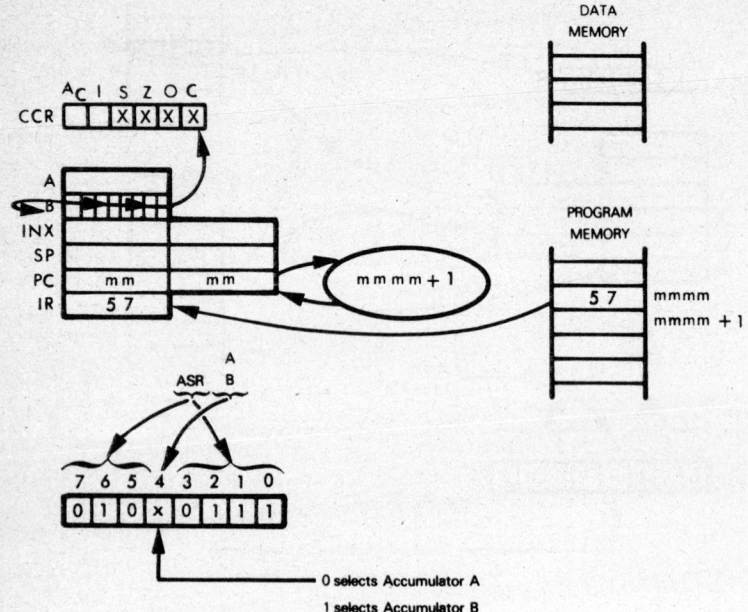

Suppose Accumulator B contains $7A_{16}$. Performing an:

ASR B

instruction will set Carry to 0, Sign to 0, Overflow to 0, Zero to 0 and store $3D_{16}$ in Accumulator B.

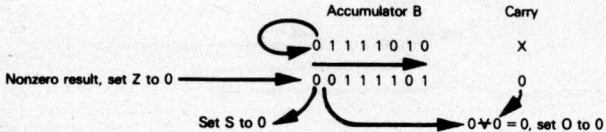

The ASR instruction uses two memory addressing options:

1) Extended
2) Indexed

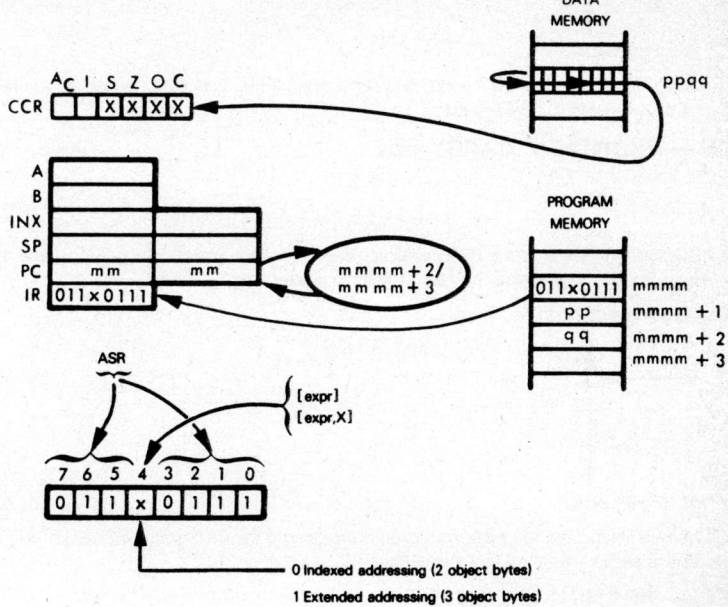

Suppose extended addressing is used, $pp = 01_{16}$, $qq = 34_{16}$, and the contents of 0134_{16} are CB_{16}. Executing an:

    ASR $0134

instruction will alter the contents of memory location 0134_{16} to $E5_{16}$.

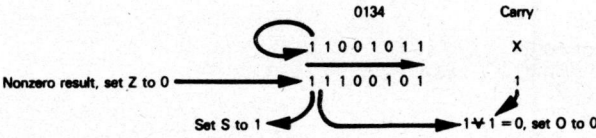

ASR is frequently used in division routines.

BCC — BRANCH IF CARRY CLEAR

$$\underbrace{BCC}_{24}$$

This instruction is identical to the BRA instruction except that the branch is only executed if the Carry status equals 0, otherwise the next instruction is executed.

In the following instruction sequence:

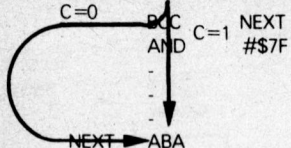

after the BCC instruction, the ABA instruction is executed if the Carry status equals 0. The AND instruction is executed if the Carry status equals 1.

BCS — BRANCH IF CARRY SET

$$\underset{25}{\underbrace{\text{BCS}}}$$

This instruction is identical to the BRA instruction except that the branch is only executed if the Carry status equals 1, otherwise the next instruction is executed.

In the following instruction sequence:

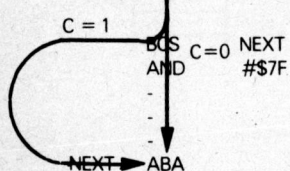

After the BCS instruction, the ABA instruction is executed if the Carry status equals 1. The AND instruction is executed if the Carry status equals 0.

BEQ — BRANCH IF EQUAL

$$\underset{27}{\underbrace{\text{BEQ}}}$$

This instruction is identical to the BRA instruction except that the branch is executed only if the Zero status equals 1; otherwise the next instruction is executed.

In the following instruction sequence:

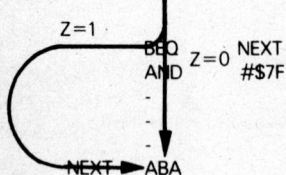

After the BEQ instruction, the ABA instruction is executed if the Zero status equals 1. The AND instruction is executed if the Zero status equals 0.

BGE — BRANCH IF GREATER THAN OR EQUAL TO ZERO

$$\underset{2C}{\underbrace{\text{BGE}}}$$

This instruction is identical to the BRA instruction except that the branch is executed only if the Exclusive-OR of the Sign and Overflow statuses is 0; i.e., Sign and Overflow are both 1 or Sign and Overflow are both 0; otherwise the next instruction is executed.

In the following instruction sequence:

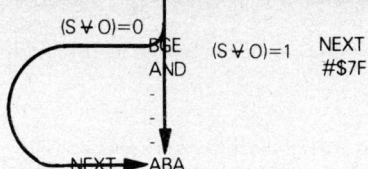

After the BGE instruction, the ABA instruction is executed if the Sign and Overflow statuses are both 1 or if they are both 0. The AND instruction is executed if the Sign status does not equal the Overflow status.

This instruction is used to perform a twos complement greater than or equal branch.

BGT — BRANCH IF GREATER THAN ZERO

$$\underbrace{\text{BGT}}_{\text{2E}}$$

This instruction is identical to the BRA instruction except that the branch is executed only if one of the following two conditions is met:

1) The Zero status is 0 and the Sign and Overflow statuses are 0.
2) The Zero status is 0 and the Sign and Overflow statuses are 1.

Otherwise, the next instruction is executed.

In the following instruction sequence:

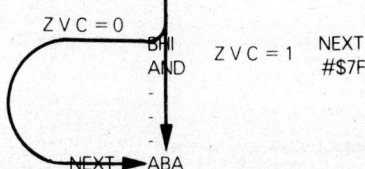

After the BGT instruction, the ABA instruction is executed if the Zero flag is 0 and the Exclusive-OR of the Sign and Overflow statuses is 0. In all other cases, the AND instruction is executed.

This instruction is used to implement a twos complement greater than branch capability.

BHI — BRANCH IF HIGHER

$$\underbrace{\text{BHI}}_{\text{22}}$$

This instruction is identical to the BRA instruction except that the branch is executed only if the Zero status and the Carry status are 0; otherwise the next instruction is executed.

In the following instruction sequence:

After the BHI instruction is executed, the ABA instruction is executed if the Zero and Carry statuses are 0. The AND instruction is executed if either the Zero or Carry status is 1 or both the Zero and Carry statuses are 1.

This instruction provides an unsigned greater than branch instruction. Contrast this instruction with the BGT instruction.

BIT — BIT TEST

This instruction ANDs the contents of Accumulator A or B with the contents of a selected memory location, sets the condition flags accordingly, but does not alter the contents of the Accumulator or memory byte. This instruction offers the same memory addressing options as the ADC instruction. This instruction will be illustrated using extended addressing; consult the ADC instruction for the other available modes.

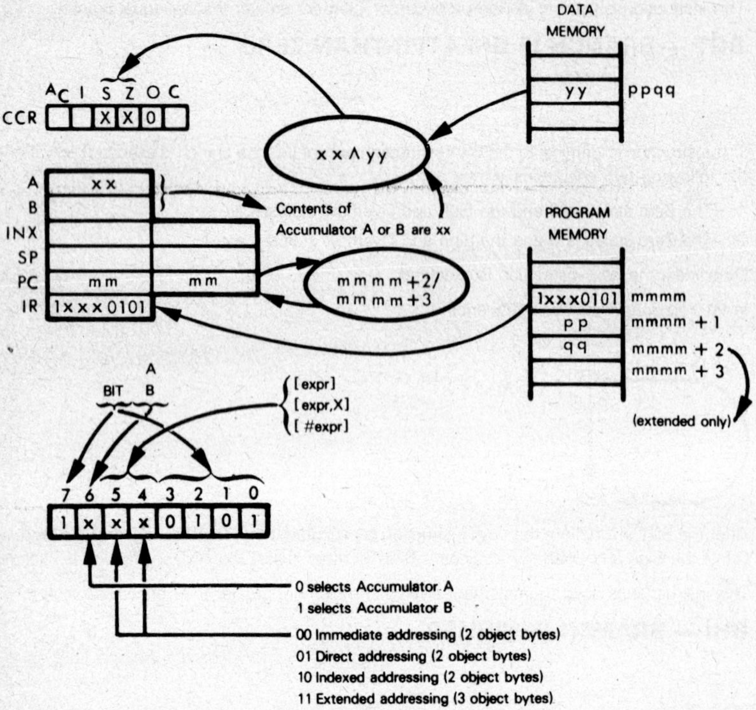

AND the contents of the specified Accumulator with the contents of the selected memory location and set the Sign and Zero condition flags accordingly. Suppose xx=$A6_{16}$, yy=$E0_{16}$ and ppqq=1641_{16}. After the instruction:

```
BIT   A     $1641
```

has executed, Accumulator A will still contain $A6_{16}$, location ppqq will still contain $E0_{16}$ but the statuses will be modified as follows:

```
A6  =  1 0 1 0 0 1 1 0
E0  =  1 1 1 0 0 0 0 0
       ---------------
       1 0 1 0 0 0 0 0  <-- Nonzero result, set Z to 0
```

Set S to 1

O is always cleared by a BIT instruction

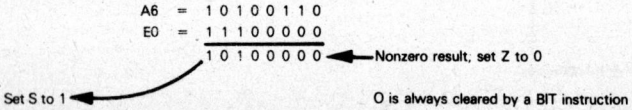

BIT instructions frequently precede conditional Branch instructions. BIT instructions are also used to perform masking functions on data.

BLE — BRANCH IF LESS THAN OR EQUAL TO ZERO

$$\underbrace{BLE}_{2F}$$

This instruction is identical to the BRA instruction with the exception that the branch is executed only if one or more of the three following conditions exist:

1) The Zero status is 1.
2) The Overflow status is 1 and the Sign status is 0.
3) The Overflow status is 0 and the Sign status is 1.

Otherwise the next instruction is executed.

In the following instruction sequence:

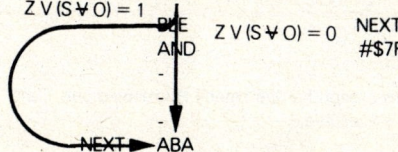

After the BLE instruction, the ABA instruction is executed if the Zero status is 1 or the Exclusive-OR of the Sign and Overflow statuses is 1. The AND instruction is executed if the Zero status is 0 and the Exclusive-OR of the Sign and Overflow statuses is 0.

This instruction provides the programmer with a twos complement less than or equal branch.

BLS — BRANCH IF LOWER OR SAME

$$\underbrace{BLS}_{23}$$

This instruction is identical to the BRA instruction except that the branch is executed only if either the Carry or Zero status is set; otherwise the next instruction is executed.

In the following instruction sequence:

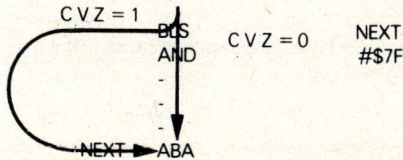

After the BLS instruction, the ABA instruction is executed if the Carry or Zero status equals 1. The AND instruction is executed if both the Carry and Zero statuses are 0.

This instruction is useful as an unsigned less than or equal branch. Compare this instruction with the BLE instruction which provides a twos complement less than or equal branch.

BLT — BRANCH IF LESS THAN ZERO

$$\underbrace{BLT}_{2D}$$

This instruction is identical to the BRA instruction except that the branch is performed only when the Exclusive-OR of the Sign and Overflow statuses is 1; otherwise the next instruction is executed.

In the following instruction sequence:

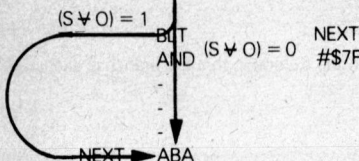

After the BLT instruction, the ABA instruction is executed if the Sign and Overflow statuses are not equal. The AND instruction will be executed if the Sign and Overflow statuses are equal.

This instruction provides a twos complement less than branch capability.

BMI — BRANCH IF MINUS

$$\underbrace{BMI}_{2B}$$

This instruction is identical to the BRA instruction except that the branch is executed only if the Sign status is 1; otherwise the next instruction is executed.

In the following instruction sequence:

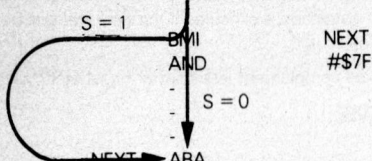

After the BMI instruction, the ABA instruction is executed if the Sign status is 1. The AND instruction is executed if the Sign status is 0.

BNE — BRANCH IF NOT EQUAL

$$\underbrace{BNE}_{26}$$

This instruction is identical to the BRA instruction except that the branch is executed only if the Zero status is 0; otherwise the next instruction is executed.

In the following instruction sequence:

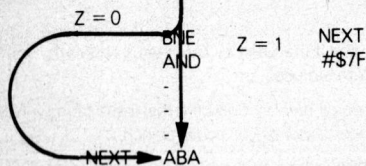

After the BNE instruction, the ABA instruction is executed if the Zero status is 0. The AND instruction is executed if the Zero status is 1.

BPL — BRANCH IF PLUS

$$\underbrace{\text{BPL}}_{\text{2A}}$$

This instruction is identical to the BRA instruction except that the branch is executed only if the Sign status is 0; otherwise the next instruction is executed.

In the following instruction sequence:

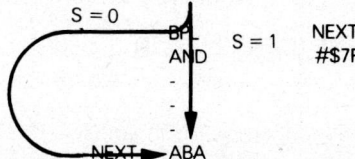

After the BPL instruction, the ABA instruction is executed if the Sign status is 0. The AND instruction is executed if the Sign status is 1.

BRA — BRANCH TO THE INSTRUCTION IDENTIFIED IN THE OPERAND

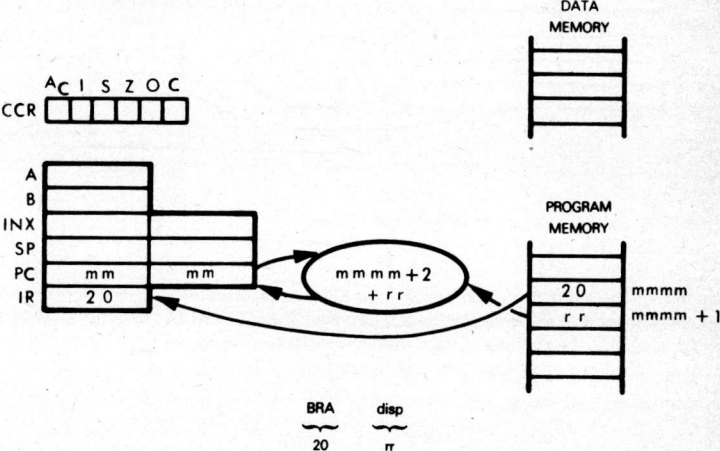

$$\underbrace{\text{BRA}}_{20} \quad \underbrace{\text{disp}}_{rr}$$

This instruction adds the contents of the second object code byte (taken as a signed 8-bit displacement) to the contents of the Program Counter plus 2; this becomes the memory address for the next instruction to be executed. The previous Program Counter contents are lost.

In the following instruction sequence:

```
        BRA    NEXT
        AND    #$7F
        -
        -
        -
NEXT    ABA
```

After the BRA instruction, the ABA instruction will be executed. The AND instruction will never be executed unless a Branch or Jump instruction somewhere else in the instruction sequence jumps to this instruction. (Note that since this instruction is not labeled, this is a very unlikely event.)

The Branch instruction uses Branch-Relative addressing, which is similar to Program Relative Paging as described in "An Introduction To Microcomputers: Volume I — Basic Concepts". The exception is that the Program Counter contents are incremented to point to the next instruction before the 8-bit signed displacement is added. Therefore, the Program Counter contents are replaced by:

$$[PC] + 2 + rr$$

Note that in the above example, the ABA instruction labeled by NEXT must be within 129 object bytes (not instructions) of the Branch-to-Next instruction. If it isn't, the Assembler will flag the BRA instruction as an error.

BSR — BRANCH TO THE SUBROUTINE IDENTIFIED IN THE OPERAND

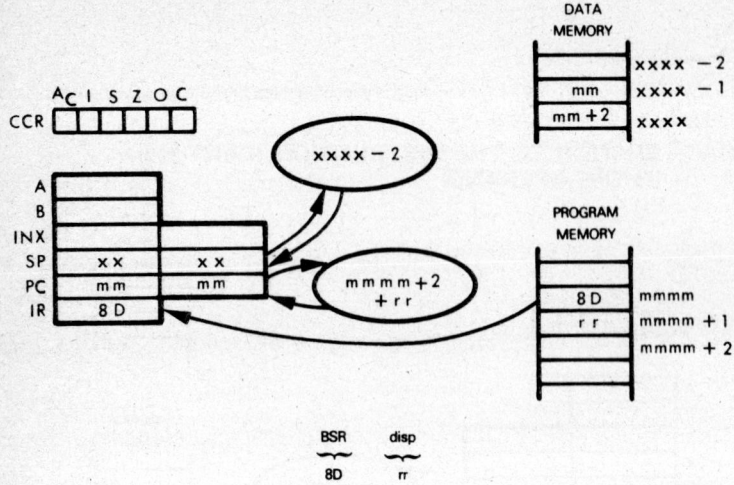

Store the address of the instruction following the BSR on the top of the stack; the top of the stack is a data memory byte addressed by the Stack Pointer. Then subtract two from the Stack Pointer in order to address the new top of stack. Add the contents of the second byte of the instruction and two to the Program Counter and begin execution.

Consider the instruction sequence:

```
        BSR     SUBR
        AND     #$7F
         -
         -
         -
SUBR    ABA
```

After the BSR instruction has executed, the address of the AND instruction is saved at the top of the stack. The Stack Pointer is decremented by 2. The ABA instruction will be executed next.

BVC — BRANCH IF OVERFLOW CLEAR

$$\underbrace{BVC}_{28}$$

This instruction is identical to the BRA instruction except that the branch is executed only if the Overflow status is 0; otherwise the next instruction is executed.

In the following instruction sequence:

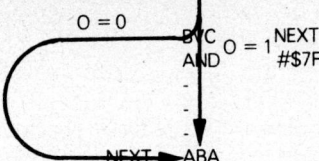

After the BVC instruction, the ABA instruction is executed if the Overflow status is 0. The AND instruction is executed if the Overflow status is 1.

BVS — BRANCH IF OVERFLOW SET

$$\underset{29}{\underline{BVS}}$$

This instruction is identical to the BRA instruction except that the branch is executed only if the Overflow status is 1; otherwise the next instruction is executed.

In the following instruction sequence:

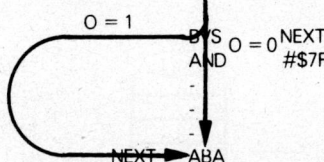

after the BVS instruction, the ABA instruction is executed if the Overflow status equals 1. The AND instruction is executed if the Overflow status equals 0.

CBA — COMPARE ACCUMULATORS

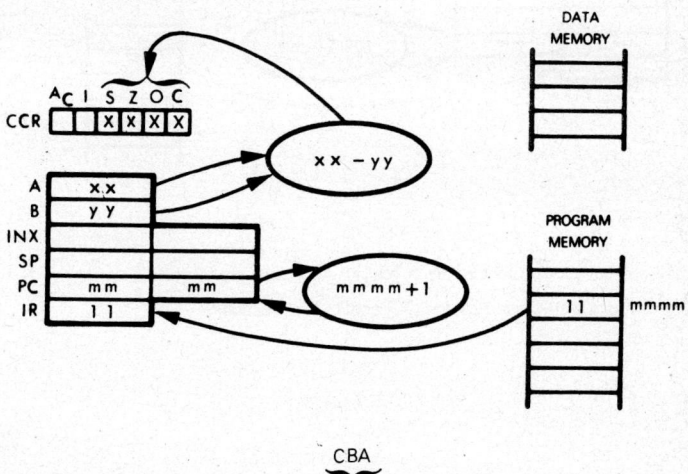

$$\underset{11}{\underline{CBA}}$$

Subtract the contents of Accumulator B from the contents of Accumulator A. Discard the result, i.e., do not affect the contents of either Accumulator, but modify the status flags to reflect the result of the operation.

Suppose $xx = E3_{16}$ and $yy = A0_{16}$. After the instruction:

    CBA

has executed, Accumulator A will still contain $E3_{16}$ and Accumulator B will still contain $A0_{16}$, but statuses will be modified as follows:

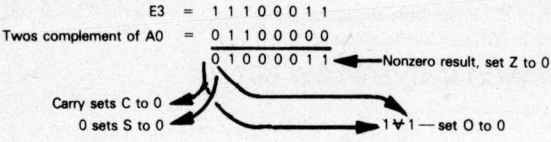

Notice that the resulting Carry is complemented.

Compare instructions usually precede conditional Branch instructions.

CLC — CLEAR CARRY

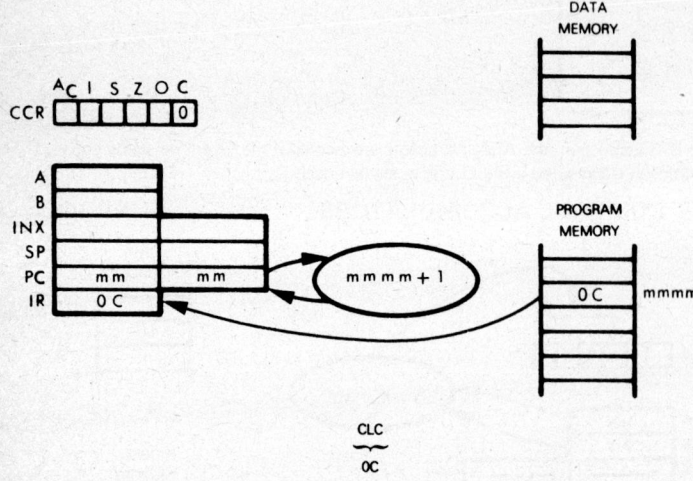

Clear the Carry status. No other status or register's contents are affected.

The Carry status is also cleared by the CLR and TST instructions.

CLI — CLEAR INTERRUPT MASK

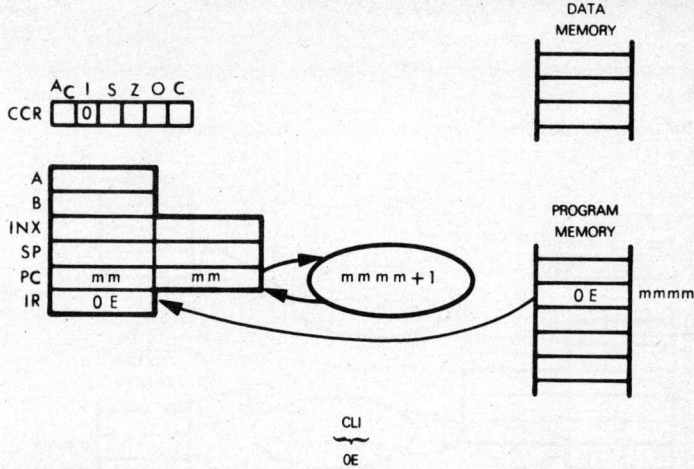

Clear the interrupt mask bit in the Condition Code register. This instruction enables the MC6800's interrupt service ability, i.e., the MC6800 will respond to the Interrupt Request control line. No other registers or statuses are affected.

CLR — CLEAR ACCUMULATOR OR MEMORY

This instruction clears a specified Accumulator or a selected memory byte. The Zero flag is set to 1; the Sign, Overflow and Carry statuses are set to 0.

First, consider clearing an Accumulator:

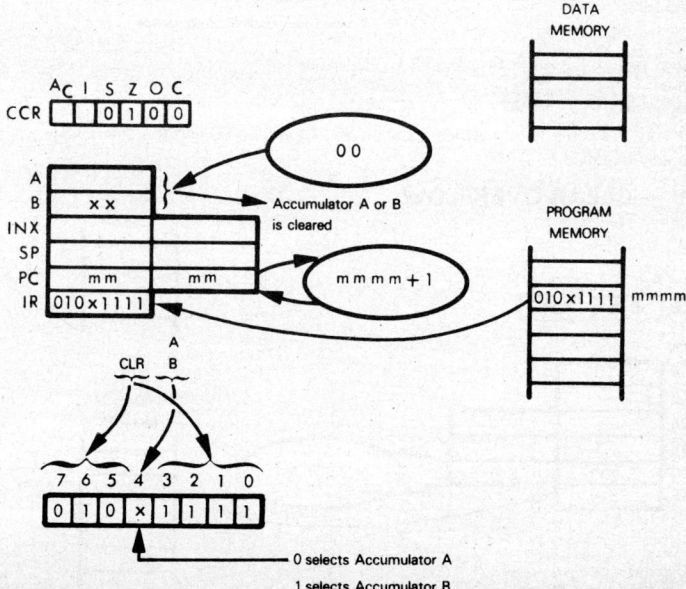

Clear the contents of the specified Accumulator. Suppose Accumulator B contains 43_{16}. After the instruction:

    CLR B

is executed, Accumulator B will contain 00_{16}. In addition, Sign, Overflow and Carry will be 0; Zero will be 1.

The CLR instruction also has two memory addressing modes, Indexed and Extended.

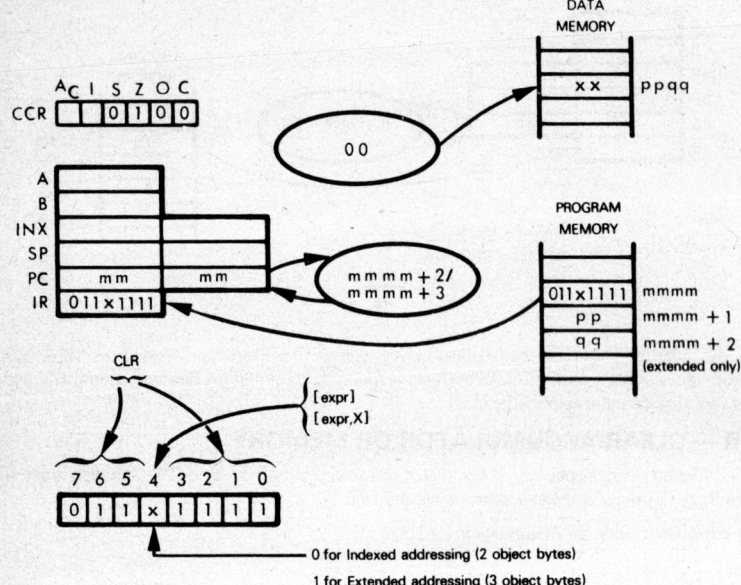

Suppose $pp = 43_{16}$, $qq = 14_{16}$ and $xx = 05_{16}$. After the execution:

    CLR $4314

instruction, the contents of memory location 4314_{16} will be 00 and the status flags will be appropriately modified.

CLV — CLEAR OVERFLOW

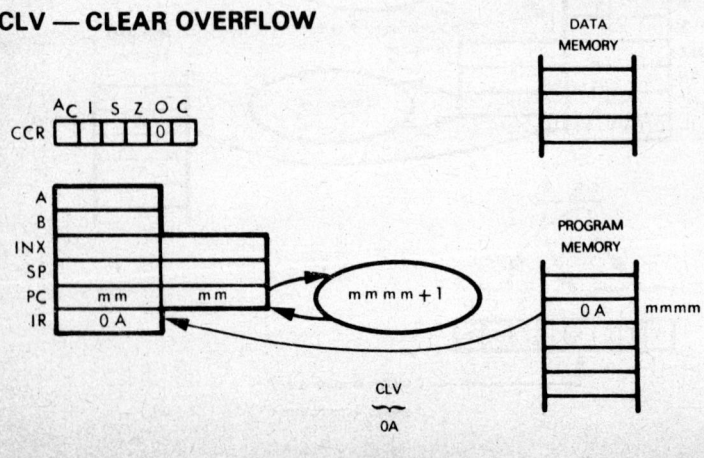

Clear the overflow bit in the Condition Code register. No other registers or statuses are affected.

CMP — COMPARE ACCUMULATOR WITH MEMORY

This instruction subtracts the contents of a selected memory byte from Accumulator A or B, sets the condition flags accordingly, but does not alter the contents of the Accumulator or memory byte. This instruction offers the same memory addressing options as the ADC instruction. This instruction will be illustrated using indexed addressing; consult the ADC instruction for examples of the other available modes.

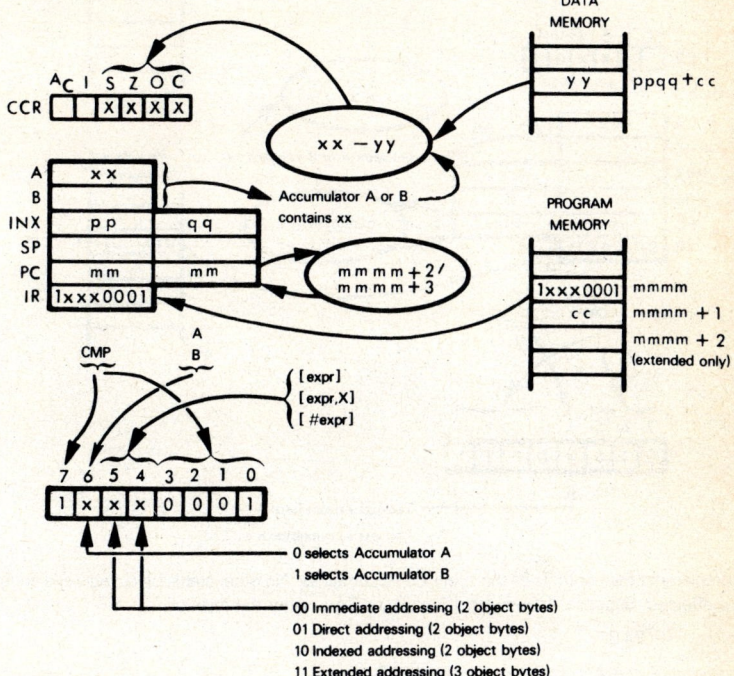

Subtract the contents of the selected memory byte from the contents of the specified Accumulator and set the Sign, Zero, Overflow and Carry statuses to reflect the result of the subtraction. Suppose $xx = F6_{16}$, $yy = 18_{16}$ and $cc = 43_{16}$.

After the instruction:

    CMP B $43,X

has executed, Accumulator B will still contain $F6_{16}$, location $ppqq + 43_{16}$ will still contain 18_{16} but the statuses will be modified as follows:

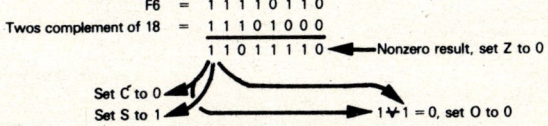

Notice that C is the complement of the resulting carry.

Compare instructions are most frequently used to set statuses before the execution of Branch-on-Condition instructions.

COM — COMPLEMENT ACCUMULATOR OR MEMORY

This instruction complements a specified Accumulator or a selected memory byte.

First, consider complementing an Accumulator:

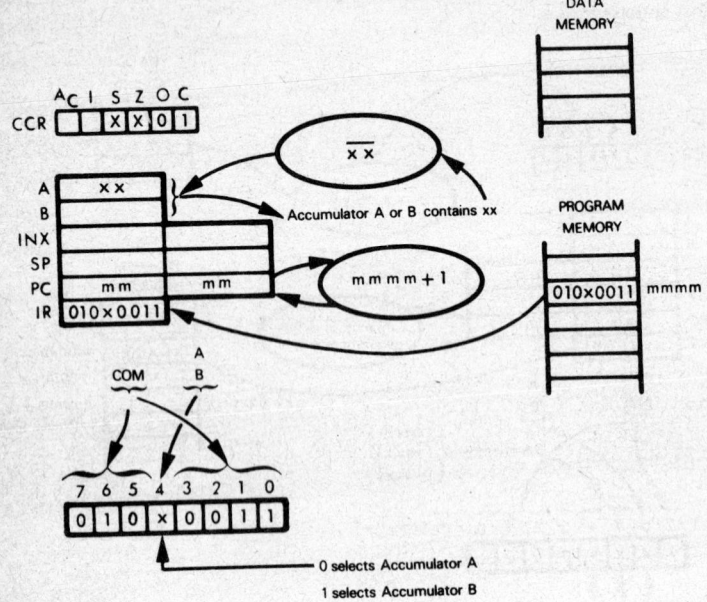

Complement the contents of the specified Accumulator. No other status bit or register's contents are affected. Suppose Accumulator B contains $3A_{16}$. After the instruction:

COM B

is executed, the Accumulator will contain $C5_{16}$.

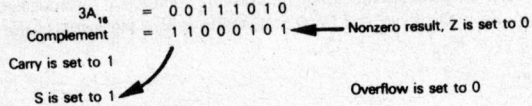

The COM instruction also offers two memory addressing modes:
1) Extended
2) Indexed

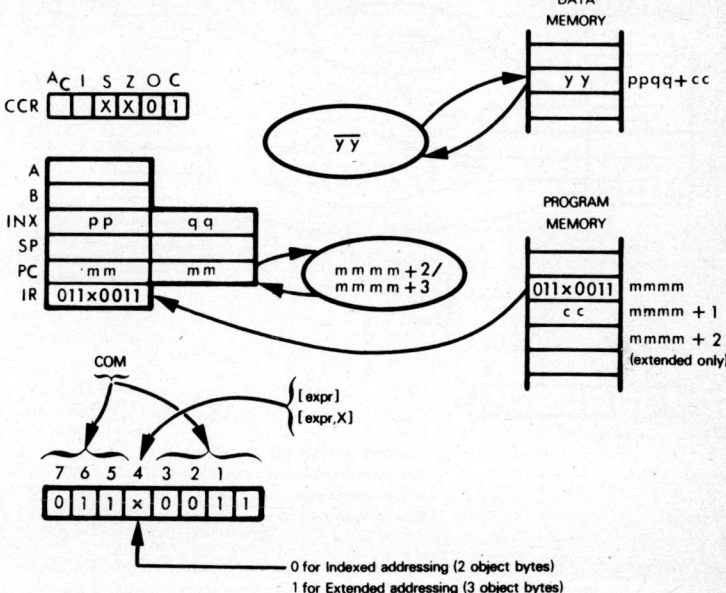

0 for Indexed addressing (2 object bytes)
1 for Extended addressing (3 object bytes)

Suppose that the contents of the Index register are 0100_{16}, and the contents of memory location 0113_{16} are 23_{16}. After a:

    COM $13,X

instruction executes, memory location 0113_{16} will be altered to DC_{16}.

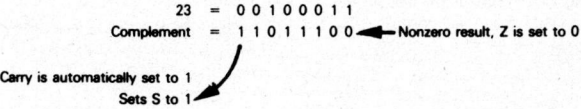

CPX — COMPARE INDEX REGISTER

This instruction compares the contents of the Index register with the contents of two selected memory locations. This instruction offers the same memory addressing options as the ADC instruction. This instruction will be illustrated using direct addressing; consult the discussion of the ADC instruction for the other addressing modes.

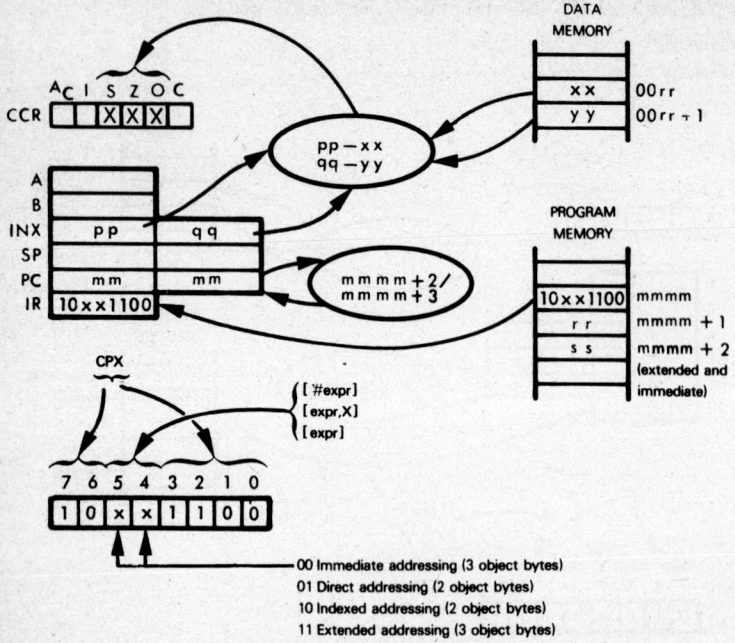

Subtract the contents of the memory byte immediately following the selected memory byte from the low byte of the Index register, and discard the result. Subtract the contents of the selected memory byte from the high byte of the Index register. Set the Sign and Overflow statuses according to the result, set the Zero status to 1 if the result of both subtractions was 0, and discard the result.

Suppose pp = $1A_{16}$, qq = $B0_{16}$, xx = $1B_{16}$, yy = $B0_{16}$ and rr = 43_{16}. After the instruction:

    CPX $43

has executed, the Index register will still contain $1AB0_{16}$, location 0043_{16} will still contain $1B_{16}$ and memory location 0044_{16} will still contain $B0_{16}$, but the statuses Sign, Zero and Overflow will be modified as follows:

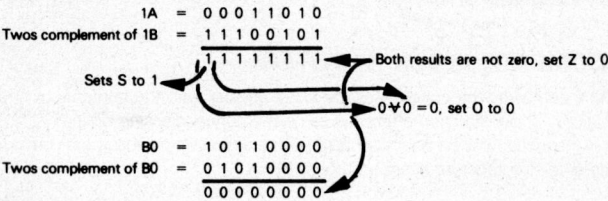

DAA — DECIMAL ADJUST ACCUMULATOR

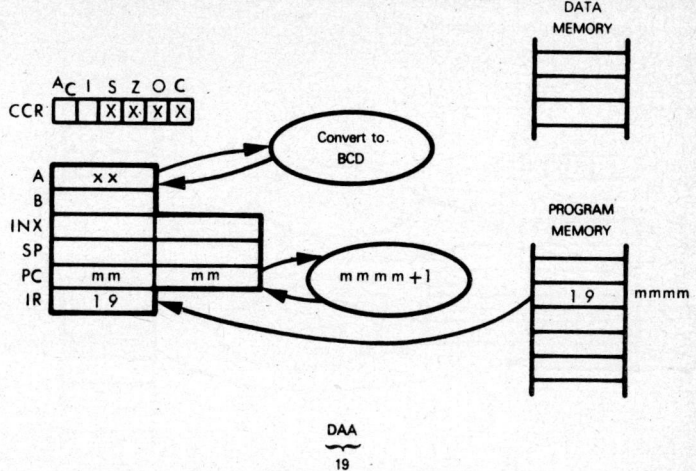

Convert the contents of Accumulator A to binary-coded-decimal form. This instruction should be used only after adding two BCD numbers, i.e., look upon ABA DAA or ADD A DAA or ADC A DAA or SUB A DAA or SBC A DAA as compound decimal arithmetic instructions which operate on BCD source to generate BCD answers.

Suppose Accumulator A contains 39_{16} and Accumulator B contains 47_{16}. After the instructions:

    ABA
    DAA

have executed, the Accumulator will contain 86_{16}, not 80_{16}.

The Sign and Zero flags are modified to reflect the status they represent. The Overflow status is destroyed and the Carry status is set or reset as if a hypothetical binary-coded-decimal addition had just taken place.

DEC — DECREMENT ACCUMULATOR OR MEMORY

This instruction decrements a specified Accumulator or a selected memory byte. Consider decrementing Accumulator A or B.

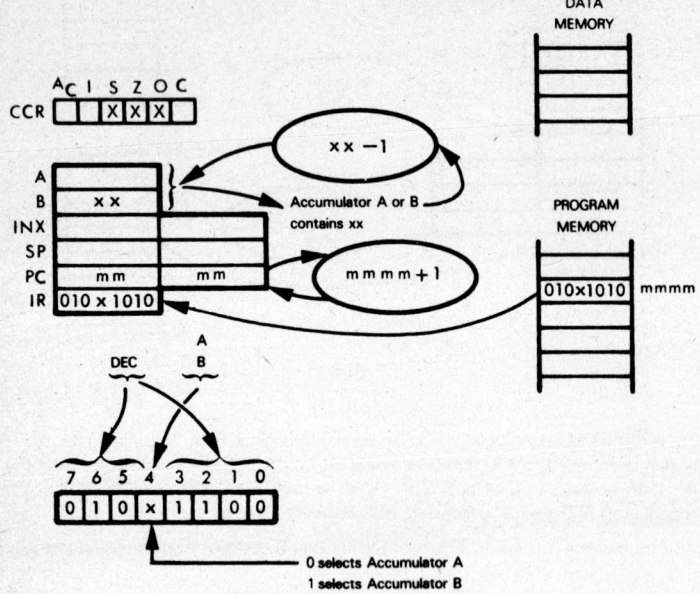

Subtract 1 from the contents of the specified Accumulator.

Suppose Accumulator B contains $3A_{16}$. After instruction:

    DEC B

has executed, Accumulator B will contain 39_{16}.

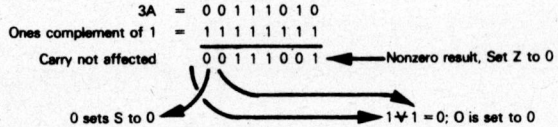

The DEC instruction also offers two memory addressing modes:
1) Extended
2) Indexed

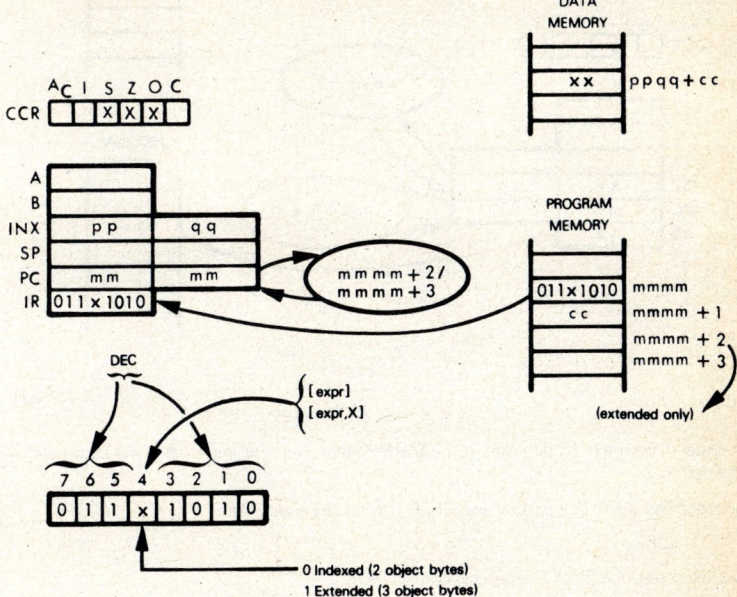

Decrement the contents of the specified memory byte.

If $xx = A5_{16}$, $ppqq = 0100_{16}$, and $cc = 0A_{16}$, then after execution of the instruction:

DEC $0A,X

memory location $010A_{16}$ will be altered to $A4_{16}$.

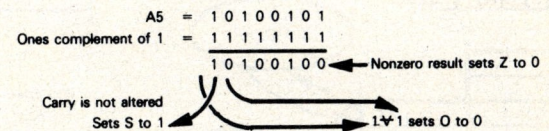

DES — DECREMENT STACK POINTER

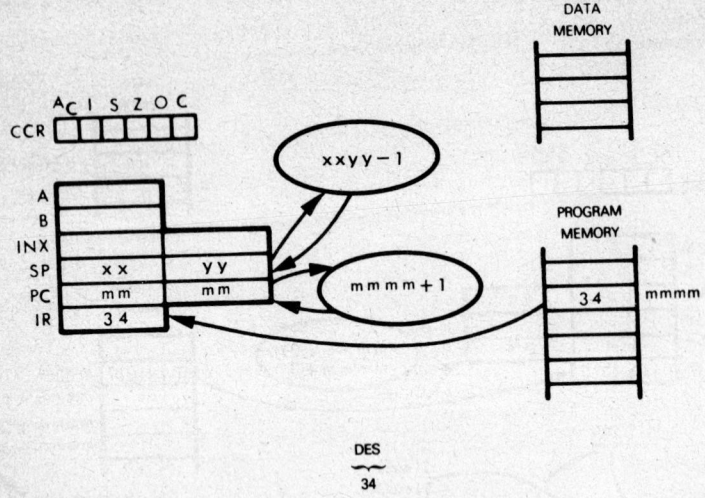

Subtract 1 from the 16-bit value in the Stack Pointer. No other registers or condition codes are affected.

Suppose the Stack Pointer contains $2F7A_{16}$. After the instruction:

    DES

has executed, the Stack Pointer will contain $2F79_{16}$.

DEX — DECREMENT INDEX REGISTER

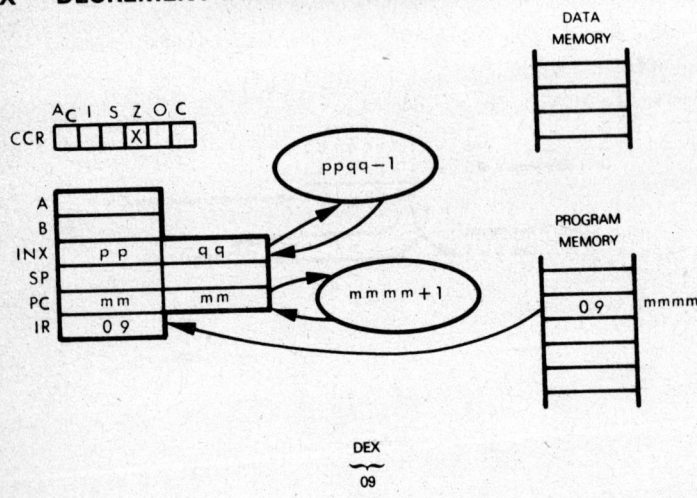

Subtract 1 from the 16-bit value in the Index register. The Zero status is set to 1 if the 16-bit result is 0.

Suppose the Index register contains $310C_{16}$. After the instruction:

DEX

has executed, the Index register will contain $310B_{16}$ and the Zero status will be set to 0.

EOR — EXCLUSIVE-OR ACCUMULATOR WITH MEMORY

Exclusive-OR the contents of Accumulator A or B with the contents of a selected memory byte. This instruction offers the same memory addressing options as the ADC instruction, and will be illustrated using immediate addressing; consult the ADC instruction for the other addressing modes.

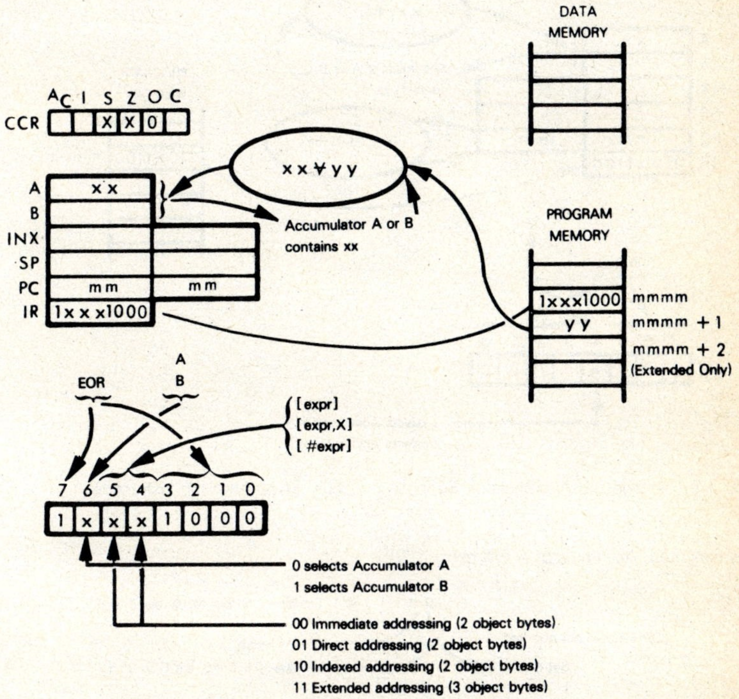

Exclusive-OR the contents of the specified Accumulator with the contents of the selected memory location, treating both operands as simple binary data. Suppose that xx = $E3_{16}$ and yy = $A0_{16}$. After the instruction:

EOR A #$A0

has executed, Accumulator A will contain 43_{16}.

```
                         E3  =  1 1 1 0 0 0 1 1
                         A0  =  1 0 1 0 0 0 0 0
Carry is not affected           0 1 0 0 0 0 1 1  <-- Nonzero result, set Z to 0

           0 sets S to 0                           Overflow is cleared
```

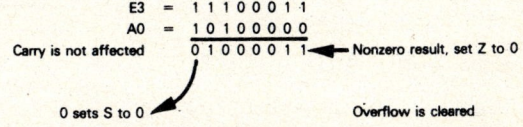

EOR is used to test for changes in bit status.

INC — INCREMENT ACCUMULATOR OR MEMORY

This instruction increments the specified Accumulator or selected memory byte.

First, consider incrementing an Accumulator:

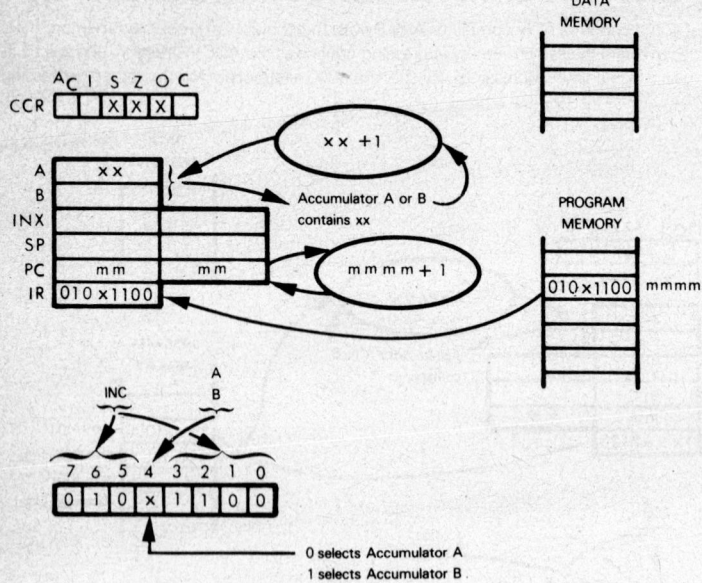

Add 1 to the selected Accumulator. Suppose that xx = $3A_{16}$. After the instruction:

    INC A

has executed, Accumulator A will contain $3B_{16}$.

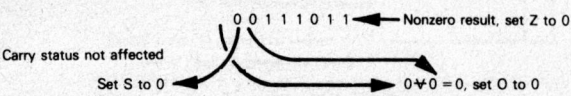

The INC instruction also offers two memory addressing modes:
1) Extended
2) Indexed

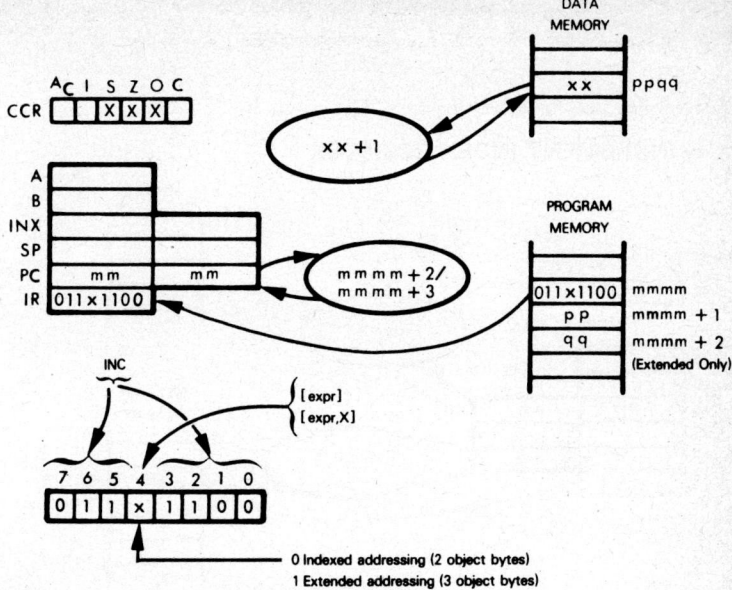

Increment the selected memory byte.

If pp = 01_{16}, qq = $A2_{16}$ and xx = $C0_{16}$, then after executing an:

    INC $01A2

instruction, the contents of memory location $01A2_{16}$ will be incremented to $C1_{16}$.

The INC instruction can be used to provide a counter in a variety of applications, e.g., counting the occurrences of an event or as an iterative counter which specifies the number of times a task is to be performed.

INS — INCREMENT STACK POINTER

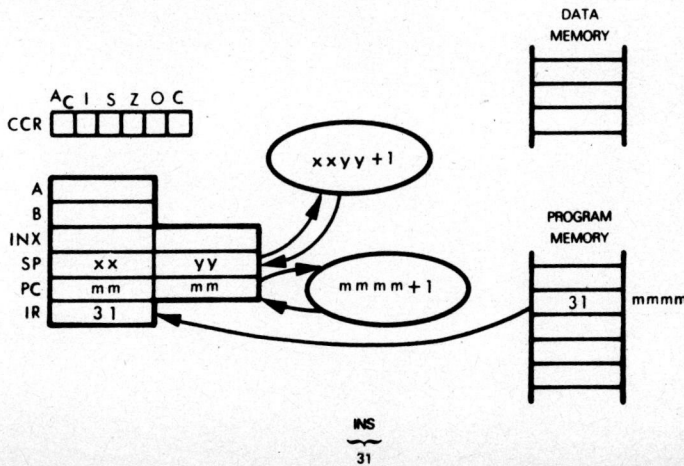

Add 1 to the 16-bit value in the Stack Pointer. No other registers or condition codes are affected. Suppose the Stack Pointer contains $2F7A_{16}$. After the instruction:

    INS

has executed, the Stack Pointer will contain $2F7B_{16}$.

INX — INCREMENT INDEX REGISTER

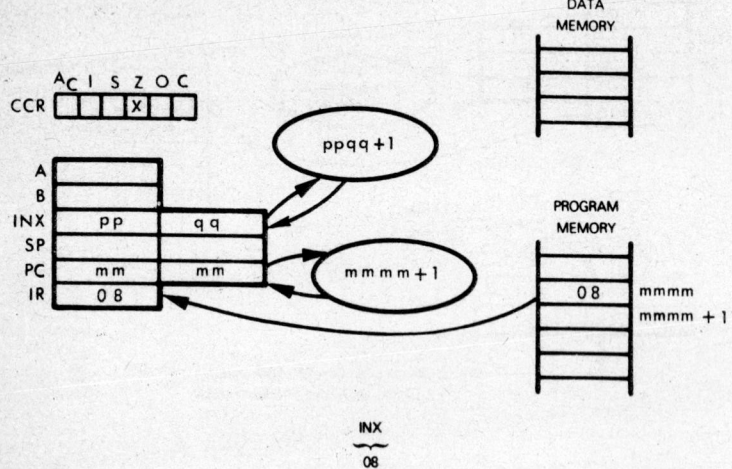

Add 1 to the 16-bit value in the Index register. The Zero status is set to 1 if the 16-bit result is 0. Suppose the Index register contains $310C_{16}$. After the instruction:

    INX

has executed, the Index register will contain $310D_{16}$.

JMP — JUMP VIA INDEXED OR EXTENDED ADDRESSING

This instruction will be illustrated using indexed addressing.

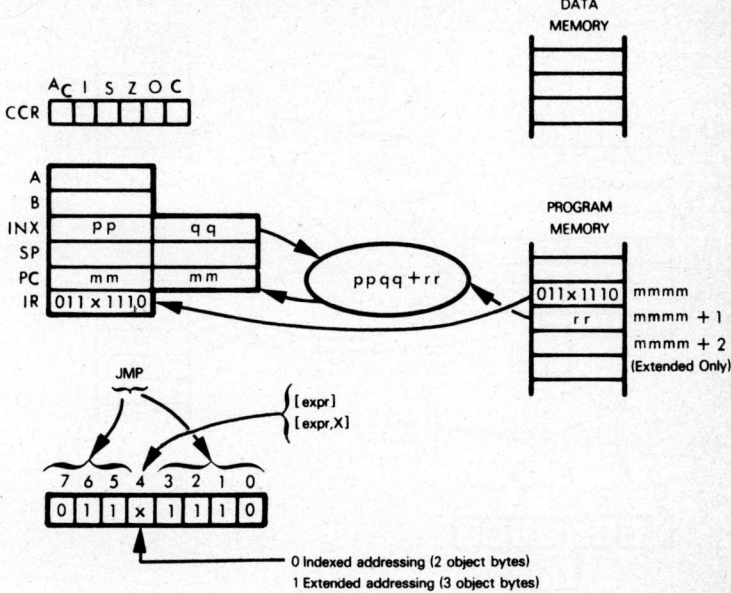

Jump to the instruction specified by the operand by loading the address of the selected memory byte into the Program Counter.

In the following instruction sequence:

```
        LDX     #JPTBL
        JMP     2,X
        -
        -
        -
JPTBL   BRA     NEWDATA
        BRA     PROCESSDATA
        BRA     FLAGDATA
```

If the Index register contains the address of JPTBL, then the JMP instruction will perform an indexed jump relative to JPTBL. In this case, the instruction executed following the:

```
        JMP     2,X
```

instruction would be the BRA PROCESSDATA instruction.

More frequently, the JMP instruction uses the extended addressing mode. In this case, the second byte of the instruction is loaded into the high byte of the Program Counter, and the third byte of the instruction is loaded into the low byte of the Program Counter. Instruction execution continues from this address.

JSR — JUMP TO SUBROUTINE USING INDEXED OR EXTENDED ADDRESSING

This instruction will be illustrated using extended addressing.

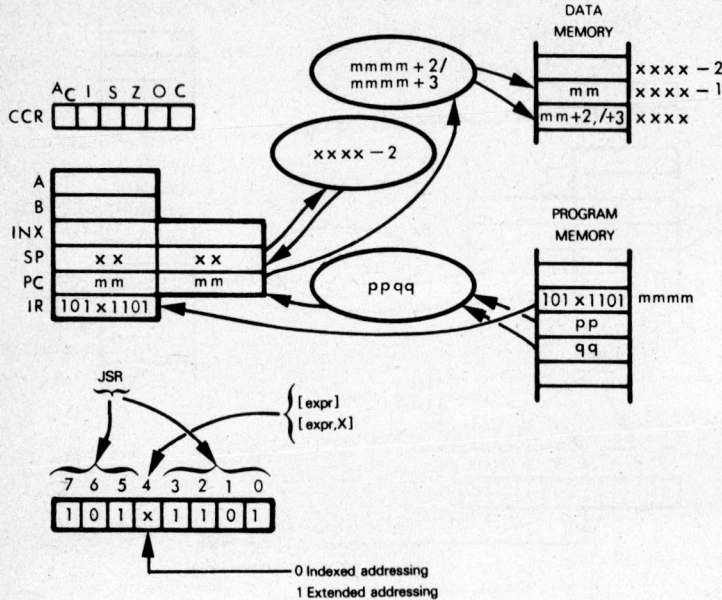

The Program Counter is incremented by 3 (if extended addressing is used), or 2 (if indexed addressing is used), and then is pushed onto the stack. The Stack Pointer is adjusted to point to the next empty location in the stack. (These functions are detailed in the description of the BSR instruction.) The address of the selected memory byte is then stored into the Program Counter. Execution continues from this point.

Consider this instruction sequence:

```
        JSR     SUBR
        AND     #$7F
        -
        -
        -
SUBR    ABA
```

After the JSR instruction has executed, the address of the AND instruction will be saved at the top of the stack. The ABA instruction will be the next instruction executed.

LDA — LOAD ACCUMULATOR FROM MEMORY

Load the contents of the selected memory byte into the specified Accumulator. This instruction offers the same memory addressing options as the ADC instruction and will be illustrated using indexed addressing; consult the ADC instruction for the other addressing modes.

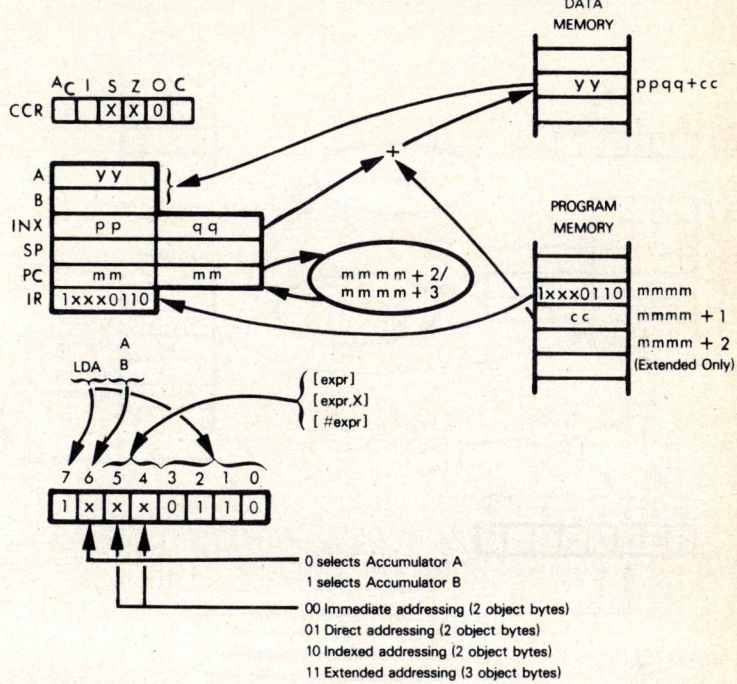

Load the contents of the selected memory byte into the specified Accumulator.

Suppose the Index register contains 0800_{16} and cc = 43_{16}. If memory location 0843_{16} contains AA_{16}, then after:

    LDA A $43,X

has executed, Accumulator A will contain AA_{16}.

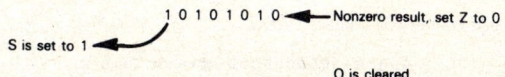

LDS — LOAD STACK POINTER

Load the contents of two selected memory locations into the Stack Pointer. This instruction offers the same memory addressing options as the ADC instruction, and will be illustrated using immediate addressing; consult the discussion of the ADC instruction for examples of the other addressing modes.

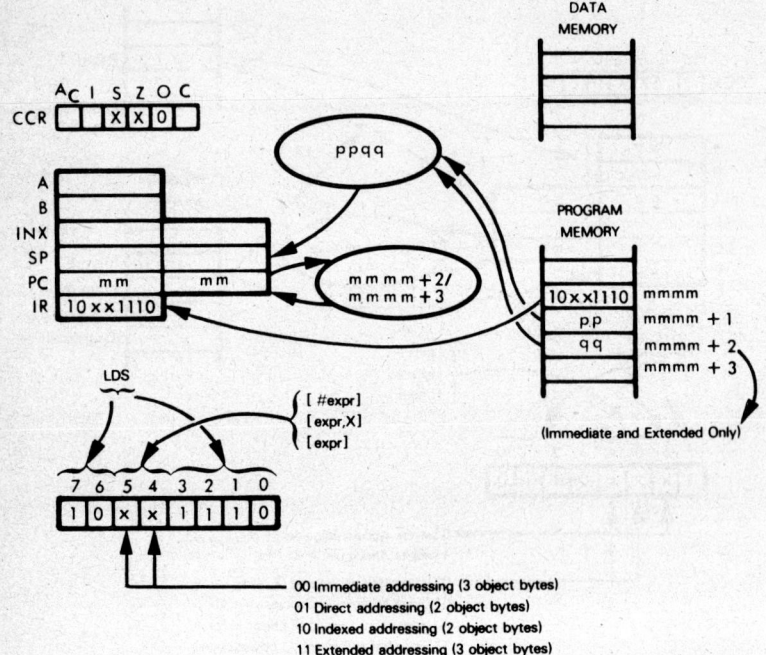

Load the contents of the selected memory byte into the high byte of the Stack Pointer. Load the contents of the memory byte immediately following the selected memory byte into the low byte of the Stack Pointer. Set the Sign status if the most significant bit of the Stack Pointer is set; set the Zero status if all 16 bits loaded are 0. Clear the Overflow flag.

Suppose pp = 14_{16} and qq = 00_{16}. After executing a:

    LDS   #$1400

instruction, the Stack Pointer will contain 1400_{16}.

3-62

LDX — LOAD INDEX REGISTER

Load the contents of two selected memory locations into the Index register. This instruction offers the same memory addressing options as the ADC instruction, and will be illustrated using direct addressing; consult the ADC instruction for the other addressing modes.

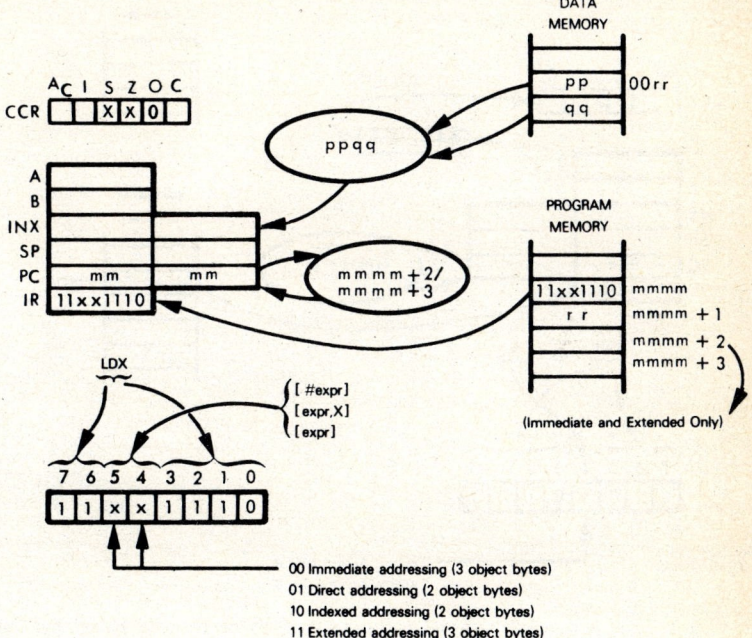

Load the contents of the selected memory byte into the high byte of the Index register. Load the contents of the memory byte immediately following the selected memory byte into the low byte of the Index register. Set the Sign status if the most significant bit of the Index register is set. Set the Zero status if all 16 bits of the Index register are set to 0. The Overflow status is cleared to 0.

Suppose that $rr = 90_{16}$, $pp = 01_{16}$ and $qq = 00_{16}$. Executing the:

    LDX $90

instruction will load 0100_{16} into the Index register.

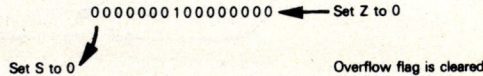

LSR — LOGICAL RIGHT SHIFT OF ACCUMULATOR OR MEMORY

This instruction performs a one-bit logical right shift of the specified Accumulator or the selected memory byte.

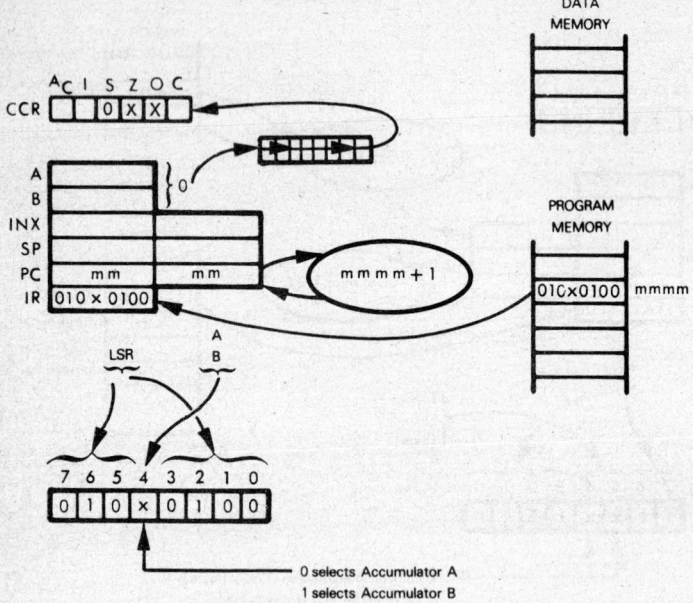

Shift the selected Accumulator's contents right one bit. Shift the low order bit into the Carry status. Shift a 0 into the high order bit.

Suppose Accumulator B contains $7A_{16}$. After the:

    LSR B

instruction is executed, Accumulator B will contain 3D and the Carry status will be set to 0.

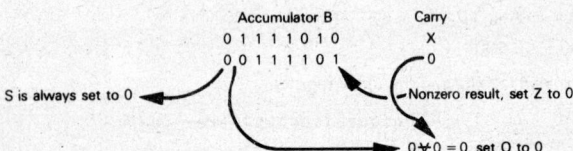

Two methods of memory addressing are available with the LSR instruction, Indexed and Extended.

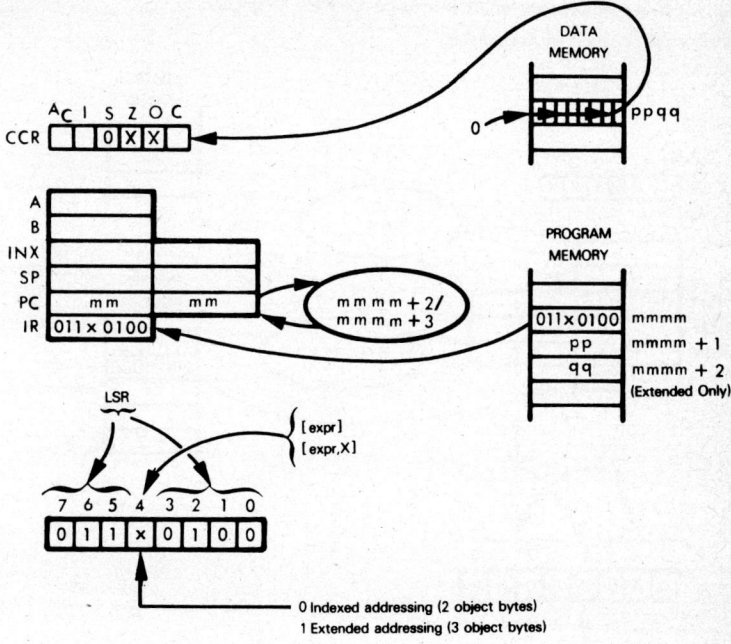

Logically shift the contents of the selected memory location right by one bit.

Suppose $pp = 04_{16}$, $qq = FA_{16}$ and the contents of memory location $04FA_{16}$ are $0D_{16}$. After the instruction:

    LSR $04FA

is executed, the Carry status will be 1 and the contents of location $04FA_{16}$ will be 06_{16}.

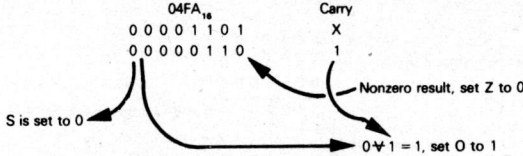

NEG — NEGATE ACCUMULATOR OR MEMORY

This instruction negates the specified Accumulator or the selected memory byte by replacing the Accumulator or memory byte with the twos complement of its contents.

First, consider negating an Accumulator:

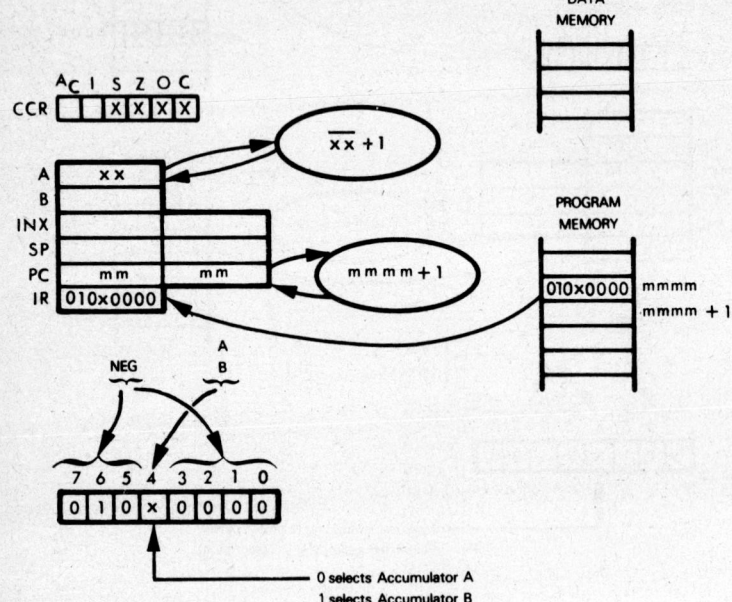

Negate the contents of the specified Accumulator by taking the ones complement of the contents of the specified Accumulator and adding one to the result.

Suppose Accumulator A contains $3A_{16}$. After the instruction:

    NEG A

is executed, Accumulator A will contain $C6_{16}$.

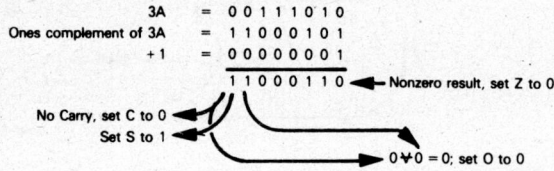

The NEG instruction also offers two memory addressing options:

1) Extended
2) Indexed

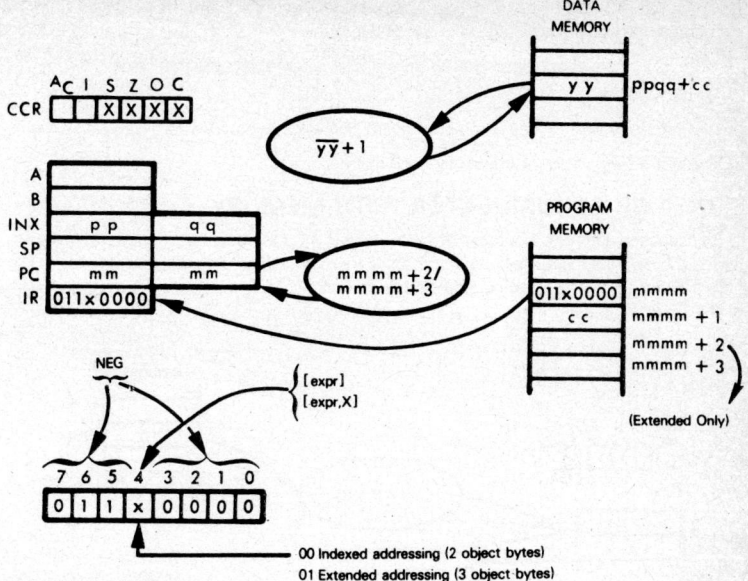

Suppose the contents of the Index register are 0100_{16}, cc = $1D_{16}$ and memory location $011D_{16}$ contains AA_{16}. After the instruction:

    NEG $1D,X

is executed, memory location $011D_{16}$ will be altered to 56_{16}.

```
              AA              =  1 0 1 0 1 0 1 0
   Ones complement of AA      =  0 1 0 1 0 1 0 1
              +1                              +1
                              0 1 0 1 0 1 1 0    ← Nonzero result, set Z to 0
   No Carry, set C to 0
   Set S to 0
                              0 ⊻ 0 = 0, set O to 0
```

NOP — NO OPERATION

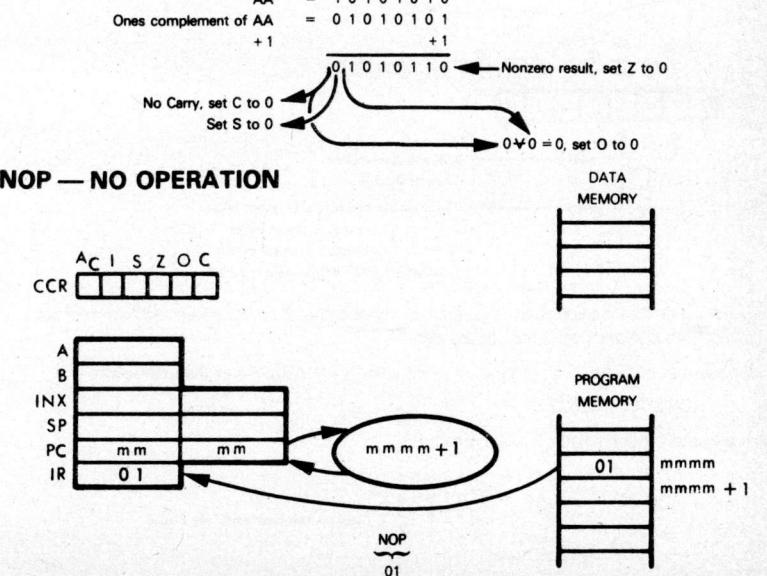

This is a one-byte instruction which performs no operation except that the Program Counter is incremented. This instruction is present for two reasons:

1) The NOP instruction allows you to give a label to an object program byte:
   HERE   NOP

2) To fine tune delay times. Each NOP instruction adds two cycles to a delay.

NOP is not a very useful or frequently used instruction.

ORA — OR ACCUMULATOR WITH MEMORY

This instruction ORs the contents of Accumulator A or B with the contents of the selected memory byte. This instruction offers the same memory addressing options as the ADC instruction, and will be illustrated using extended addressing; consult the ADC instruction for examples of the other addressing modes.

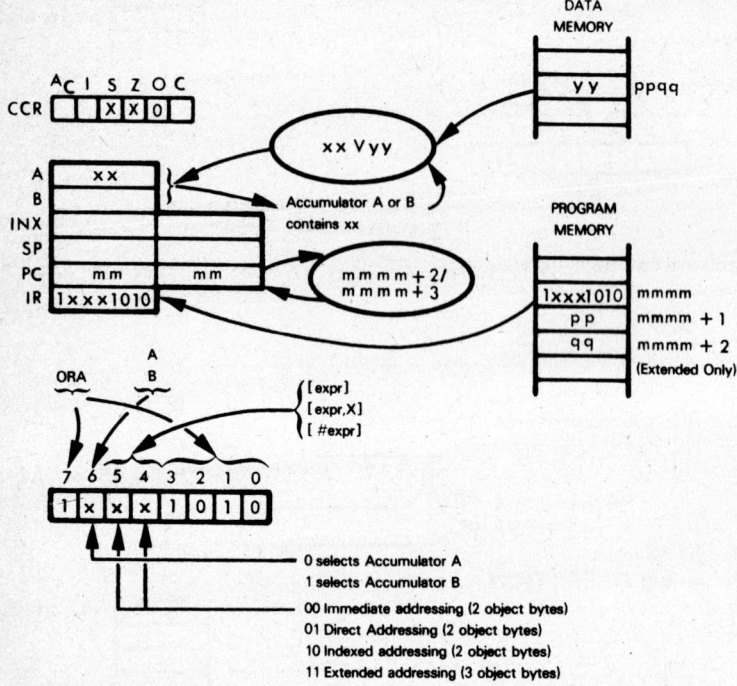

OR the contents of the specified Accumulator with the contents of the selected memory location, treating both operands as simple binary data.

Suppose that $pp = 16_{16}$, $qq = 23_{16}$, $xx = E3_{16}$ and $yy = AB_{16}$. After the instruction:

    ORA A $1623

has executed, Accumulator A will contain EB_{16}.

```
E3 = 1 1 1 0 0 0 1 1
AB = 1 0 1 0 1 0 1 1
     1 1 1 0 1 0 1 1  ← Nonzero result, set Z to 0
```

Sets S to 1

O is cleared

This is a logical instruction; it is often used to turn bits "on". For example, the instruction:

    ORA A   #$80

will unconditionally set the high order bit in Accumulator A to 1.

PSH — PUSH ACCUMULATOR ONTO STACK

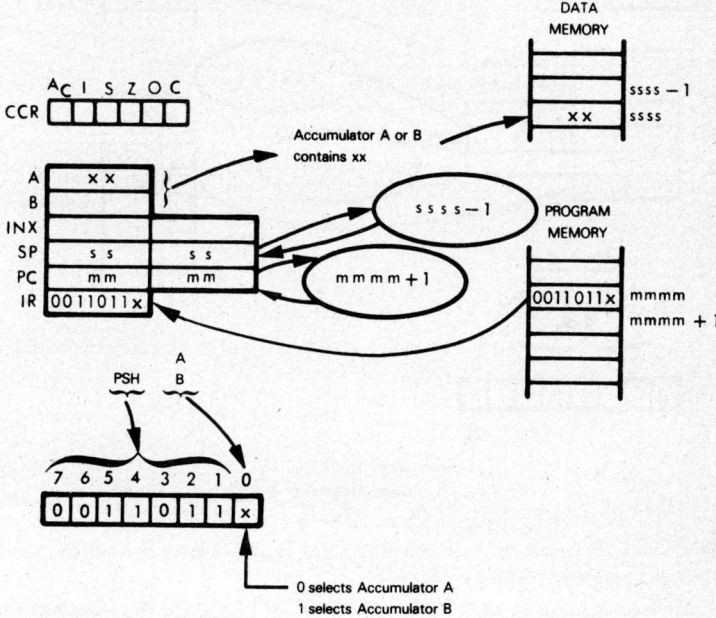

Push the contents of the selected Accumulator onto the top of the stack. The Stack Pointer is then decremented by 1. No other registers or statuses are affected.

Suppose Accumulator A contains $3A_{16}$ and the Stack Pointer contains $2AF7_{16}$. After the instruction:

    PSH A

has executed, $3A_{16}$ will have been stored into location $2AF7_{16}$ and the Stack Pointer will be altered to $2AF6_{16}$.

The PSH instruction is most frequently used to save Accumulator contents, for example, before servicing an interrupt.

PUL — PULL DATA FROM STACK

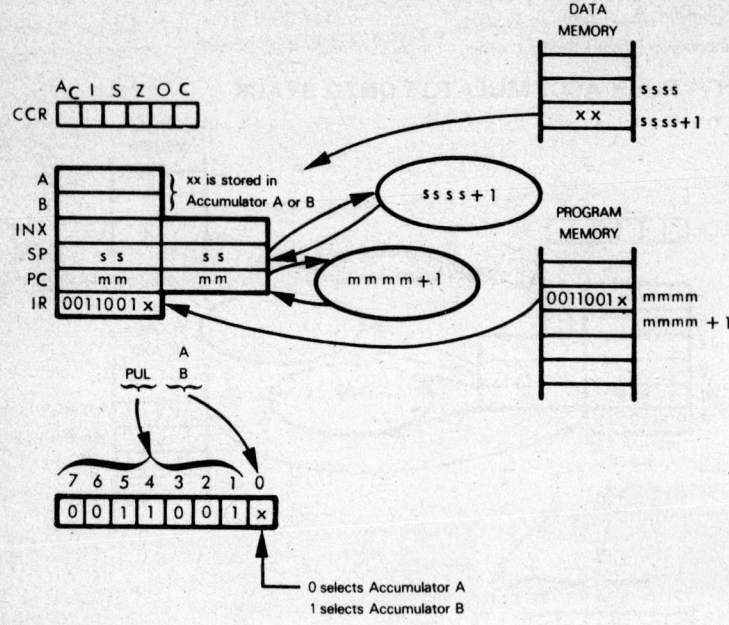

Increment the Stack Pointer, then pull the top stack byte into the selected Accumulator. No other registers or statuses are affected.

Suppose the Stack Pointer contains $2AF6_{16}$ and location $2AF7_{16}$ contains CE_{16}. After the instruction:

   PUL B

has executed, Accumulator B will contain CE_{16} and the Stack Pointer will contain $2AF7_{16}$.

The PUL instruction is most frequently used to restore Accumulator contents that have been saved on the stack, for example, after servicing an interrupt.

ROL — ROTATE ACCUMULATOR OR MEMORY LEFT THROUGH CARRY

This instruction rotates the specified Accumulator or the selected memory byte one bit to the left through the Carry.

First, consider rotating an Accumulator:

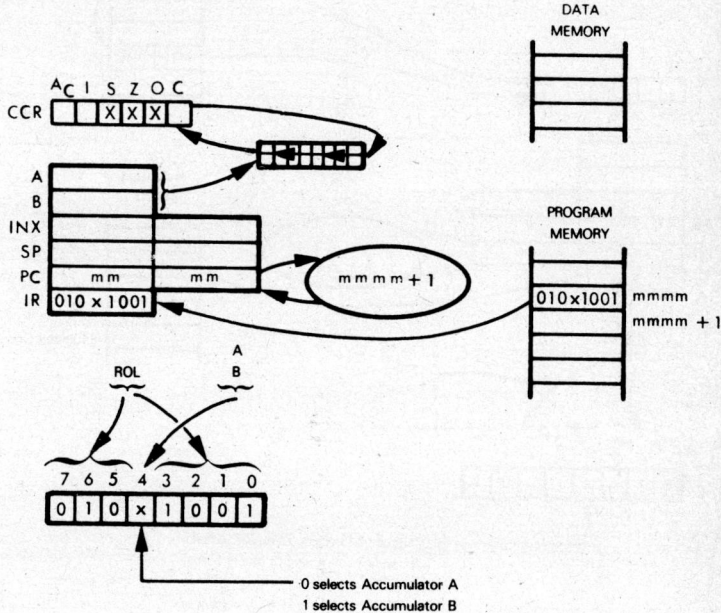

Rotate the selected Accumulator's contents left one bit through the Carry status.

Suppose Accumulator A contains $7A_{16}$ and the Carry status is set to 1. After the:

    ROL A

instruction is executed, Accumulator A will contain $F5_{16}$ and the Carry status will be reset to 0.

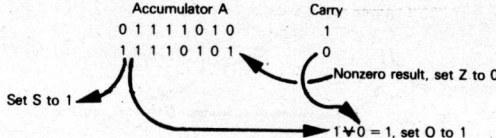

The ROL instruction provides two kinds of memory addressing:

1) Extended
2) Indexed

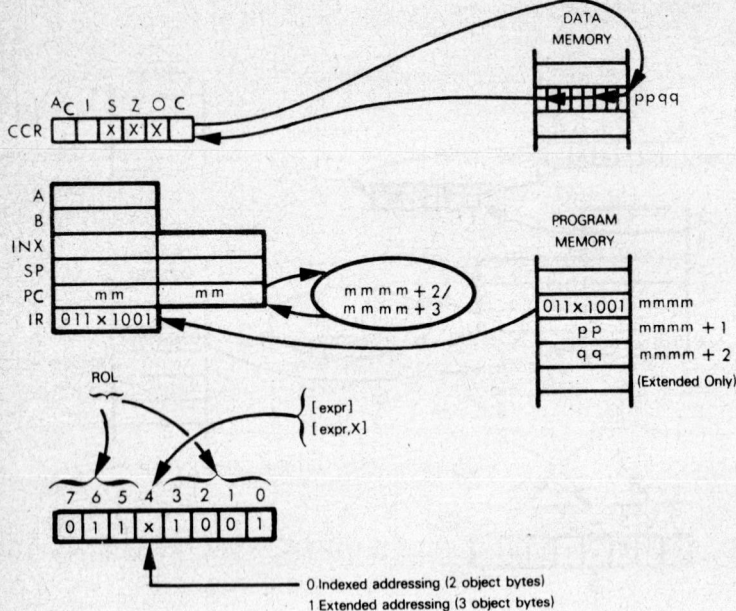

Rotate the selected memory byte left one bit through the Carry status.

Suppose pp = 14_{16}, qq = 03_{16}, the contents of memory location 1403_{16} are $2E_{16}$ and the Carry status is 0. After executing a:

    ROL $1403

instruction, memory location 1403_{16}'s contents will be $5C_{16}$.

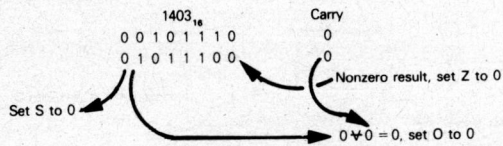

ROR — ROTATE ACCUMULATOR OR MEMORY RIGHT THROUGH CARRY

This instruction rotates a specified Accumulator or a selected memory byte one bit to the right through the Carry.

First, consider rotating an Accumulator:

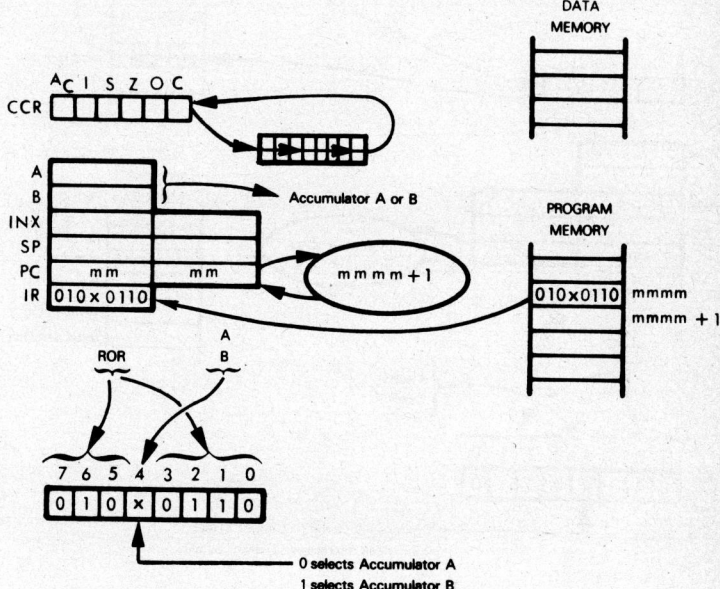

Rotate the selected Accumulator's contents right one bit through the Carry status.

Suppose Accumulator B contains $7A_{16}$ and the Carry status is set to 1. Execution of the:

    ROR B

instruction will produce these results: Accumulator B will contain BD_{16} and the Carry status will be 0.

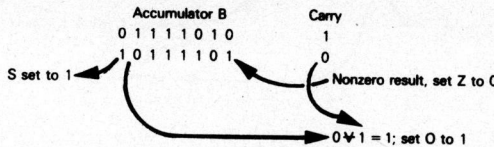

3-73

The ROR instruction provides two kinds of memory addressing:

1) Extended
2) Indexed

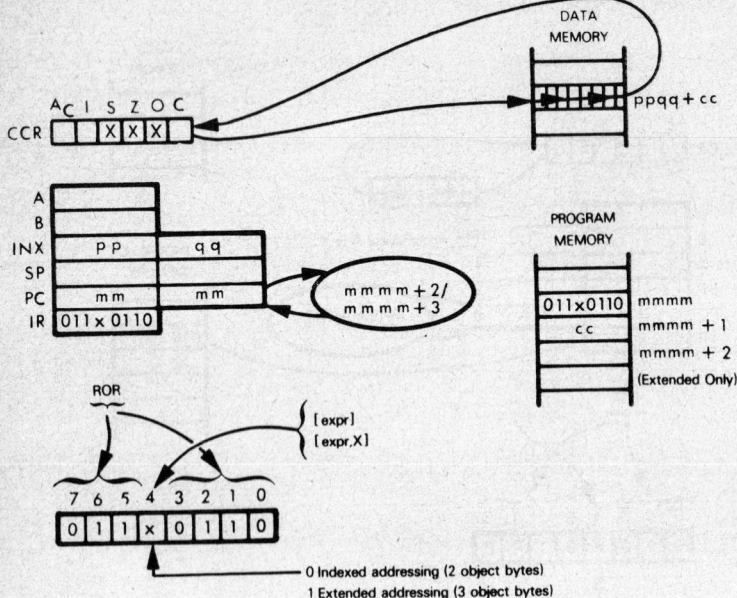

Suppose that cc = 14_{16}, the contents of the Index register are 0100_{16}, the contents of memory location 0114_{16} are ED_{16} and the Carry status is 1. After executing a:

    ROR $14,X

instruction, the Carry will be 1 and memory location 0114_{16} will contain $F6_{16}$.

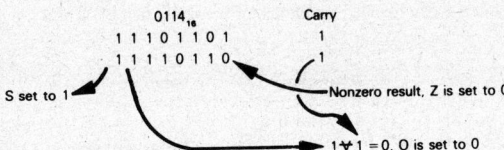

RTI — RETURN FROM INTERRUPT

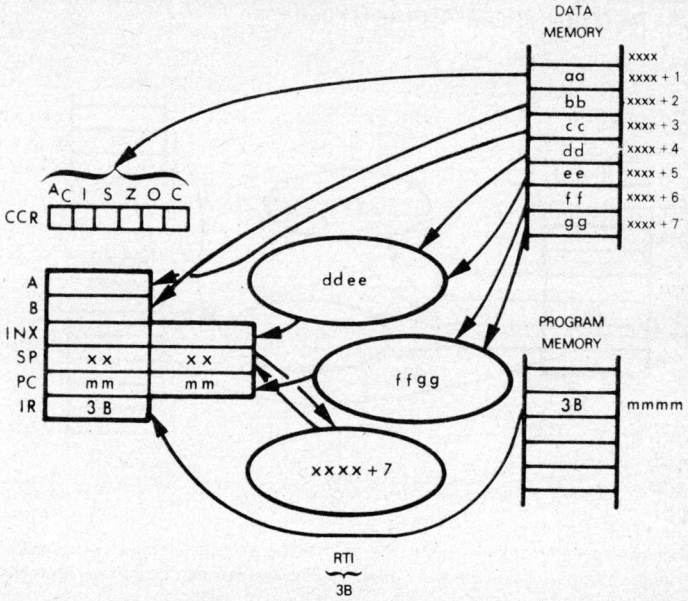

The Condition Code register, the Accumulators, the Index register and the Program Counter all have data values pulled into them off the stack. The registers and the corresponding locations on the stack which are pulled into the registers are as follows:

Memory Location (SP is xxxx at instruction execution start)	Register
xxxx + 1 (bits 5 - 0)	Condition Code register
xxxx + 2	Accumulator B
xxxx + 3	Accumulator A
xxxx + 4	High byte of Index register
xxxx + 5	Low byte of Index register
xxxx + 6	High byte of Program Counter
xxxx + 7	Low byte of Program Counter

Execution continues from the address pulled into the Program Counter.

Suppose the Stack Pointer contains $100F_{16}$, aa = CB_{16}, bb = 14_{16}, cc = 00_{16}, dd = 01_{16}, ee = 00_{16}, ff = 09_{16} and qq = $A2_{16}$. After the instruction:

RTI

has executed, Accumulator A will be 00_{16}, Accumulator B will contain 14_{16}, the Index register contents will equal 0100_{16}, the Stack Pointer will contain 1016_{16}, and the Program Counter contents will be $09A2_{16}$ (this is the address from which instruction execution will proceed). In addition, the Condition Code register will appear as follows:

CB = 11 | 0 | 0 | 1 | 0 | 1 | 1 |
with headers A/C I S Z O C

Note that the Interrupt Mask bit will be set or reset depending on its value at the time the CCR was pushed.

RTS — RETURN FROM SUBROUTINE

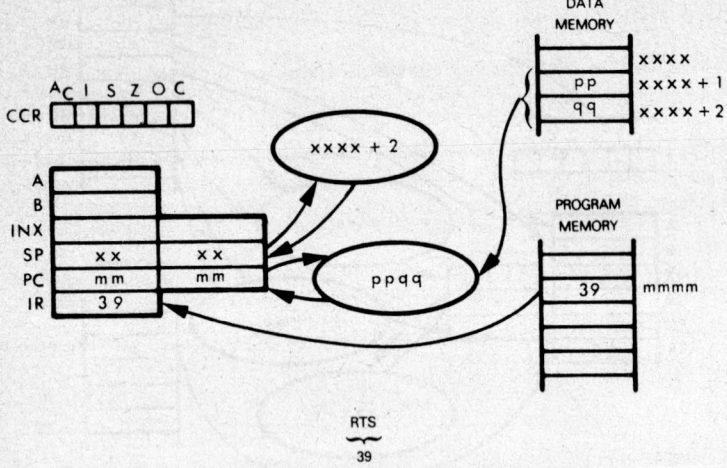

Move the contents of the top two stack bytes to the Program Counter; these two bytes provide the address of the next instruction to be executed. Previous Program Counter contents are lost. Increment the Stack Pointer by 2 to address the new top of stack.

Every subroutine must contain at least one Return instruction; this is the last instruction executed within the subroutine and causes execution to return to the calling program.

For an illustrated description of the RTS instruction's execution see Chapter 5.

SBA — SUBTRACT ACCUMULATORS

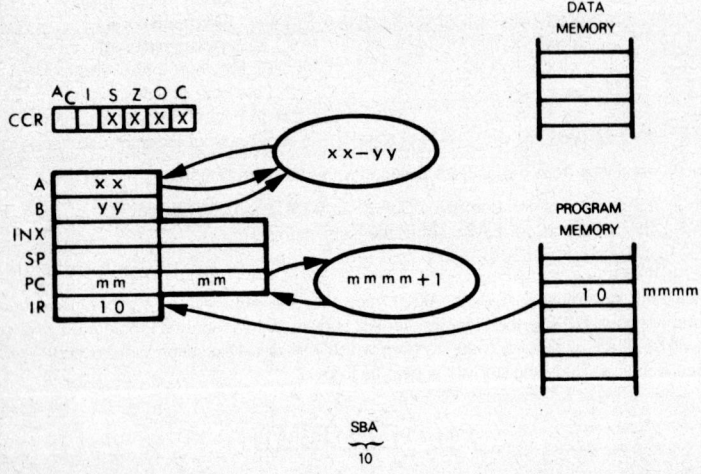

Subtract the contents of Accumulator B from the contents of Accumulator A.
Suppose xx = $3A_{16}$ and yy = $7C_{16}$. After the instruction:

   SBA

has executed, Accumulator A will contain BE_{16} and Accumulator B will contain $7C_{16}$.

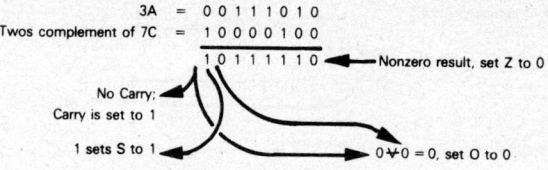

Note that the resulting Carry is complemented.

SBC — SUBTRACT MEMORY FROM ACCUMULATOR WITH BORROW

Subtract the contents of the selected memory byte from the specified Accumulator. This instruction offers the same memory addressing options as the ADC instruction, and will be illustrated using immediate addressing; consult the ADC instruction for examples of the other available modes.

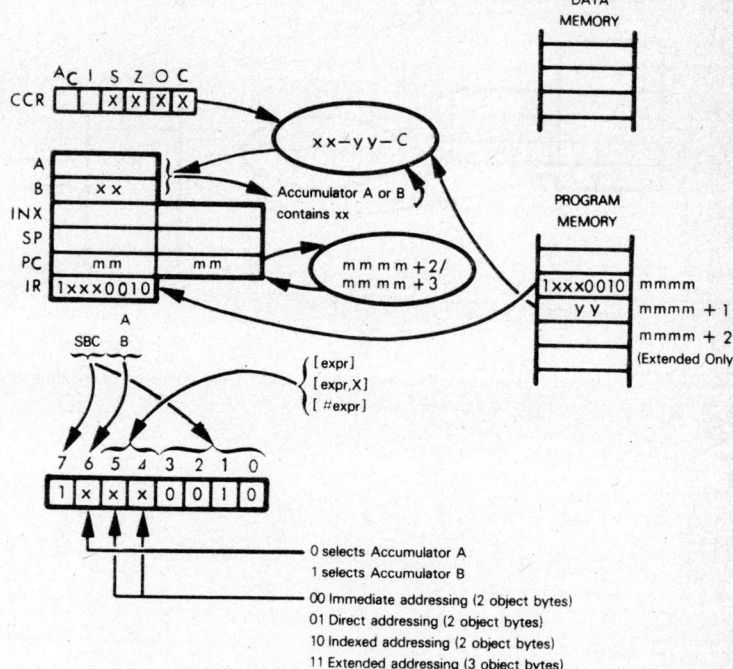

Subtract the contents of the selected memory byte, and the Carry status, from the specified Accumulator, treating all register contents as simple binary data.

3-77

Suppose xx = 14_{16}, yy = 34_{16} and C = 1. After executing a:

SBC B   #$34

instruction, the contents of Accumulator B would be altered to DF_{16}.

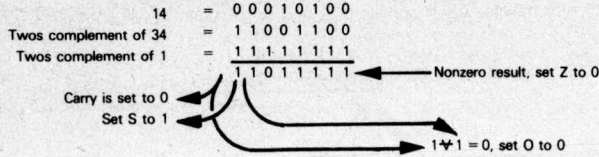

Note that the resulting Carry is complemented.

The SBC instruction is frequently used in multibyte subtraction, after the low order byte has been processed using the SUB instruction.

SEC — SET CARRY

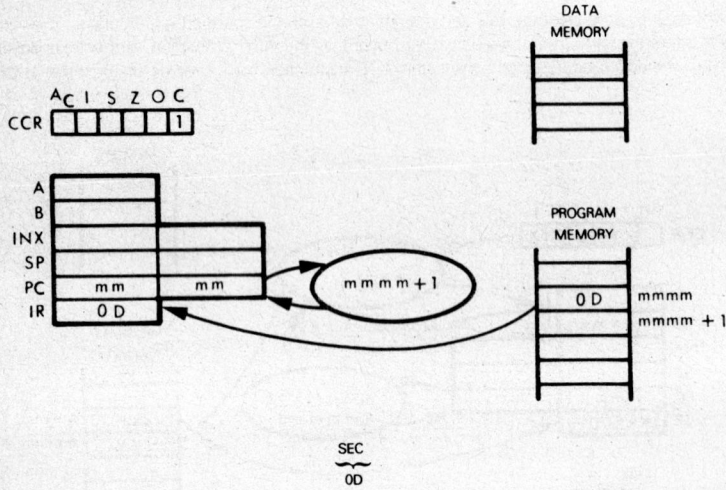

When the SEC instruction is executed, the Carry status is set to 1, regardless of its previous value. No other statuses or register contents are affected.

SEI — SET INTERRUPT MASK

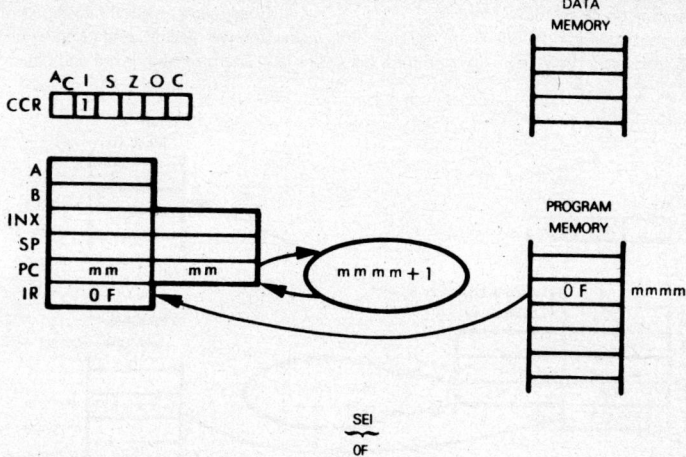

After this instruction has been executed, the microprocessor is inhibited from servicing an interrupt and will continue to execute instructions without responding to interrupts until the interrupt status is cleared. Non-maskable interrupts will be serviced regardless of the state of the Interrupt Mask bit.

With the exception of the Interrupt Mask bit in the CCR, no other registers or statuses are altered.

SEV — SET OVERFLOW STATUS

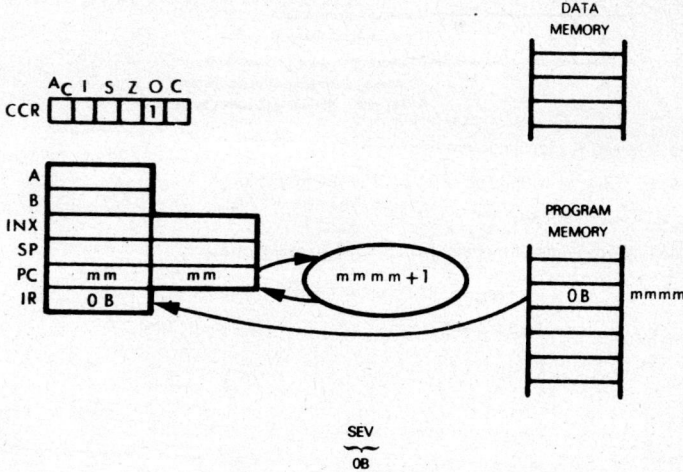

When the SEV instruction is executed, the Overflow status is set to 1, regardless of its previous value. This instruction does not affect any other statuses or register contents.

STA — STORE ACCUMULATOR IN MEMORY

Store the contents of the selected Accumulator into the specified memory location. This instruction offers the same memory addressing modes as the ADC instruction, with the exception that an immediate addressing mode is not available. This instruction will be illustrated using extended addressing; consult the ADC instruction for a discussion and example of indexed and direct addressing.

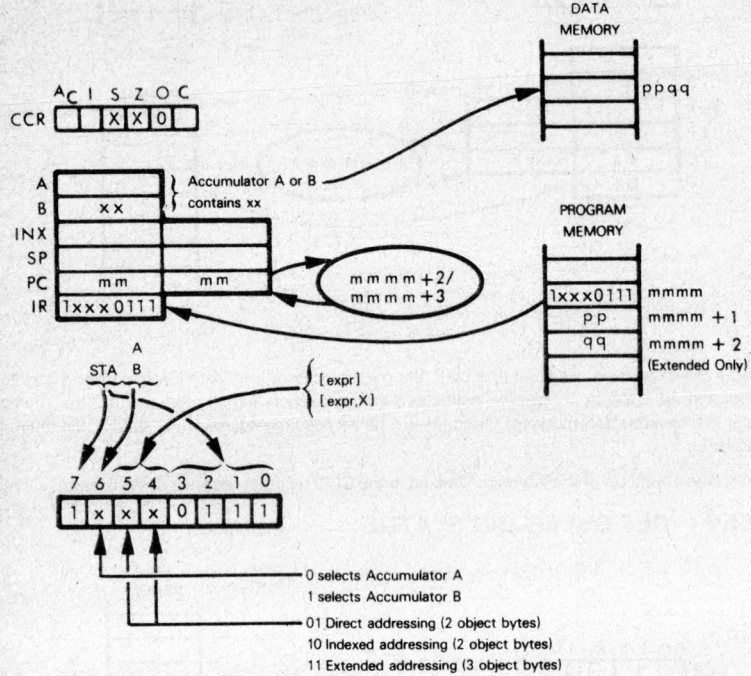

Store the specified Accumulator into memory.

Suppose $xx = 63_{16}$, $pp = 05_{16}$, $qq = 3A_{16}$. After the instruction:

    STA B $053A

is executed, the contents of memory location $053A_{16}$ will be 63_{16}.

STS — STORE STACK POINTER

Store the contents of the Stack Pointer into two contiguous memory locations. Like the STA instruction, this instruction offers direct, indexed and extended addressing modes. This instruction will be illustrated using direct addressing. Consult the ADC instruction for a discussion of indexed and extended addressing modes.

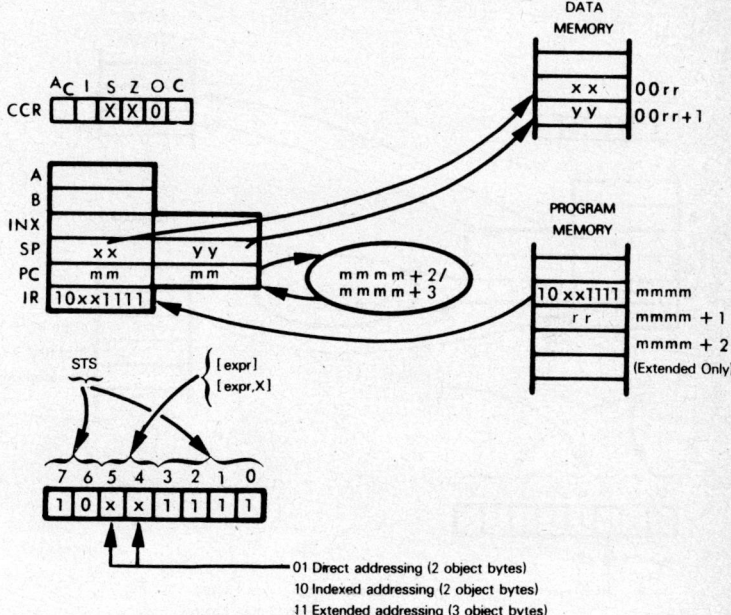

01 Direct addressing (2 object bytes)
10 Indexed addressing (2 object bytes)
11 Extended addressing (3 object bytes)

Store the high byte of the Stack Pointer into the selected memory byte. Store the low byte of the Stack Pointer into the memory byte immediately following the selected memory location.

Suppose the contents of the Stack Pointer are $28FF_{16}$ and rr = 80_{16}. After executing the:

  STS

instruction, memory location 0080_{16} will contain 28_{16} and memory location 81_{16} will contain FF_{16}.

00101000 11111111 ← Nonzero result, Z is set to 0

S is set to 0

Overflow is cleared

STX — STORE INDEX REGISTER

Store the contents of the Index register into two contiguous memory locations. Like the STA instruction, this instruction does not offer immediate addressing, but it does offer the other three memory access methods: Direct, Indexed and Extended. This instruction will be illustrated using extended addressing; consult the ADC instruction for a discussion of direct and indexed addressing.

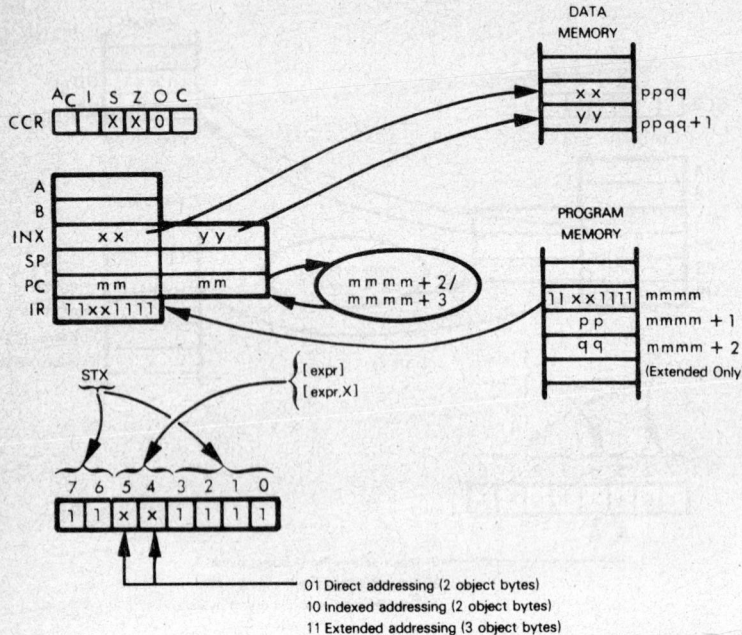

01 Direct addressing (2 object bytes)
10 Indexed addressing (2 object bytes)
11 Extended addressing (3 object bytes)

Store the high byte of the Index register into the selected memory byte. Store the low byte of the Index register into the memory byte immediately following the selected memory location.

Suppose the contents of the Index register are 0100_{16}, $pp = 14_{16}$, and $qq = 30_{16}$. After the:

STX

instruction has executed, memory location 1430_{16} will contain 01_{16}, and 1431_{16} will contain 00_{16}.

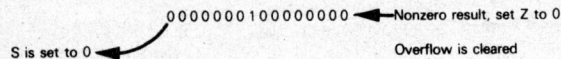

0000000100000000 ◄— Nonzero result, set Z to 0

S is set to 0 ◄—   Overflow is cleared

SUB — SUBTRACT MEMORY FROM ACCUMULATOR

Subtract the contents of the selected memory byte from the contents of Accumulator A or B. This instruction offers the same memory addressing options as the ADC instruction, and will be illustrated using direct addressing; consult the description of the ADC instruction for examples of the other addressing modes.

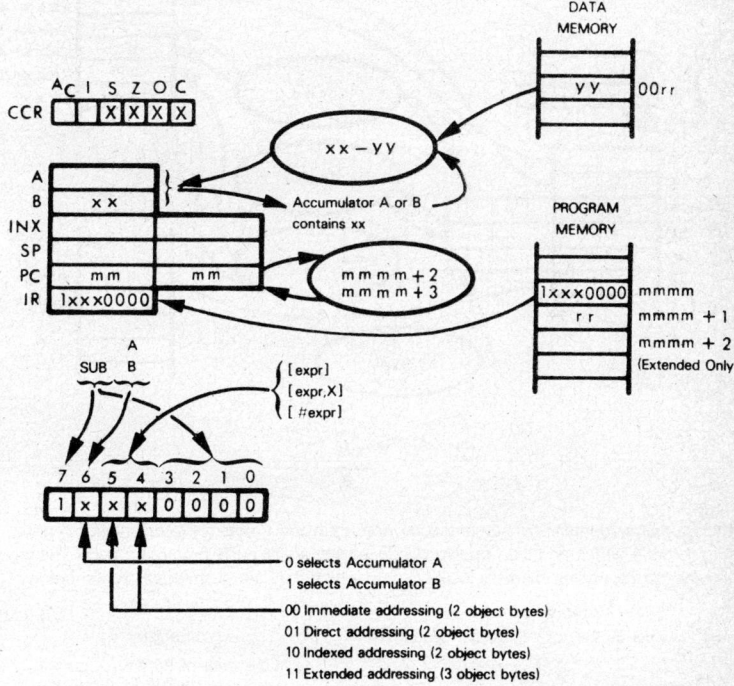

Subtract the contents of the selected memory byte from the contents of the specified Accumulator, treating both operands as simple binary data.

Suppose $xx = E3_{16}$, $yy = A0_{16}$, and $rr = 31_{16}$. After executing the instruction:

   SUB B $31

the contents of Accumulator B will be 43_{16}.

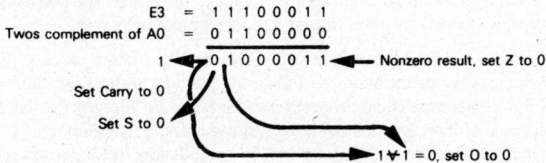

The SUB instruction is used to perform single byte subtractions, or for the low order byte in multibyte subtractions.

SWI — SOFTWARE INTERRUPT

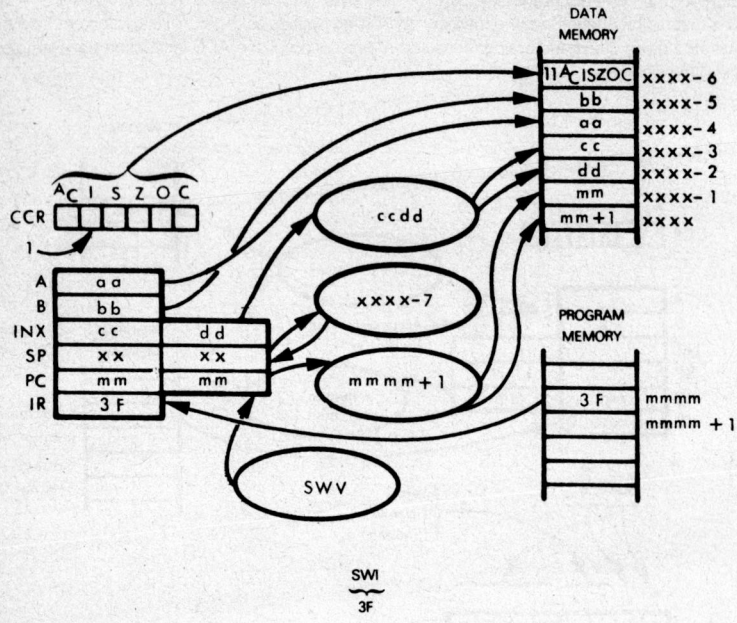

The Program Counter is incremented by one, then the Program Counter, Index register, Accumulators A and B, and the Condition Code register are all pushed onto the stack. The registers and the corresponding memory locations into which they are pushed are shown below:

Memory Location (SP is xxxx at start of instruction execution)	Register
xxxx	Low byte of Program Counter
xxxx-1	High byte of Program Counter
xxxx-2	Low byte of Index register
xxxx-3	High byte of Index register
xxxx-4	Accumulator A
xxxx-5	Accumulator B
xxxx-6	Condition Code register

The Interrupt Mask bit is then set to 1. This disables the MC6800's interrupt service ability, i.e., the processor will not respond to an interrupt from a peripheral device. The contents of the SWV (the Software Interrupt Pointer) are then loaded into the Program Counter.

The SWI instruction can be used for a variety of functions. The address of the entry point for a group of system subroutines or the address of the entry point for a disk operating system or the address of any software package could be inserted in the Software Interrupt Pointer. By executing an SWI instruction, any of these various software systems could be entered. For further information on the SWI instruction, consult Chapter 6 of "An Introduction To Microcomputers: Volume II — Some Real Products".

TAB — MOVE FROM ACCUMULATOR A TO ACCUMULATOR B

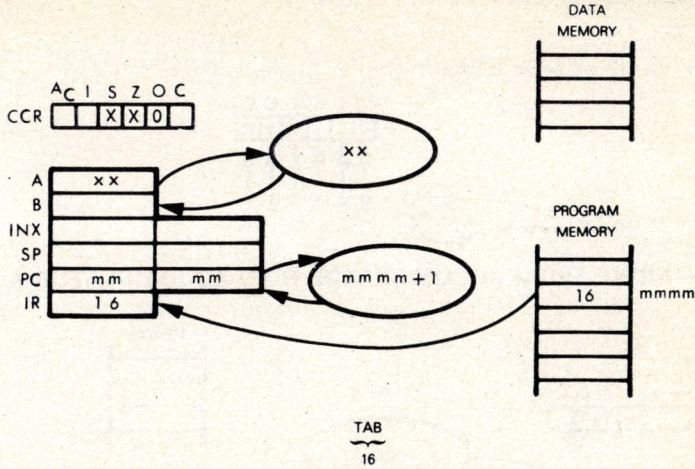

Move the contents of Accumulator A to Accumulator B. Set the Sign and Zero statuses accordingly. Clear the Overflow status.

Suppose $xx = 00_{16}$. After executing the:

    TAB

instruction, Accumulators A and B will contain 0.

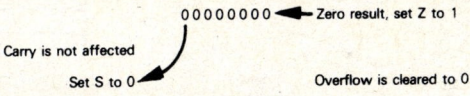

TAP — MOVE FROM ACCUMULATOR A TO CCR

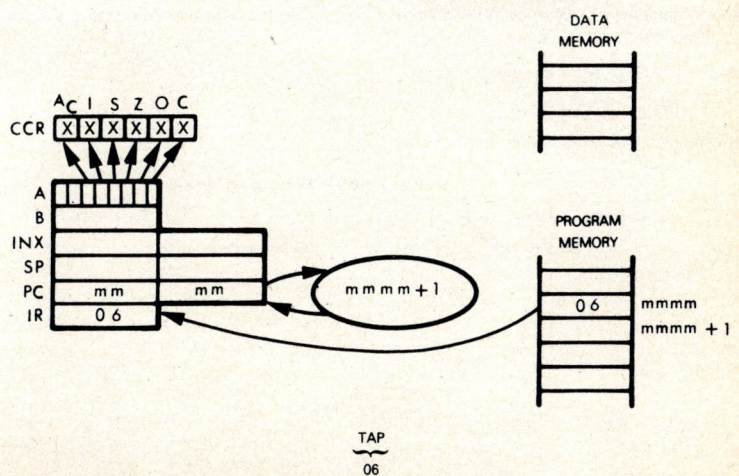

Move bits 0 - 5 in Accumulator A into the Condition Code register.

Suppose Accumulator A contains CA_{16}. After executing the:

    TAP

instruction, the CCR will be set as follows:

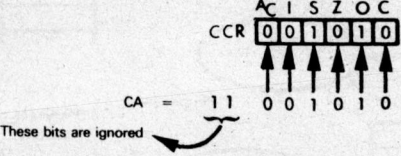

TBA — MOVE FROM ACCUMULATOR B TO ACCUMULATOR A

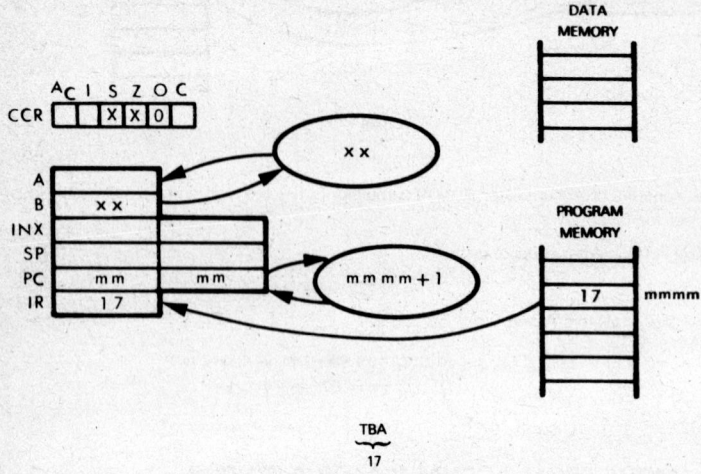

Move the contents of Accumulator B to Accumulator A. Set the Sign and Zero statuses accordingly. Clear the Overflow status.

Suppose $xx = C3_{16}$. After executing the:

    TBA

instruction, Accumulators A and B will contain $C3_{16}$.

TPA — MOVE CCR TO ACCUMULATOR A

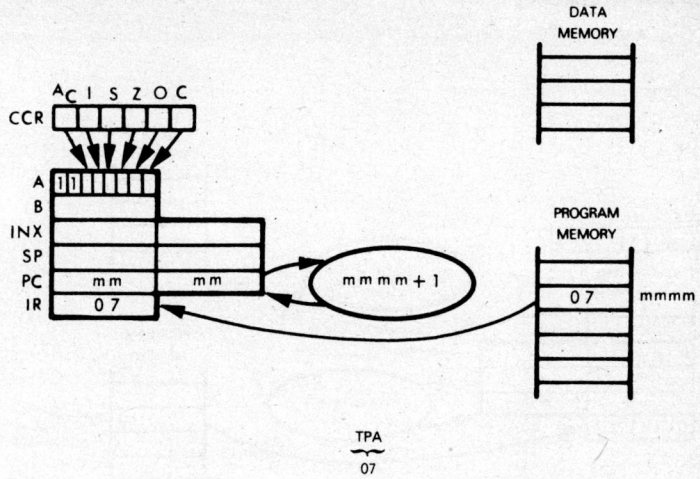

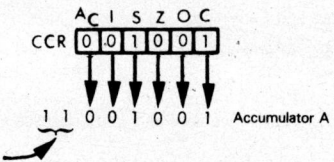

Move the contents of the CCR into Accumulator A, bits 0 - 5. Set Bits 6 and 7 of Accumulator A to 1.

Suppose the CCR was in the following state:

        S and C are 1.
        A_C, I, Z and O are 0.

After executing the:

        TPA

instruction, Accumulator A will contain $C9_{16}$.

Accumulator A is the only register affected. No statuses are altered.

TST — TEST THE CONTENTS OF ACCUMULATOR OR MEMORY

Set the Sign and Zero flags depending on the contents of the specified Accumulator or the selected memory byte.

First, consider testing an Accumulator:

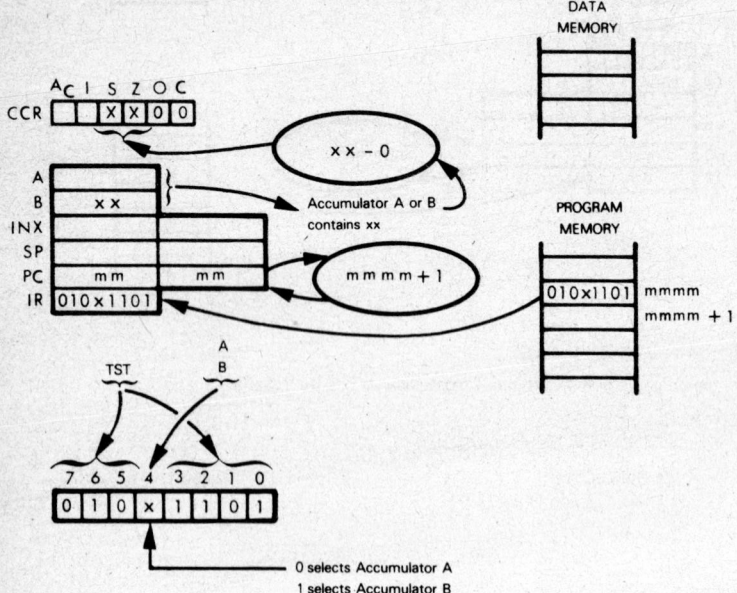

Set the Sign and Zero flags depending on the result of subtracting 00_{16} from Accumulator A or B. Clear the Overflow and Carry flags.

Suppose $xx = 31_{16}$. After executing a:

    TST B

instruction, the Sign, Zero, Overflow and Carry statuses are 0.

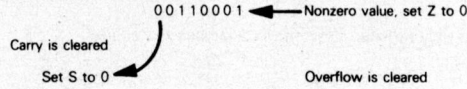

TST offers two memory access methods: indexed and extended.

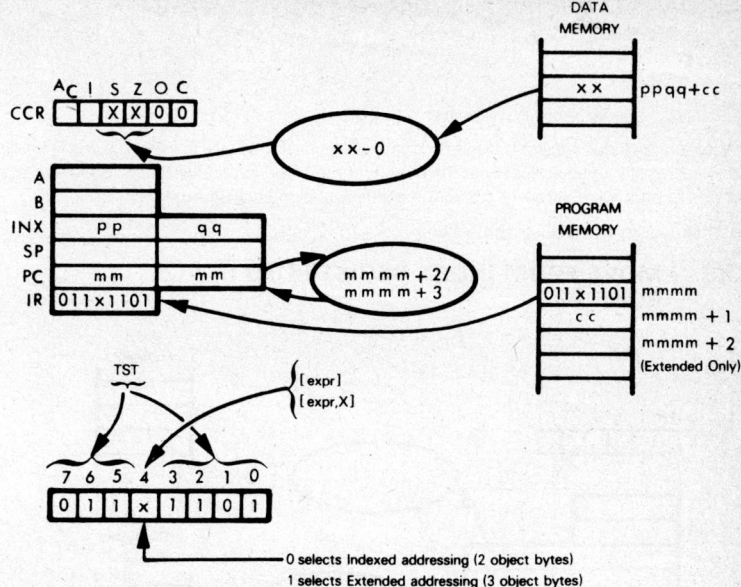

Test the selected memory byte by subtracting 00_{16} from its contents. Set the Sign and Zero flags accordingly, and clear the Overflow and Carry statuses.

Suppose the Index register contains 0100_{16}, cc = 02_{16}, and the contents of memory location 0102_{16} are 00. Executing a:

    TST   2,X

instruction would set the Sign, Overflow and Carry flags to 0 and set the Zero flag to 1.

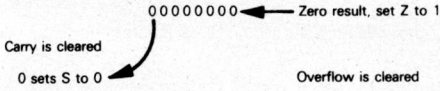

TSX — MOVE FROM STACK POINTER TO INDEX REGISTER

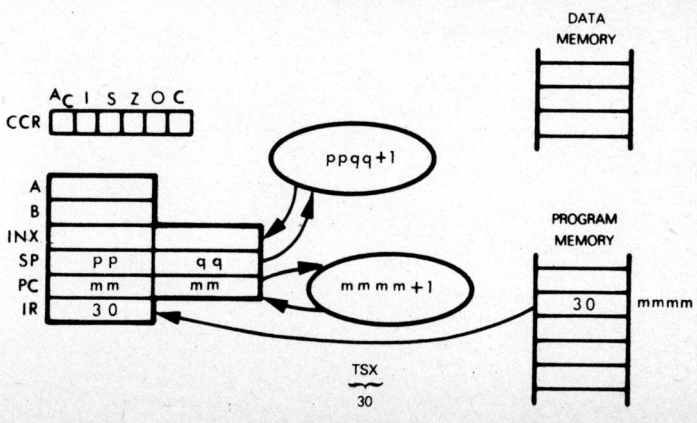

Move the contents of the Stack Pointer to the Index register and increment by one.

Suppose ppqq is $2AF7_{16}$. After the execution of the:

TSX

instruction, the Index register will contain $2AF8_{16}$.

The reason the Index register is loaded with the contents of the Stack Pointer plus one is to allow the Index register to point directly at the bottom of the stack. Recall that the MC6800 employs a decrement after write, increment before read stack implementation scheme.

No other registers or statuses are affected.

TXS — MOVE FROM INDEX REGISTER TO STACK POINTER

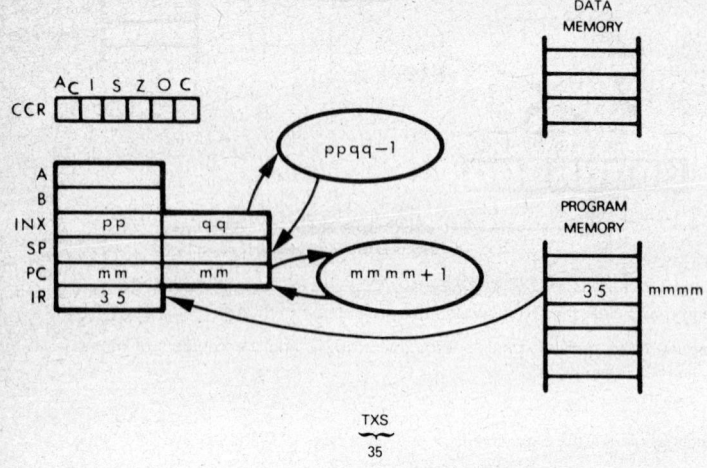

Move the contents of the Index register to the Stack Pointer and decrement by one.

Suppose ppqq = $2AF8_{16}$. After:

TXS

has executed, the Stack Pointer will contain $2AF7_{16}$.

No other registers or statuses are affected.

3-90

WAI — WAIT FOR INTERRUPT

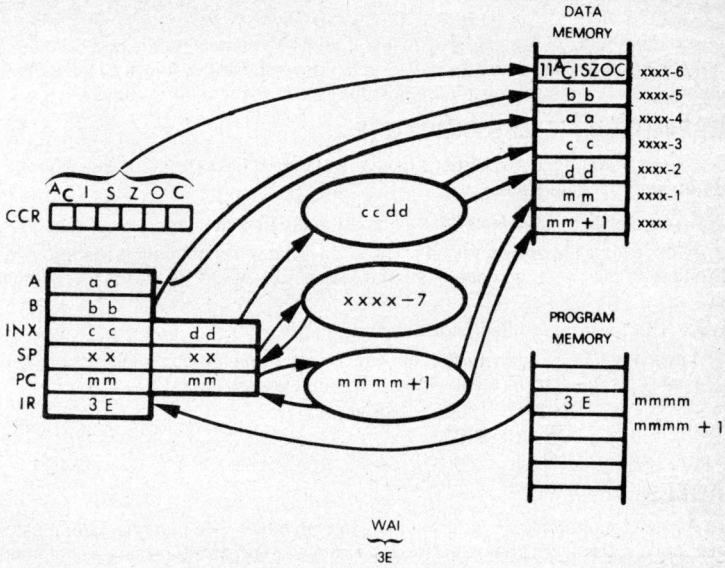

WAI
3E

The Program Counter is incremented by one, then the Program Counter, Index register, Accumulators A and B, and the Condition Code register are all pushed onto the stack. The registers and the corresponding memory locations into which they are pushed are shown below:

Memory Location (SP is xxxx at start of instruction execution)	Register
xxxx	Low byte of Program Counter
xxxx-1	High byte of Program Counter
xxxx-2	Low byte of Index register
xxxx-3	High byte of Index register
xxxx-4	Accumulator A
xxxx-5	Accumulator B
xxxx-6	Condition Code register

After the status of the system has been saved on the stack, execution is halted until a peripheral device requests an interrupt. When an interrupt is requested, the interrupt mask bit is set to 1 and a jump is made to the address contained in the normal External Interrupt Vector. Consult Chapter 6 of <u>An Introduction To Microcomputers: Volume II — Some Real Products</u> for further information on the WAI instruction.

MOTOROLA 6800 ASSEMBLER CONVENTIONS

The standard 6800 Assembler is available from 6800 manufacturers and on the major time-sharing networks; it is also part of most development systems. Cross-assembler versions are available for most large computers and many minicomputers.

ASSEMBLER FIELD STRUCTURE

The assembly language instructions have the standard field structure (see Figure 2-1). The required delimiters are:

1) A space after a label. Note that all labels must start in column 1.
2) A space after the operation code. The Accumulator designation, if needed, may be added to the operation code without a space; e.g., ADDA for "Add to Accumulator A".
3) An X in the operand field indicates indexing.
4) A space before a comment that appears on the same line as an instruction, and an asterisk at the start of a line without an operation code.

```
START     LDAA      1000      GET LENGTH
          LDX       2300
          WAI
```

LABELS

The Assembler often allows only six characters in labels; the first character must be a letter while subsequent characters must be letters or numbers. The single characters A, B, and X are reserved for the two Accumulators and the Index register, respectively.

PSEUDO-OPERATIONS

The Assembler has the following pseudo-operations:

> END - End of Program
> EQU - Equate
> FCB - Form Constant Byte
> FCC - Form Constant Characters
> FDB - Form Double Constant
> ORG - Origin
> RMB - Reserve Memory Bytes

FCB, FCC, and FDB are the Data pseudo-operations used to place data in ROM. FCB is used for 8-bit data, FCC for 7-bit ASCII characters (MSB is zero), and FDB for 16-bit data or addresses. FDB stores 16-bit data or addresses in two consecutive bytes, with the eight most significant bits going into the first word (lower address).

FCB, FCC, FDB PSEUDO-OPERATIONS

Examples:

ADDR   FDB $3165

results in (ADDR) = 31 and (ADDR+1) = 65 (hexadecimal).

TCONV   FCB   32

This pseudo-operation places the number 32 in the next byte of ROM and assigns the name TCONV to the address of that byte.

ERROR   FCC   /ERROR/

This pseudo-operation places the 7-bit ASCII characters E, R, R, O, and R in the next five bytes of ROM and assigns the name ERROR to the address of the first byte.

Any single character (not just /) may be used to surround the ASCII text. An alternative is to specify the number of characters in the operand field. For example:

```
ERROR   FCC   5,ERROR
```

We will always use the first form shown; i.e., with the slash, for consistency.

```
OPERS   FDB   FADD,FSUB,FMUL,FDIV
```

This pseudo-operation places the addresses FADD, FSUB, FMUL, and FDIV in the next eight bytes of memory and assigns the name OPERS to the address of the first byte.

RMB is the Reserve pseudo-operation used to assign locations in RAM; it allocates a specified number of bytes.

EQU is the Equate or Define pseudo-operation used to define names.

ORG is the standard Origin pseudo-operation.

6800 programs usually have several origins; the origins are used as follows:

ORG PSEUDO-OPERATION

1) To specify the Reset and interrupt service addresses. These addresses must be placed in the highest memory addresses in the system (usually $FFF8_{16}$ through $FFFF_{16}$).
2) To specify the starting addresses of the actual Reset and interrupt service routines. The routines themselves may be placed anywhere in memory.
3) To specify the starting address of the main program.
4) To specify the starting addresses of subroutines.
5) To define areas for RAM storage.
6) To define an area for the RAM Stack.
7) To specify addresses used for I/O ports and special functions.

Examples:

```
RESET   EQU   $3800
        ORG   $FFFE
        FDB   RESET
        ORG   RESET
```

Note: $ means 'hexadecimal'.

This sequence places the Reset instruction sequence in memory beginning at address 3800, and places that address in the memory locations (addresses FFFE and FFFF) from which the 6800 CPU retrieves the Reset address.

The instruction sequence which follows is stored in memory beginning at location $C000_{16}$.

```
MAIN    EQU   $C000
        ORG   MAIN
```

END simply marks the end of the assembly language program.

LABELS WITH PSEUDO-OPERATIONS

The rules and recommendations for labels with 6800 pseudo-operations are as follows:

1) EQU requires a label, since its purpose is to define the meaning of that label.
2) FCB, FCC, FDB, and RMB usually have labels.
3) ORG and END should not have labels, since the meaning of such labels is unclear.

ADDRESSES

The Motorola 6800 Assembler allows entries in the address field in any of the following forms:

1) Decimal (the default case)
   Example: 1247
2) Hexadecimal (must start with $)
   Example: $CE00
3) Octal (must start with @)
   Example: @1247
4) Binary (must start with %)
   Example: %11100011
5) ASCII (single character preceded by an apostrophe)
   Example: 'H
6) As an offset from the Program Counter (*)
   Example: *+7

> **NUMBERS AND CHARACTERS IN ADDRESS FIELD**

The various 6800 addressing modes are distinguished as follows:

Direct or Extended are the default modes (the Assembler chooses Direct if the address is less than 256, and Extended otherwise).

\# for Immediate mode (precedes the data).

X for Indexing (follows the offset). X alone is equivalent to 0,X.

> **ADDRESSING MODES**

The Assembler also allows expressions in the address field. These expressions consist of numbers and names separated by the arithmetic operators +, -, * (multiplication), or / (integer division). The Assembler evaluates expressions from left to right; no parentheses are allowed, nor is there any hierarchy of operations. Fractional results are truncated.

> **ASSEMBLER ARITHMETIC EXPRESSIONS**

We recommend that you avoid expressions within address fields whenever possible. If you must compute an address, comment any unclear expressions and be sure that the evaluation of the expressions never produces a result which is too large for its ultimate use.

OTHER ASSEMBLER FEATURES

The standard 6800 Assembler has neither a conditional assembly capability nor a macro capability. Some 6800 assemblers have one or both of these capabilities, and you should consult your manual for a description. We will not use or refer to either capability again, although both can be quite convenient.

Chapter 4
SIMPLE PROGRAMS

The only way to learn assembly language programming is to write assembly language programs. That is what we will do for the next six chapters, which contain examples of typical microprocessor tasks. Problems at the end of each chapter contain variations on the examples given in the text of the chapter. You should try to run the examples on a 6800-based microcomputer system, to ensure that you understand the material covered in the chapter.

In this chapter we begin with some very simple programs.

GENERAL FORMAT OF EXAMPLES

Each program example contains the following parts:

EXAMPLE FORMAT

1) A title that describes the general problem.
2) A statement of purpose that describes the specific task which the program performs, plus the memory locations that it uses.
3) A sample problem showing input data and results.
4) A flowchart if the program logic is complex.
5) The source program or assembly language listing of the program.
6) The object program or hexadecimal machine language listing of the program.
7) Explanatory notes that discuss the instructions and methods used in the program.

The problems at the end of the chapter are similar to the examples; problems should be programmed on a 6800-based microcomputer system, using the examples as guidelines.

The source programs in the examples have been constructed as follows:

GUIDELINES FOR EXAMPLES

1) Standard Motorola 6800 Assembler notation is used, as summarized in Chapter 3.
2) The forms in which data and addresses appear are selected for clarity rather than for consistency. We use hexadecimal numbers for memory addresses, instruction codes, and BCD data; decimal for numeric constants; binary for logical masks; and ASCII for characters.
3) Frequently used instructions and programming techniques are emphasized.
4) Examples illustrate tasks that microprocessors perform in communications, instrumentation, computer, business equipment, industrial, and military applications.
5) Detailed comments are included.
6) Simple and clear structures are emphasized, but programs are as efficient as possible within this guideline. The notes often describe more efficient procedures.
7) Programs use consistent memory allocations. Each program starts in memory location 0 and ends with the Software Interrupt instruction (SWI), which typically returns control to the microcomputer monitor. If your microcomputer has no monitor, you may prefer to end programs with an endless loop instruction, such as

      HERE   BRA   HERE

Consult the user's manual for your microcomputer to determine the required memory allocations and terminating instruction for your particular system.

When tackling the problems at the end of each chapter, try to work within the following guidelines:

1) Comment each program so that others can understand it. The comments can be brief and ungrammatical; they should explain the purpose of a section or instruction in the program. Comments should not describe the operation of instructions; that description is available in manuals. You do not have to comment each statement or explain the obvious. You may follow the format of the examples but provide less detail. **PROGRAMMING GUIDELINES**

2) Emphasize clarity, simplicity, and good structure in programs. While programs should be reasonably efficient, do not worry about saving a single word of program memory or a few microseconds.

3) Make programs reasonably general. Do not confuse parameters (such as the number of elements in an array) with fixed constants (such as π or ASCII C).

4) Never assume fixed initial values for parameters; i.e., use an instruction to load an initial value into a parameter.

5) Use Assembler notation as shown in the examples and defined in Chapter 3.

6) Use hexadecimal notation for addresses. Use the clearest possible form for data.

7) If your microcomputer allows it, start all programs in memory location 0 and use memory locations starting with 0040 for data and temporary storage. Otherwise, establish equivalent addresses for your microcomputer and use them consistently. Again, consult your user's manual.

8) Use meaningful names for labels and variables; for example, SUM or CHECK rather than X, Y, or Z.

9) Execute each program on your microcomputer. There is no other way of ensuring that your program is correct. We have provided sample data with each problem. Be sure that the program works for special cases.

We will now summarize some useful information that you should keep in mind when writing programs.

Almost all processing instructions (e.g., Add, Subtract, AND, OR) use one of the two Accumulators. In most cases you will load data into the Accumulator with LDAA or LDAB. You will store the result (from the Accumulator) in memory with STAA or STAB. **USING THE ACCUMULATORS**

Frequently accessed data should be placed on page zero of memory (addresses 0000 through 00FF). This data can then be accessed with one-word direct addresses. Note, however, that single-operand instructions such as Clear, Decrement, Increment, Shift, and Test require a full two-word extended address even if the memory location being used is on page zero. **USING DIRECT ADDRESSING**

PROGRAM EXAMPLES

Ones Complement

Purpose: Logically complement the contents of memory location 0040 and place the result in memory location 004l.

Sample Problem:

```
            (0040) = 6A
   Result:  (0041) = 95
```

Source Program:

```
LDAA    $40     GET DATA
COMA            ONES COMPLEMENT
STAA    $41     STORE RESULT
SWI
```

Object Program:

Memory Address (Hex)	Memory Contents (Hex)	Instruction (Mnemonic)
0000	96 40	LDAA $40
0002	43	COMA
0003	97 41	STAA $41
0005	3F	SWI

LDAA (Load Accumulator A) and STAA (Store Accumulator A) need an address to determine the source or destination of the data. Since the addresses used in the example are on page zero (that is, the eight most significant bits are all zero), the direct form of the instruction can be used with the address in the next word. The leading zeros are dropped (the address is really 0040) just as they are in everyday use (we say "sixty cents" rather than "zero dollars and sixty cents").

COMA (Complement Accumulator A) is a one-word instruction which inverts each bit of Accumulator A. It replaces each '0' with a '1' and each '1' with a '0', just like a set of inverter gates.

SWI (Software Interrupt) is used to end all the examples.

8-Bit Addition

Purpose: Add the contents of memory locations 0040 and 0041, and place the result in memory location 0042.

Sample Problem:

```
        (0040) = 38
        (0041) = 2B
Result: (0042) = 63
```

Source Program:

```
LDAA    $40     GET FIRST OPERAND
ADDA    $41     ADD SECOND OPERAND
STAA    $42     STORE RESULT
SWI
```

Object Program:

Memory Address (Hex)	Memory Contents (Hex)	Instruction (Mnemonic)
0000	96 40	LDAA $40
0002	9B 41	ADDA $41
0004	97 42	STAA $42
0006	3F	SWI

The direct forms of all instructions are used, since all the addresses are on page zero.

ADDA affects the Carry bit, but LDAA and STAA do not. Only arithmetic instructions (Add, Subtract, Compare, etc.) change the Carry.

LDAA and ADDA do not affect the contents of memory. STAA changes the contents of the addressed memory location, but does not affect the contents of the Accumulator.

Shift Left One Bit

Purpose: Shift the contents of memory location 0040 left one bit and place the result in memory location 0041. Clear the empty bit position.

Sample Problem:

```
          (0040) = 6F
  Result: (0041) = DE
```

Source Program:

```
LDAB    $40        GET DATA
ASLB               SHIFT LEFT
STAB    $41        STORE RESULT
```

Object Program:

Memory Address (Hex)	Memory Contents (Hex)	Instruction (Mnemonic)
0000	D6 40	LDAB $40
0002	58	ASLB
0003	D7 41	STAB $41
0005	3F	SWI

Accumulators A and B are virtually interchangeable, so most instructions can use either one. Note, however, that the instructions ABA (Add Accumulators) and SBA (Subtract Accumulators) place their results in Accumulator A.

ASLB shifts Accumulator B left one bit and clears the least significant bit. The most significant bit goes into the Carry. The result is twice the original data (why?).

Mask Off Most Significant Four Bits

Purpose: Place the least significant four bits of memory location 0040 in the least significant four bits of memory location 0041. Clear the most significant four bits of memory location 0041.

Sample Problem:

```
          (0040) = 3D
  Result: (0041) = 0D
```

Source Program:

```
LDAA    $40              GET DATA
ANDA    #%00001111       MASK OFF 4 MSBS
STAA    $41              STORE RESULT
SWI
```

Note: # means immediate addressing and % means binary constant in standard 6800 Assembler notation.

Object Program:

Memory Address (Hex)	Memory Contents (Hex)	Instruction (Mnemonic)	
0000	96 40	LDAA	$40
0002	84 0F	ANDA	#%00001111
0004	97 41	STAA	$41
0006	3F	SWI	

ANDA #%00001111 logically ANDs the contents of the Accumulator with the number 0F (hex) -- not the contents of the memory location 000F. Immediate addressing (indicated by #) means that the actual data, not the address of the data, is included in the instruction.

The mask (00001111) is written in binary to make its function clearer to the reader. Binary notation for masks is generally much clearer than hexadecimal notation, although the results are the same. Hexadecimal notation should be used for masks longer than eight bits. The comments should explain the masking operation.

Clear a Memory Location

Purpose: Clear memory location 0040.

Source Program:

    CLR $40   CLEAR MEMORY LOCATION 40

Object Program:

Memory Address (Hex)	Memory Contents (Hex)	Instruction (Mnemonic)	
0000	7F 0040	CLR	$40
0003	3F	SWI	

CLR can be applied to any memory location, but a complete 16-bit address is necessary (i.e., 0040 instead of just 40). Of course, the processor does not really act directly on memory. It generates a zero internally and stores it in the memory location.

CLR resets the Carry, Negative, and Overflow flags, and sets the Zero flag.

Word Disassembly

Purpose: Divide the contents of memory location 0040 into two 4-bit sections and store them in memory locations 0041 and 0042. Place the four most significant bits of memory location 0040 in the four least significant bit positions of memory location 0041; place the four least significant bits of memory location 0040 in the four least significant bit positions of memory location 0042. Clear the four most significant bit positions of memory locations 0041 and 0042.

Sample Problem:

            (0040) = 3F
  Result: (0041) = 03
            (0042) = 0F

Source Program:

```
        LDAA    $40             GET DATA
        ANDA    #%00001111      MASK OFF FOUR MSBS
        STAA    $42             SAVE LEAST SIGNIFICANT HEX DIGIT
        LDAA    $40             RESTORE DATA
        LSRA                    SHIFT FOUR MSBS TO LEAST
        LSRA                      SIGNIFICANT POSITIONS
        LSRA                      AND CLEAR MSBS
        LSRA
        STAA    $41             SAVE MOST SIGNIFICANT HEX DIGIT
        SWI
```

Object Program:

Memory Address (Hex)	Memory Contents (Hex)		Instruction (Mnemonic)	
0000	96	40	LDAA	$40
0002	84	0F	ANDA	#%00001111
0004	97	42	STAA	$42
0006	96	40	LDAA	$40
0008	44		LSRA	
0009	44		LSRA	
000A	44		LSRA	
000B	44		LSRA	
000C	97	41	STAA	$41
000E	3F		SWI	

A logical shift of four positions requires four executions of the LSR instruction.

Each LSR instruction clears the most significant bit of the result. Thus, the four most significant bits of Accumulator A are all cleared after LSRA has been executed four times.

Find the Larger of Two Numbers

Purpose: Place the larger of the contents of memory locations 0040 and 0041 in memory location 0042. Assume that the contents of memory locations 0040 and 0041 are unsigned binary numbers.

Sample Problems:

a.
        (0040) = 3F
        (0041) = 2B
Result: (0042) = 3F

b.
        (0040) = 75
        (0041) = A8
Result: (0042) = A8

Source Program:

```
        LDAA    $40             GET FIRST OPERAND
        CMPA    $41
        BHI     STRES           REPLACE WITH SECOND OPERAND IF
        LDAA    $41               SECOND LARGER
STRES   STAA    $42             STORE LARGER OPERAND
        SWI
```

Object Program:

Memory Address (Hex)	Memory Contents (Hex)		Instruction (Mnemonic)	
0000	96	40		LDAA	$40
0002	91	41		CMPA	$41
0004	22	02		BHI	STRES
0006	96	41		LDAA	$41
0008	97	42	STRES	STAA	$42
000A	3F			SWI	

CMPA $41 subtracts the contents of memory location 0041 from the contents of the Accumulator, but does not store the result anywhere. The instruction is used merely to set the flags.

CMPA affects the flags as follows:

1) N is 1 if the most significant bit of the result of the subtraction is 1, 0 otherwise.
2) Z is 1 if the result of the subtraction is zero, 0 otherwise.
3) V is 1 if the subtraction would cause twos complement overflow, 0 otherwise.
4) C is 1 if the subtraction would require a borrow into the most significant bit of the result, 0 otherwise.

Note the following cases:

1) If the operands are equal, Z = 1. If they are not equal, Z = 0.
2) If the contents of the Accumulator are greater than or equal to the contents of the other address (considering both as unsigned binary numbers), C = 0, since no borrow would then be needed. Otherwise, C = 1.

All 6800 conditional branch instructions use relative addressing, in which the second word of the instruction is an 8-bit twos complement number which the CPU adds to the address of the next instruction to find the target address. In the example, the relative offset is 0008 (target address) - 0006 (address immediately following the branch) or 02.

BHI causes a branch if the contents of the Accumulator are greater than the contents of memory location 0041; i.e., if C = 0 (result non-negative) and Z = 0 (result non-zero).

STRES is a label, a name which the programmer assigns to a memory location. The label makes the destination of the branch clearer, particularly when relative addressing is being used. The Assembler calculates the required offset. Using a label is preferable to just specifying the offset (i.e., BHI*+2), since the 6800's instructions vary in length. You could therefore easily make an error in determining an offset.

16-Bit Addition

Purpose: Add the 16-bit number in memory locations 0040 and 0041 to the 16-bit number in memory locations 0042 and 0043. The most significant eight bits are in memory locations 0040 and 0042. Store the result in memory locations 0044 and 0045, with the most significant bits in 0044.

Sample Problem:

```
         (0040) = 67
         (0041) = 2A
         (0042) = 14
         (0043) = F8
Result:  672A + 14 F8 = 7C22
         (0044) = 7C
         (0045) = 22
```

Source Program:

```
        LDAA    $41
        ADDA    $43     ADD LEAST SIGNIFICANT BITS
        STAA    $45
        LDAA    $40
        ADCA    $42     ADD MOST SIGNIFICANT BITS
        STAA    $44         WITH CARRY
        SWI
```

Object Program:

Memory Address (Hex)	Memory Contents (Hex)	Instruction (Mnemonic)
0000	96 41	LDAA $41
0002	9B 43	ADDA $43
0004	97 45	STAA $45
0006	96 40	LDAA $40
0008	99 42	ADCA $42
000A	97 44	STAA $44
000C	3F	SWI

ADCA $42 adds the contents of Accumulator A and the contents of memory location 0042, plus the contents of the Carry (C) bit. The carry from the addition of the less significant eight bits is thus included in the addition of the more significant eight bits.

The 6801 microprocessor has special instructions for loading and storing the double Accumulator (A and B), adding 16 bits to it, and subtracting 16 bits from it.

Table of Squares

Purpose: Calculate the square of the contents of memory location 0041 from a table and place it in memory location 0042. Assume that memory location 0041 contains a number between 0 and 7 inclusive $(0 \leq (41) \leq 7)$.

The table occupies memory locations 0050 to 0057.

Memory Address (Hex)	Entry	
	(Hex)	(Decimal)
0050	00	0 (0^2)
0051	01	1 (1^2)
0052	04	4 (2^2)
0053	09	9 (3^2)
0054	10	16 (4^2)
0055	19	25 (5^2)
0056	24	36 (6^2)
0057	31	49 (7^2)

Sample Problems:

```
a.              (0041)  =  03
       Result:  (0042)  =  09

b.              (0041)  =  06
       Result:  (0042)  =  24
```

Source Program:

CLR	$40	SET 8 MOST SIGNIFICANT BITS TO ZERO
LDX	$40	MOVE DATA TO INDEX REGISTER
LDAA	$50,X	ACCESS SQUARE TABLE
STAA	$42	STORE RESULT
SWI		

Object Program:

Memory Address (Hex)	Memory Contents (Hex)	Instruction (Mnemonic)
0000	7F 0040	CLR $40
0003	DE 40	LDX $40
0005	A6 50	LDAA $50,X
0007	97 42	STAA $42
0009	3F	SWI

Note that the programmer must also enter the table of squares into memory (the Assembler pseudo-operation FCB will handle this).

Memory location 0040 is cleared so that the most significant bits of the Index register will be zero when it is subsequently loaded from memory locations 0040 and 0041. Never assume that a memory location contains zero just because you haven't used it.

LDX $40 loads the Index register with the contents of memory locations 0040 and 0041. The contents of memory location 0040 are placed in the eight most significant bits of the Index register, and the contents of memory location 0041 are placed in the eight least significant bits of the Index register. Always remember that the Index register is 16 bits long.

Indexed addressing means that the actual address used by the instruction is the sum of the address given with the instruction and the contents of the Index register. Thus LDAA $50,X (,X indicates indexed addressing in 6800 assembly language) is equivalent to LDAA $50 + (X), or 53 if (X) = 3. In this case, the Index register contains the number to be squared and the address given with the instruction is the starting address of the table of squares.

Although the 6800 is an 8-bit processor, it has many instructions which handle 16 bits. These are primarily intended to handle addresses which must be 16 bits long to access an adequate amount of memory. Typical instructions are:

LDX - load the 16-bit Index register from memory

STX - store the 16-bit Index register in memory

DEX - subtract 1 from the Index register

INX - add 1 to the Index register

CPX - compare the 16-bit Index register to another 16-bit number; i.e., perform 16-bit subtraction and change the flags but don't store the result anywhere. The Z (Zero) bit can be used for branching.

Of course, the CPU really does everything eight bits at a time; the 16-bit instructions give the CPU directions for two cycles rather than just one.

Arithmetic that a microprocessor cannot do directly in a few instructions is often best performed with lookup tables. Lookup tables simply contain all the possible answers to the problem; they are organized so that the answer to a particular problem can be found easily. The arithmetic problem now becomes an accessing problem -- how do we get the correct answer from the table? We must know two things -- the position of the answer in the table (called the index) and the base or starting address of the table. The address of the answer is then the base address plus the index.

The base address, of course, is a fixed number for a particular table. How can we determine the index? In simple cases, where a single piece of data is involved, we can organize the table so that the data is the index. In the table of squares, the 0th entry in the table contains zero squared, the first entry one squared, etc. In more complex cases, where the spread of input values is very large or there are several data items involved (for example, roots of a quadratic or number of permutations), we must use more complicated methods to determine indexes.

The basic tradeoff in using a table is time vs. memory. Tables are faster, since no computations are required, and simpler, since no mathematical methods must be devised and tested. However, tables can occupy a large amount of memory if the range of the input data is large. We can often reduce the size of a table by limiting the accuracy of the results, scaling the input data, or organizing the table cleverly. Tables are often used to compute transcendental and trigonometric functions, linearize inputs, convert codes, and perform other mathematical tasks.

16-Bit Ones Complement

Purpose: Place the ones complement of the 16-bit number in memory locations 0040 and 0041 in memory locations 0042 and 0043. The most significant bytes are in locations 0040 and 0042.

Sample Problem:

```
           (0040) = 67
           (0041) = E2
Result:    (0042) = 98
           (0043) = 1D
```

The ones complement inverts each bit of the original number; the sum of the original number and its ones complement will always be all 1 bits.

Source Program:

```
LDAA    $40     GET 8 MSBS
COMA            COMPLEMENT MSBS
STAA    $42     STORE 8 MSBS OF COMPLEMENT
LDAA    $41     GET 8 LSBS
COMA            COMPLEMENT LSBS
STAA    $43     STORE 8 LSBS OF COMPLEMENT
SWI
```

Object Program:

Memory Address (Hex)	Memory Contents (Hex)	Instruction (Mnemonic)
0000	96 40	LDAA $40
0002	43	COMA
0003	97 42	STAA $42
0005	96 41	LDAA $41
0007	43	COMA
0008	97 43	STAA $43
000A	3F	SWI

Despite the 6800's 16-bit instructions, you must use the 8-bit instructions to perform most arithmetic and logical operations. The 16-bit instructions can, however, be used to load and store data and occasionally to do a few 16-bit arithmetic operations, such as adding or subtracting 1.

Manage the Accumulators with care. Store the old result somewhere before loading an Accumulator with new data.

PROBLEMS

1) Twos Complement

Purpose: Place the twos complement of the contents of memory location 0040 in memory location 0041. the twos complement is the ones complement plus one.

Sample Problem:

```
         (0040) = 3E
Result:  (0041) = C2
```

The sum of the original number and its twos complement is zero (try the sample case).

2) 8-Bit Subtraction

Purpose: Subtract the contents of memory location 0041 from the contents of memory location 0040. Place the result in memory location 0042.

Sample Problem:

```
         (0040) = 77
         (0041) = 39
Result:  (0042) = 3E
```

3) Shift Left Two Bits

Purpose: Shift the contents of memory location 0040 left two bits and place the result in memory location 0041. Clear the two least significant bit positions.

Sample Problem:

```
         (0040) = 5D
Result:  (0041) = 74
```

4) Mask Off Least Significant Four Bits

Purpose: Place the four most significant bits of the contents of memory location 0040 in memory location 0041. Clear the four least significant bits of memory location 0041.

Sample Problem:

```
         (0040) = C4
Result:  (0041) = C0
```

5) Set a Memory Location to All Ones

Purpose: Memory location 0040 is set to all ones (FF hex).

6) Word Assembly

Purpose: Combine the four least significant bits of memory locations 0040 and 0041 into a word and store them in memory location 0042. Place the four least significant bits of memory location 0040 in the four most significant bit positions of memory location 0042; place the four least significant bits of memory location 0041 in the four least significant bit positions of memory location 0042.

Sample Problem:

```
           (0040) = 6A
           (0041) = B3
  Result:  (0042) = A3
```

7) Find Smaller of Two Numbers

Purpose: Place the smaller of the contents of memory locations 0040 and 0041 in memory location 0042. Assume that 0040 and 0041 contain unsigned binary numbers.

Sample Problems:

a.
```
           (0040) = 3F
           (0041) = 2B
  Result:  (0042) = 2B
```

b.
```
           (0040) = 75
           (0041) = A8
  Result:  (0042) = 75
```

8) 24-Bit Addition

Purpose: Add the 24-bit number in memory locations 0040, 0041, and 0042 to the 24-bit number in memory locations 0043, 0044, and 0045. The most significant eight bits are in memory locations 0040 and 0043, the least significant eight bits in memory locations 0042 and 0045. Store the result in memory locations 0046, 0047, and 0048 with the most significant bits in 0046 and the least significant bits in 0048.

Sample Problem:

```
           (0040) = 35
           (0041) = 67
           (0042) = 2A
           (0043) = 51
           (0044) = A4
           (0045) = F8
  Result:  (0046) = 87
           (0047) = 0C
           (0048) = 22
```

that is,
```
   35672A
  +51A4F8
   870C22
```

9) Sum of Squares

Purpose: Calculate the squares of the contents of memory locations 0041 and 0043 and add them together. Place the result in memory location 0044. Assume that memory locations 0041 and 0043 both contain numbers between 0 and 7 inclusive ($0 \leq (41) \leq 7$ and $0 \leq (43) \leq 7$). Use the table of squares from the example entitled Table of Squares.

Sample Problem:

```
           (0041) = 03
           (0043) = 06
  Result:  (0044) = 2D
```

that is, $3^2 + 6^2 = 9 + 36$ (decimal)
$= 45 = 2D$ (hex)

10) 16-Bit Twos Complement

Purpose: Place the twos complement of the 16-bit number in memory locations 0040 and 0041 (most significant bits in 0040) in memory locations 0042 and 0043 (most significant bits in 0042).

Sample Problems:

a.
        (0040) = 00
        (0041) = 58
Result: (0042) = FF
        (0043) = A8

b.
        (0040) = 72
        (0041) = 00
Result: (0042) = 8E
        (0043) = 00

Chapter 5
SIMPLE PROGRAM LOOPS

The program loop is the basic structure that forces the CPU to repeat a sequence of instructions. Loops have four sections:

1) The initialization section, which establishes the starting values of counters, address registers (pointers), and other variables.
2) The processing section, where the actual data manipulation occurs. This is the section that does the work.
3) The loop control section, which updates counters and pointers for the next iteration.
4) The concluding section, which analyzes and stores the results.

Note that the computer performs Sections 1 and 4 once, while it may perform Sections 2 and 3 many times. Thus, the execution time of the loop will mainly depend on the execution time of Sections 2 and 3. You will want Sections 2 and 3 to execute as quickly as possible; do not worry about the execution time of Sections 1 and 4. A typical program loop can be flowcharted as shown in Figure 5-1, or the positions of the processing and loop control sections may be reversed as shown in Figure 5-2. The processing section in Figure 5-1 is always executed at least once, while the processing section in Figure 5-2 may not be executed at all. Figure 5-1 seems more natural, but Figure 5-2 is often more efficient and avoids the problem of what to do when there is no data (a bugaboo for computers, and the frequent cause of silly situations like the computer dunning someone for a bill of $0.00).

The loop structure can be used to process entire blocks of data. To accomplish this, the program must increment an Address register (usually the Index register) after each iteration so that the Address register points to the next element in the data block. The next iteration will then perform the same operations on the data in the next memory location. The computer can handle blocks of any length with the same set of instructions. Indexed addressing is the key to processing blocks of data with the 6800, since it allows you to vary the actual memory address by changing the contents of registers. Note that in the other 6800 addressing modes, the address from which the data is obtained is completely determined by the instruction (and thus fixed if the program memory is read-only).

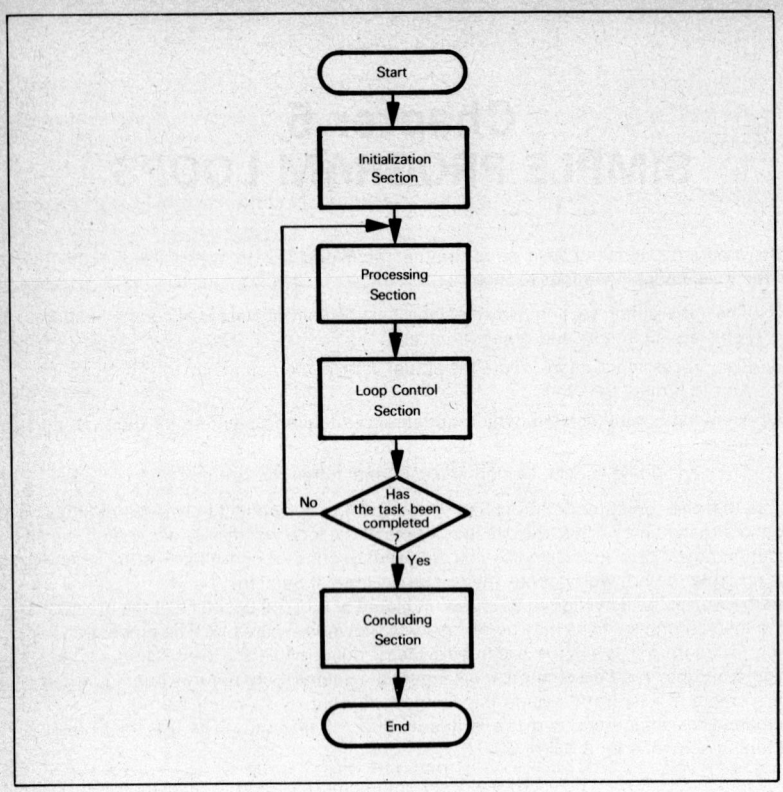

Figure 5-1. Flowchart of a Program Loop

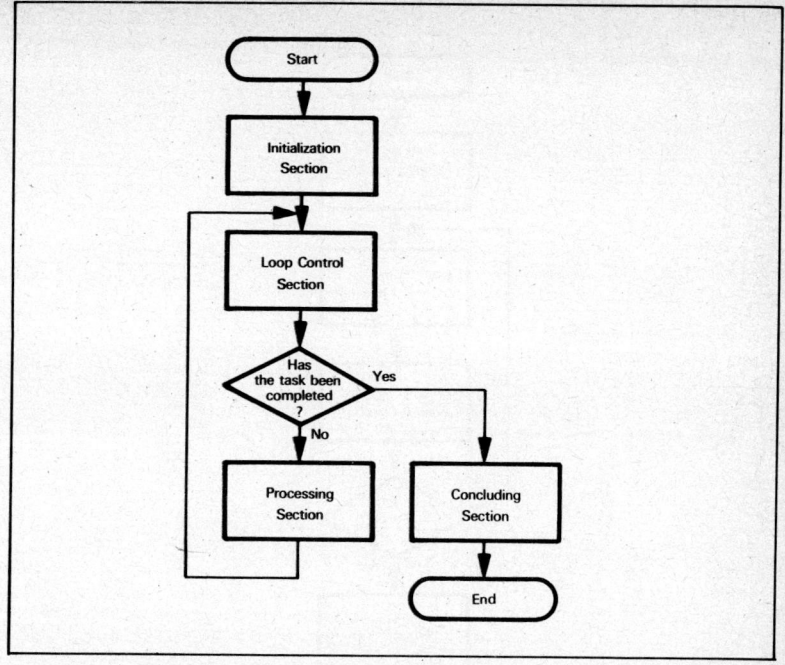

Figure 5-2. A Program Loop that Allows Zero Iterations

EXAMPLES
Sum of Data

Purpose: Calculate the sum of a series of numbers. The length of the series is in memory location 0041 and the series begins in memory location 0042. Store the sum in memory location 0040. Assume that the sum is an 8-bit number so that you can ignore carries.

8-BIT SUMMATION

Sample Problem:

```
         (0041) = 03
         (0042) = 28
         (0043) = 55
         (0044) = 26
Result:  (0040) = (0042)+(0043)+(0044)
                = 28+55+26
                = A3
```

There are three entries in the sum, since (0041)=03.

Flowchart:

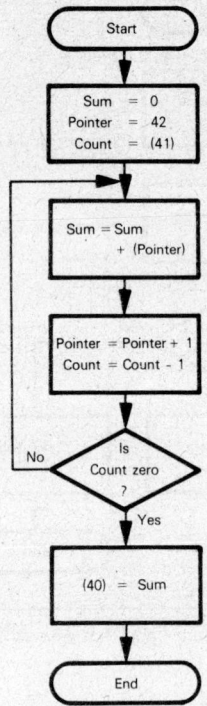

Note: (Pointer) is the contents of the memory location addressed by Pointer. Remember that on the 6800 and similar microprocessors, Pointer is a 16-bit address, while (Pointer) is an 8-bit byte of data.

Source Program:

```
        CLRA                SUM = ZERO
        LDAB    $41         COUNT = LENGTH OF ARRAY
        LDX     #$42        POINT TO START OF ARRAY
SUMD    ADDA    X           ADD NUMBER TO SUM
        INX
        DECB
        BNE     SUMD
        STAA    $40         STORE SUM
        SWI
```

Object Program:

Memory Address (Hex)	Memory Contents (Hex)			Instruction (Mnemonic)	
0000	4F			CLRA	
0001	D6	41		LDAB	$41
0003	CE	0042		LDX	#$42
0006	AB	00	SUMD	ADDA	X
0008	08			INX	
0009	5A			DECB	
000A	26	FA		BNE	SUMD
000C	97	40		STAA	$40
000E	3F			SWI	

The initialization section of the program is the first three instructions, which set the sum, counter, and data pointers to their starting values. Note that LDX loads two 8-bit words of memory into the 16-bit Index register (i.e., 0042 from memory addresses 0004 and 0005).

The processing section of the program is the single instruction ADDA X, which adds the contents of the memory location addressed by the Index register to the contents of the Accumulator. This instruction does the real work of the program. The <u>effective address</u> (that is, the address from which the CPU gets the data) is 0 + the contents of the Index register. You can omit the zero offset from the assembly language program; ADDA X and ADDA 0,X are equivalent.

The loop control section of the program consists of the instructions INX and DECB. INX updates the pointer so that the next iteration adds the next number to the sum. DECB decrements the Counter, which keeps track of how many iterations remain to be done.

The instruction BNE causes a branch if the Zero flag is zero. The offset is a twos complement number and the count begins from the memory location immediately following the BNE instruction. In this case, the required jump is from memory location 000C to memory location 0006. So the offset is:

$$\begin{array}{r} 0006 = 06 \\ -000C +F4 \\ \hline FA \end{array}$$

If the Zero flag is one, the CPU executes the next instruction in sequence (STAA $40). Since DECB was the last instruction before BNE to affect the Zero flag, BNE SUMD causes a jump to SUMD if DECB does not produce a zero result; that is,

$$(PC) = \begin{cases} SUMD \text{ if } (B) \neq 0 \\ (PC) + 2 \text{ if } (B) = 0 \end{cases}$$

(The 2 is caused by the two-word BNE instruction.) A single instruction combining the Decrement and the Jump would be a useful addition to the 6800 set.

Most computer loops count down rather than up so that the Zero flag can serve as an exit condition. Remember that the Zero flag is 1 if the result was zero and 0 if the result was not zero. Try rewriting the program so that it counts up rather than down; which method is more efficient?

The order of instructions is often very important. DECB must come right before BNE SUMD, since otherwise the Zero result set by DECB could be changed by another instruction. INX must come after ADDA X, or else the first number added to the sum will be the contents of memory location 0043 instead of the contents of memory location 0042.

16-Bit Sum of Data

Purpose: Calculate the sum of a series of numbers. The length of the series is in memory location 0042 and the series itself begins in memory location 0043. Store the sum in memory locations 0040 and 0041 (eight most significant bits in 0040).

Sample Problem:

```
         (0042) = 03
         (0043) = C8
         (0044) = FA
         (0045) = 96
Result:  C8 + FA + 96 = 0258
         (0040) = 02
         (0041) = 58
```

Flowchart:

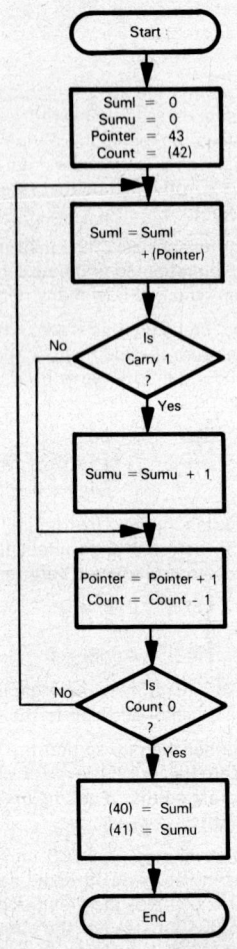

Source Program:

```
        CLRA            MSBS OF SUM = 0
        CLRB            LSBS OF SUM = 0
        LDX    #$43     POINTER = START OF ARRAY
SUMD    ADDB   X        SUM = SUM + DATA
        ADCA   #0       AND ADD IN CARRY
        INX
        DEC    $42
        BNE    SUMD
        STAA   $40      SAVE MSBS OF SUM
        STAB   $41      SAVE LSBS OF SUM
        SWI
```

Object Program:

Memory Address (Hex)	Memory Contents (Hex)			Instruction (Mnemonic)	
0000	4F			CLRA	
0001	5F			CLRB	
0002	CE	0043		LDX	#$43
0005	EB	00	SUMD	ADDB	X
0007	89	00		ADCA	#0
0009	08			INX	
000A	7A	0042		DEC	$42
000D	26	F6		BNE	SUMD
000F	97	40		STAA	$40
0011	D7	41		STAB	$41
0013	3F			SWI	

The structure of this program is the same as the structure of the last one. The most significant bits of the sum must now be initialized and stored. The processing section consists of two instructions (ADDB X and ADCA #0).

The instruction ADCA #0 adds the carry and zero to Accumulator A:

$$(A) = (A) + 0 + CARRY$$
$$(A) + CARRY$$

No actual decision about the value of the Carry is necessary.

Another useful instruction in loops is CPX (Compare Index register) which subtracts a 16-bit number in memory from the 16-bit Index register. This instruction could, for example, be used to control the number of iterations.

A single instruction (for example, DEC $42) can decrement the contents of a memory location, but a full 16-bit address or an indexed offset is necessary (no direct addressing on page zero). This is true of all the 6800's single-operand instructions, such as Shift, Clear, Increment, Decrement, etc.

Number of Negative Elements

Purpose: Determine the number of negative elements (most significant bit 1) in a block. The length of the block is in memory location 0041 and the block itself starts in memory location 0042. Place the number of negative elements in memory location 0040.

Sample Problem:

   (0041) = 06
   (0042) = 68
   (0043) = F2
   (0044) = 87
   (0045) = 30
   (0046) = 59
   (0047) = 2A

Result: (0040) = 02, since 0043 and 0044 contain numbers with an MSB of 1.

Flowchart:

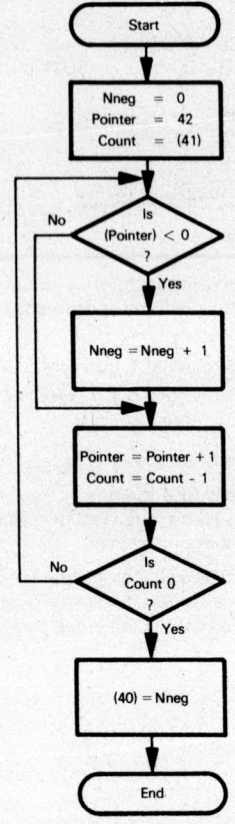

Source Program:

```
            LDX     #$42        POINT TO FIRST NUMBER
            CLRB                START NEGATIVE COUNT AT ZERO
CHKNEG      LDAA    X           IS NEXT ITEM NEGATIVE?
            BPL     CHCNT
            INCB                YES, ADD 1 TO NEGATIVE COUNT
CHCNT       INX
            DEC     $41
            BNE     CHKNEG
            STAB    $40         SAVE NEGATIVE COUNT
            SWI
```

Object Program:

Memory Address (Hex)	Memory Contents (Hex)		Instruction (Mnemonic)		
0000	CE	0042		LDX	$42
0003	5F			CLRB	
0004	A6	00	CHKNEG	LDAA	X
0006	2A	01		BPL	CHCNT
0008	5C			INCB	
0009	08		CHCNT	INX	
000A	7A	0041		DEC	$41
000D	26	F5		BNE	CHKNEG
000F	D7	40		STAB	$40
0011	3F			SWI	

LDAA X is the same as LDAA 0,X.

We could also use the Test instruction (TST) to check the sign of the number in memory. This would allow us to use Accumulator A as a counter. Try rewriting the program to use TST.

BPL, Branch if Plus, causes a jump over the specified number of locations if the Negative (Sign) bit is zero. Note that the LDA instruction affects this bit.

The offset for BPL is calculated from the first memory location following the two-word instruction. Here the offset is simply from 08 to 09, or one location (i.e., the INCB instruction is skipped if the Negative bit is zero). The Negative bit will be zero if the most significant bit of the data loaded from memory by the LDAA X instruction is zero.

Remember that negative signed numbers all have a most significant bit (bit 7) of 1. All negative numbers are actually larger (in the unsigned sense) than positive numbers.

Find Maximum

Purpose: Find the largest element in a block of data. The length of the block is in memory location 0041 and the block itself begins in memory location 0042. Store the maximum in memory location 0040. Assume that the numbers in the block are all 8-bit unsigned binary numbers.

Sample Problem:

```
        (0041) = 05
        (0042) = 67
        (0043) = 79
        (0044) = 15
        (0045) = E3
        (0046) = 72
Result: (0040) = E3, since this is the largest of
                 the five unsigned numbers.
```

Source Program:

```
        LDAB    $41          GET COUNT
        CLRA                 MAXIMUM=ZERO (MINIMUM POSSIBLE VALUE)
        LDX     #$42         POINT TO FIRST ENTRY
MAXM    CMPA    X            IS MAXIMUM GREATER THAN CURRENT ENTRY?
        BCC     NOCHG        YES, KEEP MAXIMUM
        LDAA    X            NO. REPLACE MAXIMUM WITH CURRENT ENTRY
NOCHG   INX
        DECB
        BNE     MAXM
        STAA    $40          SAVE MAXIMUM
        SWI
```

Flowchart:

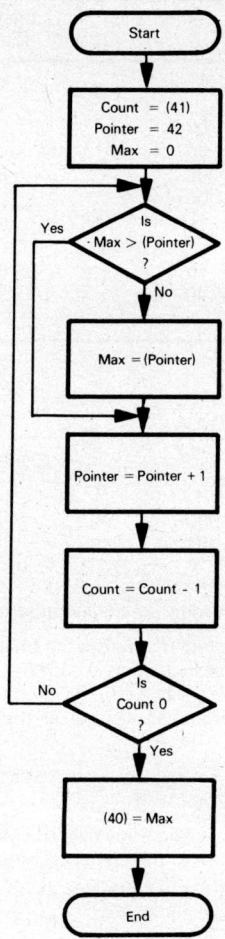

Object Program:

Memory Address (Hex)	Memory Contents (Hex)		Instruction (Mnemonic)	
0000	D6	41		LDAB $41
0002	4F			CLRA
0003	CE	0042		LDX #$42
0006	A1	00	MAXM	CMPA X
0008	24	02		BCC NOCHG
000A	A6	00		LDAA X
000C	08		NOCHG	INX
000D	5A			DECB
000E	26	F6		BNE MAXM
0010	97	40		STAA $40
0012	3F			SWI

The relative offset for BCC NOCHG is:

$$\begin{array}{r} 000C \\ -000A \\ \hline 02 \end{array}$$

The relative offset for BNE MAXM is:

$$\begin{array}{rcr} 0006 & = & 06 \\ -0010 & & +F0 \\ \hline & & F6 \end{array}$$

The first three bytes of this program form the initialization section.

This program takes advantage of the fact that zero is the smallest 8-bit unsigned binary number. When you set the register that contains the maximum value (in this case Accumulator A) to the minimum possible value before you enter the loop, then the program will set Accumulator A to a larger value unless all the elements in the array are zeros.

The program works properly if there are two elements, but not if there is one or none at all. Why? How could you solve this problem?

The instruction CMPA X sets the Carry flag as follows (ELEMENT is the contents of the address in the Index register and MAX is the contents of Accumulator A):

Carry = 1 if ELEMENT > MAX
Carry = 0 if ELEMENT ≤ MAX

If Carry = 0, the program proceeds to NOCHG and does not change the maximum. If Carry = 1, the program replaces the old maximum with the current element by executing the instruction LDAA X.

The program does not work if the numbers are signed, because negative numbers will appear to be larger than positive numbers. The problem is somewhat tricky because overflow could make the result appear to have the wrong sign. The 6800 has special branch instructions BGT, BGE, BLE, and BLT, which handle overflow properly. Remember that overflow occurs when the magnitude of a result affects its sign bit.

Justify a Binary Fraction

Purpose: Shift the contents of memory location 0040 left until the most significant bit of the number is 1. Store the result in memory location 0041 and the number of left shifts required in memory location 0042. If the contents of memory location 0040 are zero, clear both 0041 and 0042.

Note: The process is just like converting a number to a scientific notation; for example,
$$0.0057 = 5.7 \times 10^{-3}$$

Sample Problems:

a.   (0040) = 22
     Result: (0041) = 88
           (0042) = 02

b.   (0040) = 01
     Result: (0041) = 80
           (0042) = 07

c.   (0040) = CB
     Result: (0041) = CB
           (0042) = 00

d.   (0040) = 00
     Result: (0041) = 00
           (0042) = 00

Flowchart:

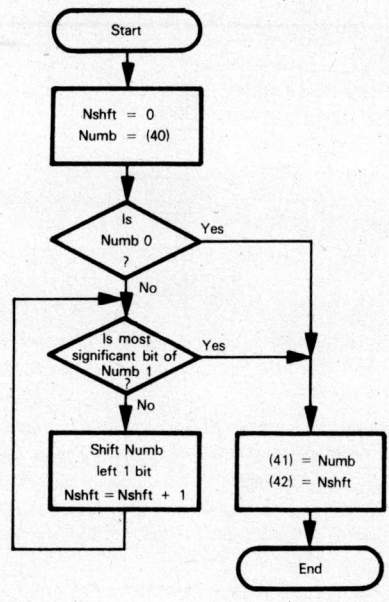

Source Program:

```
        CLRB              NUMBER OF SHIFTS = 0
        LDAA    $40       GET DATA
        BEQ     DONE      THROUGH IF DATA ZERO
CHKMS   BMI     DONE      THROUGH IF MSB = 1
        INCB              ADD 1 TO NUMBER OF SHIFTS
        ASLA              SHIFT DATA LEFT 1 BIT
        BRA     CHKMS
DONE    STAA    $41       SAVE JUSTIFIED DATA
        STAB    $42       SAVE NUMBER OF SHIFTS
        SWI
```

Object Program:

Memory Address (Hex)	Memory Contents (Hex)		Instruction (Mnemonic)		
0000	5F			CLRB	
0001	96	40		LDAA	$40
0003	27	06		BEQ	DONE
0005	2B	04	CHKMS	BMI	DONE
0007	5C			INCB	
0008	48			ASLA	
0009	20	FA		BRA	CHKMS
000B	97	41	DONE	STAA	$41
000D	97	42		STAB	$42
000F	3F			SWI	

The relative offsets are:

```
        BEQ    DONE     000B
                       -0005
                       ─────
                         06

        BMI    DONE     000B
                       -0007
                       ─────
                         04

        BRA    CHKMS    0005   =   05
                       -000B      +F5
                       ─────      ─────
                                   FA
```

ASL, Arithmetic Shift Left, shifts the contents of the specified address left one bit and clears the least significant bit. The most significant bit of the specified address ends up in the Carry. The old Carry is lost.

ASLA is equivalent to adding the number in Accumulator A to itself. The result is, of course, twice the original number (try it!).

BMI DONE causes a jump to location DONE if the Negative bit is 1. This condition may mean that the last result was a negative number, or may just mean that its most significant bit was 1 — the computer only supplies the results; the programmer must provide the interpretation.

There is an extraneous BRA instruction, BRA CHKMS, in this program. Can you change the initial conditions so that this instruction is not necessary?

PROBLEMS
1) Checksum of Data

Purpose: Calculate the checksum of a series of numbers. The length of the series is in memory location 0041 and the series itself begins in memory location 0042. Store the checksum in memory location 0040. The checksum is formed by Exclusive-ORing all the numbers in the series together.

Note: Such checksums are often used in paper tape and cassette systems to ensure that the data has been read correctly. The calculated checksum is compared to the one stored with the data — if the two checksums do not agree, the system will usually either indicate an error to the operator or automatically read the data again.

Sample Problem:

$$\begin{aligned}
(0041) &= 03 \\
(0042) &= 28 \\
(0043) &= 55 \\
(0044) &= 26 \\
\text{Result: } (0040) &= (0042) \oplus (0043) \oplus (0044) \\
&= 28 \oplus 55 \oplus 26 \\
&= 0010\,1000 \\
\oplus\ &\,0101\,0101 \\
&\,\overline{0111\,1101} \\
\oplus\ &\,0010\,0110 \\
&\,\overline{0101\,1011} \\
&= 5B
\end{aligned}$$

2) Sum of 16-Bit Data

Purpose: Calculate the sum of a series of 16-bit numbers. The length of the series is in memory location 0042 and the series itself begins in memory location 0043. Store the sum in memory locations 0040 and 0041 (eight most significant bits in 0040). Each 16-bit number occupies two memory locations, with the eight most significant bits in the lower address. Assume that the sum can be contained in 16 bits.

Sample Problem:

$$\begin{aligned}
(0042) &= 03 \\
(0043) &= 28 \\
(0044) &= F1 \\
(0045) &= 30 \\
(0046) &= 1A \\
(0047) &= 4B \\
(0048) &= 89 \\
\text{Result: } 28F1 + 301A + 4B89 &= A494 \\
(0040) &= A4 \\
(0041) &= 94
\end{aligned}$$

3) Number of Zero, Positive, and Negative Numbers

Purpose: Determine the number of zero, positive (most significant bit zero but entire number not zero), and negative (most significant bit 1) elements in a block. The length of the block is in memory location 0043 and the block itself starts in memory location 0044. Place the number of negative elements in memory location 0040, the number of zero elements in memory location 0041, and the number of positive elements in memory location 0042.

Sample Problem:

```
         (0043) = 06
         (0044) = 68
         (0045) = F2
         (0046) = 87
         (0047) = 00
         (0048) = 59
         (0049) = 2A
Result:  2 negative, 1 zero, and 3 positive, so
         (0040) = 02
         (0041) = 01
         (0042) = 03
```

4) Find Minimum

Purpose: Find the smallest element in a block of data. The length of the block is in memory location 0041 and the block itself begins in memory location 0042. Store the minimum in memory location 0040. Assume that the numbers in the block are 8-bit unsigned binary numbers.

Sample Problem:

```
         (0041) = 05
         (0042) = 67
         (0043) = 79
         (0044) = 15
         (0045) = E3
         (0046) = 72
Result:  (0040) = 15, since this is the smallest of the
                     five unsigned numbers.
```

5) Count 1 Bits

Purpose: Determine how many bits in memory location 0040 are one and place the result in memory location 0041.

Sample Problem:

```
         (0040) = 3B = 00111011
Result:  (0041) = 05
```

Chapter 6
CHARACTER-CODED DATA

Microprocessors often handle character-coded data. Not only do keyboards, teletypewriters, communications devices, displays, and computer terminals expect or provide character-coded data; many instruments, test systems, and controllers also require data in this form. The most commonly used code is ASCII. Baudot and EBCDIC are found less frequently. We will assume all of our character-coded data to be 7-bit ASCII with the most significant bit zero (see Table 6-1).

Some principles to remember in handling ASCII-coded data are:

HANDLING DATA IN ASCII

1) The codes for the numbers and letters form ordered sub-sequences. The codes for the decimal numbers are hex 30 through 39, so that you can convert between decimal and ASCII with a simple additive factor. The codes for the upper-case letters are hex 41 through 5A, so that you can do alphabetic ordering by sorting the data in increasing numerical order.

2) The computer draws no distinction between printing and non-printing characters. This distinction is only made by I/O devices.

3) An ASCII device will only handle ASCII data. To print a 7 on an ASCII printer, the microprocessor must send hex 37 to the printer; hex 07 is the 'bell' character. Similarly, the microprocessor will receive the character 9 from an ASCII keyboard as hex 39; hex 09 is the 'tab' character.

4) Some ASCII devices do not use the full character set. For example, control characters and lower-case letters may be ignored or printed as spaces or question marks.

5) Some widely used ASCII characters are:

   $0A_{16}$ - line feed (LF)
   $0D_{16}$ - carriage return (CR)
   20_{16} - space
   $3F_{16}$ - ?
   $7F_{16}$ - rub out or delete character

Table 6-1. Hex-ASCII Table

Hex LSD \ Hex MSD	0	1	2	3	4	5	6	7
0	NUL	DLE	SP	0	@	P	`	p
1	SOH	DC1	!	1	A	Q	a	q
2	STX	DC2	"	2	B	R	b	r
3	ETX	DC3	#	3	C	S	c	s
4	EOT	DC4	$	4	D	T	d	t
5	ENQ	NAK	%	5	E	U	e	u
6	ACK	SYN	&	6	F	V	f	v
7	BEL	ETB	`	7	G	W	g	w
8	BS	CAN	(	8	H	X	h	x
9	HT	EM	)	9	I	Y	i	y
A	LF	SUB	*	:	J	Z	j	z
B	VT	ESC	+	;	K	[	k	{
C	FF	FS	,	<	L	\	l	|
D	CR	GS	-	=	M	]	m	}
E	SO	RS	.	>	N	∧	n	~
F	SI	US	/	?	O	—	o	DEL

EXAMPLES

Length of a String of Characters

Purpose: Determine the length of a string of ASCII characters (7 bits with most significant bit 0). The string starts in memory location 0041; the end of the string is marked by a carriage return character ('CR', hex 0D). Place the length of the string (excluding the carriage return) in memory location 0040.

Sample Problems:

a.   (0041) = 0D
    Result: (0040) = 00, since the first character is a carriage return.

b.   (0041) = 52 'R'
              (0042) = 41 'A'
              (0043) = 54 'T'
              (0044) = 48 'H'
              (0045) = 45 'E'
              (0046) = 52 'R'
              (0047) = 0D CR
    Result: (0040) = 06

Flowchart:

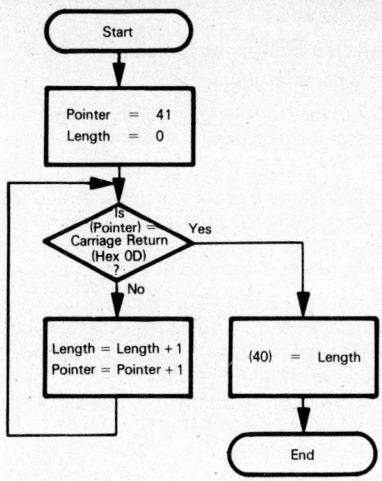

Source Program:

```
        CLRB              STRING LENGTH = ZERO
        LDX     #$41      POINTER = START OF STRING
        LDAA    #$0D      GET ASCII CARRIAGE RETURN FOR COMPARISON
CHKCR   CMPA    X         IS CHARACTER A CARRIAGE RETURN?
        BEQ     DONE      YES, END OF STRING
        INCB              NO, ADD 1 TO STRING LENGTH
        INX
        BRA     CHKCR     TRY NEXT CHARACTER
DONE    STAB    $40       SAVE STRING LENGTH
        SWI
```

Object Program:

Memory Address (Hex)	Memory Contents (Hex)			Instruction (Mnemonic)	
0000	5F			CLRB	
0001	CE	0041		LDX	#$41
0004	86	0D		LDAA	#$0D
0006	A1	00	CHKCR	CMPA	X
0008	27	04		BEQ	DONE
000A	5C			INCB	
000B	08			INX	
000C	20	F8		BRA	CHKCR
000E	D7	40	DONE	STAB	$40
0010	3F			SWI	

The carriage return (CR) is just another ASCII character (hex 0D) as far as the computer is concerned. The fact that the output device treats the carriage return as a control character rather than as a printing character does not affect the computer.

The Compare instruction, CMPA, sets the flags as if a subtraction had been performed, but leaves the carriage return character in Accumulator A for later comparisons. The Zero (Z) flag is affected as follows:

   Z = 1 if the character in the string is a carriage return
   Z = 0 if it is not a carriage return

The instruction INCB adds 1 to the string length counter in Accumulator B. CLRB initializes this counter to zero before the loop begins. Remember to initialize variables before using them in a loop.

This loop does not terminate because a counter is decremented to zero. The computer will simply continue examining characters until it finds a carriage return. You may have to place a maximum count in a loop like this to avoid problems with erroneous strings that do not contain a carriage return. What would happen if the example program were used with such a string?

Note that, by rearranging the logic and changing the initial conditions, you can shorten the program and decrease its execution time. If we adjust the flowchart so that the program increments the Counter and Pointer before it looks for the carriage return, only one Jump instruction is necessary instead of two. The new flowchart and program are as follows:

Flowchart:

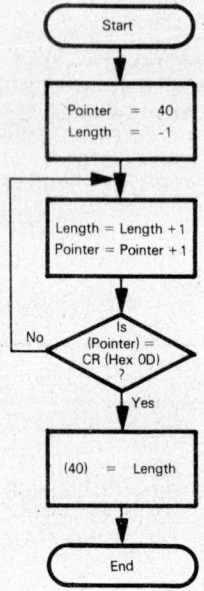

Source Program:

```
        LDX    #$40      POINTER = BYTE BEFORE STRING
        LDAB   #-1       STRING LENGTH = -1
        LDAA   #$0D      GET ASCII CARRIAGE RETURN FOR COMPARISON
CHKCR   INX
        INCB             ADD 1 TO STRING LENGTH
        CMPA   X         IS CHARACTER A CARRIAGE RETURN?
        BNE    CHKCR     NO, TRY NEXT CHARACTER
        STAB   $40       YES, SAVE STRING LENGTH
        SWI
```

Object Program:

Memory Address (Hex)	Memory Contents (Hex)		Instruction (Mnemonic)	
0000	CE	0040	LDX	#$40
0003	C6	FF	LDAB	#-1
0005	86	0D	LDAA	#$0D
0007	08		CHKCR INX	
0008	5C		INCB	
0009	A1	00	CMPA	X
000B	26	FA	BNE	CHKCR
000D	D7	40	STAB	$40
000F	3F		SWI	

Find First Non-Blank Character

Purpose: Search a string of ASCII characters (7 bits with most significant bit zero) for a non-blank character. The string starts in memory location 0042. Place the address of the first non-blank character in memory locations 0040 and 0041 (most significant bits in 0040). A blank character is hex 20 in ASCII.

Sample Problems:

a. (0042) = 37 ASCII 7
    Result: (0040) = 00
            (0041) = 42, since memory location 0042 contains a non-blank character.

b. (0042) = 20 SP
    (0043) = 20 SP
    (0044) = 20 SP
    (0045) = 46 F
    (0046) = 20 SP
    Result: (0040) = 00
            (0041) = 45, since the three previous memory locations all contain blanks.

Flowchart:

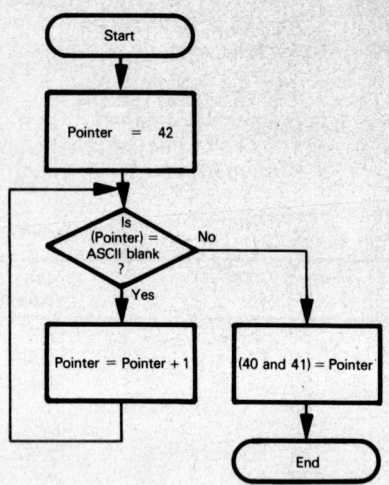

Source Program:

```
        LDX     #$42        POINTER = START OF STRING
        LDAA    #$20        GET ASCII SPACE FOR COMPARISON
CHBLK   CMPA    X           IS CHARACTER A SPACE?
        BNE     DONE        NO, THROUGH
        INX
        BRA     CHBLK       YES, EXAMINE NEXT CHARACTER
DONE    STX     $40         SAVE ADDRESS OF FIRST NON-BLANK CHARACTER
        SWI
```

Object Program:

Memory Address (Hex)	Memory Contents (Hex)		Instruction (Mnemonic)	
0000	CE	0042		LDX #$42
0003	86	20		LDAA #$20
0005	A1	00	CHBLK	CMPA X
0007	26	03		BNE DONE
0009	08			INX
000A	20	F9		BRA CHBLK
000C	DF	40	DONE	STX $40
000E	3F			SWI

Looking for spaces in strings is a common task. Spaces often are eliminated from strings when they are used simply to increase readability or to fit particular formats. It is obviously wasteful to store and transmit beginning, ending or extra spaces, particularly if you are paying for the communications capability and memory required. Data and program entry, however, are much simpler if extra spaces are tolerated. Microcomputers are often used in situations like this to convert data between forms that are easy for humans to use and forms that are efficiently handled on computers and communications lines.

The computer treats the space code (hex 20) just like any other character.

The instruction STX stores the contents of the Index register (most significant bits first) at the specified address and the next higher address. So STX $40 stores the 16-bit Index register in memory locations 0040 and 0041. Note that STX can use an 8-bit address on page zero.

Again, if we alter the initial conditions so that the loop control section precedes the processing section, we can reduce the number of bytes in the program and decrease the loop's execution time. The rearranged flowchart is:

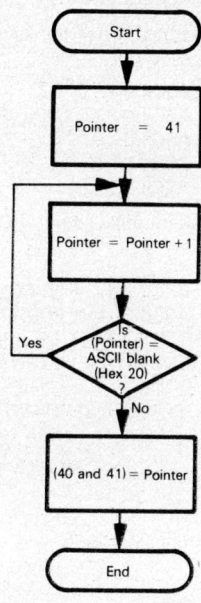

Source Program:

```
         LDX     #$41        POINT TO BYTE BEFORE STRING
         LDAA    #$20        GET ASCII SPACE FOR COMPARISON
CHBLK    INX
         CMPA    X           IS CHARACTER A SPACE?
         BEQ     CHBLK       YES, KEEP EXAMINING CHARACTERS
         STX     $40         NO, SAVE ADDRESS OF FIRST NON-BLANK
                             CHARACTER
         SWI
```

Object Program:

Memory Address (Hex)	Memory Contents (Hex)		Instruction (Mnemonic)	
0000	CE 0041		LDX	#$41
0003	86 20		LDAA	#$20
0005	08	CHBLK	INX	
0006	A1 00		CMPA	X
0008	27 FB		BEQ	CHBLK
000A	DF 40		STX	$40
000C	3F		SWI	

Replace Leading Zeros with Blanks

Purpose: Edit a string of ASCII decimal characters by replacing all leading zeros with blanks. The string starts in memory location 0041; assume that it consists entirely of ASCII-coded decimal digits. The length of the string is in memory location 0040.

Sample Problems:

a. (0040) = 02
    (0041) = 36   ASCII 6

The program leaves the string unchanged, since the leading digit is not zero.

b. (0040) = 08
    (0041) = 30   ASCII 0
    (0042) = 30   ASCII 0
    (0043) = 38   ASCII 8
    Result: (0041) = 20   ASCII SP
            (0042) = 20   ASCII SP

The two leading ASCII zeros have been replaced by ASCII blanks.

Source Program:

```
          LDAA    #'0         GET ASCII ZERO FOR COMPARISON
          LDAB    #$20        GET ASCII BLANK FOR STORAGE
          LDX     #$41        POINTER = START OF ARRAY
CHKZ      CMPA    X           IS ELEMENT ASCII ZERO?
          BNE     DONE        NO, DONE
          STAB    X           YES, REPLACE ZERO WITH BLANK
          INX
          DEC     $40
          BNE     CHKZ
DONE      SWI
```

An apostrophe before a character indicates ASCII.

Flowchart:

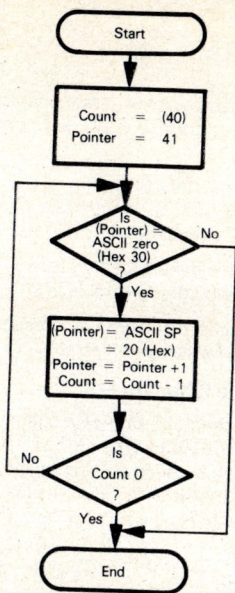

Object Program:

Memory Address (Hex)	Memory Contents (Hex)			Instruction (Mnemonic)	
0000	86	30		LDAA	#'0
0002	C6	20		LDAB	#$20
0004	CE	0041		LDX	#$41
0007	A1	00	CHKZ	CMPA	X
0009	26	08		BNE	DONE
000B	E7	00		STAB	X
000D	08			INX	
000E	7A	0040		DEC	$40
0011	26	F4		BNE	CHKZ
0013	3F		DONE	SWI	

You will frequently want to edit decimal strings before they are printed or displayed, in order to improve their appearance. Common editing tasks include eliminating leading zeros, justifying numbers, adding signs or other identifying markers, and rounding. Clearly, printed numbers like 0006 or $27.34382 can be confusing and annoying.

Here the loop has two exits -- one if the processor finds a non-zero digit and the other if it has examined the entire string.

You can place a single ASCII character in a 6800 assembly language program by preceding it with an apostrophe ('). You can place a string of ASCII characters in program memory by using the FCC (Form Constant Characters) pseudo-operation on the 6800

Assembler. Either of the following forms is acceptable:

Label	Operation Code	Operand
EMSG	FCC	5,ERROR
EMSG	FCC	/ERROR/

In the first form, the number specifies how many characters are in the string; it is followed by a comma. In the second form, any single character delimiter may mark the beginning and end of the string.

All digits in the string are assumed to be ASCII; that is, the digits are hex 30 through 39 rather than the ordinary decimal 0 to 9. The conversion from decimal to ASCII is simply a matter of adding hex 30 to the decimal digit.

You may have to be careful, when blanking leading zeros, to leave one zero in the event that all the digits are zero. How would you do this?

Note that each ASCII digit requires eight bits, as compared to four for a BCD digit. Therefore, ASCII is an expensive format in which to store or transmit numerical data.

Add Even Parity to ASCII Characters

Purpose: Add even parity to a string of 7-bit ASCII characters. The length of the string is in memory location 0040 and the string itself begins in memory location 0041. Place even parity in the most significant bit of each character by setting the most significant bit to 1 if that makes the total number of 1 bits in the word an even number.

Sample Problem:

```
         (0040) = 06
         (0041) = 31
         (0042) = 32
         (0043) = 33
         (0044) = 34
         (0045) = 35
         (0046) = 36
Result:  (0041) = B1
         (0042) = B2
         (0043) = 33
         (0044) = B4
         (0045) = 35
         (0046) = 36
```

Flowchart:

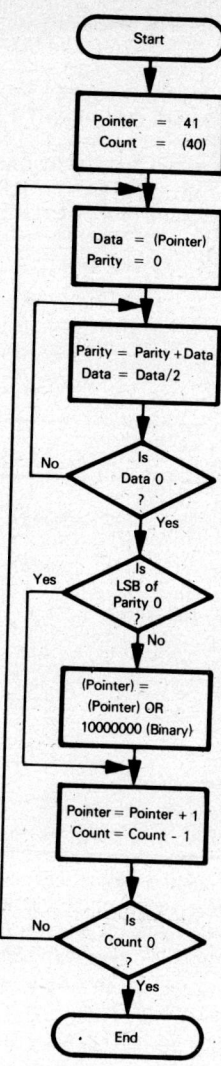

Source Program:

```
         LDX    #$41            POINTER = START OF DATA BLOCK
GTDATA   LDAB   X               GET DATA FROM BLOCK
         CLRA                   PARITY = ZERO
CALPAR   ABA                    PARITY = PARITY + DATA
         LSRB                   SHIFT DATA RIGHT 1 BIT
         BNE    CALPAR
         LSRA                   MOVE PARITY TO CARRY
         BCC    CHCNT           GO ON IF PARITY ALREADY EVEN
         LDAA   #%10000000      MAKE PARITY EVEN BY SETTING MSB
         ORAA   X
         STAA   X
CHCNT    INX
         DEC    $40
         BNE    GTDATA
         SWI
```

Object Program:

Memory Address (Hex)	Memory Contents (Hex)		Instruction (Mnemonic)	
0000	CE	0041		LDX	#$41
0003	E6	00	GTDATA	LDAB	X
0005	4F			CLRA	
0006	1B		CALPAR	ABA	
0007	54			LSRB	
0008	26	FC		BNE	CALPAR
000A	44			LSRA	
000B	24	06		BCC	CHCNT
000D	86	80		LDAA	#%10000000
000F	AA	00		ORAA	X
0011	A7	00		STAA	X
0013	08		CHCNT	INX	
0014	7A	0040		DEC	$40
0017	26	EA		BNE	GTDATA
0019	3F			SWI	

Parity is often added to ASCII characters before they are transmitted on noisy communication lines, so as to provide a simple error-checking facility. Parity detects all single-bit errors but does not allow error correction; i.e., you know that an error occurred when the received parity is wrong but you cannot tell which bit was changed.

The procedure for calculating parity is to add all the bits together and see if the result is even or odd. This determines if the number of one bits in the data is even or odd.

LSR clears the most significant bit of the number being shifted. Therefore, the result of a series of LSR instructions will eventually be zero, regardless of the original value of the number (try it).

The following sequence after BNE CALPAR will also work (why?).

```
LSRA            MOVE PARITY TO CARRY
RORB            MOVE INTO MSB OF B
ORAB    X       MOVE INTO MSB OF DATA
STAB    X
```

Remember that B must have contained zero at this point, or else the instruction BNE CALPAR would have caused a branch.

Logically ORing a bit with one produces a result of one regardless of the original value of the bit.

Pattern Match

Purpose: Compare two strings of ASCII characters to see if they are the same. The length of the strings is in memory location 0041; one string starts in memory location 0042 and the other in memory location 0052. If the two strings match, clear memory location 0040; otherwise, set memory location 0040 to FF hex (all ones).

Sample Problems:

a.
    (0040) = 03

    (0042) = 43 'C'
    (0043) = 41 'A'
    (0044) = 54 'T'

    (0052) = 43 'C'
    (0053) = 41 'A'
    (0054) = 54 'T'

  Result: (0040) = 00, since the two strings are the same.

b.
    (0041) = 03

    (0042) = 52 'R'
    (0043) = 41 'A'
    (0044) = 54 'T'

    (0052) = 43 'C'
    (0053) = 41 'A'
    (0054) = 54 'T'

  Result: (0040) = FF, since the first characters in the strings differ.

Note: The matching process ends as soon as the CPU finds a difference -- the rest of the strings need not be examined.

Flowchart:

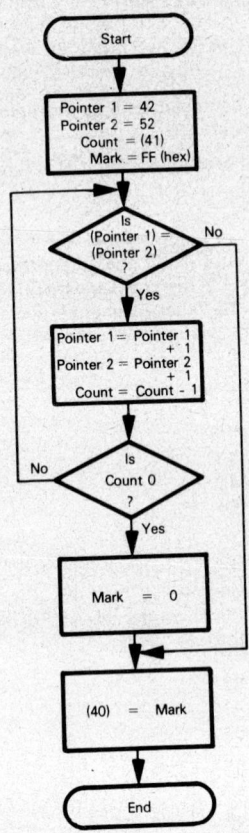

Source Program:

```
              LDAA    #$FF
              STAA    $40       MARK = FF HEX FOR INEQUALITY
              LDAB    $41       COUNT = LENGTH OF STRINGS
              LDX     #$42      POINT TO START OF STRINGS
      PATTC   LDAA    X         GET ELEMENT OF STRING 1
              CMPA    $10,X     IS IT SAME AS ELEMENT OF STRING 2?
              BNE     DONE      NO, NO MATCH
              INX
              DECB              ALL CHARACTERS CHECKED?
              BNE     PATTC     NO, CHECK NEXT CHARACTERS
              CLR     $40       YES, MARK = 0 FOR EQUALITY
      DONE    SWI
```

Object Program:

Memory Address (Hex)	Memory Contents (Hex)			Instruction (Mnemonic)	
0000	86	FF		LDAA	#$FF
0002	97	40		STAA	$40
0004	D6	41		LDAB	$41
0006	CE	0042		LDX	#$42
0009	A6	00	PATTC	LDAA	X
000B	A1	10		CMPA	$10,X
000D	26	07		BNE	DONE
000F	08			INX	
0010	5A			DECB	
0011	26	F6		BNE	PATTC
0013	7F	0040		CLR	$40
0016	3F		DONE	SWI	

Matching strings of ASCII characters is an essential part of looking for commands, recognizing names, identifying variables or operation codes in assemblers and compilers, finding files, and many other tasks.

The Index register is used to access both strings -- only the offsets are different. This method would not work, however, if the strings were separated in memory by more than 255 locations, since the offset is only eight bits long.

The instruction CMPA $10,X compares Accumulator A to the contents of the memory location whose address is 10 (hex) plus the contents of the Index register.

You can use the instruction COM (ones complement) to complement the contents of a memory location, but no short direct addresses are allowed -- just as with Clear, Shift, etc.

This program could take advantage of the fact that Accumulator B contains zero after all the characters have been examined. Otherwise, the execution of the BNE PATTC instruction would cause a branch. Therefore, we can store Accumulator B in memory location 0040 (STAB $40) to indicate that a match has been found. Another possibility is INC $40. Which do you prefer and why?

PROBLEMS

1) Length of a Teletypewriter Message

Purpose: Determine the length of an ASCII message. All characters are 7-bit ASCII with MSB = 0. The string of characters in which the message is embedded starts in memory location 0041. The message itself starts with an ASCII STX character (hex 02) and ends with ETX (hex 03). Place the length of the message (the number of characters between the STX and the ETX but including neither) in memory location 0040.

Sample Problem:

```
          (0041) = 40
          (0042) = 02   STX
          (0043) = 47   'G'
          (0044) = 4F   'O'
          (0045) = 03   ETX
Result:   (0040) = 02, since there are two characters between
                   the STX in location 0042 and ETX in
                   location 0045.
```

2) Find Last Non-Blank Character

Purpose: Search a string of ASCII characters for the last non-blank character. The string starts in memory location 0042 and ends with a carriage return character (hex 0D). Place the address of the last non-blank character in memory locations 0040 and 0041 (most significant bits in 0040).

Sample Problems:

a.   (0042) = 37 '7'
                        (0043) = 0D CR
    Result: (0040) = 00
                        (0041) = 42, since the last (and only) non-blank character is in memory location 0042.

b.   (0042) = 41 'A'
                        (0043) = 20 SP
                        (0044) = 48 'H'
                        (0045) = 41 'A'
                        (0046) = 54 'T'
                        (0047) = 20 SP
                        (0048) = 20 SP
                        (0049) = 0D CR
    Result: (0040) = 00
                        (0041) = 46

3) Truncate Decimal String to Integer Form

Purpose: Edit a string of ASCII decimal characters by replacing all digits to the right of the decimal point with ASCII blanks (hex 20). The string starts in memory location 0041 and is assumed to consist entirely of ASCII-coded decimal digits and a possible decimal point (hex 2E). The length of the string is in memory location 0040. If no decimal point appears in the string, assume that the decimal point is implicitly at the far right.

Sample Problems:

a.   (0040) = 04
                        (0041) = 37 '7'
                        (0042) = 2E '.'
                        (0043) = 38 '8'
                        (0044) = 31 '1'
    Result: (0041) = 37 '7'
                        (0042) = 2E '.'
                        (0043) = 20 SP
                        (0044) = 20 SP

b.   (0040) = 03
                        (0041) = 26 '6'
                        (0042) = 37 '7'
                        (0043) = 31 '1'
    Result: Unchanged, as number is assumed to be 671.

4) Check Even Parity in ASCII Characters

Purpose: Check even parity in a string of ASCII characters. The length of the string is in memory location 0041, and the string itself begins in memory location 0042. If the parity of all the characters in the string is correct, clear memory location 0040; otherwise, place FF hex (all ones) in memory location 0040.

Sample Problems:

a.   (0041) = 03

    (0042) = B1
    (0043) = B2
    (0044) = 33
    Result: (0040) = 00, since all the characters have even parity.

b.   (0041) = 03

    (0042) = B1
    (0043) = B6
    (0044) = 33
    Result: (0040) = FF, since the character in memory location 0042 does not have even parity.

5) String Comparison

Purpose: Compare two strings of ASCII characters to see which is larger (i.e., which follows the other in 'alphabetical' ordering). The length of the strings is in memory location 0041; one string starts in memory location 0042 and the other in memory location 0052. If the string starting in memory location 0042 is greater than or equal to the other string, clear memory location 0040; otherwise, set memory location 0040 to FF hex (all ones).

Sample Problems:

a.   (0041) = 03

    (0042) = 43 'C'
    (0043) = 41 'A'
    (0044) = 54 'T'

    (0052) = 42 'B'
    (0053) = 41 'A'
    (0054) = 54 'T'
    Result: (0040) = 00, since CAT is 'larger' than BAT.

b.   (0041) = 03

    (0042) = 44 'D'
    (0043) = 4F 'O'
    (0044) = 47 'G'

    (0052) = 44 'D'
    (0053) = 4F 'O'
    (0054) = 47 'G'
    Result: (0040) = 00, since the two strings are equal.

c.   (0041) = 03
              (0042) = 43 'C'
              (0043) = 41 'A'
              (0044) = 54 'T'

              (0052) = 43 'C'
              (0053) = 55 'U'
              (0054) = 54 'T'
Result: (0040) = FF, since CUT is 'larger' than CAT.

Chapter 7
CODE CONVERSION

Code conversion is a continual problem for microprocessors. Peripherals provide data in ASCII, BCD, or various special codes. The computer may be required to convert this data to binary or decimal in order to process it. Output devices require data in ASCII, BCD, seven-segment, or other codes. Therefore, the computer must convert the results to a suitable form after the processing is completed. Some code conversions are simple to perform in hardware; for example, standard integrated circuits exist for converting BCD to seven-segment. Universal Asynchronous Receiver/Transmitters (UARTs) convert data between ASCII and teletypewriter formats. However, the program may still be required to perform much of the conversion work.

EXAMPLES
Hex to ASCII

Purpose: Convert the contents of memory location 0040 to an ASCII character. Memory location 0040 contains a single hexadecimal digit (the four most significant bits are zero). Store the ASCII character in memory location 0041.

Sample Problems:

a.
	(0040)	=	0C	
Result:	(0041)	=	43	'C'

b.
	(0040)	=	06	
Result:	(0041)	=	36	'6'

Flowchart:

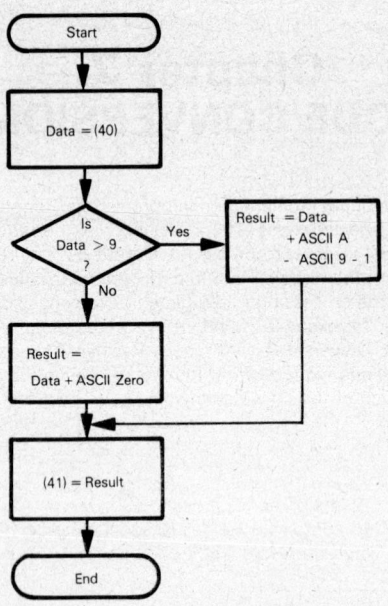

Source Program:

```
        LDAA    $40         GET DATA
        CMPA    #9          IS DATA 9 OR LESS?
        BLS     ASCZ
        ADDA    #'A-'9-1    NO, ADD OFFSET FOR LETTERS
ASCZ    ADDA    #'0         CONVERT DATA TO ASCII
        STAA    $41         STORE ASCII DATA
        SWI
```

Object Program:

Memory Address (Hex)	Memory Contents (Hex)		Instruction (Mnemonic)	
0000	96	40	LDAA	$40
0002	81	09	CMPA	#9
0004	23	02	BLS	ASCZ
0006	8B	07	ADDA	#'A-'9-1
0008	8B	30	ASCZ ADDA	#'0
000A	97	41	STAA	$41
000C	3F		SWI	

In this program, the basic idea is to add ASCII 0 to all the hexadecimal digits. This addition converts the decimal digits correctly; however, there is a break between ASCII 9 (39 hex) and ASCII A (41 hex) which must be considered. This break must be added to the nondecimal digits; i.e., A, B, C, D, E, and F. This is accomplished by the ADDA instruction, which adds the offset 'A-'9-1 to the contents of Accumulator A. Can you explain why the offset is 'A-'9-1?

Note that the addition factors are placed in the assembly language program in ASCII form (a single quotation mark precedes an ASCII character). The offset for the letters is left as an arithmetic expression. The effort is to make the purpose of the factors as clear as possible in the assembly language listing. The extra assembly time is a very small price to pay for a large increase in clarity.

This routine could be used in a variety of programs; for example, monitor programs must convert hexadecimal digits to ASCII in order to display the contents of memory locations in hexadecimal on an ASCII printer or CRT display.

Another (quicker) conversion method that requires no conditional jumps at all is the following program, described by Allison in Computer magazine.[1]

```
LDAA   $40     GET HEX DIGIT
ADDA   #$90    DECIMAL ADD 90 BCD
DAA
ADCA   #$40    DECIMAL ADD 40 BCD + CARRY
DAA
STAA   $41     STORE ASCII DIGIT
SWI
```

Try this program on some digits. Can you explain why it works?

Decimal to Seven-Segment

Purpose: Convert the contents of memory location 0041 to a seven-segment code in memory location 0042. If memory location 0041 does not contain a single decimal digit, clear memory location 0042.

Seven-segment table: The following table can be used to convert decimal numbers to seven-segment code. The seven-segment code is organized with the most significant bit always zero followed by the code (1 = on, 0 = off) for segments g, f, e, d, c, b, and a (see Figure 7-1).

Digit	Code
0	3F
1	06
2	5B
3	4F
4	66
5	6D
6	7D
7	07
8	7F
9	6F

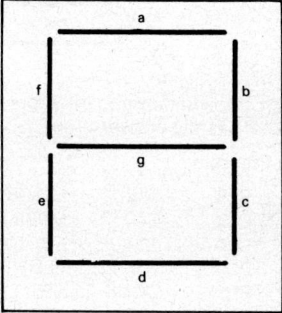

Figure 7-1. Seven-Segment Arrangement

Note that the table uses 7D for 6 rather than the alternative (top bar off) 7C to avoid confusion with lower case b, and 6F for 9 rather than 67 (bottom bar off) for no particular reason.

Sample Problems:

a. (0041) = 03
    Result: (0042) = 4F
b. (0041) = 28
    Result: (0042) = 00

Flowchart:

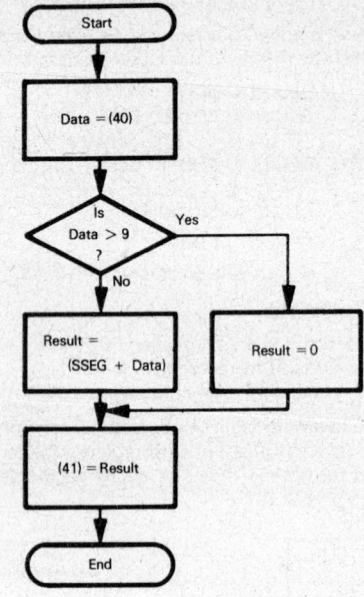

Note that the addition of base address SSEG and index (Data) produces the address which contains the answer.

Source Program:

```
         CLR    $42        ERROR CODE BLANKS DISPLAY
         CLR    $40        MSBS OF TABLE ADDRESS = 0
         LDAA   $41        GET DATA
         CMPA   #9         IS DATA GREATER THAN 9?
         BHI    DONE       YES, LEAVE ERROR CODE FOR DISPLAY
         LDX    $40        GET FIXED TABLE OFFSET
         LDAA   SSEG,X     CONVERT DATA TO SEVEN-SEGMENT CODE
         STAA   $42        SAVE SEVEN-SEGMENT CODE
DONE     SWI
SSEG     FCB    $3F, $06, $5B, $4F, $66
         FCB    $6D, $7D, $07, $7F, $6F
```

Object Program:

Memory Address (Hex)	Memory Contents (Hex)		Instruction (Mnemonic)	
0000	7F	0042		CLR $42
0003	7F	0040		CLR $40
0006	96	41		LDAA $41
0008	81	09		CMPA #9
000A	22	06		BHI DONE
000C	DE	40		LDX $40
000E	A6	13		LDAA SSEG,X
0010	97	42		STAA $42
0012	3F		DONE	SWI
0013	3F 06 5B 4F 66		SSEG	FCB $3F,$06,$5B,$4F,$66
0018	6D 7D 07 7F 6F			FCB $6D,$7D,$07,$7F,$6F

Tables are often used to perform code conversions which are more complex than the previous example. Such tables typically contain all the results organized according to the input data (the first entry is the code corresponding to the number zero).

Seven-segment displays provide recognizable forms of the decimal digits and a few letters and other characters. Calculator-type seven-segment displays are inexpensive, easy to combine, and use little power. However, the seven-segment coded digits are somewhat difficult to read.

The indexed Load instruction adds the index (the digit to be displayed) to the base address of the seven-segment table to get the address of the desired code. Note that the 16-bit Index register contains the data as its eight least significant bits, and the most significant bits of the starting address of the table as its eight most significant bits. This odd arrangement is necessary because the offset included with the instruction is only eight bits long and can therefore only hold the eight least significant bits of the starting address of the table.

A blank display (code 00) indicates an error.

The assembly language pseudo-operation FCB (Form Constant Byte) places constant data in program memory. Such data may include tables, headings, error messages, priming messages, format characters, thresholds, etc. The label attached to an FCB pseudo-operation is assigned the value of the address in which the first byte of data is placed.

The Assembler simply places the data for the table in memory. Note that one FCB pseudo-operation can fill many memory locations.

A more general program would allow the table to be placed anywhere in memory. If the table address is SSEGM (8 MSBs) and SSEGL (8 LSBs), the instruction CLR $40 must be replaced by

    LDAA   #SSEGM   GET MSBS OF TABLE ADDRESS
    STAA $40

Why is this change necessary?

ASCII to Decimal

Purpose: Convert the contents of memory location 0040 from an ASCII character to a decimal digit and store the result in memory location 0041. If the contents of memory location 0040 are not the ASCII representation of a decimal digit, set the contents of memory location 0041 to FF (hex).

Sample Problems:

a.   (0040) = 37   (ASCII 7)
    Result: (0041) = 07

b.   (0040) = 55
    Result: (0041) = FF

Flowchart:

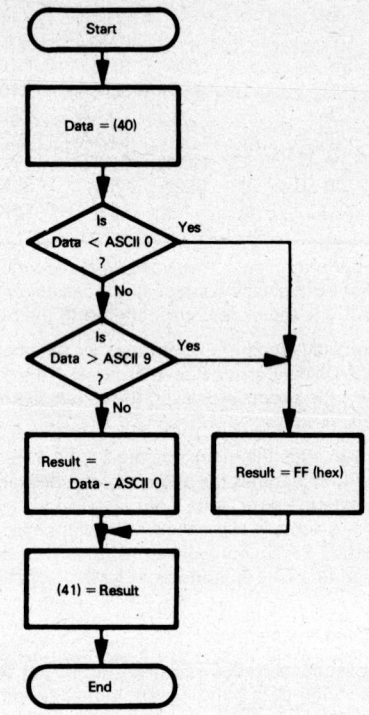

Source Program:

```
         LDAB    #$FF      MARKER = FF FOR ERROR
         LDAA    $40
         SUBA    #'0       SUBTRACT ASCII ZERO
         BCS     STDEC     NOT DIGIT IF RESULT NEGATIVE
         CMPA    #9        COMPARE REMAINDER TO 9
         BHI     STDEC     NOT DIGIT IF GREATER THAN 9
         TAB               DIGIT TO MARKER
STDEC    STAB    $41       SAVE DIGIT OR ERROR CODE
         SWI
```

Note: ' means ASCII character in 6800 assembly language.

Object Program:

Memory Address (Hex)	Memory Contents (Hex)			Instruction (Mnemonic)	
0000	C6	FF		LDAB	#FF
0002	96	40		LDAA	$40
0004	80	30		SUBA	#'0
0006	25	05		BCS	STDEC
0008	81	09		CMPA	#9
000A	22	01		BHI	STDEC
000C	16			TAB	
000D	D7	41	STDEC	STAB	$41
000F	3F			SWI	

This program handles ASCII-coded characters just like ordinary numbers. Note that the decimal digits and the letters form groups of consecutive codes. Strings of letters (like names) can be alphabetized by placing their ASCII representations in increasing numerical order (ASCII B = ASCII A + 1, for example).

Subtracting ASCII zero (30 hex) from any ASCII decimal digit gives the BCD representation of that digit.

The instruction BHI (Branch-on-Higher) causes a branch if both the carry and zero bits are zero. This would occur if the Accumulator contents were larger than the other operand in a Compare instruction when both are considered as unsigned binary numbers (neither overflow nor sign is included). BHI and BCC differ only in what happens when the result of a comparison is zero — BCC causes a branch, while BHI does not.

ASCII-to-decimal conversion is necessary when decimal numbers are being entered from an ASCII device such as a teletypewriter or CRT terminal.

The basic idea of the program is to determine if the character is between ASCII 0 and ASCII 9, inclusive. If the character is, it's an ASCII decimal digit, since the digits form a sequence. It may then be converted to decimal simply by subtracting hex 30 (ASCII 0), e.g., ASCII 7 - ASCII 0 = 7 - 0 = 7.

Note that one comparison is done with an actual subtraction (SUBA #'0), since the subtraction is necessary to convert ASCII to decimal. The other comparison is done with an implied subtraction (CMPA #9), since the final result is now in the Accumulator if the original number was valid.

BCD to Binary

Purpose: Convert two BCD digits in memory locations 0040 and 0041 to a binary number in memory location 0042. The most significant BCD digit is in memory location 0040.

Sample Problems:

a.   (0040) = 02
               (0041) = 09
     Result: (0042) = 1D (hex) = 29 (decimal)

b.   (0040) = 07
               (0041) = 01
     Result: (0042) = 47 (hex) = 71 (decimal)

Note: No flowchart is included since the program multiplies the most significant digit by 10 simply by using the formula $10x = 8x + 2x$. Multiplying by 2 requires one arithmetic left shift and multiplying by 8 requires three such shifts.

Source Program:

LDAA	$40	GET MOST SIGNIFICANT DIGIT
ASLA		MULTIPLY MSD BY 2
TAB		SAVE DOUBLED MSD
ASLA		MULTIPLY MSD BY 8
ASLA		
ABA		ADD DOUBLED MSD TO GIVE TEN TIMES MSD
ADDA	$41	ADD LEAST SIGNIFICANT DIGIT
STAA	$42	STORE BINARY EQUIVALENT
SWI		

Object Program:

Memory Address (Hex)	Memory Contents (Hex)		Instruction (Mnemonic)	
0000	96	40	LDAA	$40
0002	48		ASLA	
0003	16		TAB	
0004	48		ASLA	
0005	48		ASLA	
0006	1B		ABA	
0007	9B	41	ADDA	$41
0009	97	42	STAA	$42
000B	3F		SWI	

BCD entries are converted to binary in order to save on storage and make calculations simpler. However, the conversion may offset some of the advantages of binary storage and arithmetic.

The idea of the program is to replace multiplication by arithmetic left shifts. Shifts are faster and require less program memory than a full software multiplication. Each arithmetic left shift is equivalent to a multiplication by 2. Similarly, an arithmetic right shift is equivalent to a division by 2. How would you use the arithmetic left shift to multiply by 16? by 12? by 7?

BCD numbers require about 20% more storage than do binary numbers. Representing 0 to 999 requires 3 BCD digits (12 bits) and 10 bits in binary (since $2^{10} = 1024 \sim 1000$).

Convert Binary Number to ASCII String

Purpose: Convert the 8-bit binary number in memory location 0041 to eight ASCII characters (either ASCII 0 or ASCII 1) in memory locations 0042 through 0049 (the most significant bit is in 0042).

Sample Problem:

	(0041)	=	D2 = 11010010	
Result:	(0042)	=	31	'1'
	(0043)	=	31	'1'
	(0044)	=	30	'0'
	(0045)	=	31	'1'
	(0046)	=	30	'0'
	(0047)	=	30	'0'
	(0048)	=	31	'1'
	(0049)	=	30	'0'

Flowchart:

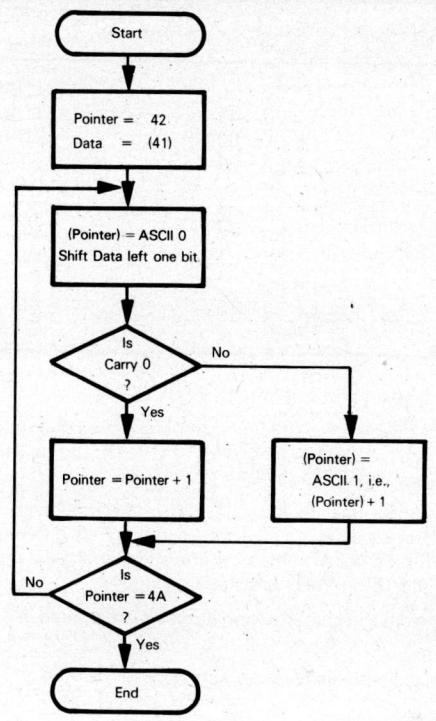

Source Program:

```
        LDAB    #'0         GET ASCII ZERO TO STORE IN STRING
        LDAA    $41         GET DATA
        LDX     #$42        POINTER = START OF ASCII STRING
CONV    STAB    X           PUT ASCII ZERO IN STRING
        ASLA                SHIFT DATA LEFT
        BCC     COUNT       IS NEXT BIT 1?
        INC     X           YES, MAKE STRING ELEMENT ASCII ONE
COUNT   INX
        CPX     #$4A        CHECK FOR CONVERSION COMPLETED
        BNE     CONV
        SWI
```

Object Program:

Memory Address (Hex)	Memory Contents (Hex)		Instruction (Mnemonic)	
0000	C6	30	LDAB	#'0
0002	96	41	LDAA	$41
0004	CE	0042	LDX	#$42
0007	E7	00 CONV	STAB	X
0009	48		ASLA	
000A	24	02	BCC	COUNT
000C	6C	00	INC	X
000E	08	COUNT	INX	
000F	8C	004A	CPX	#$4A
0012	26	F3	BNE	CONV
0014	3F		SWI	

The ASCII digits form a sequence so ASCII 1 − ASCII 0 = 1.

The CPX (Compare Index Register) instruction compares 16-bit quantities. The Zero flag should be used as the jump condition. The other flags are not set properly on the 6800 processor, but are set properly on the 6801.

The INC instruction requires only an 8-bit offset if indexed addressing is used, even though 8-bit direct addresses are not allowed. Be careful of the difference between INC X, which adds 1 to an 8-bit number in memory (the address is in the Index register) and INX, which adds 1 to the 16-bit Index register.

Binary-to-ASCII conversion is necessary when numbers are printed in binary form on an ASCII device.

The conversion to ASCII simply involves adding ASCII 0 (hex 30).

PROBLEMS

1) ASCII to Hex

Purpose: Convert the contents of memory location 0040 to a hexadecimal digit and store the result in memory location 0041. Assume that memory location 0040 contains the ASCII representation of a hexadecimal digit (7 bits with MSB 0).

Sample Problems:

a.   (0040) = 43 'C'
   Result: (0041) = 0C

b.   (0040) = 36 '6'
   Result: (0041) = 06

2) Seven-Segment to Decimal

Purpose: Convert the contents of memory location 0040 from a seven-segment code to a decimal number in memory location 0041. If memory location 0040 does not contain a valid seven-segment code, set memory location 0041 to FF (hex). Use the seven-segment table given under the Decimal to Seven-Segment example and try to match codes.

Sample Problems:

a.   (0040) = 4F
   Result: (0041) = 03

b.   (0040) = 28
   Result: (0041) = FF

3) Decimal to ASCII

Purpose: Convert the contents of memory location 0040 from a decimal digit to an ASCII character and store the result in memory location 0041. If the number in memory location 0040 is not a decimal digit, set the contents of memory location 0041 to an ASCII blank character (20 hex).

Sample Problems:

a.   (0040) = 07
   Result: (0041) = 37 ('7')

b.   (0040) = 55
   Result: (0041) = 20 ('SP')

4) Binary to BCD

Purpose: Convert the contents of memory location 0040 to two BCD digits in memory locations 0041 and 0042 (most significant digit in 0041). The number in memory location 0040 is unsigned and less than 100.

Sample Problems:

a.   (0040) = 1D (29 decimal)
   Result: (0041) = 02
                (0042) = 09

b.   (0040) = 47 (71 decimal)
   Result: (0041) = 07
                (0042) = 01

5) Binary Number to ASCII String

Purpose: Convert the eight ASCII characters in memory locations 0042 through 0049 to an 8-bit binary number in memory location 0041 (the most significant bit is in 0042). Clear memory location 0040 if all the ASCII characters are either ASCII 1 or ASCII 0 and set it to FF otherwise.

Sample Problems:

a.   (0042) = 31 '1'
                    (0043) = 31 '1'
                    (0044) = 30 '0'
                    (0045) = 31 '1'
                    (0046) = 30 '0'
                    (0047) = 30 '0'
                    (0048) = 31 '1'
                    (0049) = 30 '0'
   Result: (0041) = D2
                    (0040) = 00

b.   (0045) = 37 '7'
   Result: (0040) = FF

REFERENCES

[1] Allison, D.R., "A Design Philosophy for Microcomputer Architectures". *Computer*, February 1977. pp. 35-41. This is an excellent article which we recommend highly.

Chapter 8
ARITHMETIC PROBLEMS

Most arithmetic in microprocessor applications consists of multiple-word binary or decimal manipulations. A decimal correction (decimal adjust) or some other means for performing decimal arithmetic is frequently the only arithmetic instruction provided besides basic addition and subtraction. You must implement other arithmetic operations with sequences of instructions.

Multiple-precision binary arithmetic requires simple repetitions of the basic single-word instructions. The Carry bit transfers information between words. Add with Carry and Subtract with Carry use the information from the previous arithmetic operations. You must be careful to clear the Carry before operating on the first words (obviously there is no carry into or borrow from the least significant bits).

Decimal arithmetic is a common enough task for microprocessors that most have special instructions for this purpose. These instructions may either perform decimal operations directly or correct the results of binary operations to the proper decimal form. Decimal arithmetic is essential in such applications as point-of-sale terminals, calculators, check processors, order entry systems, and banking terminals.

You can implement multiplication and division as series of additions and subtractions, respectively, much as they are done by hand. Double-word operations are necessary, since a multiplication produces a result twice as long as the operands, while a division similarly contracts the length of the result. Multiplications and divisions are time-consuming when done in software because of the repeated arithmetic and shift operations that are necessary. Of course, multiplying or dividing by a power of 2 is simple because such operations can be implemented with an appropriate number of left or right arithmetic shifts.

EXAMPLES
Multiple-Precision Addition

Purpose: Add two multiple-word binary numbers. The length of the numbers (in bytes) is in memory location 0040, the numbers themselves start (least significant bits first) in memory locations 0041 and 0051, respectively, and the sum replaces the number starting in memory location 0041.

Sample Problem:

```
            (0040) = 04

            (0041) = C3
            (0042) = A7
            (0043) = 5B
            (0044) = 2F

            (0051) = B8
            (0052) = 35
            (0053) = DF
            (0054) = 14

Result:     (0041) = 7B
            (0042) = DD
            (0043) = 3A
            (0044) = 44

that is,       2F5BA7C3
            +  14DF35B8
               ─────────
               443ADD7B
```

Flowchart:

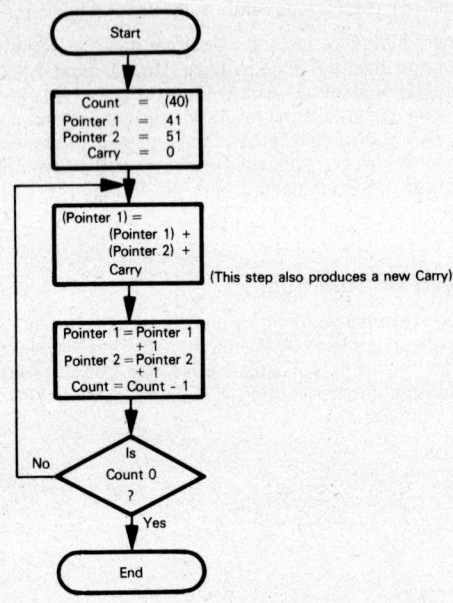

8-2

Source Program:

```
        LDAB    $40         COUNT = LENGTH OF NUMBERS (IN BYTES)
        CLC                 START CARRY AT ZERO
        LDX     #$41        POINT TO FIRST BITS IN NUMBERS
MPADD   LDAA    X           GET 8 BITS OF FIRST NUMBER
        ADCA    $10,X       ADD 8 BITS OF SECOND NUMBER
        STAA    X           STORE SUM IN FIRST NUMBER
        INX
        DECB
        BNE     MPADD
        SWI
```

Object Program:

Memory Address (Hex)	Memory Contents (Hex)		Instruction (Mnemonic)	
0000	D6	40		LDAB	$40
0002	0C			CLC	
0003	CE	0041		LDX	#$41
0006	A6	00	MPADD	LDAA	X
0008	A9	10		ADCA	$10,X
000A	A7	00		STAA	X
000C	08			INX	
000D	5A			DECB	
000E	26	F6		BNE	MPADD
0010	3F			SWI	

The relative address for BNE MPADD is

$$\frac{06}{-10} = \frac{06}{\underline{+F0}}$$
$$F6$$

The instruction CLC clears the Carry bit. The Carry must be cleared, since there is no carry involved in the addition of the least significant bytes.

The instruction ADC, ADD WITH CARRY, includes the Carry from the previous words in the addition. ADC is the only instruction in the loop that affects the Carry. Remember that neither INX nor DEC does.

The two strings must be less than 256 locations apart, so that an 8-bit indexed offset can hold the distance between them.

This procedure can add binary numbers of any length. Note that ten binary bits correspond to three decimal digits, since $2^{10} = 1024 \sim 1000$. So, you can calculate the number of bits required to give a certain accuracy in decimal digits. For example, twelve-decimal digit accuracy requires

DECIMAL ACCURACY IN BINARY

$$12 \times \frac{10}{3} = 40 \text{ bits}$$

Decimal Addition

Purpose: Add two multiple-word decimal (BCD) numbers. The length of the numbers is in memory location 0040, the numbers themselves start (least significant bits first) in memory locations 0041 and 0051, respectively, and the sum replaces the number starting in memory location 0041.

Sample Problem:

(0040) = 04

(0041) = 85
(0042) = 19
(0043) = 70
(0044) = 36

(0051) = 59
(0052) = 34
(0053) = 66
(0054) = 12

Result:
(0041) = 44
(0042) = 54
(0043) = 36
(0044) = 49

that is,
```
   36701985
 +12663459
  ---------
   49365444
```

Flowchart:

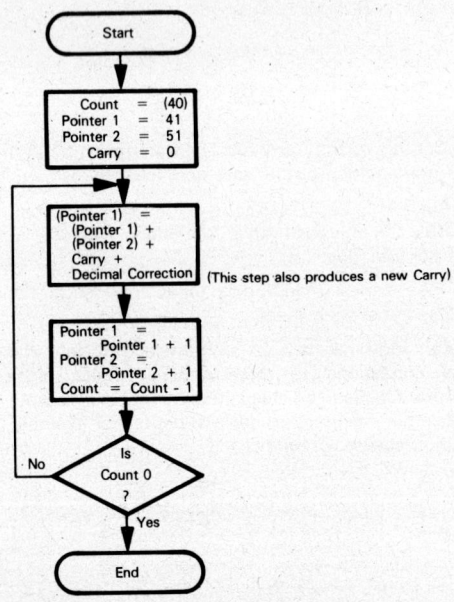

Source Program:

```
        LDAB    $40         COUNT = LENGTH OF STRINGS (IN BYTES)
        CLC                 START CARRY AT ZERO
        LDX     #$41        POINT TO FIRST DIGITS IN STRINGS
DCADD   LDAA    X           GET TWO DIGITS OF FIRST STRING
        ADCA    $10,X       ADD TWO DIGITS OF SECOND STRING
        DAA                 DECIMAL CORRECTION
        STAA    X           STORE SUM IN FIRST STRING
        INX
        DECB
        BNE     DCADD
        SWI
```

Object Program:

Memory Address (Hex)	Memory Contents (Hex)			Instruction (Mnemonic)	
0000	D6	40			LDAB	$40
0002	0C				CLC	
0003	CE	00	41		LDX	#$41
0006	A6	00		DCADD	LDAA	X
0008	A9	10			ADCA	
000A	19				DAA	
000B	A7	00			STAA	X
000D	08				INX	
000E	5A				DECB	
000F	26	F5			BNE	DCADD
0011	3F				SWI	

The Decimal Adjust (DAA) instruction uses the Carry (C) and Half Carry (H) bits to correct the following situations: **DECIMAL ADJUST**

1) The sum of two digits is between 10 and 15, inclusive. In this case, six must be added to the sum to give the right result, i.e.,

```
    0101    (5)
  + 1000    (8)
    ────
    1101    (D)
  + 0110
    ─────────
  0001 0011   (BCD 13, which is correct)
```

2) The sum of two digits is 16 or more. In this case the result is a proper BCD number, but six less than it should be, i.e.,

```
    1000    (8)
  + 1001    (9)
  ─────────
  0001 0001  (BCD 11)
  +   0110
  ─────────
  0001 0111  (BCD 17, which is correct)
```

Six must be added in both situations. However, case 1 can be recognized by the fact that the sum is not a BCD digit; it is between 10 and 15 (or A and F hexadecimal). Case 2 can only be recognized by the fact that the Carry (most significant digit) or Half Carry (least significant digit) has been set to 1, since the result is a valid BCD number. DAA is the only instruction which uses the Half Carry. Note that DAA only operates on Accumulator A.

This procedure can add decimal (BCD) numbers of any length. Here four binary bits are required for each decimal digit, so twelve-digit accuracy requires

$$12 \times 4 = 48 \text{ bits}$$

as opposed to 40 bits in the binary case. This is essentially six 8-bit words instead of five. The decimal procedure also takes a little longer per word because of the extra DAA instruction.

8-Bit Binary Multiplication

Purpose: Multiply the 8-bit unsigned number in memory location 0041 by the 8-bit unsigned number in memory location 0040. Place the eight most significant bits of the result in memory location 0042 and the eight least significant bits in memory location 0043.

Sample Problems:

a.
                (0040) = 03
                (0041) = 05
    Result: (0042) = 00
                (0043) = 0F
                or, in decimal, 3 x 5 = 15

b.
                (0040) = 6F
                (0041) = 61
    Result: (0042) = 2A
                (0043) = 0F
                or, 111 x 97 = 10,767

You can perform multiplication on a computer in the same way that you do long multiplication by hand. Since the numbers are binary, the only problem is whether to multiply by 0 or 1; multiplying by zero obviously gives zero as a result, while multiplying by one produces the same number that you started with (the multiplicand). So, each step in a binary multiplication can be reduced to the following operation:

If the current bit in the multiplier is 1, add the multiplicand to the partial product.

> **MULTIPLICATION ALGORITHM**

The only remaining problem is to ensure that you line everything up correctly each time. The following operations perform this task:

1) Shift multiplier left one bit so that the bit to be examined is placed in the Carry.
2) Shift product left one bit so that the next addition is lined up correctly.

The complete process for binary multiplication is as follows:

Step 1 - Initialization
    Product = 0
    Counter = 8

Step 2 - Shift Product so as to line up properly
    Product = 2 x Product (LSB = 0)

Step 3 - Shift Multiplier so bit goes to Carry
    Multiplier = 2 x Multiplier

Step 4 - Add Multiplicand to Product if Carry is 1
    If Carry = 1, Product = Product + Multiplicand

Step 5 - Decrement Counter and check for zero
    Counter = Counter - 1
    If Counter ≠ 0, go to Step 2

In the case of Sample Problem b, where the multiplier is 61 (hex) and the multiplicand is 6F (hex), the process works as follows:

Initialization:

Product	0000
Multiplier	61
Multiplicand	6F
Counter	08

After first iteration of steps 2-5:

Product	0000
Multiplier	C2
Multiplicand	6F
Counter	07
Carry from Multiplier	0

After second iteration:

Product	006F
Multiplier	84
Multiplicand	6F
Counter	06
Carry from Multiplier	1

After third iteration:

Product	014D
Multiplier	08
Multiplicand	6F
Counter	05
Carry from Multiplier	1

After fourth iteration:

Product	029A
Multiplier	10
Multiplicand	6F
Counter	04
Carry from Multiplier	0

After fifth iteration:

Product	0534
Multiplier	20
Multiplicand	6F
Counter	03
Carry from Multiplier	0

After sixth iteration:

Product	0A68
Multiplier	40
Multiplicand	6F
Counter	02
Carry from Multiplier	0

After seventh iteration:

Product	14D0
Multiplier	80
Multiplicand	6F
Counter	01
Carry from Multiplier	0

After eighth iteration:

Product	2A0F
Multiplier	00
Multiplicand	6F
Counter	00
Carry from Multiplier	1

Flowchart:

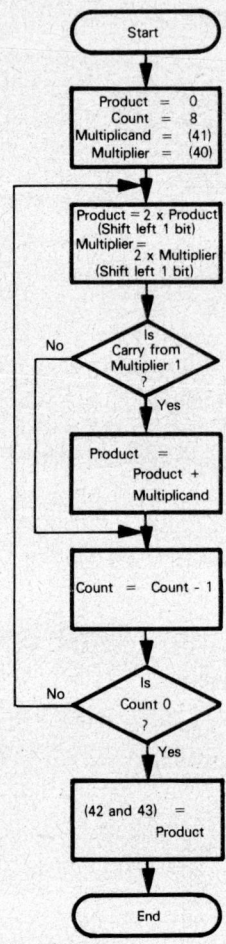

Source Program:

```
            CLRA            PRODUCT MSB = ZERO
            CLRB            PRODUCT LSB = ZERO
            LDX    #8       NUMBER OF BITS IN MULTIPLIER = 8
SHIFT       ASLB            SHIFT PRODUCT LEFT 1 BIT
            ROLA
            ASL    $40      SHIFT MULTIPLIER LEFT TO
            BCC    DECR       EXAMINE NEXT BIT
            ADDB   $41      ADD MULTIPLICAND TO
            ADCA   #0         PRODUCT IF CARRY IS 1
DECR        DEX
            BNE    SHIFT    LOOP UNTIL 8 BITS ARE DONE
            STAA   $42      STORE RESULT
            STAB   $43
            SWI
```

Object Program:

Memory Address (Hex)	Memory Contents (Hex)		Instruction (Mnemonic)	
0000	4F			CLRA	
0001	5F			CLRB	
0002	CE	0008		LDX	#8
0005	58		SHIFT	ASLB	
0006	49			ROLA	
0007	78	0040		ASL	$40
000A	24	04		BCC	DECR
000C	DB	41		ADDB	$41
000E	89	00		ADCA	#0
0010	09		DECR	DEX	
0011	26	F2		BNE	SHIFT
0013	97	42		STAA	$42
0015	D7	43		STAB	$43
0017	3F			SWI	

Besides its obvious use in calculators and point-of-sale terminals, multiplication is a key part of almost all signal processing and control algorithms. The speed at which multiplications can be performed determines the usefulness of a CPU in process control, signal detection, and signal analysis.

This algorithm takes between 190 and 230 microseconds to multiply on a 6800 with a 1 MHz clock. The precise time depends on the number of 1 bits in the multiplier. Other algorithms can reduce the average time somewhat, but 250 microseconds will still be typical for a software multiplication.

The Index register is used as a counter, since it is not otherwise needed in the program. The DEX instruction decrements the contents of the Index register. A memory location could also serve as the counter.

The instruction ASL $40 shifts the contents of memory location 0040 left one bit, placing the most significant bit in the Carry and clearing the least significant bit.

The instruction ADDB $41 adds the multiplicand to the product. The instruction ADCA #0 adds the carry from that 8-bit addition to the most significant eight bits of the product (in Accumulator A). ADCA #0 results in

$$(A) = (A) + 0 + (Carry)$$
$$= (A) + (Carry)$$

The instructions ASLB and ROLA together act as a 16-bit arithmetic left shift of the product in Accumulators A and B (MSBs in A). Similarly, LSRA, RORB is a 16-bit logical right shift, and ASRA, RORB a 16-bit arithmetic right shift. You can also use the same sequences to shift the contents of two memory locations as a 16-bit number.

Other methods for implementing multiplication, division, and other arithmetic tasks are discussed in:

REFERENCES ON MULTIPLICATION

    Geist, D.J., "MOS Processor Picks Up Speed with Bipolar Multipliers", Electronics, July 7, 1977, pp. 113 - 115.

    Mick, J.R., and J. Springer, "Single-chip Multiplier Expands Digital Role in Signal Processing", Electronics, May 13, 1976, pp. 103 - 108.

    Parasuraman, B., "Hardware Multiplication Techniques for Microprocessor Systems", Computer Design, April 1977, pp. 75 - 82.

    Tao, T.F. et al., "Applications of Microprocessors in Control Problems", Proceedings of the 1977 Joint Automatic Control Conference, San Francisco, CA., June 22-24, 1977.

    Waser, S., and A. Peterson, "Real-time Processing Gains Ground with Fast Digital Multiplier", Electronics, September 29, 1977, pp. 93 - 99.

    Weissberger, A.J., and T. Toal, "Tough Mathematical Tasks Are Child's Play for Number Cruncher", Electronics, February 17, 1977, pp. 102 - 107.

8-Bit Binary Division

Purpose: Divide the 8-bit unsigned number in memory location 0040 by the 8-bit unsigned number in memory location 0041. Store the quotient in memory location 0042 and the remainder in memory location 0043.

Sample Problems:

a.
    (0040) = 00 (64 decimal)
    (0041) = 08
  Result: (0042) = 08
    (0043) = 00
  or, in decimal, 64/8 = 8

b.
    (0040) = FF (255 decimal)
    (0041) = 17 (23 decimal)
  Result: (0042) = 0B (11 decimal)
    (0043) = 02 (2 decimal)
  that is, 255/23 = 11 with a remainder of 2.

You can perform division on a computer just like you would perform division with pencil and paper; i.e., by using trial subtractions. Since the numbers are binary, the only question is whether the divisor can be subtracted from what is left of the dividend. Each step in a binary division can be reduced to the following operation:

DIVISION ALGORITHM

> If the divisor can be subtracted from the eight most significant bits of the dividend without a borrow, the corresponding bit in the quotient is 1; otherwise it is zero.

The only remaining problem is to line up the dividend and quotient properly. You can do this by shifting the dividend and quotient logically left one bit before each trial subtraction. The dividend and quotient can share a 16-bit register, since the procedure clears one bit of the dividend at the same time as it determines one bit of the quotient. The 8-bit dividend is initially expanded to 16 bits by adding eight leading zero bits.

The complete process for binary division is:

Step 1 - Initialization

    Quotient = 0
    Count = 8

Step 2 - Shift Dividend and Quotient so as to line up properly

    Dividend = 2 x Quotient
    Quotient = 2 x Quotient

Step 3 - Perform trial subtraction. If no Borrow, add 1 to Quotient

    If 8 MSBs of Dividend $\geq$ Divisor, then MSBs of Dividend = MSBs of Dividend - Divisor Quotient = Quotient + 1

Step 4 - Decrement Counter and check for zero

    Count = Count - 1
    If Count $\neq$ 0, go to Step 2
    Remainder = 8 MSBs of Dividend

In the case of Sample Problem b, where the dividend is FF (hex) and the divisor is 17 (hex), the process works as follows:

Initialization:

Dividend	00FF
Divisor	17
Quotient	00
Count	08

After first iteration of Steps 2-4: (Note that the dividend is shifted prior to the trial subtraction.)

Dividend	01FE
Divisor	17
Quotient	00
Count	07

After second iteration of Steps 2-4:

Dividend	03FC
Divisor	17
Quotient	00
Count	06

After third iteration:

	Dividend	07F8
	Divisor	17
	Quotient	00
	Count	05

After fourth iteration:

	Dividend	0FF0
	Divisor	17
	Quotient	00
	Count	04

After fifth iteration:

	Dividend	08E0
	Divisor	7
	Quotient	01
	Count	03

After sixth iteration:

	Dividend	11C0
	Divisor	17
	Quotient	02
	Count	02

After seventh iteration:

	Dividend	0C80
	Divisor	17
	Quotient	05
	Count	01

After eighth iteration:

	Dividend	0200
	Divisor	17
	Quotient	0B
	Count	00

So, the quotient is 0B and the remainder is 02.

Flowchart:

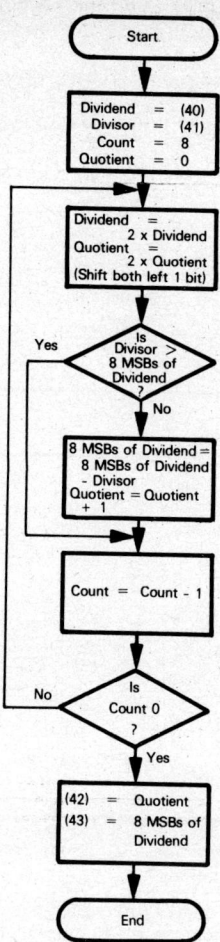

Source Program:

```
           LDX     #8         NUMBER OF BITS IN DIVISOR
           CLRA               GET DIVIDEND
           LDAB    $40
DIVIDE     ASLB               SHIFT DIVIDEND, QUOTIENT
           ROLA
           CMPA    $41        IS TRIAL SUBTRACTION SUCCESSFUL?
           BCS     CHKCNT
           SUBA    $41        YES, SUBTRACT AND SET BIT IN QUOTIENT
           INCB
CHKCNT     DEX
           BNE     DIVIDE
           STAB    $42        STORE QUOTIENT
           STAA    $43        STORE REMAINDER
           SWI
```

Object Program:

Memory Address (Hex)	Memory Contents (Hex)		Instruction (Mnemonic)	
0000	CE	0008		LDX	#8
0003	4F			CLRA	
0004	D6	41		LDAB	$40
0006	58		DIVIDE	ASLB	
0007	49			ROLA	
0008	91	42		CMPA	$41
000A	25	03		BCS	CHKCNT
000C	90	42		SUBA	$41
000E	5C			INCB	
000F	09		CHKCNT	DEX	
0010	26	F4		BNE	DIVIDE
0012	D7	42		STAB	$42
0014	97	43		STAA	$43
0016	3F			SWI	

Division is used in calculators, terminals, communications error checking, control algorithms, and many other applications.

The algorithm takes between 170 and 210 microseconds to divide on a 6800 with a 1 MHz clock. The precise time depends on the number of 1 bits in the quotient. Other algorithms can reduce the average time somewhat, but 200 microseconds will still be typical for a software division.

The instructions ASLB and ROLA together provide a 16-bit arithmetic left shift of Accumulators A and B (MSBs in A).

An 8-bit subtraction is necessary, since there is no simple way to do a 16-bit subtraction or comparison.

Accumulators A and B hold both the dividend and the quotient. The quotient simply replaces the dividend in Accumulator B as the dividend is shifted left logically.

Self-Checking Numbers
Double Add Double Mod 10

Purpose: Calculate a checksum digit from a string of BCD digits. The length of the string of digits (number of words) is in memory location 0041; the string of digits (2 BCD digits to a word) starts in memory location 0042. Calculate the checksum digit by the Double Add Double Mod 10 technique and store it in memory location 0040. (See J.R. Herr, "Self-checking Number Systems", Computer Design, June 1974, pp. 85 - 91.)

The Double Add Double Mod 10 technique works as follows:

SELF-CHECKING NUMBERS

1) Clear the checksum to start.
2) Multiply the leading digit by two and add the result to the checksum.
3) Add the next digit to the checksum.
4) Continue the alternating process until you have used all the digits.
5) The least significant digit of the checksum is the self-checking digit.

Self-checking digits are commonly added to identification numbers on credit cards, inventory tags, luggage, parcels, etc., when they are handled by computerized systems. They may also be used in routine messages, identifying files, and other applications. The purpose of the digits is to minimize entry errors such as transposing digits (69 instead of 96), shifting digits (7260 instead of 3726), missing digits by 1 (65 instead of 64), etc. You can check the self-checking number automatically for correctness upon entry and can eliminate many errors immediately.

The analysis of self-checking methods is quite complex. For example, a plain checksum will not find transposition errors $(4 + 9 = 9 + 4)$. The Double Add Double algorithm will find simple transposition errors $(2 \times 4 + 9 = 17 \neq 2 \times 9 + 4)$, but will miss some errors, such as transpositions across even numbers of digits (367 instead of 763). However, this method will find many common errors! The value of a method depends on what errors it will detect and on the probability of particular errors in an application.

For example, if the string of digits is

$$549321$$

the result will be:

Checksum $= 5 \times 2 + 4 + 9 \times 2 + 3 + 2 \times 2 + 1 = 40$
Self-checking digit $= 0$ (least significant digit of checksum)

Note that an erroneous entry like 543921 would produce a different self-checking digit (4), but erroneous entries like 049321 or 945321 would not be detected.

Sample Problems:

a.
        (0041) = 03
        (0042) = 36
        (0043) = 68
        (0044) = 51
  Result: Checksum $= 3 \times 2 + 6 + 6 \times 2 + 8 + 5 \times 2 + 1 = 43$
        (0040) = 03

b.
        (0041) = 04
        (0042) = 50
        (0043) = 29
        (0044) = 16
        (0045) = 83
  Result: Checksum $= 5 \times 2 + 0 + 2 \times 2 + 9 + 1 \times 2 + 6 + 8 \times 2 + 3 = 50$
        (0040) = 00

Flowchart:

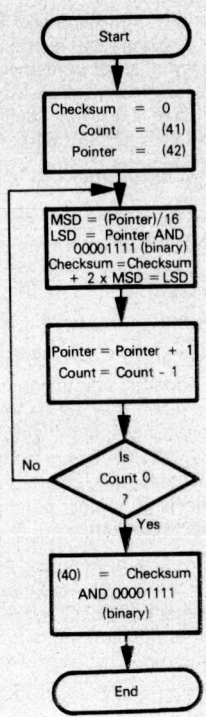

Source Program:

```
             LDX     #$42            POINT TO START OF STRING
             CLR     $40             CHECKSUM = 0
CHKDIG       LDAA    X
             LSRA
             LSRA                    GET MSD BY 4 LOGICAL SHIFTS
             LSRA
             LSRA
             TAB                     DOUBLE MSD
             ABA
             DAA                     AND KEEP IT DECIMAL
             LDAB    X
             ANDB    #%00001111      MASK OFF MSD
             ABA                     ADD LSD TO TWICE MSD
             DAA
             ADDA    $40             ADD LSD + TWICE MSD TO OLD
                                         CHECKSUM DIGIT
             DAA
             STAA    $40
             INX
             DEC     $41             COUNT LENGTH OF NUMBER IN BYTES
             BNE     CHKDIG
             ANDA    #%00001111      MASK OFF MSD
             STAA    $40             SAVE SELF-CHECKING DIGIT
             SWI
```

Object Program:

Memory Address (Hex)	Memory Contents (Hex)			Instruction (Mnemonic)	
0000	CE	0042		LDX	#$42
0003	7F	0040		CLR	$40
0006	A6	00	CHKDIG	LDAA	X
0008	44			LSRA	
0009	44			LSRA	
000A	44			LSRA	
000B	44			LSRA	
000C	16			TAB	
000D	1B			ABA	
000E	19			DAA	
000F	F6	00		LDAB	X
0011	C4	0F		ANDB	#%00001111
0013	1B			ABA	
0014	19			DAA	
0015	9B	40		ADDA	$40
0017	19			DAA	
0018	97	40		STAA	$40
001A	08			INX	
001B	7A	0041		DEC	$41
001E	26	E6		BNE	CHKDIG
0020	84	0F		ANDA	#%00001111
0022	97	40		STAA	$40
0024	3F			SWI	

The digits are removed by shifting and masking. Four logical right shifts are needed to separate the most significant digit.

A decimal adjust (DAA) must follow each addition in order to produce the proper decimal result. A single DAA after a series of additions will not work (try it!). Remember that DAA only works on Accumulator A.

There is no problem with carries from the decimal sum, since the procedure only uses the least significant digit of the checksum anyway.

You can double a decimal number (in A) by adding it to itself and then performing a decimal correction:

DOUBLING AND HALVING BINARY NUMBERS

```
        TAB
        ABA     DOUBLE NUMBER
        DAA     AND MAKE RESULT DECIMAL
```

You cannot use ASLA, because that instruction does not affect the Half-Carry (only Add and Add With Carry affect that bit).

You can divide a decimal number by 2 simply by shifting it right logically and then subtracting 3 from any digit that is 8 or larger (since 10 BCD is 16 binary). The following program divides a decimal number in memory location 0040 by 2 and places the result in memory location 0041.

```
        LDAA    $40     GET DECIMAL NUMBER
        LSRA            DIVIDE BY 2 IN BINARY
        CMPA    #8      IS LEAST SIGNIFICANT DIGIT 8 OR MORE?
        BCC     DONE
        SUBA    #3      YES, SUBTRACT 3 FOR DECIMAL CORRECTION
DONE    STAA    $41     STORE RESULT
        SWI
```

Try this program and the method on the decimal numbers 28, 30 and 37. Do you understand why it works?

Rounding is simple whether the numbers are binary or decimal. A binary number can be rounded as follows:

BINARY ROUNDING

> If the most significant bit to be dropped is 1, add 1 to the remaining bits. Otherwise, leave the remaining bits alone.

This rule works because 1 is halfway between 0 and 10 in binary, much as 5 is halfway in decimal (note that 0.5 decimal = 0.1 binary).

So, the following program will round a 16-bit number in memory locations 0040 and 0041 (MSBs in 0040) to an 8-bit number in memory location 0040.

```
        TST     $41     IS MSB OF EXTRA BYTE 1?
        BPL     DONE
        INC     $40     YES, ROUND UP
DONE    SWI
```

If the number is longer than 16 bits, the rounding must ripple through the other bytes as needed.

Decimal rounding is a bit more difficult, because the crossover point is now BCD 50 and the rounding must produce a decimal result. The rule is:

DECIMAL ROUNDING

> If the most significant digit to be dropped is 5 or more, add 1 to the remaining digits.

The following program will round a four-digit BCD number in memory locations 0040 and 0041 (MSDs in 0040) to a two-digit BCD number in memory location 0040.

```
        LDAA    $41
        CMPA    #$50        IS BYTE TO BE DROPPED 50 OR MORE?
        BCS     DONE
        LDAA    $40         YES, ROUND MSDS UP
        ADDA    #1
        DAA                 KEEP MSDS DECIMAL
        STAA    $40
DONE    SWI
```

Remember that you cannot use the INC instruction to add 1 because it does not affect the H bit (which may have been set by an earlier operation). Again, longer numbers mean that the rounding must ripple through the more significant digits as needed.

PROBLEMS

1) Multiple-Precision Subtraction

Purpose: Subtract one multiple-word number from another. The length of the numbers is in memory location 0040, the numbers themselves start (least significant bits first) in memory locations 0041 and 0051, respectively, and the difference replaces the number starting in memory location 0041. Subtract the number starting in 0051 from the one starting in 0041.

Sample Problem:

```
            (0040) = 04

            (0041) = C3
            (0042) = A7
            (0043) = 5B
            (0044) = 2F

            (0051) = B8
            (0052) = 35
            (0053) = DF
            (0054) = 14

Result:     (0041) = 0B
            (0042) = 72
            (0043) = 7C
            (0044) = 1A

that is,        2F5BA7C3
            +   14DF35B8
                --------
                1A7C720B
```

2) Decimal Subtraction

Purpose: Subtract one multiple-word decimal (BCD) number from another. The length of the numbers is in memory location 0040, the numbers themselves start (least significant bits first) in memory locations 0041 and 0051, respectively, and the difference replaces the number starting in memory location 0041. Subtract the number starting in 0051 from the one starting in 0041.

Sample Problem:

```
              (0040)  =  04
              (0041)  =  85
              (0042)  =  19
              (0043)  =  70
              (0044)  =  36

              (0051)  =  59
              (0052)  =  34
              (0053)  =  66
              (0054)  =  12

Result:  (0041)  =  26
         (0042)  =  85
         (0043)  =  03
         (0044)  =  24
```

that is,
```
      36701985
    - 12663459
      --------
      24038526
```

Hint: $X - Y = X + 99 - Y + \overline{BORROW}$

where X and Y are each two digits from the strings and the BORROW is the borrow from the less significant digits. Calculating 99-Y is no problem, since any decimal number can be subtracted from 99 without any borrows. But remember that the role of the Carry is reversed from the usual (why?).

3) 8-Bit by 16-Bit Binary Multiplication

Purpose: Multiply the 16-bit unsigned number in memory locations 0040 and 0041 (most significant bits in 0040) by the 8-bit unsigned number in memory location 0042. Store the result in memory locations 0043 through 0045, with the most significant bits in memory location 0043.

Sample Problems:

a.
```
              (0040)  =  00
              (0041)  =  03
              (0042)  =  05
    Result:   (0043)  =  00
              (0044)  =  00
              (0045)  =  0F
```
that is, $3 \times 5 = 15$

b.
```
              (0040)  =  72   (29,295 decimal)
              (0041)  =  6F
              (0042)  =  61   (97 decimal)
    Result:   (0043)  =  2B
              (0044)  =  5C
              (0045)  =  0F
```
that is, $29,295 \times 97 = 2,841,615$

4) Signed Binary Division

Purpose: Divide the 16-bit signed number in memory locations 0040 and 0041 (most significant bits in 0040) by the 8-bit signed number in memory location 0042. The numbers are normalized so that the magnitude of memory location 0040 (that is, the quotient) is an 8-bit number. Store the quotient (signed) in memory location 0043 and the remainder (always positive) in memory location 0044.

Sample Problems:

a.
                (0040) = FF (-64)
                (0041) = C0
                (0042) = 08
    Result: (0043) = F8 (-8) quotient
                (0044) = 00 (0) remainder

b.
                (0040) = ED (-4717)
                (0041) = 93
                (0042) = 47 (71 decimal)
    Result: (0043) = BD (-67 decimal)
                (0044) = 28 (+40 decimal)

Hint: Determine the sign of the result, perform an unsigned division, and adjust the quotient and remainder properly.

5) Self-Checking Numbers Aligned 1, 3, 7 Mod 10

Purpose: Calculate a checksum digit from a string of BCD digits. The length of the string of digits (number of words) is in memory location 0041; the string of digits (2 BCD digits to a word) starts in memory location 0042. Calculate the checksum digit by the Aligned 1, 3, 7 Mod 10 method and store it in memory location 0040.

The Aligned 1, 3, 7 Mod 10 technique works as follows:

1) Clear the checksum to start.
2) Add the leading digit to the checksum.
3) Multiply the next digit by 3 and add the result to the checksum.
4) Multiply the next digit by 7 and add the result to the checksum.
5) Continue the process (Steps 2-4) until you have used all the digits.
6) The self-checking digit is the least significant digit of the checksum.

For example, if the string of digits is

$$549321$$

the result will be
        Checksum = $5 + 3 \times 4 + 7 \times 9 + 3 + 3 \times 2 + 7 \times 1 = 96$
   Self-checking digit = 6

Sample Problems:

a.
                (0041) = 03
                (0042) = 36
                (0043) = 68
                (0044) = 51
    Result: Checksum = $3 + 3 \times 6 + 7 \times 6 + 8 + 3 \times 5 + 7 \times 1 = 93$
            (0040) = 03

b.
                (0041) = 04
                (0042) = 50
                (0043) = 29
                (0044) = 16
                (0045) = 83
    Result: Checksum = $5 + 3 \times 0 + 7 \times 2 + 9 + 3 \times 1 + 7 \times 6 + 8 + 3 \times 3 = 90$
            (0040) = 00

Hint: Note that $7 = 2 \times 3 + 1$ and $3 = 2 \times 1 + 1$, so the formula $M_i = 2 \times M_{i-1} + 1$ can be used to calculate the next multiplying factor.

Chapter 9
TABLES AND LISTS

Tables and lists are two of the basic data structures used with all computers. We have already seen tables used to perform code conversions and arithmetic. Tables may also be used to identify or respond to commands and instructions, linearize data, provide access to files or records, define the meaning of keys or switches, and choose instruction sequences. Lists are usually less structured than tables. Lists may record tasks that the processor must perform, messages or data that the processor must record, or conditions that have changed or should be monitored. Tables are a simple way of making decisions or solving problems, since no computations or logical functions are necessary. The task, then, is reduced to organizing the table so that the proper entry is easy to find. Lists allow the execution of sequences of tasks, the preparation of sets of results, and the construction of interrelated data files (or data bases). Problems include how to add elements to a list and remove elements from it.

EXAMPLES

Add Entry to List

Purpose: Add the contents of memory location 0040 to a list if it is not already present in the list. The length of the list is in memory location 0041 and the list itself begins in memory location 0042.

Sample Problems:

a.
            (0040) = 6B
            (0041) = 04
            (0042) = 37
            (0043) = 61
            (0044) = 38
            (0045) = 1D
    Result: (0041) = 05
            (0046) = 6B

The entry is added to the list, since it is not already present. The length of the list is increased by 1.

b.
            (0040) = 6B
            (0041) = 04
            (0042) = 37
            (0043) = 6B
            (0044) = 38
            (0045) = 1D
    Result: No change, since the entry is already in the list.

Flowchart:

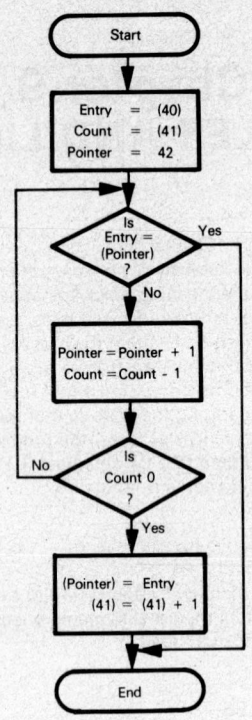

Source Program:

```
        LDX     #$42        POINT TO START OF LIST
        LDAB    $41         COUNT = LENGTH OF LIST
        LDAA    $40         GET ENTRY
SRLST   CMPA    X           IS ENTRY = ELEMENT IN LIST?
        BEQ     DONE        YES, DONE
        INX
        DECB                ALL ENTRIES EXAMINED?
        BNE     SRLST       NO, KEEP LOOKING
        STAA    X           YES, ADD ENTRY TO LIST
        INC     $41         ADD 1 TO LIST LENGTH
DONE    SWI
```

Object Program:

Memory Address (Hex)	Memory Contents (Hex)			Instruction (Mnemonic)	
0000	CE	0042		LDX	#$42
0003	D6	41		LDAB	$41
0005	96	40		LDAA	$40
0007	A1	00	SRLST	CMPA	X
0009	27	09		BEQ	DONE
000B	08			INX	
000C	5A			DECB	
000D	26	F8		BNE	SRLST
000F	A7	00		STAA	X
0011	7C	0041		INC	$41
0014	3F		DONE	SWI	

Clearly, this method of adding elements is very inefficient if the list **HASHING** is long. We could improve the procedure by limiting the search to part of the list or by ordering the list. We could limit the search by using the entry to get a starting point in the list. This method is called "hashing", and is much like selecting a starting page in a dictionary or directory on the basis of the first letter in an entry. We could order the list by numerical value. The search could then end when the list values went beyond the entry (larger or smaller, depending on the ordering technique used). A new entry would have to be inserted properly, and all the other entries would have to be moved down in the list.

The program could be restructured to use two tables. One table could provide a starting point in the other table; for example, the search point could be based on the most or least significant 4-bit digit in the entry.

The program does not work if the length of the list could be zero (what happens?). We could avoid this problem by checking the length initially. The initialization procedure would then be:

```
        LDAB   $41       COUNT = LENGTH OF LIST
        BEQ    ADELM     ADD ENTRY TO LIST IF LENGTH IS ZERO
         .
         .
         .
ADELM   STAA   X         YES, ADD ENTRY TO LIST
         .
         .
         .
```

Unlike many other processors, the 6800's Zero bit is affected by transfer instructions such as Load and Store.

If each entry were longer than one word, a pattern-matching program would be necessary. The program would have to proceed to the next entry if a match failed; that is, skip over the last part of the current entry once a mis-match was found.

Check an Ordered List

Purpose: Check the contents of memory location 0041 to see if it is in an ordered list. The length of the list is in memory location 0042; the list itself begins in memory location 0043 and consists of unsigned binary numbers in increasing order. If the contents of location 0041 is in the list, clear memory location 0040; otherwise, set memory location 0040 to FF (hex).

Sample Problems:

a.
    (0041) = 6B
    (0042) = 04
    (0043) = 37
    (0044) = 55
    (0045) = 7D
    (0046) = A1
    Result: (0040) = FF, since 6B is not in the list.

b.
    (0041) = 6B
    (0042) = 04
    (0043) = 37
    (0044) = 55
    (0045) = 6B
    (0046) = A1
    Result: (0040) = 00, since 6B is in the list.

Flowchart:

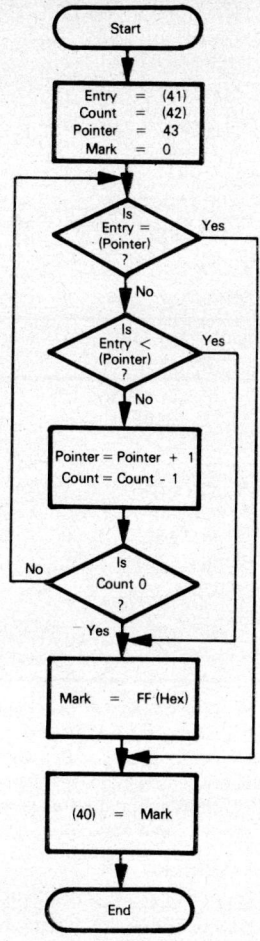

The searching process is a bit different here since the elements are ordered. Once we find an element larger than the entry, the search is over, since subsequent elements will be even larger. You may want to try an example to convince yourself that the procedure works.

As in the previous problem, a table or other method that could choose a good starting point would speed up the search. One method would be to start in the middle and determine which half of the list the entry was in, then divide the half into halves, etc. This method is called a binary search, since it divides the remaining part of the list in half each time. Knuth describes other searching techniques in his book The Art of Computer Programming, Volume III: Sorting and Searching, Addison-Wesley, Reading, Mass., 1978. Knuth also has discussed searching and hashing in a more elementary way in an article entitled "Algorithms" (see the April 1977 issue of Scientific American).

SEARCHING METHODS

Source Program:

```
            CLR     $40             MARK ELEMENT AS IN LIST
            LDX     #$43            POINT TO START OF LIST
            LDAB    $42             COUNT = LENGTH OF LIST
            LDAA    $41             GET ENTRY
SRLST       CMPA    X               IS ENTRY = ELEMENT IN LIST?
            BEQ     DONE            YES, DONE
            BCS     NOTIN           ENTRY NOT IN LIST IF ELEMENT LARGER
            INX
            DECB
            BNE     SRLST           ALL ELEMENTS EXAMINED?
NOTIN       COM     $40             YES, MARK ELEMENT AS NOT IN LIST
DONE        SWI
```

Object Program:

Memory Address (Hex)	Memory Contents (Hex)		Instruction (Mnemonic)	
0000	7F	0040	CLR	$40
0003	CE	0043	LDX	#$43
0006	D6	42	LDAB	$42
0008	96	41	LDAA	$41
000A	A1	00	SRLST CMPA	X
000C	27	09	BEQ	DONE
000E	25	04	BCS	NOTIN
0010	08		INX	
0011	5A		DECB	
0012	26	F6	BNE	SRLST
0014	73	0040	NOTIN COM	$40
0017	3F		DONE SWI	

This algorithm is a bit slower than the one in the example given under Add Entry to List because of the extra conditional Jump (BCS NOTIN). The average execution time for this simple search technique increases linearly with the length of the list, while the average execution time for a binary search increases logarithmically. For example, if the length of the list doubles, the simple technique takes twice as long on the average, while the binary search only requires one extra iteration.

Remove Element from Queue

Purpose: Place the address of the first element (head) of a queue in memory locations 0040 and 0041 (MSBs in 0040) and update the queue so as to remove the element. Memory locations 0042 and 0043 contain the address of the head of the queue (MSBs in 0042). Each element in the queue is two bytes long and contains the address of the next two-byte element in the queue. The last element in the queue contains zero to indicate that there is no next element.

Queues are used to store data in the order in which it will be used, or tasks in the order in which they will be executed. The queue is a first-in, first-out data structure; i.e., elements are removed from the queue in the same order in which they were entered. Operating systems place tasks in queues so that they will be executed in the proper order. I/O drivers transfer data to or from queues so that it will be transmitted or handled in the proper order. Buffers may be queued so that the next available one can easily be found and those that are released can easily be added to the available storage. Queues may also be used to link requests for storage, timing, or I/O so that they can be satisfied in the correct order.

In real applications, each element in the queue will typically contain a large amount of information or storage space besides the address required to link the element to the next one.

Sample Problems:

a.
    (0042) = 00   address of first element in queue
    (0043) = 46
    (0046) = 00   address of second element in queue
    (0047) = 4D
    (004D) = 00   end of queue
    (004E) = 00
Result: (0040) = 00   address of element removed from queue
    (0041) = 46
    (0042) = 00   address of new first element in queue
    (0043) = 4D

b.
    (0042) = 00   empty queue
    (0043) = 00
Result: (0040) = 00   no element available from queue
    (0041) = 00

Flowchart:

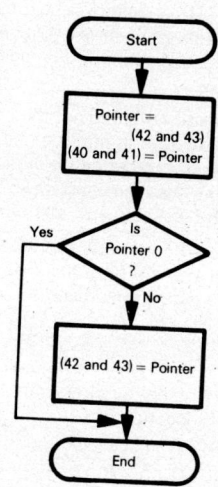

Source Program:

```
         LDX   $42    GET ADDRESS OF HEAD OF QUEUE
         STX   $40    REMOVE HEAD OF QUEUE
         BEQ   DONE   DONE IF QUEUE WAS EMPTY
         LDX   X      GET ADDRESS OF NEXT ELEMENT IN QUEUE
         STX   $42    MOVE ELEMENT TO HEAD OF QUEUE
DONE     SWI
```

Object Program:

Memory Address (Hex)	Memory Contents (Hex)	Instruction (Mnemonic)	
0000	DE 42	LDX	$42
0002	DF 40	STX	$40
0004	27 04	BEQ	DONE
0006	EE 00	LDX	X
0008	DF 42	STX	$42
000A	3F DONE	SWI	

Queuing can handle lists that are not in sequential memory locations. Each element must contain the address of the next element. Such lists allow a user to change variables or fill in definitions in a program. Extra storage is required, but elements can easily be added or deleted.

Note the use of the 6800 16-bit instruction LDX. LDX with direct or indexed addressing loads the Index register with the contents of the specified address and the next sequential address. LDX is thus ideal for handling indirect addresses, since it fetches an entire 16-bit address from memory. This is useful in queuing and in jump tables, as well as in handling 16-bit data.

One problem is that the instruction LDX X destroys the previous contents of the Index register. So, those contents must be saved somewhere if you need to backtrack or get another element from an array or table. Another Index register would be a good addition to the 6800 architecture.

It may be useful to maintain pointers to both ends of the queue, rather than just to its head. The data structure may then be used in either a first-in, first-out manner or in a last-in, first-out manner, depending on whether new elements are added to the head or to the tail. How would you change the example program so that memory locations 0044 and 0045 contain the address of the last element (tail) of the queue?

If there are no elements in the queue, the program clears memory locations 0040 and 0041. A program that requested an element from the queue would then have to check those memory locations to see if its request had been satisfied. Can you suggest other ways to provide this information?

8-Bit Sort

Purpose: Sort an array of unsigned binary numbers into descending order. The length of the array is in memory location 0041.

Sample Problem:

```
         (0040) = 06
         (0041) = 2A
         (0042) = B5
         (0043) = 60
         (0044) = 3F
         (0045) = D1
         (0046) = 19
Result:  (0041) = D1
         (0042) = B5
         (0043) = 60
         (0044) = 3F
         (0045) = 2A
         (0046) = 19
```

A simple sorting technique works as follows:

SIMPLE SORTING ALGORITHM

Step 1) Set a flag INTER.

Step 2) Examine each consecutive pair of numbers in the array. If any are out of order, exchange them and clear INTER.

Step 3) If INTER = 0 after the entire array has been examined, return to Step 1.

INTER will be cleared if any consecutive pair of numbers is out of order. Therefore, if INTER = 1 at the end of a pass through the entire array, the array is in proper order.

This sorting method is referred to as a "bubble sort". It is an easy algorithm to implement. However, other sorting techniques should be considered when sorting long lists where speed is important.

The technique operates as follows in a simple case. Let us assume that we want to sort an array into descending order; the array has four elements — 12, 03, 15, 08.

1st Iteration:

Step 1) INTER = 1

Step 2) Final order of the array is:
12
15
08
03
since the second pair (03, 15) is exchanged and so is the third pair (03, 08). INTER = 0.

2nd Iteration:

Step 1) INTER = 1

Step 2) Final order of the array is:
15
12
08
03
since the first pair (12, 15) is exchanged. INTER = 0.

3rd Iteration:

Step 1) INTER = 1

Step 2) The elements are already in order, so no exchanges are necessary and INTER remains one.

Flowchart:

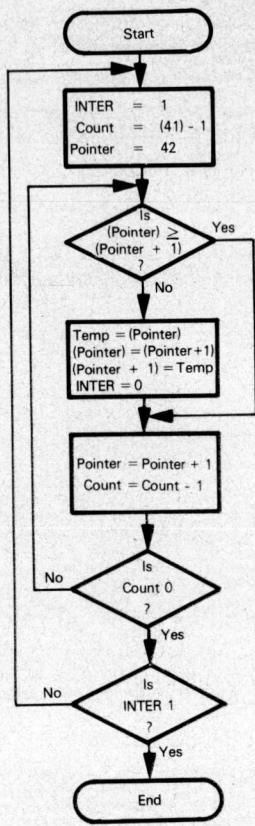

Source Program:

```
SORT    LDAA    #1          INTERCHANGE FLAG = 1
        STAA    $40
        LDAA    $41         ADJUST ARRAY LENGTH TO NUMBER OF PAIRS
        DECA
        LDX     #$42        POINT TO START OF ARRAY
PASS    LDAB    X
        CMPB    1,X         IS PAIR OF ELEMENTS IN ORDER?
        BLS     COUNT       YES, TRY NEXT PAIR
        CLR     $40         NO, CLEAR INTERCHANGE FLAG
        PSHA                SAVE ARRAY COUNTER
        LDAA    1,X         INTERCHANGE ELEMENTS IF OUT OF ORDER
        STAB    1,X
        STAA    X
        PULA                RESTORE ARRAY COUNTER
COUNT   INX
        DECA                COUNT DOWN FOR A PASS
        BNE     PASS
        TST     $40         WERE ALL ELEMENTS IN ORDER?
        BEQ     SORT        NO, GO THROUGH ARRAY AGAIN
        SWI
```

Object Program:

Memory Address (Hex)	Memory Contents (Hex)		Instruction (Mnemonic)		
0000	86	01	SORT	LDAA	#1
0002	97	40		STAA	$40
0004	96	41		LDAA	$41
0006	4A			DECA	
0007	CE	0042		LDX	#$42
000A	E6	00	PASS	LDAB	X
000C	E1	01		CMPB	1,X
000E	23	0B		BLS	COUNT
0010	7F	0040		CLR	$40
0013	36			PSHA	
0014	A6	01		LDAA	1,X
0016	E7	01		STAB	1,X
0018	A7	00		STAA	X
001A	32			PUL	A
001B	08		COUNT	INX	
001C	4A			DECA	
001D	26	EB		BNE	PASS
001F	7D	0040		TST	$40
0022	27	DC		BEQ	SORT
0024	3F			SWI	

Before starting each sorting pass, we must be careful to reinitialize the Counter, Pointer, and Interchange flag.

There are many sorting algorithms that vary widely in efficiency. Knuth describes some in the book mentioned earlier (The Art of Computer Programming, Volume III: Sorting and Searching). Sorting and searching algorithms are also discussed in K.A. Schember and J.R. Rumsey "Minimal Storage Sorting and Searching Techniques for RAM Applications, a Tutorial", Computer, June 1977, pp. 92-100.

OTHER SORTING METHODS

The program must reduce the Counter by 1, since the number of consecutive pairs is one less than the number of elements (the last element has no successor).

Indexing is convenient here since the program can refer to the elements in the pair with the same address in the Index register but different offsets.

Using an Ordered Jump Table

Purpose: Use the contents of memory location 0041 as an index to a jump table starting in memory location 0042. Each entry in the jump table contains a 16-bit address with the MSBs in the first word. The program should transfer control to the address with the appropriate index; that is, if the index is 6, the program jumps to address entry #6 in the table.

Sample Problem:

```
           (0041) = 02
           (0042) = 00
           (0043) = 48
           (0044) = 00
           (0045) = 4C
           (0046) = 00
           (0047) = 50
           (0048) = 00
           (0049) = 54
Result:    (PC)   = 0050, since that is entry #2
                   (starting from zero) in the jump table.
```

Flowchart:

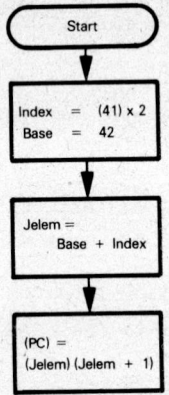

The last box results in a transfer of control to the address obtained from the table.

Source Program:

```
CLR   $40      MSBS OF JUMP TABLE ADDRESS = 0
ASL   $41      INDEX = DATA TIMES TWO
LDX   $40      GET OFFSET ADDRESS
LDX   $42,X    GET ADDRESS FROM JUMP TABLE
JMP   X        AND JUMP TO IT
```

Object Program:

Memory Address (Hex)	Memory Contents (Hex)	Instruction (Mnemonic)
0000	7F 0040	CLR $40
0003	78 0041	ASL $41
0006	DE 40	LDX $40
0008	EE 42	LDX $42,X
000A	6E 00	JMP X

Jump tables are very useful in situations where one of several routines must be selected. Such situations arise in decoding commands, selecting test programs, choosing alternate methods, or selecting an I/O configuration.

The jump table replaces a whole series of conditional jump operations. The program that accesses the jump table could be used to access several different tables merely by changing the starting address.

The data must be multiplied by two to give the correct index, since each entry in the jump table is a two-word address.

Generally, the Index register must contain the eight most significant bits of the starting address of the jump table and the data; i.e., if the jump table started at an address given by JTABU (8 MSBs) and JTABL (8 LSBs), the accessing program would be:

```
LDAA   #JTABU
STAA   $40         GET MSBS OF JUMP TABLE ADDRESS
ASL    $41         INDEX = DATA TIMES TWO
LDX    $40         GET OFFSET ADDRESS
LDX    JTABL,X     GET ADDRESS FROM JUMP TABLE
JMP    X           AND JUMP TO IT
```

The instruction LDX fetches an entire 16-bit address and places it in the Index register.

No ending operation is necessary, since JMP X transfers control to the address in the jump table.

There are additional examples of the use of jump tables in L.A. Leventhal, "Cut Your Processor's Computation Time", Electronic Design, August 16, 1977, pp. 82-89, and in Chapter 7 of J.B. Peatman, Microcomputer-Based Design, McGraw-Hill, New York, 1977.

PROBLEMS
1) Remove an Entry From a List
Purpose: Remove the contents of memory location 0040 from a list if it is present. The length of the list is in memory location 0041 and the list itself begins in memory location 0042. Move the entries below the one removed up one position and reduce the length of the list by 1.

Sample Problems:

a.
        (0040) = 6B
        (0041) = 04
        (0042) = 37
        (0043) = 61
        (0044) = 28
        (0045) = 1D
    Result: No change, since the entry is not in the list.

b.
        (0040) = 6B
        (0041) = 04
        (0042) = 37
        (0043) = 6B
        (0044) = 28
        (0045) = 1D
    Result: (0041) = 03
        (0043) = 28
        (0044) = 1D

The entry is removed from the list and the ones below it are moved up one position. The length of the list is reduced by 1.

2) Add an Entry to an Ordered List
Purpose: Place the contents of memory location 0041 in an ordered list if it is not already there. The length of the list is in memory location 0042, and the list itself begins in memory location 0043, which consists of unsigned binary numbers in increasing order. Place the new entry in the correct position in the list, adjust the elements below it down, and increase the length of the list by 1.

Sample Problems:

a.
        (0041) = 6B
        (0042) = 04
        (0043) = 37
        (0044) = 55
        (0045) = 7D
        (0046) = A1
    Result: (0042) = 05
        (0045) = 6B
        (0046) = 7D
        (0047) = A1

b.
        (0041) = 6B
        (0042) = 04
        (0043) = 37
        (0044) = 55
        (0045) = 6B
        (0046) = A1
    Result is no change, since the entry is already in the list.

3) Add an Element to a Queue

Purpose: Add the address in memory locations 0040 and 0041 (MSBs in 0040) to a queue. The address of the first element of the queue is in memory locations 0042 and 0043 (MSBs in 0042). Each element in the queue contains either the address of the next element in the queue or zero if there is no next element; all addresses are 16 bits long with the most significant bits in the first word of the element. The new element goes at the end (tail) of the queue; its address will be in the element that was at the end of the queue and it will contain zero to indicate that it is now the end of the queue.

Sample Problem:

	(0040)	=	00	new element to be added to queue
	(0041)	=	4D	
	(0042)	=	00	pointer to head of queue
	(0043)	=	46	
	(0046)	=	00	last element in queue
	(0047)	=	00	
Result:	(0046)	=	00	old last element points to
	(0047)	=	4D	new last element
	(004D)	=	00	new last element in queue
	(004E)	=	00	

How would you add an element to the queue if memory locations 0043 and 0044 contained the address of the tail of the queue?

4) 16-Bit Sort

Purpose: Sort an array of unsigned 16-bit binary numbers into descending order. The length of the array is in memory location 0040 and the array itself begins in memory location 0041. Each 16-bit number is stored with the most significant bits in the first word.

Sample Problem:

	(0040)	=	03
	(0041)	=	19
	(0042)	=	D1
	(0043)	=	3F
	(0044)	=	60
	(0045)	=	B5
	(0046)	=	2A
Result:	(0041)	=	B5
	(0042)	=	2A
	(0043)	=	3F
	(0044)	=	60
	(0045)	=	19
	(0046)	=	D1

The numbers are B52A, 3F60, and 19D1.

5) Using a Jump Table With a Key

Purpose: Use the contents of memory location 0040 as the key to a jump table starting in memory location 0041. Each entry in the jump table contains an 8-bit key value followed by a 16-bit address (MSBs in first word) to which the program should transfer control if the key is equal to that key value.

Sample Problem:

```
        (0040) = 38
        (0041) = 32
        (0042) = 00
        (0043) = 4B
        (0044) = 35
        (0045) = 00
        (0046) = 4D
        (0047) = 38
        (0048) = 00
        (0049) = 4F
Result: (PC)   = 004F, since that address corresponds
                to key value 38.
```

Chapter 10
SUBROUTINES

None of the examples that we have shown so far is typically a program all by itself. Most real programs perform a series of tasks, many of which may be the same or may be common to several different programs. We need a way to formulate these tasks once and make the formulations conveniently available both in different parts of the current program and in other programs.

The standard method is to write subroutines that perform particular tasks. The resulting sequences of instructions can be written once, tested, and then used repeatedly. They can form a subroutine library that provides documented solutions to common problems.

SUBROUTINE LIBRARY

Most microprocessors have special instructions for transferring control to subroutines and restoring control to the main program. We often refer to the special instruction that transfers control to a subroutine as Call, Jump-to-Subroutine, Jump and Mark Place, or Jump and Link. The special instruction that restores control to the main program is usually called Return. On the 6800 microprocessor, the Jump-to-Subroutine (JSR) or Branch-to-Subroutine (BSR) instruction saves the old value of the Program Counter in the RAM Stack before placing the starting address of the subroutine in the Program Counter; the Return from Subroutine (RTS) instruction gets the old value from the Stack and puts it back in the Program Counter. The effect is to transfer program control, first to the subroutine and then back to the main program. Clearly the subroutine may itself transfer control to a subroutine, and so on.

SUBROUTINE INSTRUCTIONS

In order to be really useful, a subroutine must be general. A routine that can only perform a specialized task, such as looking for a particular letter in an input string of fixed length, will not be very useful. If, on the other hand, the subroutine can look for any letter in strings of any length, it will be far more helpful. We call the data or addresses that the subroutine allows to vary "parameters". An important part of writing subroutines is deciding which variables should be parameters.

One problem is transferring the parameters to the subroutine; this process is called passing parameters. The simplest method is for the main program to place the parameters in registers. Then the subroutine can simply assume that the parameters are there. Of course, this technique is limited by the number of registers that are available. The parameters may, however, be addresses as well as data. For example, a sorting routine could begin with the starting address of an array in the Index register.

PASSING PARAMETERS

Other methods are necessary when there are more parameters. One possibility is to use the Stack. The main program can place the parameters in the Stack and the subroutine can retrieve them. The advantages of this method are that the Stack is essentially unlimited in size, and that data in the Stack is not lost even if the Stack is used again. The disadvantages are that few 6800 instructions use the Stack, and the Jump-to-Subroutine instruction also stores the return address in the Stack. Another method is to use an area of memory for parameters. The main program can place the address of the area in the Index register, and the subroutine can then retrieve the data as needed. However, this procedure is awkward if the parameters themselves are addresses.

Sometimes a subroutine must have special characteristics. A subroutine is relocatable if it can be placed anywhere in memory. **RELOCATION**
You can use such a subroutine easily regardless of the placement of other programs or the arrangement of the memory. A strictly relocatable program can use no absolute addresses; all addresses must be relative to the start of the program. A relocating loader must be used to place the program in memory; the loader will start the program after other programs and will add the starting address or relocation constant to all addresses in the program.

A subroutine is re-entrant if it can be interrupted and re-entered by the interrupting program. Re-entrancy is important for standard subroutines in an interrupt-based system. Otherwise the interrupt **RE-ENTRANT SUBROUTINE**
service routines cannot use the standard subroutines without causing errors. Microprocessor subroutines are easy to make re-entrant, since the Call instruction uses the Stack and that procedure is automatically re-entrant. The only remaining requirement is that the subroutine use the registers and Stack rather than fixed memory locations for temporary storage. This is a bit awkward, but usually can be done if necessary.

A subroutine is recursive if it calls itself. Such a subroutine clearly must also be re-entrant. However, recursive subroutines are uncommon in microprocessor applications.

Most programs consist of a main program and several subroutines. This is advantageous because you can use proven routines and debug and test the other subroutines separately. You must, however, be careful to use the subroutines properly and remember their exact effects on registers and memory locations.

SUBROUTINE DOCUMENTATION

Subroutine listings must provide enough information so that users need not examine the subroutine's internal structure. Among the necessary specifications are: **DOCUMENTING SUBROUTINES**

- A description of the purpose of the subroutine
- A list of parameters
- Registers and memory locations used
- A sample case

If these guidelines are followed, the subroutine will be easy to use.

EXAMPLES

Important note: The following examples all reserve an area of memory for the RAM Stack and save and restore the Monitor Stack Pointer. We have used address 0058 as the starting point for the Stack, and addresses 003E and 003F to store the Monitor Stack Pointer. You may prefer to use the Stack area assigned by the monitor in your microcomputer. You may also have to consistently replace the addresses that we have used with ones more suitable for your configuration. You should consult your microcomputer's manual to determine the required changes.

Hex to ASCII

Purpose: Convert the contents of Accumulator A to an ASCII character. Place the result in Accumulator A. Assume that A contains a single hexadecimal digit.

Sample Problems:

```
a.              (A)  =  0C
    Result:     (A)  =  43    'C'
b.              (A)  =  06
    Result:     (A)  =  36    '6'
```

Flowchart:

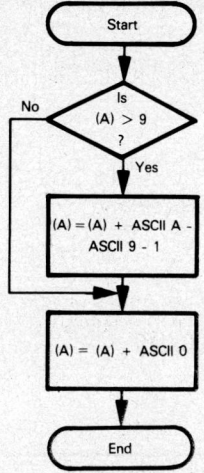

The calling program starts the Stack at memory location 0058, gets the data from memory location 0040, calls the conversion subroutine, and stores the result in memory location 0041.

```
        ORG     0
        STS     $3E       SAVE MONITOR STACK POINTER
        LDS     #$58      START STACK AT MEMORY LOCATION 0058
        LDAA    $40       GET DATA
        JSR     ASDEC     CONVERT TO ASCII
        STAA    $41       STORE RESULT
        LDS     $3E       RESTORE MONITOR STACK POINTER
        SWI
```

The subroutine converts a hexadecimal digit to ASCII.

```
        ORG     $20
ASDEC   CMPA    #9          IS DATA 9 OR LESS?
        BLS     ASCZ
        ADDA    #'A-'9-1    NO, ADD OFFSET FOR LETTERS
ASCZ    ADDA    #'0         CONVERT DATA TO ASCII
        RTS
```

Subroutine Documentation:

* **SUBROUTINE ASDEC**
*
* **PURPOSE:** ASDEC CONVERTS A HEXADECIMAL
*   DIGIT IN ACCUMULATOR A TO AN
*   ASCII DIGIT IN ACCUMULATOR A
*
* **INITIAL CONDITIONS:** HEX DIGIT IN A
*
* **FINAL CONDITIONS:** ASCII CHARACTER IN A
*
* **REGISTERS USED:** A
*
* **SAMPLE CASE**
*   INITIAL CONDITIONS: 6 IN ACCUMULATOR A
*   FINAL CONDITIONS: ASCII 6 (HEX 36)
*   IN ACCUMULATOR A

Object Program:

Memory Address (Hex)	Memory Contents (Hex)		Instruction (Mnemonic)	
0000	9F	3E		STS	$3E
0002	8E	0058		LDS	#$58
0005	96	40		LDAA	$40
0007	BD	0020		JSR	ASDEC
000A	97	41		STAA	$41
000C	9E	3E		LDS	$3E
000E	3F			SWI	
.					
.					
0020	81	09	ASDEC	CMPA	#9
0022	23	02		BLS	ASCZ
0024	8B	07		ADDA	#'A-'9-1
0026	8B	30	ASCZ	ADDA	#'0
0028	39			RTS	

The old Stack Pointer must generally be saved and restored so that SWI will transfer control back to the monitor properly. You may not have to manage the Stack Pointer if the monitor does it automatically.

The instruction LDS #$58 starts the Stack at memory location 0058. Remember that the Stack grows downward (to lower addresses). We usually place the Stack at the end of the RAM so that it does not interfere with other temporary storage.

The Jump-to-Subroutine (JSR) instruction places the subroutine starting address (0020) in the Program Counter and saves the current Program Counter (000A) in the Stack. The procedure is:

Step 1) Save LSBs of current Program Counter in Stack Pointer, decrement Stack Pointer.

Step 2) Save MSBs of current Program Counter in Stack, decrement Stack Pointer.

Note that the Stack Pointer always contains the address of the next empty location.

The result in this case is:

            (0058) = 0A
            (0057) = 00
            (SP)   = 0056

Remember that the value saved is the value of the Program Counter after the processor has fetched the entire JSR instruction from memory. Note that the address ends up in its usual 6800 form with the most significant bits in the lower of the two addresses.

The Return-from-Subroutine (RTS) instruction places the contents of the bottom (lowest) two memory locations of the Stack in the Program Counter. The procedure is:

Step 1) Increment Stack Pointer, move eight bits from Stack to MSBs of Program Counter.

Step 2) Increment Stack Pointer, move eight bits from Stack to LSBs of Program Counter.

The result in this case is:

            PC   = (0057 and 0058)
                 = 000A
            (SP) = 0058

This subroutine has a single parameter and produces a single result. An Accumulator is the obvious place to put both.

The calling program involves three steps: placing the data in the Accumulator, calling the subroutine, and storing the result. The overall initialization must also place the Stack in the appropriate area of memory.

The subroutine is re-entrant since it uses no data memory; it is relocatable since the address ASCZ is relative. BSR, Branch-to-Subroutine, would make the calling program and subroutine relocatable.

Note that the Call instruction results in the execution of four or five instructions, taking 13 or 15 clock cycles. A subroutine call may result in an extended execution time even though it appears to be a single instruction in the program.

If you plan to use the Stack for parameters, remember that JSR places the return address at the top of the Stack. You can execute INS twice to get past the return address, but you must also remember to adjust the Stack Pointer properly before returning. You can also use the instruction TSX, which transfers the Stack Pointer plus 1 (i.e., the address of the first occupied location) to the Index register. Now the parameters start at the location with offset 2 (0 and 1 contain the 16-bit return address).

Length of a String of Characters

Purpose: Determine the length of a string of ASCII characters. The starting address of the string is in the Index register. The end of the string is marked by a carriage return character (hex 0D). Place the length of the string (excluding the carriage return) in Accumulator B.

Sample Problems:

a.
```
              (X)    = 43
              (0043) = 0D
     Result:  (B)    = 00
```

b.
```
              (X)    = 0043
              (0043) = 52   'R'
              (0044) = 41   'A'
              (0045) = 54   'T'
              (0046) = 48   'H'
              (0047) = 45   'E'
              (0048) = 52   'R'
              (0049) = 0D   CR
     Result:  (B)    = 06
```

Flowchart:

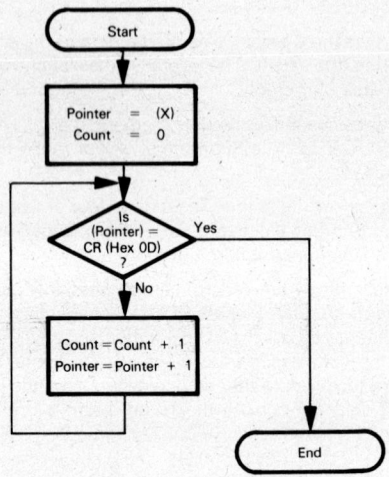

10-6

Source Program:

The calling program starts the Stack at memory location 0058, gets the starting address from memory locations 0040 and 0041, calls the string length subroutine, and stores the result in memory location 0042.

```
        ORG    0
        STS    $3E        SAVE MONITOR STACK POINTER
        LDS    #$58       START STACK AT LOCATION 0058
        LDX    $40        GET STARTING ADDRESS OF STRING
        JSR    STLEN      DETERMINE STRING LENGTH
        STAB   $42        STORE STRING LENGTH
        LDS    $3E        RESTORE MONITOR STACK POINTER
        SWI
```

The subroutine determines the length of a string of ASCII characters and places the length in Accumulator B.

```
        ORG    $20
STLEN   CLRB              STRING LENGTH = 0
        LDAA   #$0D       GET 'CR' FOR COMPARISON
CHKCR   CMPA   X          IS CHARACTER 'CR'?
        BEQ    DONE       YES, END OF STRING
        INCB              NO, ADD 1 TO STRING LENGTH
        INX
        BRA    CHKCR
DONE    RTS
```

Subroutine Documentation:

*
*SUBROUTINE STLEN
*
*PURPOSE: STLEN DETERMINES THE LENGTH
* OF A STRING (NUMBER OF CHARACTERS
* BEFORE A CARRIAGE RETURN)
*
*INITIAL CONDITIONS: STARTING ADDRESS
* OF STRING IN INDEX REGISTER
*
*FINAL CONDITIONS: NUMBER OF CHARACTERS IN B
*
*REGISTERS USED: A,B,X
*
*SAMPLE CASE
* INITIAL CONDITIONS: (X) = 42
*   (0042) = 4D, (0043) = 41, (0044) = 4E, (0045) = 0D
* FINAL CONDITIONS: (B) = 03

Object Program:

	Memory Address (Hex)	Memory Contents (Hex)			Instruction (Mnemonic)	
1) Calling program						
	0000	9F	3E		STS	$3E
	0002	8E	0058		LDS	#$58
	0005	DE	40		LDX	$40
	0007	BD	0020		JSR	STLEN
	000A	D7	42		STAB	$42
	000C	9E	3E		LDS	$3E
	000E	3F			SWI	
2) Subroutine						
	0020	5F		STLEN	CLRB	
	0021	86	0D		LDAA	#$0D
	0023	A1	00	CHKCR	CMPA	X
	0025	27	04		BEQ	DONE
	0027	5C			INCB	
	0028	08			INX	
	0029	20	F8		BRA	CHKCR
	002B	39		DONE	RTS	

This subroutine has a single parameter which is an address; the Index register is the obvious place to put it. The result is returned in Accumulator B.

The calling program involves three steps: placing the starting address of the string in the Index register, calling the subroutine, and storing the result. The overall initialization also must place the Stack in the appropriate area of memory.

The subroutine is re-entrant, since it does not use any fixed memory addresses for storage.

How would you rearrange the calling program and the subroutine so as to eliminate the unconditional jump in the subroutine?

The subroutine changes the address in the Index register as well as the contents of both Accumulators. The programmer must be aware that data stored in Accumulator A will be lost; the registers used must be part of the subroutine documentation. An alternative would be to save the old register contents in the Stack and restore them afterward, but this takes extra time and memory.

Add Even Parity to ASCII Characters

Purpose: Add even parity to a string of 7-bit ASCII characters. The length of the string is in Accumulator B and the starting address of the string is in the Index register. Place even parity in the most significant bit of each character; that is, set the most significant bit to 1 if that makes the total number of 1 bits in the word even.

Sample Problem:

```
            (B)    = 6
            (X)    = 0041
         (0041)    = 31
         (0042)    = 32
         (0043)    = 33
         (0044)    = 34
         (0045)    = 35
         (0046)    = 36
Result:  (0041)    = B1
         (0042)    = B2
         (0043)    = 33
         (0044)    = B4
         (0045)    = 35
         (0046)    = 36
```

Flowchart:

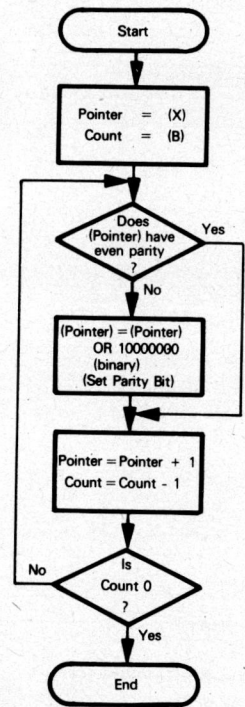

10-9

Source Program:

The calling program starts the Stack at memory location 0058, sets the starting address to 0041, gets the string length from memory location 0040, and calls the even parity subroutine.

```
        ORG     0
        STS     $3E         SAVE MONITOR STACK POINTER
        LDS     #$58        START STACK AT LOCATION 0058
        LDX     #$41        GET STARTING ADDRESS OF STRING
        LDAB    $40         GET STRING LENGTH
        JSR     EPAR        ADD EVEN PARITY TO STRING
        LDS     $3E         RESTORE MONITOR STACK POINTER
        SWI
```

The subroutine adds even parity to a string of ASCII characters.

```
        ORG     $20
EPAR    PSHB                SAVE COUNT
        CLRA                PARITY = 0
        LDAB    X           GET CHARACTER FROM STRING
CHPAR   ABA                 ADD BIT TO PARITY
        LSRB                EXAMINE NEXT BIT
        BNE     CHPAR       DONE IF REMAINING BITS ZERO
        RORA                MOVE PARITY TO CARRY
        RORB                MOVE PARITY TO MSB
        ORAB    X           ADD PARITY TO CHARACTER
        STAB    X
        INX
        PULB                RESTORE COUNT
        DECB
        BNE     EPAR
        RTS
```

Subroutine Documentation:

*
*SUBROUTINE EPAR
*
*PURPOSE: EPAR ADDS EVEN PARITY
*   TO A STRING OF 7 BIT ASCII
*   CHARACTERS
*
*INITIAL CONDITIONS: STARTING ADDRESS
*   OF STRING IN INDEX REGISTER, LENGTH
*   OF STRING IN ACCUMULATOR B
*
*FINAL CONDITIONS: EVEN PARITY IN
*   MSB OF EACH CHARACTER
*
*REGISTERS USED: A, B, X
*
*SAMPLE CASE
*   INITIAL CONDITIONS: (X) = 0041
*   (B) = 2, (0041) = 32, (0042) = 33
*   FINAL CONDITIONS: (0041) = B2, (0042) = 33
*

This subroutine has two parameters, an address, and a number. The Index register is used to pass the address, and Accumulator B is used to pass the number. No explicit results are returned, since the subroutine only affects the MSB of each character in the string.

The calling program must place the starting address of the string in the Index register and the length of the string in Accumulator B before transferring control to the subroutine.

The subroutine changes the values in Registers A, B, and X and uses the Stack for temporary storage. It is re-entrant, since it does not use any fixed addresses for temporary storage. PSHB saves the counter in the Stack, and PULB retrieves it after the parity has been calculated. When you use the Stack for temporary storage, be sure that no paths through the program accidentally leave data in the Stack.

Object Program:

	Memory Address (Hex)	Memory Contents (Hex)		Instruction (Mnemonic)	
1)	Calling program				
	0000	9F	3E	STS	$3E
	0002	8E	0058	LDS	#$58
	0005	CE	0041	LDX	#$41
	0008	D6	40	LDAB	$40
	000A	BD	0020	JSR	EPAR
	000D	9E	3E	LDS	$3E
	000F	3F		SWI	
2)	Subroutine				
	0020	37		EPAR	PSHB
	0021	4F			CLRA
	0022	E6	00		LDAB X
	0024	1B		CHPAR	ABA
	0025	54			LSRB
	0026	26	FC		BNE CHPAR
	0028	46			RORA
	0029	56			RORB
	002A	EA	00		ORAB X
	002C	E7	00		STAB X
	002E	08			INX
	002F	33			PULB
	0030	5A			DECB
	0031	26	ED		BNE EPAR
	0033	39			RTS

Pattern Match

Purpose: Compare two strings of ASCII characters to see if they are the same. The length of the strings is in Accumulator A. The starting address of one string is in memory locations 0042 and 0043; the starting address of the other is in memory locations 0044 and 0045. If the two strings match, clear Accumulator B; otherwise, set Accumulator B to FF hex.

Sample Problems:

a.
```
            (A)    = 03
          (0042)   = 00
          (0043)   = 46
          (0044)   = 00
          (0045)   = 4A
          (0046)   = 43   'C'
          (0047)   = 41   'A'
          (0048)   = 54   'T'

          (004A)   = 43   'C'
          (004B)   = 41   'A'
          (004C)   = 54   'T'
Result:     (B)    = 00, since the strings are the same.
```

b.
```
            (A)    = 03
          (0042)   = 00
          (0043)   = 46
          (0044)   = 00
          (0045)   = 4A
          (0046)   = 52   'R'
          (0047)   = 41   'A'
          (0048)   = 54   'T'

          (004A)   = 43   'C'
          (004B)   = 41   'A'
          (004C)   = 54   'T'
Result:     (B)    = FF, since the first characters differ.
```

Flowchart:

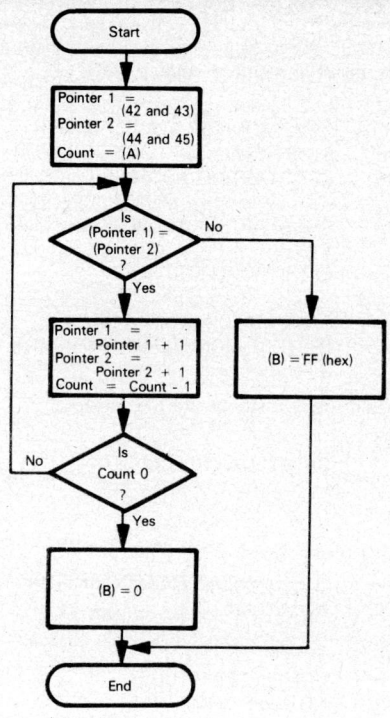

Source Program:

The calling program starts the Stack at memory location 0058, places the starting addresses of the strings in memory locations 0042 and 0043 and 0044 and 0045, respectively, gets the string length from memory location 0040, calls the pattern match subroutine, and places the result in memory location 0041.

```
        ORG     0
        STS     $3E         SAVE MONITOR STACK POINTER
        LDS     #$58        START STACK AT LOCATION 0058
        LDX     #$46        GET STARTING ADDRESS OF STRING 1
        STX     $42
        LDX     #$4A        GET STARTING ADDRESS OF STRING 2
        STX     $44
        LDAB    $40         GET STRING LENGTH
        JSR     PMTCH
        STAB    $41         SAVE MATCH INDICATOR
        LDS     $3E         RESTORE MONITOR STACK POINTER
        SWI
```

The subroutine determines if the two strings are the same.

```
        ORG     $20
PMTCH   LDX     $42         GET ELEMENT FROM STRING 1
        LDAA    X
        INX
        STX     $42
        LDX     $44
        CMPA    X           IS IT SAME AS ELEMENT IN STRING 2?
        BNE     DONE        NO, NO MATCH
        INX
        STX     $44
        DECB                COMPLETE MATCH?
        BNE     PMTCH       NO, KEEP COMPARING
        RTS                 YES, MARKER = 0 FOR MATCH
DONE    LDAB    #$FF        MARKER = FF FOR NO MATCH
        RTS
```

Subroutine Documentation:

*
*SUBROUTINE PMTCH
*
*PURPOSE: PMTCH DETERMINES IF TWO STRINGS ARE EQUIVALENT
*
*INITIAL CONDITIONS: STARTING ADDRESSES OF STRINGS IN
*   0042 AND 0043, 0044 AND 0045. LENGTH OF STRINGS IN ACCUMULATOR A
*
*FINAL CONDITIONS: 0 IN B IF STRINGS MATCH, FF IN B OTHERWISE
*
*REGISTERS USED: A, B, X
*MEMORY LOCATIONS USED: 0042 THROUGH 0045
*
*SAMPLE CASE
*   INITIAL CONDITIONS: (0042 AND 0043) = 0046, (0044 AND 0045) = 004A,
*   (A) = 2, (0046) = 36, (0047) = 39, (004A) = 36, (004B) = 39
*   FINAL CONDITIONS: (B) = 0
*

Object Program:

Memory Address (Hex)	Memory Contents (Hex)		Instruction (Mnemonic)	
1) Calling program				
0000	9E	3E	STS	$3E
0002	8E	0058	LDS	#$58
0005	CE	0046	LDX	#$46
0008	DF	42	STX	$42
000A	CE	004A	LDX	#$4A
000D	DF	44	STX	$44
000F	D6	40	LDAB	$40
0011	BD	0020	JSR	PMTCH
0014	D7	41	STAB	$41
0016	9E	3E	LDS	$3E
0018	3F		SWI	
2) Subroutine				
0020	DE	42	PMTCH LDX	$42
0022	A6	00	LDAA	X
0024	08		INX	
0025	DF	42	STX	$42
0027	DE	44	LDX	$44
0029	A1	00	CMPA	X
002B	26	07	BNE	DONE
002D	08		INX	
002E	DF	44	STX	$44
0030	5A		DECB	
0031	26	ED	BNE	PMTCH
0033	39		RTS	
0034	C6	FF	DONE LDAB	#$FF
0036	39		RTS	

This subroutine has three parameters — the two starting addresses and the length of the strings. Obviously, two starting addresses cannot fit into one Index register. Another Index register would be very convenient.

This subroutine, like the preceding ones, changes all the flags. You should generally assume that a subroutine call changes the flags unless it is specifically stated otherwise. If the main program needs the old flag values, it must save them in the Stack (the sequence TPA, PSHA will save the flags, and PULA, TAP will restore them).

The subroutine is not re-entrant, since it uses fixed addresses for storage. See if you can write a re-entrant version.

Obviously, subroutines become far more complicated as soon as the number of parameters exceeds the number of registers.

Note that this subroutine has two exit points (i.e., two RTS instructions).

Multiple-Precision Addition

Purpose: Add two multiple-word binary numbers. The length of the numbers (in words) is in Accumulator B, the starting addresses of the numbers are in memory locations 0042 and 0043 and 0044 and 0045, and the starting address of the result is in memory locations 0046 and 0047. All the numbers begin with the least significant bits.

Sample Problem:

(B)	=	04
(0042 and 0043)	=	0048
(0044 and 0045)	=	004C
(0046 and 0047)	=	0050
(0048)	=	C3
(0049)	=	A7
(004A)	=	5B
(004B)	=	2F
(004C)	=	B8
(004D)	=	35
(004E)	=	DF
(004F)	=	14
Result: (0050)	=	7B
(0051)	=	DD
(0052)	=	3A
(0053)	=	44

i.e.,
$$\begin{array}{r} 2F5BA7C3 \\ 14DF35B8 \\ \hline 443ADD7B \end{array}$$

Flowchart:

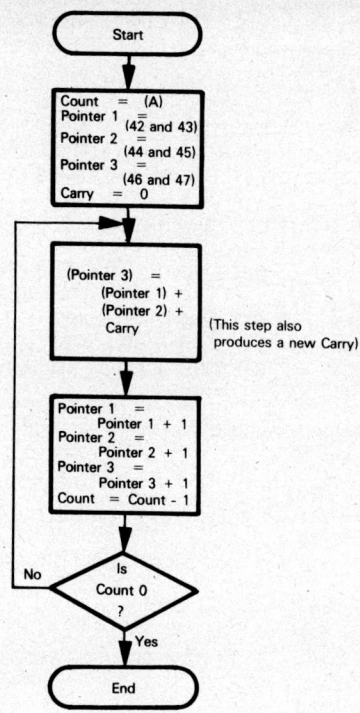

(This step also produces a new Carry)

Source Program:

The calling program starts the Stack at memory location 0058, sets the starting addresses of the various numbers to 0046, 004C, and 0050, respectively, gets the length of the numbers from memory location 0040, and calls the multiple-precision addition subroutine.

```
        ORG     0
        STS     $3E         SAVE MONITOR STACK POINTER
        LDS     #$58        START STACK AT LOCATION 0058
        LDX     #$48        GET STARTING ADDRESS OF FIRST NUMBER
        STX     $42
        LDX     #$4C        GET STARTING ADDRESS OF SECOND NUMBER
        STX     $44
        LDX     #$50        GET STARTING ADDRESS OF RESULT
        STX     $46
        LDAB    $40         GET LENGTH OF NUMBERS
        JSR     MPADD
        LDS     $3E         RESTORE MONITOR STACK POINTER
        SWI
```

The subroutine performs multiple-precision binary addition.

```
            ORG     $20
MPADD       CLC                 CLEAR CARRY TO START
MP1         LDX     $42
            LDAA    X           GET WORD FROM FIRST NUMBER
            INX
            STX     $42
            LDX     $44
            ADCA    X           ADD WORD FROM SECOND NUMBER
            INX
            STX     $44
            LDX     $46
            STAA    X           STORE RESULT
            INX
            STX     $46
            DECB
            BNE     MP1
            RTS
```

10-18

Subroutine Documentation:

*SUBROUTINE MPADD

*PURPOSE: MPADD ADDS TWO
*   MULTIPLE-WORD BINARY NUMBERS

*INITIAL CONDITIONS: STARTING ADDRESSES
*   OF NUMBERS IN 0042 AND 0043, 0044 AND 0045
*   STARTING ADDRESS OF RESULT IN
*   0046 AND 0047, LENGTH OF NUMBERS IN B

*REGISTERS USED: ALL
*MEMORY LOCATIONS USED: 0042 THROUGH 0047

*SAMPLE CASE:
*   INITIAL CONDITIONS: (0042 AND 0043) = 0048, (0044 AND
*   0045) = 004C, (0046 AND 0047) = 0050, (B) = 2, (0048) = C3,
*   (0049) = A7, (004C) = B8, (004D) = 35
*   FINAL CONDITIONS: (0050) = 7B, (0051) = DD

Object Program:

Memory Address (Hex)	Memory Contents (Hex)		Instruction (Mnemonic)	
1) Calling program				
0000	9F	3E	STS	$3E
0002	8E	0058	LDS	#$58
0005	CE	0048	LDX	#$48
0008	DF	42	STX	$42
000A	CE	004C	LDX	#$4C
000D	DF	44	STX	$44
000F	CE	0050	LDX	#$50
0012	DF	46	STX	$46
0014	D6	40	LDAB	$40
0016	BD	0020	JSR	MPADD
0019	9E	3E	LDS	$3E
001B	3F		SWI	
2) Subroutine				
0020	0C		MPADD CLC	
0021	DE	42	MP1 LDX	$42
0023	A6	00	LDAA	X
0025	08		INX	
0026	DF	42	STX	$42
0028	DE	44	LDX	$44
002A	A9	00	ADCA	X
002C	08		INX	
002D	DF	44	STX	$44
002F	DE	46	LDX	$46
0031	A7	00	STAA	X
0033	08		INX	
0034	DF	46	STX	$46
0036	5A		DECB	
0037	26	E8	BNE	MP1
0039	39		RTS	

This subroutine is not re-entrant, since it uses fixed addresses for storage. How would you write a re-entrant version?

PROBLEMS
Note that you are to write both a calling program for the sample problem and a properly documented subroutine.

1) ASCII to Hex
Purpose: Convert the contents of Accumulator A from the ASCII representation of a hexadecimal digit to the actual digit. Place the result in Accumulator A.

Sample Problems:

a.   (A) = 43 'C'
   Result: (A) = 0C

b.   (A) = 36 '6'
   Result: (A) = 06

2) Length of a Teletypewriter Message
Purpose: Determine the length of an ASCII-coded teletype message. The starting address of the string of characters in which the message is embedded is in the Index register. The message itself starts with an ASCII STX character (hex 02) and ends with ASCII ETX (hex 03). Place the length of the message (the number of characters between the STX and the ETX) in Accumulator B.

Sample Problem:

    (X) = 0041
   (0041) = 49
   (0042) = 02   STX
   (0043) = 47   'G'
   (0044) = 4F   'O'
   (0045) = 03   ETX
Result: (B) = 02

3) Check Even Parity in ASCII Characters
Purpose: Check the even parity of a string of ASCII characters. The length of the string is in Accumulator A and the starting address of the string is in the Index register. If the parity of all the characters in the string is correct, clear Accumulator B; otherwise, set Accumulator B to FF hex (all ones).

Sample Problems:

a.   (A) = 03
    (X) = 0042
  (0042) = B1
  (0043) = B2
  (0044) = 33
   Result: (B) = 00, since all the characters have even parity.

b.   (A) = 03
    (X) = 0042
  (0042) = B1
  (0043) = B6
  (0044) = 33
   Result: (B) = FF, since the character in memory location 0043 does not have even parity.

4) String Comparison

Purpose: Compare two strings of ASCII characters to see which is larger (i.e., which follows the other in 'alphabetical' ordering). The length of the strings is in Accumulator A; the starting address of string 1 is in memory locations 0042 and 0043, and the starting address of string 2 is in memory locations 0044 and 0045. If string 1 is larger than or equal to string 2, clear Accumulator B; otherwise, set Accumulator B to FF hex (all ones).

Sample Problems:

a.
- (A) = 03
- (0042 and 0043) = 0046
- (0044 and 0045) = 004A
- (0046) = 43 'C'
- (0047) = 41 'A'
- (0048) = 54 'T'

- (004A) = 42 'B'
- (004B) = 41 'A'
- (004C) = 54 'T'

Result: (B) = 00, since CAT is 'larger' than BAT.

b.
- (A) = 03
- (0042 and 0043) = 0046
- (0044 and 0045) = 004A
- (0046) = 44 'D'
- (0047) = 4F 'O'
- (0048) = 47 'G'

- (004A) = 44 'D'
- (004B) = 4F 'O'
- (004C) = 47 'G'

Result: (B) = 00, since the two strings are equal.

c.
- (A) = 03
- (0042 and 0043) = 0046
- (0044 and 0045) = 004A
- (0046) = 43 'C'
- (0047) = 41 'A'
- (0048) = 54 'T'

- (004A) = 43 'C'
- (004B) = 55 'U'
- (004C) = 54 'T'

Result: (B) = FF, since CUT is 'larger' than CAT.

5) Decimal Subtraction

Purpose: Subtract one multiple-word decimal (BCD) number from another. The length of the numbers (in bytes) is in Accumulator A and the starting addresses of the numbers are in memory locations 0042 and 0043 and 0044 and 0045. Subtract the number with the starting address in 0044 and 0045 from the one with the starting address in 0042 and 0043. The starting address of the result is in memory locations 0046 and 0047. All the numbers begin with the least significant digits. The sign of the result is returned in Accumulator B — zero if the result is positive, FF (hex) if it is negative.

Sample Problem:

```
                    (A)  = 04
         (0042 and 0043) = 0048
         (0044 and 0045) = 004C
         (0046 and 0047) = 0050
                 (0048)  = 85
                 (0049)  = 19
                 (004A)  = 70
                 (004B)  = 36
                 (004C)  = 59
                 (004D)  = 34
                 (004E)  = 66
                 (004F)  = 12
Result:          (B)     = 00 (positive result)
                 (0050)  = 26
                 (0051)  = 85
                 (0052)  = 03
                 (0053)  = 24
       i.e.,             36701985
                      -  12663459
                      +  24038526
```

Chapter 11
INPUT/OUTPUT

There are two problems in the design of input/output sections: one is how to interface peripherals to the computer and transfer data, status, and control signals; the other is how to address I/O devices so that the CPU can select a particular one for a data transfer. Clearly, the first problem is both more complex and more interesting. We will therefore discuss the interfacing of peripherals here and leave addressing to a more hardware-oriented book.

In theory, the transfer of data to or from an I/O device is similar to the transfer of data to or from memory. In fact, we can consider the memory as just another I/O device. The memory is, however, rather special for the following reasons:

1) It operates at almost the same speed as the processor.
2) It uses the same type of binary voltage signals as the CPU. The only circuits usually needed to interface the memory to the CPU are drivers, receivers, and level translators.
3) It requires no special formats or any control signals besides a Read/Write pulse.
4) It automatically latches data sent to it.
5) Its word length is the same as that of the computer.

Most I/O devices do not have such convenient features. They may operate at speeds much slower than the processor; for example, a teletypewriter can transfer only 10 characters per second, while a slow processor can transfer 10,000 characters per second. The range of speeds is also very wide — sensors may provide one reading per minute, while video displays or floppy disks may transfer 250,000 bits per second. Furthermore, I/O devices may require continuous signals (motors or thermometers), currents rather than voltages (teletypewriters), or voltages at far different levels than the signals used by the processor (gas-discharge displays). I/O devices may also require special formats, protocols, or control signals. Their word length may be much shorter or much longer than the word length of the computer. All of these variations mean that the design of I/O sections is difficult and has few general principles. Each peripheral presents its own special interfacing problem.

We may, however, provide a general description of devices and interfacing methods. We may roughly separate devices into three categories, based on their data rates:

1) Slow devices that change state no more than once per second. Changing their states typically requires milliseconds or longer. Such devices include lighted displays, switches, relays, and many mechanical sensors and actuators.
2) Medium-speed devices that transfer data at rates of 1 to 10,000 bits per second. Such devices include keyboards, printers, card readers, paper tape readers and punches, cassettes, ordinary communications lines, and many analog data acquisition systems.
3) High-speed devices that transfer data at rates of over 10,000 bits per second. Such devices include magnetic tapes, magnetic disks, high-speed line printers, high-speed communications lines, and video displays.

INTERFACING SLOW DEVICES

The interfacing of slow devices is simple. Few control signals are necessary except for multiplexing; that is, handling several devices from one port, as shown in Figures 11-1 to 11-4. Input data from slow devices need not be latched, since it remains stable for a long time interval. Output data must, of course, be latched. The only problems with input are transitions that occur while the computer is reading the data. One-shots, cross-coupled latches, or software delay routines can smooth the transitions.

A single port can handle several slow devices. Figure 11-1 shows a demultiplexer that automatically directs the next output data to the next device by counting output operations. Figure 11-2 shows a control port that provides select inputs to a demultiplexer. The data outputs here can come in any order, but an additional output instruction is necessary to change the state of the control port. Output demultiplexers are commonly used to drive several displays from the same output port. Figures 11-3 and 11-4 show the same alternatives for an input multiplexer.

Note the differences between input and output with slow devices:

1) Input data need not be latched, since the input device holds the data for an enormous length of time by computer standards. Output data must be latched, since the output device will not respond to data that is only present for a few CPU clock cycles.

2) Input transitions cause problems because of their duration; brief output transitions cause no problems because the output devices react slowly.

3) The major constraints on input are reaction time and responsiveness; the major constraints on output are response time and observability.

Medium-speed devices must be synchronized in some way to the processor clock. The CPU cannot simply treat these devices as if they held their data forever or could receive data at any time. Instead, the CPU must be able to determine when a device has new input data or is ready to receive output data. It must also have a way of telling an output device that new data is available.

HANDSHAKE

The standard unclocked procedure is the handshake. Here the sender indicates the availability of data to the receiver and transfers the data; the receiver completes the handshake by acknowledging the receipt of the data. The receiver may control the situation by initially requesting the data or by indicating its readiness to accept data; the sender then sends the data and completes the handshake by indicating that data is available. In either case, the sender knows that the transfer has been completed successfully and the receiver knows when new data is available.

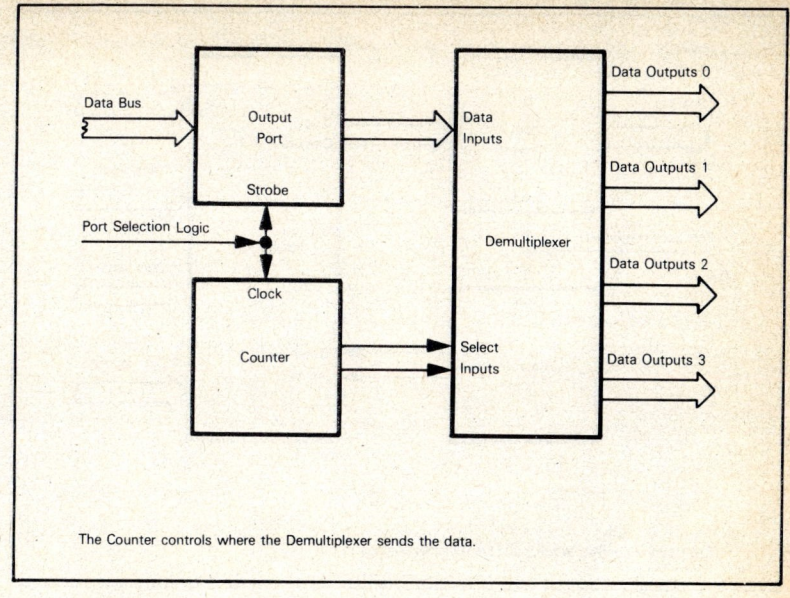

Figure 11-1. An Output Demultiplexer Controlled by a Counter

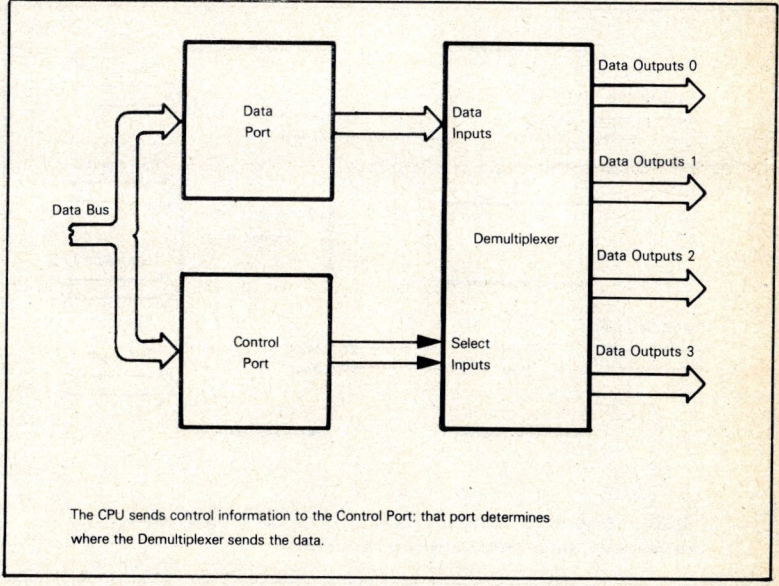

Figure 11-2. An Output Demultiplexer Controlled by a Port

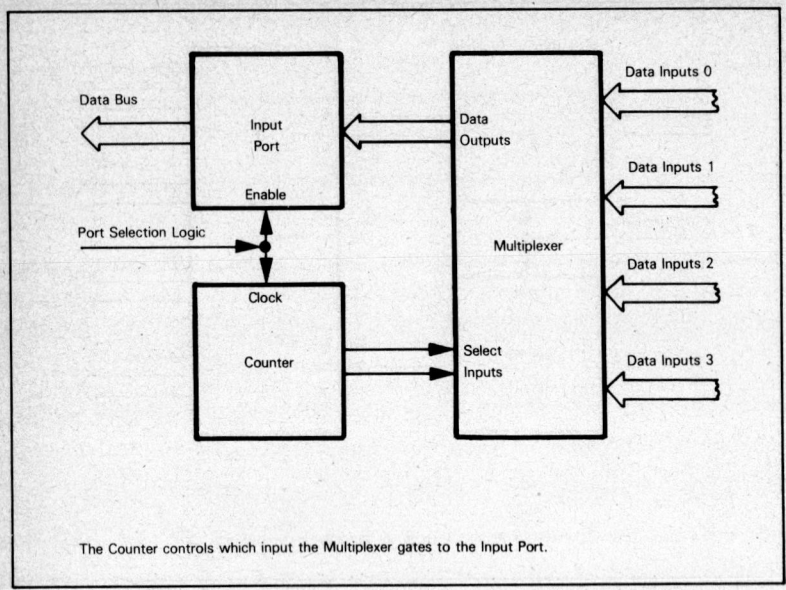

Figure 11-3. An Input Multiplexer Controlled by a Counter

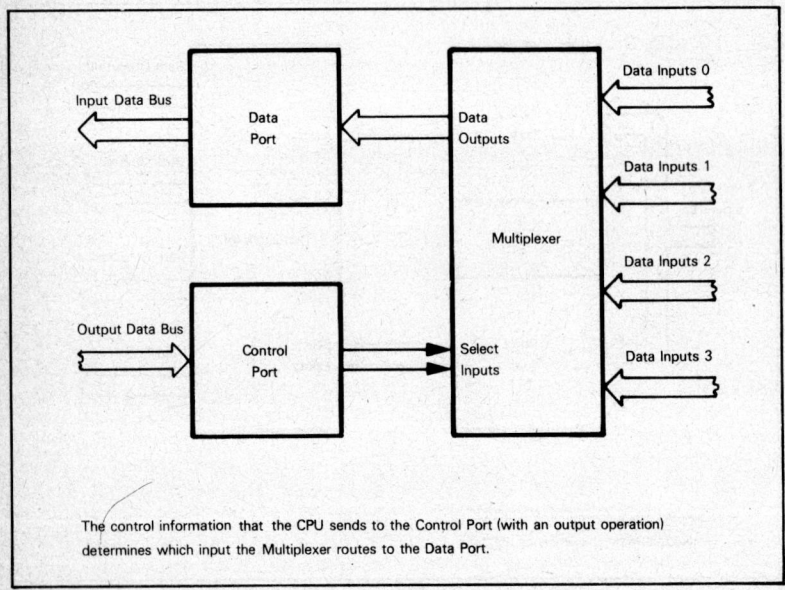

Figure 11-4. An Input Multiplexer Controlled by a Port

Figures 11-5 and 11-6 show typical input and output operations using the handshake method. The procedure whereby the CPU checks the readiness of the peripheral before transferring data is called "polling". Clearly, polling can occupy a large amount of processor time if there are many I/O devices. There are several ways of providing the handshake signals. Among these are:

- Separate dedicated I/O lines. The processor may handle these as additional I/O ports or through special lines or interrupts. The 6800 processor does not have serial I/O lines, but the 6820 Peripheral Interface Adapter does.
- Special patterns on the I/O lines. These may be single start and stop bits or entire characters or groups of characters. The patterns must be easy to distinguish from background noise or inactive states.

We often call a separate I/O line that indicates the availability of data or the occurrence of a transfer a "strobe". A strobe may, for example, clock data into a latch or fetch data from a buffer.

STROBE

Many peripherals transfer data at regular intervals; i.e., synchronously. Here the only problem is starting the process by lining up to the first input or marking the first output. In some cases, the peripheral provides a clock input from which the processor can obtain timing information.

Transmission errors are a problem with medium-speed devices. Several methods can lessen the likelihood of such errors; they include:

REDUCING TRANSMISSION ERRORS

- Sampling input data at the center of the transmission interval in order to avoid edge effects; that is, keep away from the edges where the data is changing.
- Sampling each input several times and using majority logic such as best three out of five.[1]
- Generating and checking parity; an extra bit is used that makes the number of 1 bits in the correct data even or odd.
- Using other error detecting and correcting codes such as checksums, LRC (longitudinal redundancy check), and CRC (cyclic redundancy check).[2]

High-speed devices that transfer more than 10,000 bits per second require special methods. The usual technique is to construct a special-purpose controller that transfers data directly between the memory and the I/O device. This process is called direct memory

DIRECT MEMORY ACCESS

access (DMA). The DMA controller must force the CPU off the busses, provide addresses and control signals to the memory, and transfer the data. Such a controller will be fairly complex, typically consisting of 50 to 100 chips, although LSI devices are now available. For example, the 6844 Direct Memory Access Controller for 6800-based microcomputers is described in <u>An Introduction to Microcomputers: Volume II — Some Real Products</u>. The CPU must initially load the Address and Data Counters in the controller so that the controller will know where to start and how much to transfer.

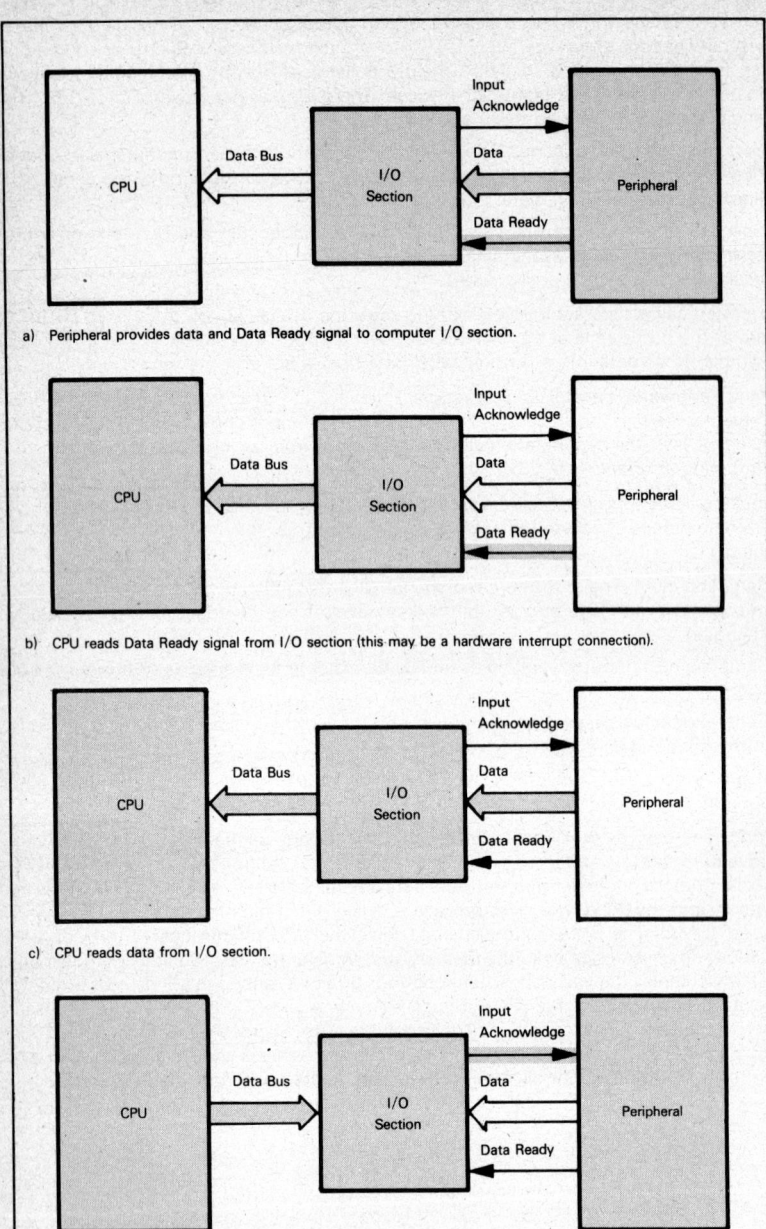

Figure 11-5. An Input Handshake

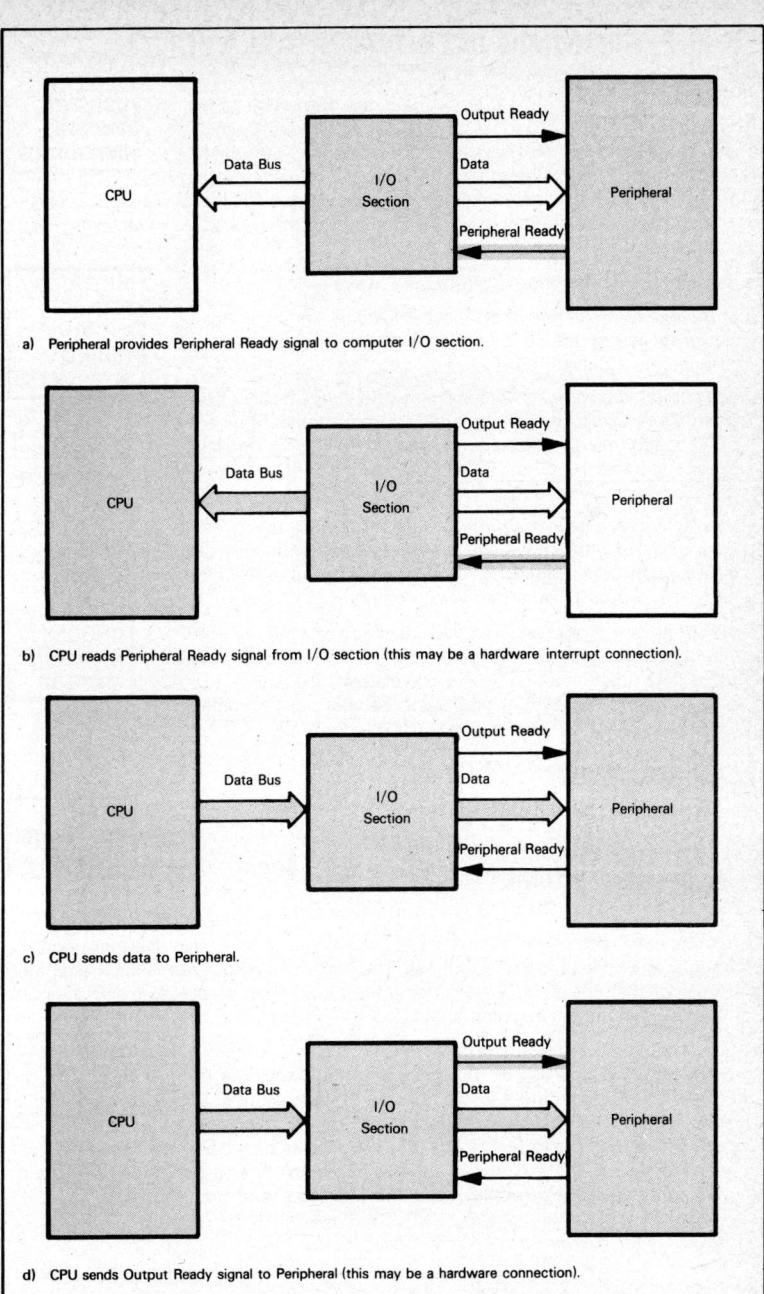

Figure 11-6. An Output Handshake

TIMING INTERVALS (DELAYS)

USES OF TIMING INTERVALS

One problem that we will face throughout the discussion of input/output is the generation of timing intervals with specific lengths. Such intervals are necessary to debounce mechanical switches (to smooth their irregular transitions), to provide pulses with specified lengths and frequencies for displays, and to provide timing for devices that transfer data regularly (for example, a teletypewriter that sends or receives one bit every 9.1 ms).

We can produce timing intervals in several ways:

METHODS FOR PRODUCING TIMING INTERVALS

1) In hardware with one-shots or monostable multivibrators. These devices produce a single pulse of fixed duration in response to a pulse input.

2) In a combination of hardware and software with a flexible programmable timer such as the 6840 Programmable Timer for 6800-based microcomputers, as described in <u>An Introduction to Microcomputers: Volume II — Some Real Products</u>. The 6840 can provide timing intervals of various lengths with a variety of starting and ending conditions.[3]

3) In software with delay routines. These routines use the processor as a counter. This is possible since the processor has a stable clock reference, but it clearly under-utilizes the processor. However, delay routines require no additional hardware and often use processor time that would otherwise be wasted.

CHOOSING A TIMING METHOD

The choice among these three methods depends on your application. The software method is inexpensive but may overburden the processor. The programmable timers are relatively expensive, but are easy to interface and may be able to handle many complex timing tasks.

DELAY ROUTINES

A simple delay routine works as follows:

BASIC SOFTWARE DELAY

Step 1) Load a register with a specified value.

Step 2) Decrement the register.

Step 3) If the result of Step 2 is not zero, repeat Step 2.

This routine does nothing except use time. The amount of time used depends upon the execution time of the various instructions. The maximum length of the delay is limited by the size of the register; however, the entire routine can be placed inside a similar routine that uses another register, and so on.

TRANSPARENT DELAY ROUTINE

The first of the following examples uses the two Accumulators to provide delays as long as 255 ms. You may wish to save the contents of the Accumulators in the Stack and restore them afterward so that the routine is "transparent" to the calling program. The second example uses the Index register to provide a 1 ms delay. Here you may want to save the Index register in specified memory locations, since there is no easy way to transfer the contents of the Index register to or from the Stack.

EXAMPLES
Delay Program Using Accumulators

Purpose: The program provides a delay of 1 ms times the contents of Accumulator B.

Flowchart:

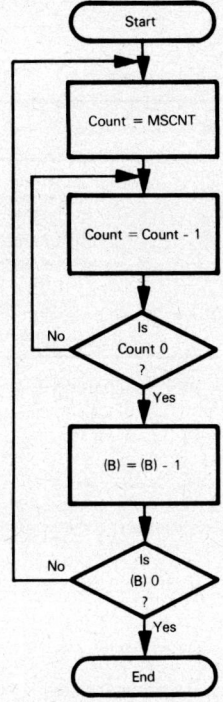

The value of MSCNT depends on the speed of the CPU and the memory cycle.

Source Program:

```
DELAY   LDAA    #MSCNT    GET COUNT FOR 1 MS DELAY
DELAY1  DECA              COUNT = COUNT-1
        BNE     DELAY1    CONTINUE UNTIL COUNT=0
        DECB              NUMBER OF MS = NUMBER OF MS-1
        BNE     DELAY     CONTINUE UNTIL NUMBER OF MS=0
        RTS
```

Object Program:

Memory Address (Hex)	Memory Contents (Hex)		Instruction (Mnemonic)		
0030	86	MSCNT	DELAY	LDAA	#MSCNT
0032	4A		DELAY1	DECA	
0033	26	FD		BNE	DELAY1
0035	5A			DECB	
0036	26	F8		BNE	DELAY
0038	39			RTS	

Time Budget:

Instruction		Number of Times Executed
LDAA	#MSCNT	(B)
DECA		(B) X MSCNT
BNE	DLY1	(B) X MSCNT
DECB		(B)
BNE	DELAY	(B)
RTS		1

The total time used should be (B) x 1 ms. If the memory is operating at full speed, the instructions require the following numbers of clock cycles:

LDAA #   2
DECA or DECB   2
BNE   4

Ignoring the JSR or BSR and RTS instructions (which only occur once), the program takes

$$(B) \times (8 + 6 \times MSCNT)$$

clock cycles. So, to make the delay 1 ms,

$$8 + 6 \times MSCNT = N_C$$

where N_C is the number of clock cycles per millisecond. At the standard 1 MHz 6800 clock rate, $N_C = 1000$, so

$$6 \times MSCNT = 992$$

> MSCNT = 165 (hex A5) at a
> 6800 clock rate
> of 1 MHz

Delay Program Using Index Register

Purpose: This program uses the Index register to provide a delay of 1 ms.

```
6800
DELAY LOOP
CONSTANT
```

Flowchart:

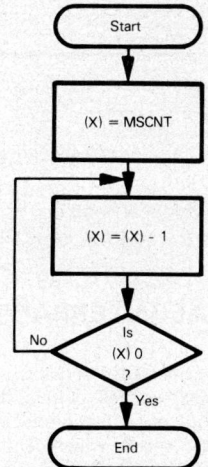

The value of MSCNT depends on the execution time of the instructions in the program.

Source Program:

```
DELAY   LDX     #MSCNT    GET COUNT FOR 1 MS DELAY
DLY     DEX               COUNT = COUNT-1
        BNE     DLY       CONTINUE UNTIL COUNT = 0
        RTS
```

Object Program:

Memory Address (Hex)	Memory Contents (Hex)		Instruction (Mnemonic)		
0030	CE	MSCNT	DELAY	LDX	#MSCNT
0033	09		DLY	DEX	
0034	26	FD		BNE	DLY
0036	39			RTS	

Remember that MSCNT is a 16-bit number.

Time Budget:

Instruction	Number of Times Executed	Number of Clock Cycles
LDX #	1	3
DEX	MSCNT	4
BNE	MSCNT	4

Ignoring the JSR or BSR and RTS instructions, the program takes

$$3 + 8 \times MSCNT = N_C$$

where N_C is the number of clock cycles per millisecond. At a 1 MHz clock rate, $N_C = 1000$, so

$$8 \times MSCNT = 997$$
$$MSCNT = 124 \text{ (hex 007C)}$$

THE 6820 PERIPHERAL INTERFACE ADAPTER (PIA)

The key element in most 6800 input/output sections is the 6820 Peripheral Interface Adapter, or PIA. This device combines latches, buffers, flip-flops, and other logic circuits required by handshaking and other simple interfacing techniques. The PIA contains many logic connections, certain sets of which can be selected according to the contents of two programmable registers, the Data Direction register and the Control register.

Figure 11-7 is the block diagram of a PIA. The device contains two nearly identical 8-bit ports — A, which is usually an input port, and B, which is usually an output port. Each port contains:

- A Data or Peripheral register that holds either input or output data. This register is latched when used for output but unlatched when used for input. **PIA REGISTERS AND CONTROL LINES**
- A Data Direction register. The bits in this register determine whether the corresponding data register bits (and pins) are inputs (0) or outputs (1).
- A Control register that holds the status signals required for handshaking, and other bits that select logic connections within the PIA.
- Two control lines that are configured by the control registers. These lines can be used for the handshaking signals shown in Figures 11-5 and 11-6.

The meanings of the bits in the Data Direction and Control registers are related to the underlying hardware and are entirely arbitrary as far as the assembly language programmer is concerned. You must either memorize them or look them up in the appropriate tables (Tables 11-2 through 11-6).

Each PIA occupies four memory addresses. The RS (register select) lines choose one of the four registers, as described in Table 11-1. Since there are six registers (two peripheral, two data direction, and two control) in each PIA, one further bit is needed for addressing. Bit 2 of each control register determines whether the other address on that side refers to the Data Direction register (0) or to the Peripheral register (1). This sharing of an external address **PIA ADDRESSES**

means that:
1) A program must change the bit in the Control register in order to use the register that is not currently being addressed.
2) The programmer must know the contents of the Control register in order to know which register is being addressed. RESET clears the Control register and thus addresses the Data Direction register.

Table 11-1 also shows a convenient way to address the various registers in the PIA. If, as is usually the case, the register select lines are tied to the corresponding least significant address lines (RS0 to A0 and RS1 to A1), the programmer can place the address of Peripheral Register A in the Index register and refer to all the other registers with appropriate offsets.

Table 11-1. Addressing 6820 Internal Registers

Address Lines		Control Register Bit		Register Selected	Offset Address
RS1	RS0	CRA-2	CRB-2		(Index Register) = Address of Peripheral Register A
0	0	1	X	Peripheral Register A	0
0	0	0	X	Data Direction Register A	0
0	1	X	X	Control Register A	1
1	0	X	1	Peripheral Register B	2
1	0	X	0	Data Direction Register B	2
1	1	X	X	Control Register B	3

X = Either 0 or 1

Table 11-2. Organization of the PIA Control Registers (Courtesy of Motorola)

	7	6	5	4	3	2	1	0
CRA	IRQA1	IRQA2	CA2 Control			DDRA Access	CA1 Control	
	7	6	5	4	3	2	1	0
CRB	IRQB1	IRQB2	CB2 Control			DDRB Access	CB1 Control	

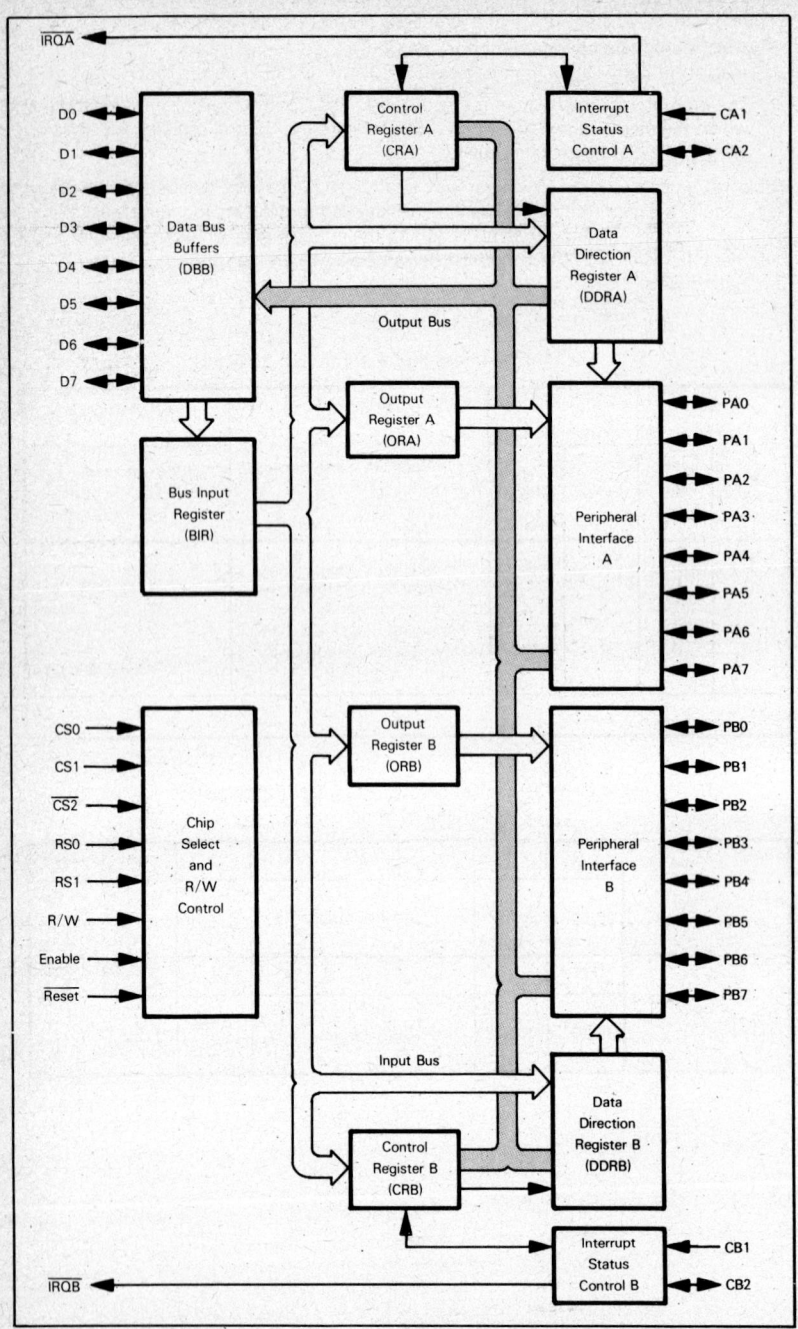

Figure 11-7. Block Diagram of the 6820 Peripheral Interface Adapter

PIA CONTROL REGISTER

Table 11-2 shows the organization of the PIA Control registers. We may describe the general purpose of each bit as follows:

PIA CONTROL REGISTER BITS

Bit 7: status bit set by transitions on control line 1 and cleared by reading the Peripheral (Data) register

Bit 6: same as bit 7 except set by transitions on control line 2

Bit 5: determines whether control line 2 is an input (0) or output (1)

Bit 4: Control line 2 input: determines whether bit 6 is set by high-to-low transitions (0) or low-to-high transitions (1) on control line 2
Control line 2 output: determines whether control line 2 is a pulse (0) or a level (1)

Bit 3: Control line 2 input: if 1, enables interrupt output from bit 6
Control line 2 output: determines ending condition for pulse (0 = handshake acknowledgment lasting until next transition on control line 1, 1 = brief strobe lasting one clock cycle) or value of level

Bit 2: selects Data Direction register (0) or Data register (1)

Bit 1: determines whether bit 7 is set by high-to-low transitions (0) or low-to-high transitions (1) on control line 1

Bit 0: if 1, enables interrupt output from bit 7 of Control register

Tables 11-3 through 11-6 describe the bits in more detail. Since E is normally tied to the Φ2 clock, you can interpret "E" pulse as "clock pulse".

Table 11-3. Control of Interrupt Inputs CA1 and CB1

CRA-1 (CRB-1)	CRA-0 (CRB-0)	Interrupt Input CA1 (CB1)	Interrupt Flag CRA-7 (CRB-7)	MPU Interrupt Request $\overline{IRQA}$ ($\overline{IRQB}$)
0	0	↓ Active	Set high on ↓ of CA1 (CB1)	Disabled — $\overline{IRQ}$ remains high
0	1	↓ Active	Set high on ↓ of CA1 (CB1)	Goes low when the interrupt flag bit CRA-7 (CRB-7) goes high
1	0	↑ Active	Set high on ↑ of CA1 (CB1)	Disabled — $\overline{IRQ}$ remains high
1	1	↑ Active	Set high on ↑ of CA1 (CB1)	Goes low when the interrupt flag bit CRA-7 (CRB-7) goes high

Notes:
1. ↑ indicates positive transition (low to high)
2. ↓ indicates negative transition (high to low)
3. The Interrupt flag bit CRA-7 is cleared by an MPU Read of the A Data Register, and CRB-7 is ceared by an MPU Read of the B Data Register.
4. If CRA-0 (CRB-0) is low when an interrupt occurs (Interrupt disabled) and is later brought high, $\overline{IRQA}$ ($\overline{IRQB}$) occurs after CRA-0 (CRB-0) is written to a "one".

Table 11-4. Control of CA2 and CB2 as Interrupt Inputs
(CRA5 (CRB5) is low)

CRA-5 (CRB-5)	CRA-4 (CRB-4)	CRA-3 (CRB-3)	Interrupt Input CA2 (CB2)	Interrupt Flag CRA-6 (CRB-6)	MPU Interrupt Request $\overline{IRQA}$ ($\overline{IRQB}$)
0	0	0	↓ Active	Set high on ↓ of CA2 (CB2)	Disabled — $\overline{IRQ}$ remains high
0	0	1	↓ Active	Set high on ↓ of CA2 (CB2)	Goes low when the interrupt flag bit CRA-6 (CRB-6) goes high
0	1	0	↑ Active	Set high on ↑ of CA2 (CB2)	Disabled — $\overline{IRQ}$ remains high
0	1	1	↑ Active	Set high on ↑ of CA2 (CB2)	Goes low when the interrupt flag bit CRA-6 (CRB-6) goes high

Notes:
1. ↑ indicates positive transition (low to high)
2. ↓ indicates negative transition (high to low)
3. The Interrupt flag bit CRA-6 is cleared by an MPU Read of the A Data Register and CRB-6 is cleared by an MPU Read of the B Data Register.
4. If CRA-3 (CRB-3) is low when an interrupt occurs (Interrupt disabled) and is later brought high, $\overline{IRQA}$ ($\overline{IRQB}$) occurs after CRA-3 (CRB-3) is written to a "one".

CONFIGURING THE PIA

The program must select the logic connections in the PIA before using it. This selection (or configuration) is usually part of the startup routine. The steps in the configuration are:

STEPS IN CONFIGURING A PIA

1) Address the Data Direction register by clearing bit 2 of the Control register. Since the Reset signal clears all the internal registers, this step is unnecessary in the overall startup routine.
2) Establish the directions of the I/O pins by loading the Data Direction register.
3) Select the required logic connections in the PIA by loading the Control register. Set bit 2 of the Control register so as to address the Data register.

Step 1 can be performed as follows:

```
        CLR     PIACR           CLEAR PIA CONTROL REGISTER
```

or

```
        LDAA    PIACR
        ANDA    #%11111011      SELECT DATA DIRECTION REGISTER
        STAA    PIACR
```

Table 11-5. Control of CB2 as an Output
(CRB5 is high)

CRB-5	CRB-4	CRB-3	CB2 Cleared	CB2 Set
1	0	0	Low on the positive transition of the first E pulse following an MPU Write "B" Data Register operation.	High when the interrupt flag bit CRB-7 is set by an active transition of the CB1 signal.
1	0	1	Low on the positive transition of the first E pulse after an MPU Write "B" Data Register operation.	High on the positive edge of the first "E" pulse following an "E" pulse which occurred while the part was deselected.
1	1	0	Low when CRB-3 goes low as a result of an MPU Write in Control Register "B".	Always low as long as CRB-3 is low. Will go high on an MPU Write in Control Register "B" that changes CRB-3 to "one".
1	1	1	Always high as long as CRB-3 is high. Will be cleared when an MPU Write Control Register "B" results in clearing CRB-3 to "zero".	High when CRB-3 goes high as a result of an MPU Write into Control Register "B".

Table 11-6. Control of CA2 as an Output
(CRA5 is high)

CRA-5	CRA-4	CRA-3	CA2 Cleared	CA2 Set
1	0	0	Low on negative transition of E after an MPU Read "A" Data operation.	High when the interrupt flag bit CRA-7 is set by an active transition of the CA1 signal.
1	0	1	Low on negative transition of E after an MPU Read "A" Data operation.	High on the negative edge of the first "E" pulse which occurs during a deselect.
1	1	0	Low when CRA-3 goes low as a result of an MPU Write to Control Register "A".	Always low as long as CRA-3 is low. Will go high on an MPU Write to Control Register "A" that changes CRA-3 to "one".
1	1	1	Always high as long as CRA-3 is high. Will be cleared on an MPU Write to Control Register "A" that clears CRA-3 to a "zero".	High when CRA-3 goes high as a result of an MPU Write to Control Register "A".

Once the program has performed Step 1, Step 2 is simply a matter of clearing each input bit and setting each output bit in the Data Direction register. Some simple examples are:

CLR	PIADDR	ALL LINES INPUTS
LDAA	#$FF	ALL LINES OUTPUTS
STAA	PIADDR	
LDAA	#$F0	MAKE LINES 4-7 OUTPUTS, 0-3 INPUTS
STAA	PIADDR	

Step 3 is clearly the difficult part of the configuration, since it involves selecting the logic connections in the PIA. Some points to remember are:

1) Bits 6 and 7 of the Control register are set by transitions on the control lines and are cleared by reading the Data register. You <u>cannot</u> change these bits by writing data into the Control register.
2) Bit 2 of the Control register must be set to address the Data register.
3) Bit 1 determines which pulse edge will set bit 7. Bit 1 is 0 for a high-to-low transition; bit 1 is 1 for a low-to-high transition.
4) Bit 0 is the interrupt enable for control line 1. Remember that it must be set to enable interrupts, unlike the 6800 interrupt bit, which must be cleared to enable interrupts. Chapter 12 describes interrupts in more detail.
5) Bit 5 must be set if control line 2 is to be an output. Bits 3 and 4 then determine how control line 2 works. Remember that sides A and B differ, since side A can only produce a read strobe while side B can only produce a write strobe. Once the strobe option has been selected, the strobes automatically follow each reading of Data Register A or writing of Data Register B. You must configure each side of each PIA in the startup program.

EXAMPLES OF PIA CONFIGURATION

1) A simple input port with no control lines:

CLR	PIACR	CLEAR OUT CONTROL REGISTER
CLR	PIADDR	ALL LINES INPUTS
LDAA	#%00000100	
STAA	PIACR	SELECT DATA REGISTER

PIA CONFIGURATION EXAMPLES

Bit 2 of the Control register must be set in order to address the Data register. The same sequence can be used if a high-to-low edge on control line 1 indicates Data Ready or Peripheral Ready.

2) A simple output port with no control lines:

CLR	PIACR	CLEAR OUT CONTROL REGISTER
LDAA	#$FF	ALL LINES OUTPUTS
STAA	PIADDR	
LDAA	#%00000100	
STAA	PIACR	SELECT DATA REGISTER

3) An input port with a low-to-high transition:

CLR	PIACR	CLEAR OUT CONTROL REGISTER
CLR	PIADDR	ALL LINES INPUTS
LDAA	#%00000110	STROBE ACTIVE LOW-TO-HIGH
STAA	PIACR	SELECT DATA REGISTER

Bit 1 = 1 to recognize low-to-high transitions on control line 1.

4) An output port with a brief Data Ready strobe:

```
CLR     PIACR           CLEAR OUT CONTROL REGISTER
LDAA    #$FF            ALL LINES OUTPUTS
STAA    PIADDR
LDAA    #%00101100      CONTROL LINE 2 = BRIEF STROBE
STAA    PIACR           SELECT DATA REGISTER
```

Bit 5 = 1 to make control line 2 an output, bit 4 = 1 to make it a pulse, and bit 2 = 1 to make it a brief active-low strobe (one clock period in length). The strobe will automatically follow each instruction that writes data into the B side of the PIA; for example, the instruction

```
STAA    PIADRB
```

will both transfer data and cause a strobe. However, the A side will produce a strobe only after a read operation. The sequence

```
STAA    PIADRA          WRITE DATA
LDAA    PIADRA          PRODUCE STROBE
```

will both transfer data and cause a strobe. The LDAA instruction is a "dummy read"; it has no effect other than to cause the strobe (and waste some time). Other instructions besides LDAA could also be used (name some of them).

5) An input port with a handshake Input Acknowledge strobe:

```
CLR     PIACR           CLEAR OUT CONTROL REGISTER
CLR     PIADDR          ALL LINES INPUTS
LDAA    #%00100100      CONTROL LINE 2 = HANDSHAKE ACKNOWLEDGE
STAA    PIACR           SELECT DATA REGISTER
```

Bit 5 = 1 to make control line 2 an output, bit 4 = 0 to make it a pulse, and bit 3 = 0 to make it an active-low acknowledgment that remains low until the next active transition on control line 1. The acknowledgment will automatically follow a read operation on the A side of the PIA; for example, the instruction

```
LDAA    PIADRA
```

will both read data and cause the acknowledgment. However, the B side will produce an acknowledgment only after a write operation. The sequence

```
LDAA    PIADRB          READ DATA
STAA    PIADRB          PRODUCE ACKNOWLEDGMENT
```

will both read data and produce an acknowledgment. The STAA instruction is a "dummy write"; it has no effect other than to cause the acknowledgment (and waste some time). Note that the order of the sequence is reversed from the previous example.

6) An output port with a latched zero control bit (latched serial output or level output):

```
CLR    PIACR           CLEAR OUT CONTROL REGISTER
LDAA   #$FF            ALL LINE OUTPUTS
STAA   PIADDR
LDAA   #%00110100      CONTROL LINE 2 = LATCHED ZERO
STAA   PIACR
```

Bit 5 = 1 to make control line 2 an output, bit 4 = 1 to make it a level or latched bit, and bit 3 = 0 to make the level zero. This bit is not affected by operations on the Data register; its value can be changed by changing the value of bit 3; i.e.,

```
LDAA   PIACR
ORAA   #%00001000      MAKE LEVEL ONE
STAA   PIACR

LDAA   PIACR
ANDA   #%11110111      MAKE LEVEL ZERO
STAA   PIACR
```

You can use this configuration to produce active-high strobes or to provide pulses with software-controlled lengths.

USING THE PIA TO TRANSFER DATA

Once the PIA has been configured, you may use its data registers like any other memory locations. The simplest instructions for data transfer are:

PIA INPUT/OUTPUT

Load Accumulator transfers 8 bits of data from the specified input pins to an Accumulator.

Store Accumulator transfers 8 bits of data from an Accumulator to the specified output pins.

You must be careful in situations where input and output ports do not behave like memory locations. For example, it often makes no sense to write data into input ports or read data from output ports. Be particularly careful if the input port is not latched or if the output port is not buffered.

Other instructions that transfer data to or from memory can also serve as I/O instructions. Typical examples are:

Clear places zeros on a set of output pins.

Test sets the flags according to the values of a set of input pins.

Compare sets the flags as if the values of a set of input pins had been subtracted from the contents of an Accumulator.

Here also you must be aware of the physical limitations of the I/O ports. Be particularly careful of instructions like Test, Shift, Complement, Increment, and Decrement, which involve both read and write cycles.

We cannot overemphasize the importance of careful documentation. Often, complex I/O transfers can be concealed in instructions with no obvious functions. You must describe the purposes of such instructions carefully. For example, one could easily be tempted to remove the dummy read and write operations mentioned earlier since they do not appear to accomplish anything.

Bit 7 of the PIA Control register often serves as a status bit, such as
Data Ready or Peripheral Ready. You can check its value with
either of the following sequences:

    LDAA   PIACR   IS READY FLAG 1?
    BMI   DEVRDY   YES, DEVICE READY
    TST   PIACR   IS READY FLAG 1?
    BMI   DEVRDY   YES, DEVICE READY

Note that you should not use the shift instructions, since they will change the contents of the Control register (why?). The following program will wait for the ready flag to go high:

WAITR   LDAA   PIACR   IS READY FLAG 1?
        BPL   WAITR   NO, WAIT

How would you change these programs so that they examine bit 6 instead of bit 7?

The only way to clear bit 7 (or bit 6) is to read the Data register. A dummy read will be necessary if a read operation is not normally part of the reaction to the bit being set. If the port is used for output, the sequence

    STAA   PIADR   SEND DATA
    LDAA   PIADR   CLEAR READ FLAG

will do the job. Note that here the dummy read is necessary on either side of the PIA. The Test instruction can also clear the strobe without changing anything except the condition codes. Be particularly careful in cases where the CPU is not ready for input data or has no output data to send.

EXAMPLES
A Pushbutton Switch

Purpose: To interface a single pushbutton switch to a 6800 microprocessor. The pushbutton is a mechanical switch that provides a single contact closure logic level while pressed.

Figure 11-8 shows the circuitry required to interface the pushbutton. It uses one bit of a 6820 PIA, which acts as a buffer; no latch is needed since the pushbutton remains closed for many CPU clock cycles. Pressing the button grounds the PIA input bit. The pullup resistor ensures that the input bit is one if the button is not being pressed.

Programming Examples:

We will perform two tasks with this circuit. They are:

1) Set a memory location based on the state of the button.
2) Count the number of times that the button is pressed.

Task 1: Set memory location 0040 to one if the button is not being pressed, and to zero if it is being pressed.

Sample Cases:

1) Button open (not pressed)
   Result: (0040) = 01

2) Button closed (pressed)
   Result: (0040) = 00

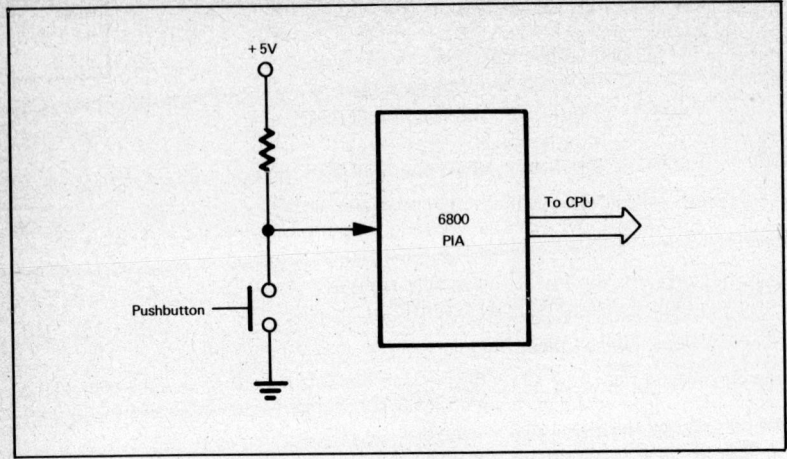

Figure 11-8. A Pushbutton Circuit

Flowchart:

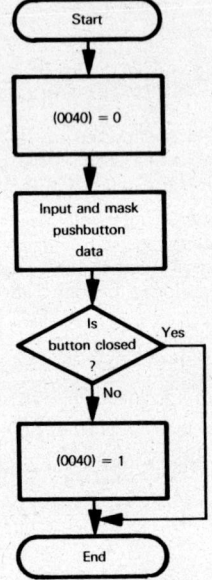

Source Program:

```
        CLR    PIACRA          CLEAR OUT CONTROL REGISTER
        CLR    PIADDRA         ALL LINES INPUTS
        LDAA   #%00000100      SELECT DATA REGISTER
        STAA   PIACRA
        CLR    $40             MARKER = 0
        LDAA   PIADRA          READ BUTTON POSITION
        ANDA   #MASK           IS BUTTON CLOSED (0)?
        BEQ    DONE            YES, DONE
        INC    $40             NO, MARKER = 1
DONE    SWI
```

Object Program:

Memory Address (Hex)	Memory Contents (Hex)		Instruction (Mnemonic)	
0000	7F	PIACRA	CLR	PIACRA
0003	7F	PIADDRA	CLR	PIADDRA
0006	86	04	LDAA	#%00000100
0008	B7	PIACRA	STAA	PIACRA
000B	7F	0040	CLR	$40
000E	B6	PIADRA	LDAA	PIADRA
0011	84	MASK	ANDA	#MASK
0013	27	03	BEQ	DONE
0015	7C	0040	INC	$40
0018	3F		DONE SWI	

The addresses PIACRA, PIADDRA and PIADRA depend on how the PIA is connected in your microcomputer. The PIA control lines are not used in this example.

MASK depends on the bit to which the pushbutton is connected; it has a one in the button position and zeros elsewhere.

Button Position (Bit Number)	Mask	
	Binary	Hex
0	00000001	01
1	00000010	02
2	00000100	04
3	00001000	08
4	00010000	10
5	00100000	20
6	01000000	40
7	10000000	80

If the button is attached to data bit 7, no masking instruction is necessary to determine the button's state:

```
        LDAA   PIADRA          READ BUTTON POSITION
        BPL    DONE            DONE IF BUTTON CLOSED
```

The TST instruction could also be used.

If the button is attached to bits 0 or 6, a shift instruction can determine the button's state, as follows:

BIT 6
```
   ASL    PIADRA    IS BUTTON CLOSED (0)?
   BPL    DONE      YES, DONE
```

BIT 7
```
   LSR    PIADRA    IS BUTTON CLOSED (0)?
   BCC    DONE      YES, DONE
```

ROL (bit 6) or ROR (bit 0) could also be used. Do the contents of the PIA Data register actually change? Explain your answer.

Task 2: Count number of button closures in memory location 0040.

Sample Case:

Pressing the button ten times after the start of the program should give

$$(0040) = 0A$$

Note: In order to count the number of times that the button has been pressed, we must be sure that each closure causes a single transition. However, each closure of a mechanical pushbutton does not produce a single transition, because the mechanical contacts bounce back and forth before settling into their final positions. We can use a one-shot to eliminate the bounce or we can handle it in software.

SWITCH BOUNCE

The program can debounce the pushbutton by waiting after it finds a closure. The required delay is called the debouncing time and is part of the specifications of the pushbutton. It is typically a few milliseconds long. The program should not examine the pushbutton during this period because it might mistake the bounces for new closures. The program may either enter a delay routine like the one described previously or may simply perform other tasks for the specified amount of time.

DEBOUNCING IN SOFTWARE

Even after debouncing, the program must still wait for the present closure to end before looking for a new closure. This procedure avoids double counting. The following program uses a software delay of 10 ms to debounce the pushbutton. You may want to try varying the delay or eliminating it entirely in order to see what happens. To run this program, you must also enter the delay subroutine into memory starting at location 0030.

Flowchart:

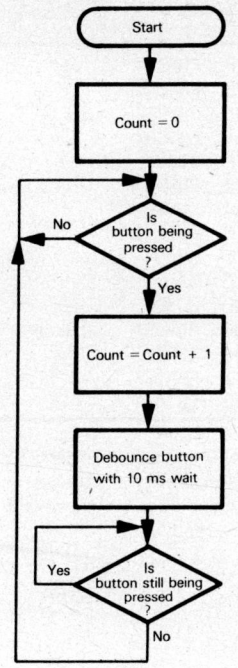

Source Program:

```
        CLR    PIACRA           CLEAR OUT CONTROL REGISTER
        CLR    PIADDRA          ALL LINES INPUTS
        LDAA   #%00000100       SELECT DATA REGISTER
        STAA   PIACRA
        CLR    $40              COUNT = 0
CHKCL   LDAA   PIADRA
        ANDA   #MASK            IS BUTTON BEING PRESSED (0)?
        BNE    CHKCL            NO, WAIT UNTIL IT IS
        INC    $40              YES, COUNT = COUNT + 1
        LDAB   #10
        JSR    DELAY            WAIT 10 MS TO DEBOUNCE
CHKOP   LDAA   PIADRA
        ANDA   #MASK            IS BUTTON STILL BEING PRESSED (0)?
        BEQ    CHKOPN           YES, WAIT FOR RELEASE
        BRA    CHKCLO           NO, LOOK FOR NEXT CLOSURE
```

Object Program:

Memory Address (Hex)	Memory Contents (Hex)			Instruction (Mnemonic)	
0000	7F	PIACRA		CLR	PIACRA
0003	7F	PIADDRA		CLR	PIADDRA
0006	86	04		LDAA	#%00000100
0008	B7	PIACRA		STAA	PIACRA
000B	7F	0040		CLR	$40
000E	B6	PIADRA	CHKCLO	LDAA	PIADRA
0011	84	MASK		ANDA	#MASK
0013	26	F9		BNE	CHKCLO
0015	7C	0040		INC	$40
0018	C6	0A		LDAB	#10
001A	BD	0030		JSR	DELAY
001D	B6	PIADRA	CHKOPN	LDAA	PIADRA
0020	84	MASK		ANDA	#MASK
0022	27	F9		BEQ	CHKOPN
0024	20	E8		BRA	CHKCLO

The three instructions beginning with the label CHKOPN are used to wait until the button is released. If the PIA is addressed as shown in the last column of Table 11-1, the Index register can be loaded with the address of Peripheral Register A, and the instructions that reference the PIA can be modified as follows:

Original		Replacement	
		(X) = PIADRA	
CLR	PIACRA	CLR	1,X
CLR	PIADDRA	CLR	X
STAA	PIACRA	STAA	1,X
LDAA	PIADRA	LDAA	X

A Toggle Switch

Purpose: To interface a single-pole, double-throw toggle switch to a 6800 microprocessor. The toggle is a mechanical device that is either of two positions.

Figure 11-9 shows the circuitry required to interface the switch. Like the pushbutton, the switch uses one bit of a 6820 PIA that serves as an addressable buffer. Unlike the button, the switch may be left in either position. Typical program tasks are to determine the switch position and to see if the position has changed. Either a one-shot with a pulse length of a few milliseconds or a pair of cross-coupled NAND gates (see Figure 11-10) can debounce a mechanical switch.

DEBOUNCING WITH CROSS-COUPLED NAND GATES

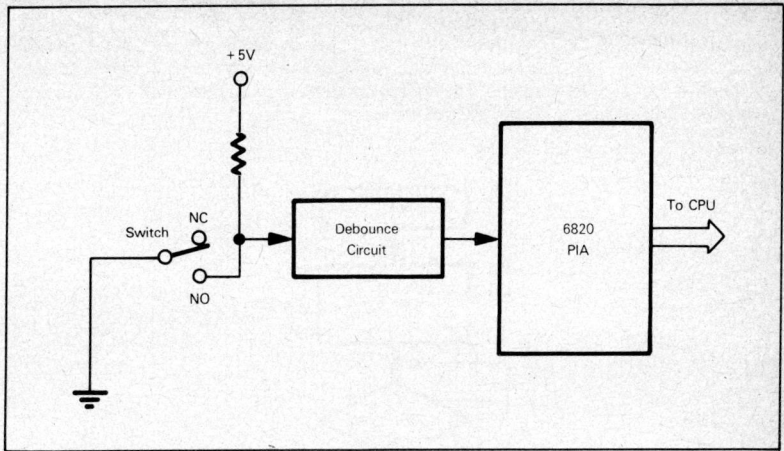

Figure 11-9. A Toggle Switch Circuit

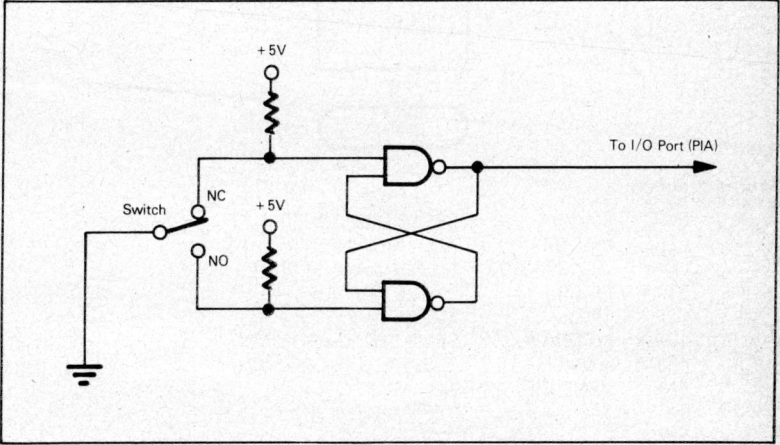

Figure 11-10. A Debounce Circuit Based on
Cross-coupled NAND Gates

The circuits will produce a single step or pulse in response to a change in switch position even if the switch bounces before settling into its new position.

Programming Examples:

We will perform two tasks involving this circuit. They are:

1) Set a memory location to one when the switch is closed.
2) Set a memory location to one when the state of the switch changes.

Task 1: Wait for switch to close.

Memory location 0040 is zero until the switch is closed and then is set to one; that is, the processor clears memory location 0040, waits for the switch to be closed, and then sets memory location 0040 to one. The switch could be marked Run/$\overline{\text{Halt}}$, since the processor will not proceed until the switch is closed.

Flowchart:

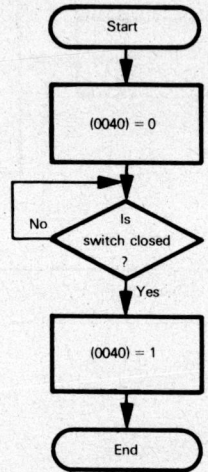

Source Program:

```
        CLR     PIACRA          CLEAR OUT CONTROL REGISTER
        CLR     PIADDRA         ALL LINES INPUTS
        LDAA    #%00000100      SELECT DATA REGISTER
        STAA    PIACRA
        CLR     $40             MARKER = 0
WAITCL  LDAA    PIADRA          READ SWITCH POSITION
        ANDA    #MASK           IS SWITCH CLOSED (0)?
        BNE     WAITCL          NO, WAIT
        INC     $40             YES, MARKER = 1
        SWI
```

Object Program:

Memory Address (Hex)	Memory Contents (Hex)			Instruction (Mnemonic)	
0000	7F	PIACRA		CLR	PIACRA
0003	7F	PIADDRA		CLR	PIADDRA
0006	86	04		LDAA	#%00000100
0008	B7	PIACRA		STAA	PIACRA
000B	7F	0040		CLR	$40
000E	B6	PIADRA	WAITCL	LDAA	PIADRA
0011	84	MASK		ANDA	#MASK
0013	26	F9		BNE	WAITCL
0015	7C	0040		INC	$40
0018	3F			SWI	

Task 2: Wait for switch to change.

Memory location 0040 remains zero until the switch position changes; that is, the processor waits until the switch changes, then sets memory location 0040 to one.

Source Program:

```
         CLR   PIACRA        CLEAR OUT CONTROL REGISTER
         CLR   PIADDRA       ALL LINES INPUTS
         LDAA  #%00000100    SELECT DATA REGISTER
         STAA  PIACRA
         CLR   $40           MARKER = 0
         LDAA  PIADRA        GET OLD SWITCH POSITION
         ANDA  #MASK
SEARCH   LDAB  PIADRA        GET NEW SWITCH POSITION
         ANDB  #MASK
         CBA                 ARE NEW AND OLD POSITIONS THE SAME?
         BEQ   SEARCH        YES, WAIT
         INC   $40           NO, MARKER = 1
         SWI
```

Flowchart:

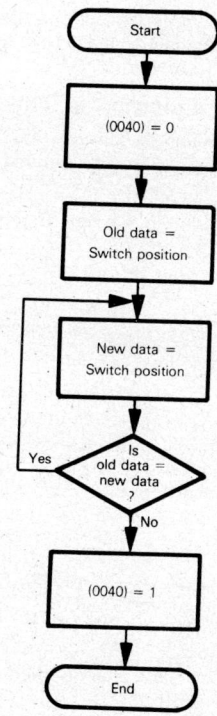

Object Program:

Memory Address (Hex)	Memory Contents (Hex)		Instruction (Mnemonic)	
0000	7F	PIACRA	CLR	PIACRA
0003	7F	PIADDRA	CLR	PIADDRA
0006	86	04	LDAA	#%00000100
0008	B7	PIACRA	STAA	PIACRA
000B	7F	0040	CLR	$40
000E	B6	PIADRA	LDAA	PIADRA
0011	84	MASK	ANDA	#MASK
0013	F6	PIADRA SEARCH	LDAB	PIADRA
0016	C4	MASK	ANDB	#MASK
0018	11		CBA	
0019	27	F8	BEQ	SEARCH
001B	7C	0040	INC	$40
001E	3F		SWI	

A Subtract or Exclusive-OR could replace the Compare in the program. Either of these instructions would, however, change the contents of the Accumulator. The Exclusive-OR would be useful if several switches were attached to the same PIA, since it would produce a one bit for each switch that changed state. How would you rewrite this program so as to debounce the switch in software?

A Multiple-position (Rotary, Selector, or Thumbwheel) Switch

Purpose: To interface a multiple-position switch to a 6800 microprocessor. The lead corresponding to the switch position is grounded, while the other leads are high (logic one).

Figure 11-11 shows the circuitry required to interface an 8-position switch. The switch uses all eight data bits of one side of a 6820 PIA. Typical tasks are to determine the position of the switch and to check whether or not that position has changed. Two special situations must be handled:

1) The switch is temporarily between positions so that no leads are grounded.
2) The switch has not yet reached its final position.

The first of these situations can be handled by waiting until the input is not all ones; i.e., until a switch lead is grounded. We can handle the second situation by examining the switch again after a delay (such as 1 or 2 seconds) and only accepting the input when it remains the same. This delay will not usually affect the responsiveness of the system to the switch. We can also use another switch (a Load switch) to tell the processor when the selector switch should be read.

Programming Examples:

We will perform two tasks involving the circuit of Figure 11-11. These are:

a) Monitor the switch until it is in a definite position, then determine the position and store its binary value in a memory location.

b) Wait for the position of the switch to change, then store the new position in a memory location.

If the switch is in a position, the lead from that position is grounded through the common line. Pullup resistors are usually necessary on all the input lines to avoid problems caused by noise.

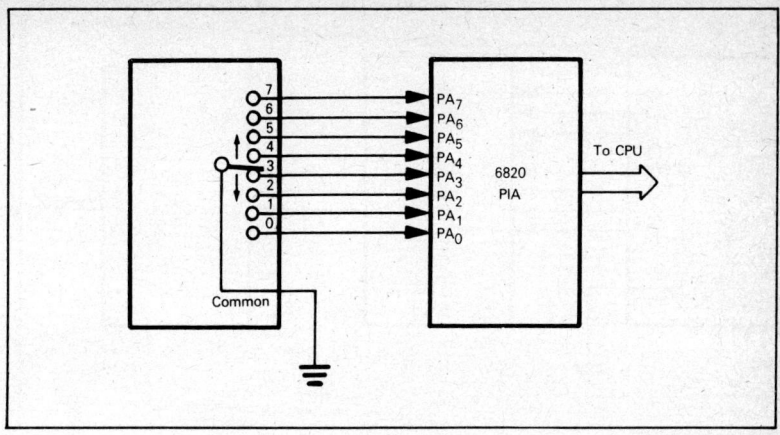

Figure 11-11. A Multiple-Position Switch

ASSEMBLY LANGUAGE PROGRAMS

EXAMPLES.
Determine Switch Position

Purpose: The program waits for the switch to be in a specific position and then places the number of that position in memory location 0040.

Note: The following table relates the data input to the switch position:

Table 11-7. Data Input vs. Switch Position

Switch Position	Data Input	
	Binary	Hex
0	11111110	FE
1	11111101	FD
2	11111011	FB
3	11110111	F7
4	11101111	EF
5	11011111	DF
6	10111111	BF
7	01111111	7F

This scheme is inefficient, since it requires eight bits to distinguish among eight different positions.

A TTL or MOS encoder could reduce the number of bits needed. Figure 11-12 shows a circuit using the 74LS148 TTL 8-to-3 encoder. We attach the switch outputs in inverse order, since the 74LS148 device has active-low inputs and outputs. The output of the encoder circuit is a 3-bit representation of the switch position. Many switches have encoders included so that they automatically produce a coded output, usually consisting of a BCD digit (in negative logic).

USING A TTL ENCODER

11-31

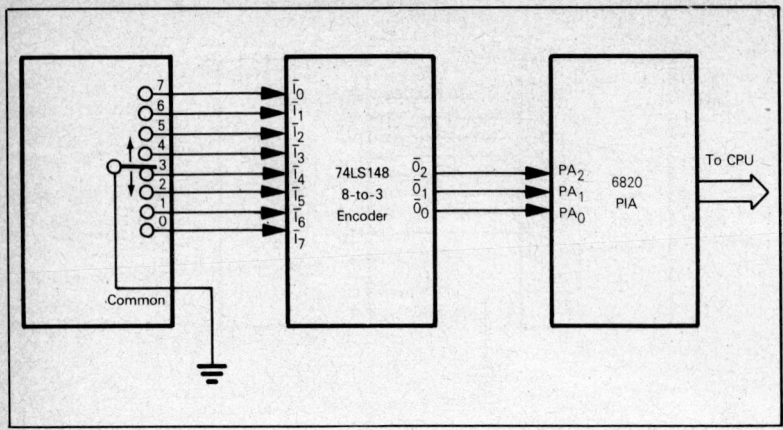

Figure 11-12. A Multiple-Position Switch with an Encoder

The encoder produces active-low outputs, so, for example, switch position 5, which is attached to input 2, produces an output of 2 in negative logic (or 5 in positive logic). You may want to verify the double negative for yourself.

Flowchart:

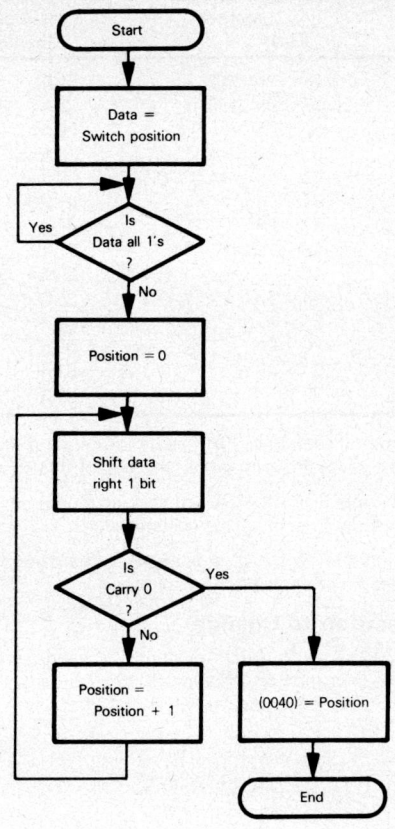

Source Program:

```
        CLR   PIACRA         CLEAR OUT CONTROL REGISTER
        CLR   PIADDRA        ALL LINES INPUTS
        LDAA  #%00000100     SELECT DATA REGISTER
        STAA  PIACRA
CHKSW   LDAA  PIADRA
        CMPA  #$FF           IS SWITCH IN A POSITION?
        BEQ   CHKSW          NO. WAIT FOR POSITION
        CLRB                 POSITION = 0
CHKPOS  RORA                 IS NEXT BIT GROUNDED POSITION?
        BCC   DONE           YES. SWITCH POSITION FOUND
        INCB                 NO. POSITION = POSITION + 1
        BRA   CHKPOS
DONE    STAB  $40            STORE SWITCH POSITION
        SWI
```

Object Program:

Memory Address (Hex)	Memory Contents (Hex)		Instruction (Mnemonic)	
0000	7F	PIACRA	CLR	PIACRA
0003	7F	PIADDRA	CLR	PIADDRA
0006	86	04	LDAA	#%00000100
0008	B7	PIACRA	STAA	PIACRA
000B	B6	PIADRA CHKSW	LDAA	PIADRA
000E	81	FF	CMPA	#$FF
0010	27	F9	BEQ	CHKSW
0012	5F		CLRB	
0013	46	CHKPOS	RORA	
0014	24	03	BCC	DONE
0016	5C		INCB	
0017	20	FA	BRA	CHKPOS
0019	D7	40 DONE	STAB	$40
001B	3F		SWI	

Suppose that a faulty switch or defective PIA results in the input always being FF_{16}. How could you change the program so that it would detect this error?

There is an unconditional jump, BRA CHKPOS, in the source program. Can you restructure the initial conditions so as to eliminate this instruction?

This example assumes that the switch is debounced in hardware. How would you change the program to debounce the switch in software?

Wait for Switch Position to Change

Purpose: The program waits for the switch position to change and places the new position (decoded) in memory location 0040. The program waits until the switch reaches its new position.

Flowchart:

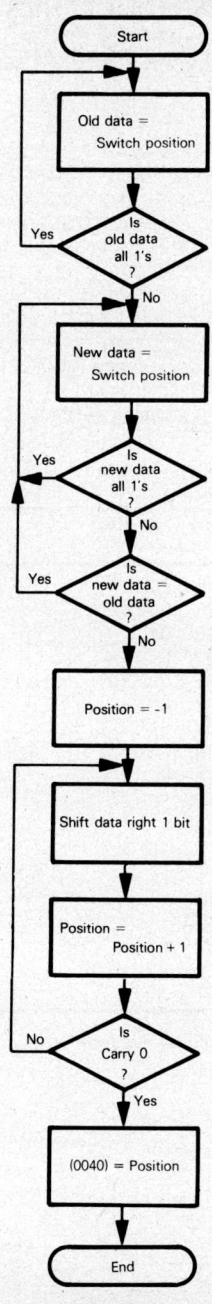

Source Program:

```
        CLR    PIACRA           CLEAR OUT CONTROL REGISTER
        CLR    PIADDRA          ALL LINES INPUTS
        LDAA   #%00000100       SELECT DATA REGISTER
        STAA   PIACRA
CHK1ST  LDAA   PIADRA           GET SWITCH DATA
        CMPA   #$FF             IS SWITCH IN A POSITION?
        BEQ    CHK1ST           NO, WAIT FOR POSITION
CHK2ND  LDAB   PIADRA           GET NEW SWITCH DATA
        CMPB   #$FF             IS SWITCH IN A POSITION?
        BEQ    CHK2ND           NO, WAIT FOR POSITION
        CBA                     IS POSITION SAME AS BEFORE?
        BEQ    CHK2ND           YES, WAIT FOR IT TO CHANGE
        LDAA   #$FF             POSITION = -1
CHKPOS  RORB                    IS NEXT BIT GROUNDED POSITION?
        INCA                    POSITION = POSITION + 1
        BCS    CHKPOS           NO, KEEP LOOKING FOR GROUNDED
                                  POSITION
        STAA   $40              STORE SWITCH POSITION
        SWI
```

Object Program:

Memory Address (Hex)	Memory Contents (Hex)		Instruction (Mnemonic)		
0000	7F	PIACRA		CLR	PIACRA
0003	7F	PIADDRA		CLR	PIADDRA
0006	86	04		LDAA	#%00000100
0008	B7	PIACRA		STAA	PIACRA
000B	B6	PIADRA	CHK1ST	LDAA	PIADRA
000E	81	FF		CMPA	#$FF
0010	27	F9		BEQ	CHK1ST
0012	F6	PIADRA	CHK2ND	LDAB	PIADRA
0015	C1	FF		CMPB	#$FF
0017	27	F9		BEQ	CHK2ND
0019	11			CBA	
001A	27	F6		BEQ	CHK2ND
001C	86	FF		LDAA	#$FF
001E	56		CHKPOS	RORB	
001F	4C			INCA	
0020	25	FC		BCS	CHKPOS
0022	97	40		STAA	$40
0024	3F			SWI	

An alternative method for determining if the switch is in a position is:

```
CHKSW  INC   PIADRA
       BEQ   CHKSW
```

Why does this work? What happens to the input data?

A Single LED

Purpose: To interface a single light-emitting diode to a 6800 microprocessor. The LED can be attached so that either a zero or a one turns it on.

Figure 11-13 shows the circuitry required to interface an LED. The LED lights when its anode is positive with respect to its cathode (Figure 11-13a). Therefore, you can either light the LED by grounding the cathode and having the computer supply a one to the anode (Figure 11-13b) or by connecting the anode to +5 volts and having the computer supply a zero to the cathode (Figure 11-13c). Controlling the cathode is the most common approach. The LED is brightest when it operates from pulsed currents of about 10 to 50 mA applied a few hundred times per second. LEDs have a very short turn-on time (in the microsecond range), so they are well suited to multiplexing (operating several from a single port). LED circuits usually need peripheral or transistor drivers and current-limiting resistors. MOS devices normally cannot drive LEDs directly and make them bright enough for easy viewing.

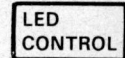

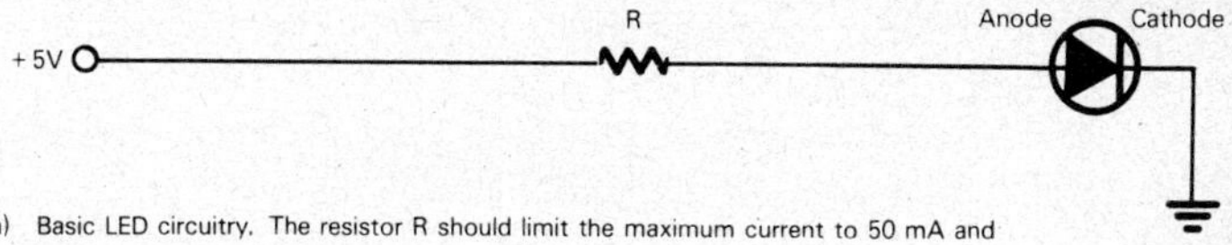

a) Basic LED circuitry. The resistor R should limit the maximum current to 50 mA and the average current to 10 mA.

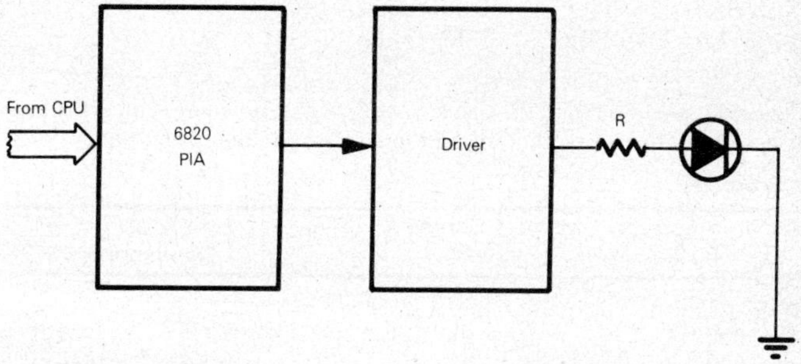

b) Interfacing an LED with positive logic. A logic '1' from the CPU turns the LED on.

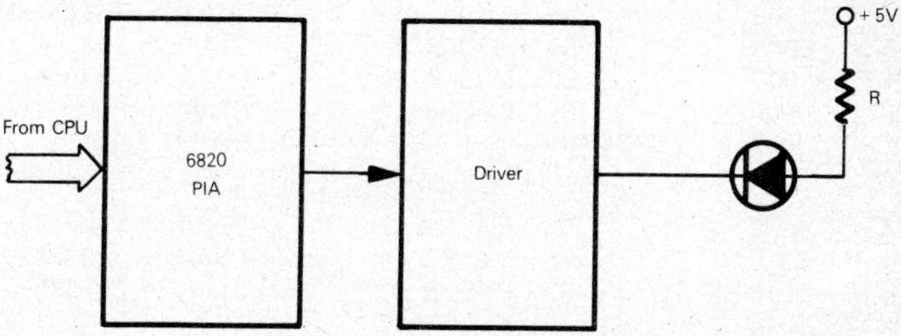

c) Interfacing an LED with negative logic. A logic '0' from the CPU turns the LED on. The driver or the CPU may reverse the logic levels.

Figure 11-13. Interfacing an LED

Note: The PIA has an output latch but no input latch. Remember that the B side of a PIA is buffered so that the output data can be read correctly regardless of the loading on the lines. The A side is unbuffered. The MOS PIA can (at best) sink a current of 1.6 mA, and therefore cannot handle LEDs directly.

Turn the Light On or Off

Purpose: The program turns a single LED either on or off.

Send a Logic One to the LED (turn a positive display on or a negative display off).

Source Program:

(form data initially)

```
        CLR     PIACRB              CLEAR OUT CONTROL REGISTER
        LDAA    #$FF                ALL LINES OUTPUTS
        STAA    PIADDRB
        LDAA    #%00000100          ACCESS DATA REGISTER
        STAA    PIACRB
        LDAA    #MASKP              GET DATA FOR LED
        STAA    PIADRB              AND SEND IT TO LED
        SWI
```

The B side of the PIA is used because of the buffering. The CPU can therefore read the data from the output port.

(update data)

```
        LDAA    PIADRB              GET OLD DATA
        ORAA    #MASKP              TURN ON LED BIT
        STAA    PIADRB              SEND DATA TO LED
        SWI
```

MASKP has a one bit in the LED position and zeros elsewhere. Logically ORing with MASKP does not affect the other bit positions, which may contain bits for other LEDs.

Object Program:

Memory Address (Hex)	Memory Contents (Hex)		Instruction (Mnemonic)	
(form data initially)				
0000	7F	PIACRB	CLR	PIACRB
0003	86	FF	LDAA	#$FF
0005	B7	PIADDRB	STAA	PIADDRB
0008	86	04	LDAA	#%00000100
000A	B7	PIACRB	STAA	PIACRB
000D	86	MASKP	LDAA	#MASKP
000F	B7	PIADRB	STAA	PIADRB
0012	3F		SWI	
(update data)				
0013	B6	PIADRB	LDAA	PIADRB
0016	8A	MASKP	ORAA	#MASKP
0018	B7	PIADRB	STAA	PIADRB
001B	3F		SWI	

Send a Logic Zero to the LED (turn a positive display off or a negative display on).

The differences are that MASKP must be replaced by its logical complement MASKN, and ORAA #MASKP must be replaced by ANDA #MASKN.

MASKN has a zero bit in the LED position and ones elsewhere. Logically ANDing with MASKN does not affect the other bit positions.

Seven-Segment LED Display

Purpose: To interface a seven-segment LED display to a 6800 microprocessor. The display may be either common-anode (negative logic) or common-cathode (positive logic).

Figure 11-14 shows the circuitry required to interface a seven-segment display. Each segment may have one, two, or more LEDs attached in the same way. There are two ways of connecting the displays. One is tying all the cathodes together to ground (see Figure 11-15a); this is a "common-cathode" display, and a logic one at an anode lights a segment. The other is tying all the anodes together to a positive voltage supply (see Figure 11-15b); this is a "common-anode" display, and a logic zero at a cathode lights a segment. So, the common-cathode display uses positive logic and the common-anode display uses negative logic. Either display requires appropriate drivers and resistors.

COMMON-ANODE OR COMMON-CATHODE DISPLAYS

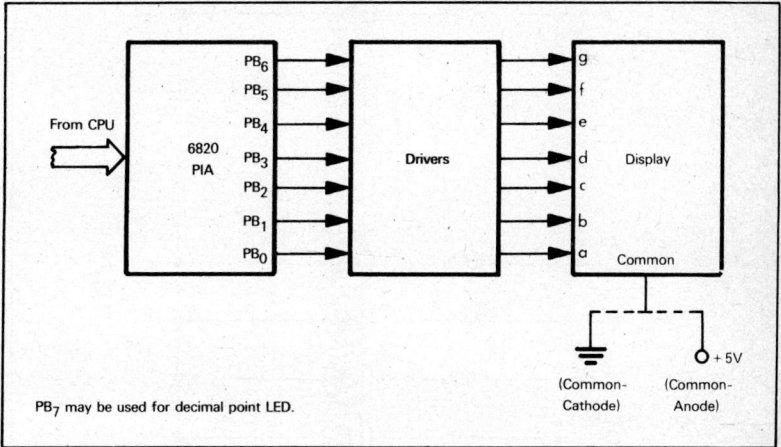

Figure 11-14. Interfacing a Seven-Segment Display

The Common line from the display is tied either to ground or to +5 volts. The display segments are customarily labelled

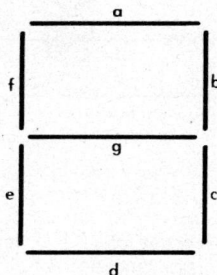

11-39

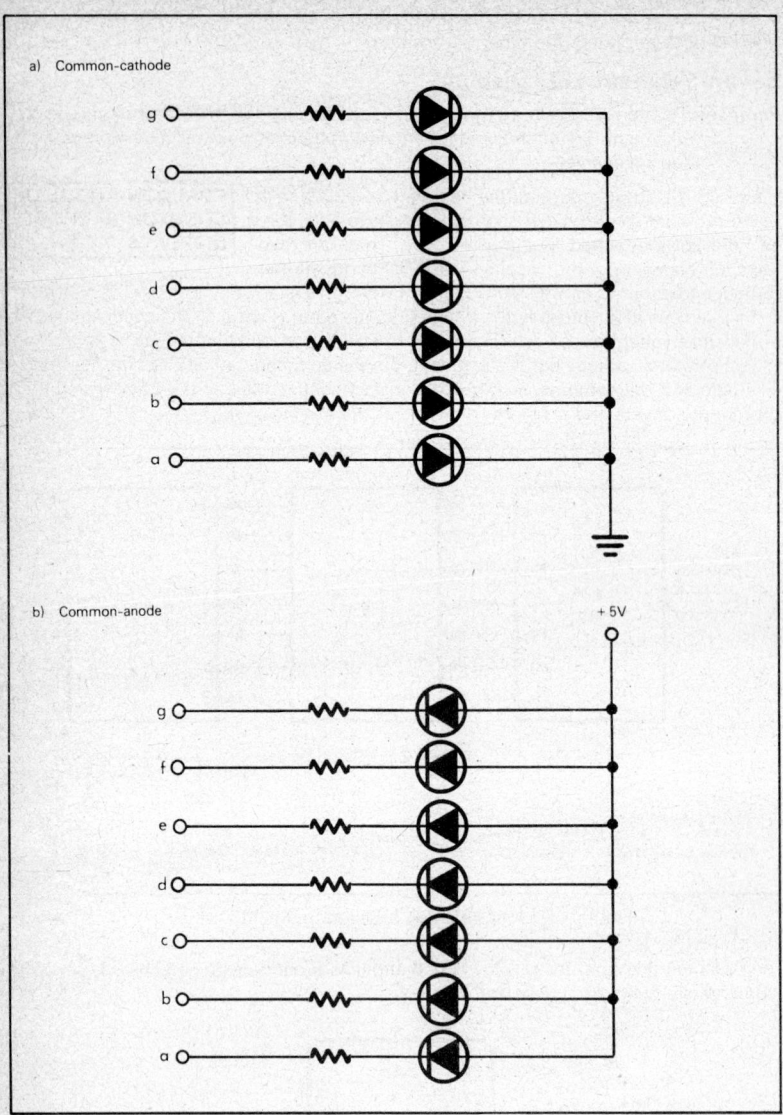

Figure 11-15. Seven-Segment Display Organization

Note: The seven-segment display is widely used because it contains the smallest number of separately controlled segments that can provide recognizable representations of all the decimal digits (see Figure 11-16 and Table 11-8). Seven-segment displays can also produce some letters and other characters (see Table 11-8). Better representations require a substantially larger number of segments and more circuitry. Since seven-segment displays are so popular, low-cost seven-segment decoder/drivers have become

SEVEN-SEGMENT REPRESENTATIONS

widely available. The most popular devices are the 7447 common-anode driver and the 7448 common-cathode driver; these devices have Lamp Test inputs (which turn all the segments on) and blanking inputs and outputs (for blanking leading or trailing zeros).

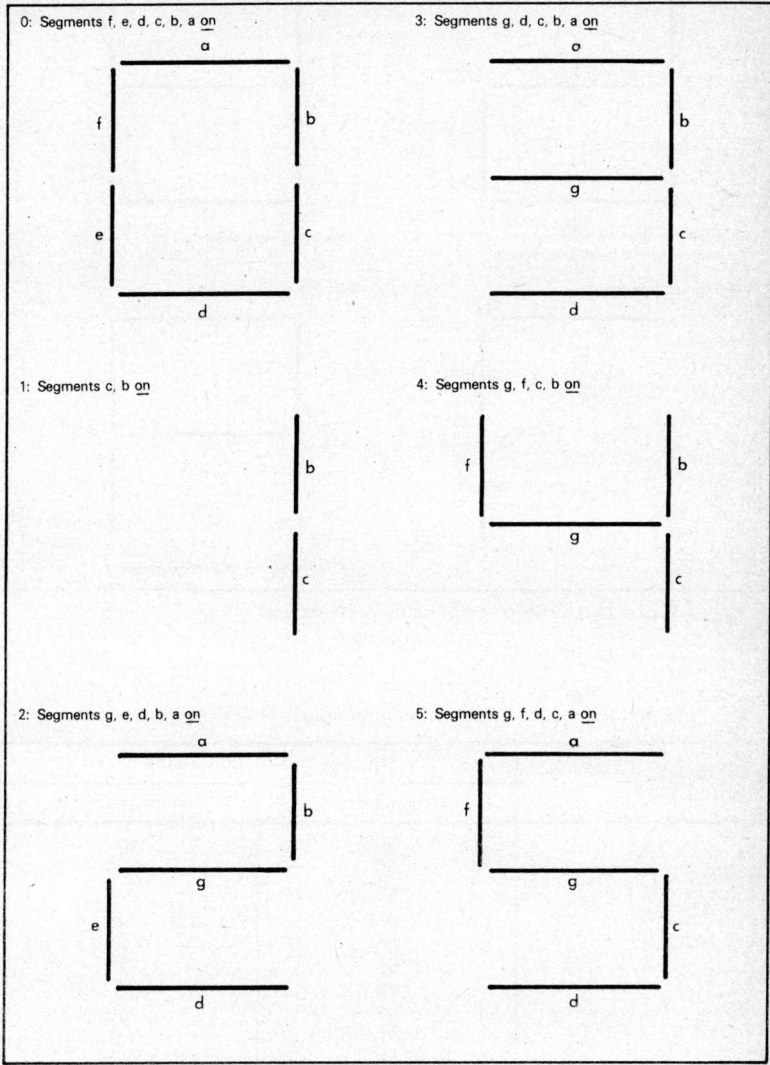

Figure 11-16. Seven-Segment Representations of Decimal Digits

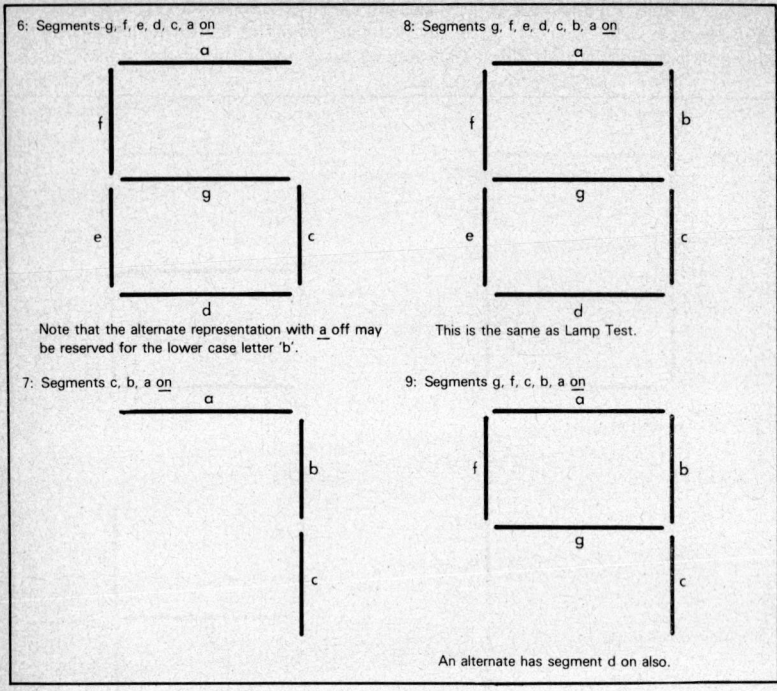

Figure 11-16. Seven-Segment Representations of Decimal Digits (Continued)

Table 11-8. Seven-Segment Representations of Decimal Numbers

Number	Hexadecimal Representation	
	Common-cathode	Common-anode
0	3F	40
1	06	79
2	5B	24
3	4F	30
4	66	19
5	6D	12
6	7D	02
7	07	78
8	7F	00
9	67	18

Bit 7 is always zero and the others are g, f, e, d, c, b, and a in decreasing order of significance.

Table 11-9. Seven-Segment Representations of Letters and Symbols

Upper-case Letters

Letter	Hexadecimal Representation	
	Common-cathode	Common-anode
A	77	08
C	39	46
E	79	06
F	71	0E
H	76	09
I	06	79
J	1E	61
L	38	47
O	3F	40
P	73	0C
U	3E	41
Y	66	19

Lower-case Letters and Special Characters

Character	Hexadecimal Representation	
	Common-cathode	Common-anode
b	7C	03
c	58	27
d	5E	21
h	74	0B
n	54	2B
o	5C	23
r	50	2F
u	1C	63
-	40	3F
?	53	2C

Programming Example

Purpose: Display the contents of memory location 0041 on a seven-segment display if it contains a decimal digit. Otherwise, blank the display.

Sample Problems:

a)   (0041) = 05
        Result is 5 on display

b)   (0041) = 66
        Result is a blank display

Flowchart:

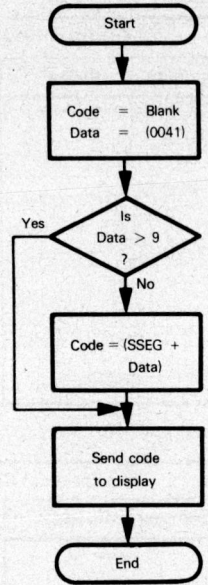

Source Program:

```
         CLR    PIACRB           CLEAR OUT CONTROL REGISTER
         LDAA   #$FF             ALL LINES OUTPUTS
         STAA   PIADDRB
         LDAA   #%00000100       ACCESS DATA REGISTER
         STAA   PIADRB
         LDAB   #BLANK           GET BLANK CODE
         LDAA   $41              GET DATA
         CMPA   #9               IS DATA GREATER THAN 9?
         BHI    DSPLY            YES, DISPLAY BLANKS
         CLR    $40
         LDX    $40              GET OFFSET ADDRESS FOR TABLE
         LDAB   SSEG,X           GET SEVEN-SEGMENT CODE
DSPLY    STAB   PIADRB           CODE TO DISPLAY
         SWI
```

BLANK is 00 for a common-cathode display, FF for a common-anode display. Another procedure would be to put the blank code at the end of the table and replace all improper data values with 10; i.e.,

```
         LDAA   #10
         CMPA   $41              IS DATA 10 OR MORE?
         BHI    CNVRT            NO, GO CONVERT TO SEVEN-SEGMENT
         STAA   $41              YES, MAKE DATA INTO INDEX FOR BLANK CODE
CNVRT    CLR    $40              GET MSBS OF BASE ADDRESS
```

Table SSEG is either the common-cathode or common-anode representation of the decimal digits from Table 11-8.

Object Program:

Memory Address (Hex)	Memory Contents (Hex)			Instruction (Mnemonic)	
0000	7F	PIACRB		CLR	PIACRB
0003	86	FF		LDAA	#$FF
0005	B7	PIADDRB		STAA	PIADDRB
0008	86	04		LDAA	#%00000100
000A	B7	PIADRB		STAA	PIADRB
000D	C6	BLANK		LDAB	#BLANK
000F	96	41		LDAA	$41
0011	81	09		CMPA	#9
0013	22	07		BHI	DSPLY
0015	7F	0040		CLR	$40
0018	DE	40		LDX	$40
001A	E6	20		LDAB	SSEG,X
001C	F7	PIADRB	DSPLY	STAB	PIADRB
001F	7F			SWI	
0020-0029			SSEG		

More generally, if the table is located at the address given by SSEGM (8 MSBs) and SSEGL (8 LSBs), you must replace CLR $40 with

    LDAB #SSEGM   GET 8 MSBS OF BASE ADDRESS
    STAB $40

and LDAB SSEG,X with

    LDAB SSEGL,X   GET SEVEN-SEGMENT CODE

Several displays may be multiplexed, as shown in Figure 11-17. A brief strobe on control line CB2 clocks the counter and directs data to the next display. RESET starts the decimal counter at 9 so that the first output operation clears the counter and directs data to the first display.

The following program uses the delay routine to pulse each of ten common-cathode displays for 1 ms.

Programming Example

Purpose: Display the contents of memory locations 0040 through 0049 on ten seven-segment displays which are multiplexed with a counter and a decoder.

Sample Problem:

        (0040) = 66
        (0041) = 3F
        (0042) = 7F
        (0043) = 7F
        (0044) = 06
        (0045) = 5B
        (0046) = 07
        (0047) = 4F
        (0048) = 6D
        (0049) = 7D
        Display reads 4088127356

Source Program:

```
            CLR    PIACRB          CLEAR OUT CONTROL REGISTER
            LDAA   #$FF            ALL LINES OUTPUTS
            STAA   PIADDRB
            LDAA   #%00101100      MAKE CB2 A BRIEF CLOCK PULSE
            STAA   PIACRB
    SCAN    LDX    #$40            POINT TO START OF DATA
            LDAB   #10             NUMBER OF DISPLAYS = 10
    DSPLY   LDAA   X               GET DATA FOR A DISPLAY
            STAA   PIADRB          SEND IT TO DISPLAY
            JSR    DELAY           WAIT 1 MS
            INX
            DECB                   COUNT DISPLAYS
            BNE    DSPLY
            BRA    SCAN            START ANOTHER SCAN
```

Control register bit 5 = 1 to make CB2 an output, bit 4 = 0 to make it a pulse, and bit 3 = 1 to make it a brief strobe.

Object Program:

Memory Address (Hex)	Memory Contents (Hex)		Instruction (Mnemonic)	
0000	7F	PIACRB		CLR	PIACRB
0003	86	FF		LDAA	#$FF
0005	B7	PIADDRB		STAA	PIADDRB
0008	86	2C		LDAA	#%00101100
000A	B7	PIACRB		STAA	PIACRB
000D	CE	0040	SCAN	LDX	#$40
0010	C6	0A		LDAB	#10
0012	A6	00	DSPLY	LDAA	X
0014	B7	PIADRB		STAA	PIADRB
0017	BD	0030		JSR	DELAY
001A	08			INX	
001B	5A			DECB	
001C	26	F4		BNE	DSPLY
001E	20	ED		BRA	SCAN

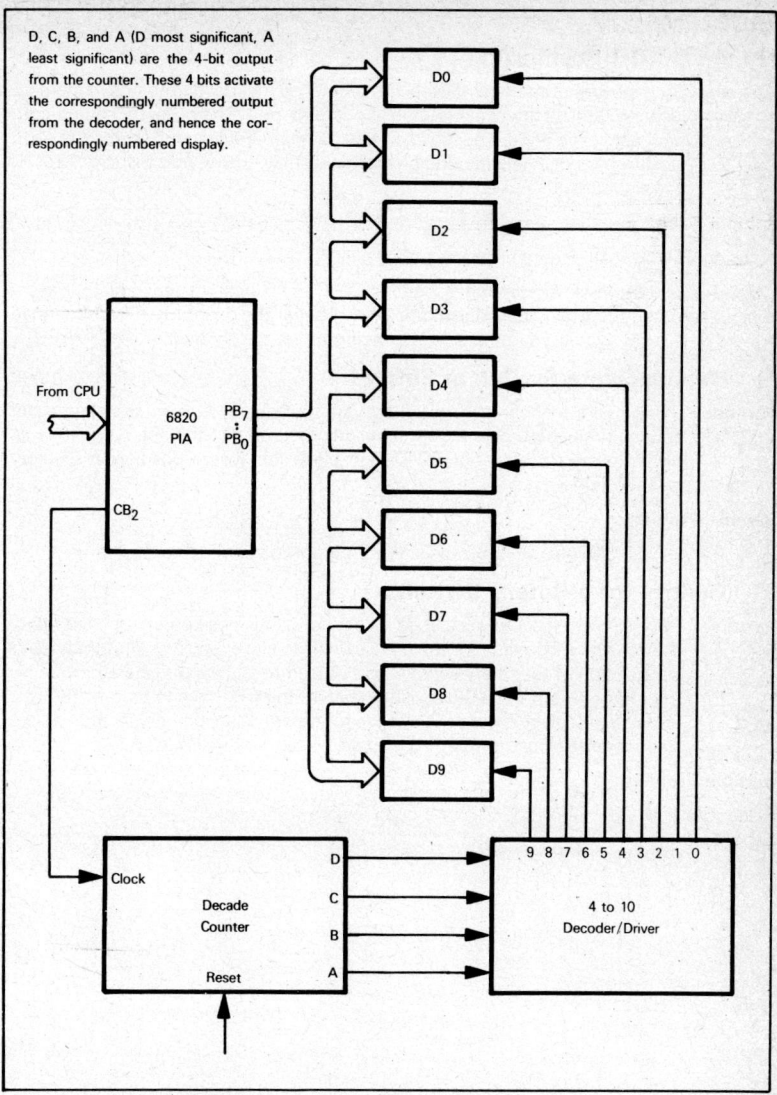

Figure 11-17. Multiplexed Seven-Segment Displays

PROBLEMS
1) An On-Off Pushbutton
Purpose: Each closure of the pushbutton complements (inverts) all the bits in memory location 0040. The location initially contains zero. The program should continuously examine the pushbutton and complement location 0040 with each closure. You may wish to complement a display output port instead, so as to make the results easier to see.

Sample Case:

Location 0040 initially contains zero.

The first pushbutton closure changes location 0040 to FF (hex), the second changes it back to zero, the third back to FF (hex), etc. Assume that the pushbutton is debounced in hardware. How would you include debouncing in your program?

2) Debouncing a Switch in Software
Purpose: Debounce a mechanical switch by waiting until two readings, taken a debounce time apart, give the same result. Assume that the debounce time (in ms) is in memory location 0040, and place the switch position in memory location 0041.

Sample Problem:

(0040) = 03 causes the program to wait 3 ms between readings.

3) Control for a Rotary Switch
Purpose: Another switch serves as a Load switch for a four-position unencoded rotary switch. The CPU waits for the Load switch to close (be zero), and then reads the position of the rotary switch. This procedure allows the operator to move the rotary switch to its final position before the CPU tries to read it. The program should place the position of the rotary switch in memory location 0040. Debounce the Load switch in software.

Sample Problem:

Place rotary switch in position 2. Close Load switch.

Result: (0040) = 02

4) Record Switch Positions on Lights

Purpose: A set of eight switches should have their positions reflected in eight LEDs. That is to say, if the switch is closed (zero), the LED should be on; otherwise, the LED should be off. Assume that the CPU output port is connected to the cathodes of the LEDs.

Sample Problem:

SWITCH	0	CLOSED
SWITCH	1	OPEN
SWITCH	2	CLOSED
SWITCH	3	OPEN
SWITCH	4	OPEN
SWITCH	5	CLOSED
SWITCH	6	CLOSED
SWITCH	7	OPEN

Result:

LED	0	ON
LED	1	OFF
LED	2	ON
LED	3	OFF
LED	4	OFF
LED	5	ON
LED	6	ON
LED	7	OFF

How would you change the program so that a switch attached to bit 7 of Side A of PIA #2 determines whether or not the displays are active (i.e., if the control switch is closed, the displays attached to Side B reflect the switches attached to Side A; if the control switch is open, the displays are always off)? A control switch is useful when the displays may distract the operator, as in an airplane.

How would you change the program so as to make the control switch an on-off pushbutton; that is, each closure reverses the previous state of the displays? Assume that the displays start in the active state and that the program examines and debounces the pushbutton before sending data to the displays. How would you change your program if the control switch were attached to a PIA control line?

5) Count on a Seven-Segment Display

Purpose: The program should count from 0 to 9 continuously on a seven-segment display, starting with zero.

Hint: Try different timing lengths for the displays and see what happens. When does the count become visible? What happens if the display is blanked part of the time?

MORE COMPLEX I/O DEVICES

More complex I/O devices differ from simple keyboards, switches, and displays in that:

1) They transfer data at higher rates.
2) They may have their own internal clocks and timing.
3) They produce status information and require control information, as well as transferring data.

Because of their high data rates, you cannot handle these I/O devices casually. If the processor does not provide the appropriate service, the system may miss input data or produce erroneous output data. You are therefore working under much more exacting constraints than in dealing with simpler devices. Interrupts are a convenient method for handling complex I/O devices, as we shall see in Chapter 12.

SYNCHRONIZING WITH I/O DEVICES

Peripherals such as keyboards, teletypewriters, cassettes, and floppy disks produce their own internal timing. These devices provide streams of data, separated by specific timing intervals. The computer must synchronize the initial input or output operation with the peripheral clock and then provide the proper interval between subsequent operations. A simple delay loop like the one shown previously can produce the timing interval. The synchronization may require one or more of the following procedures:

1) Looking for a transition on a clock or strobe line provided by the peripheral for timing purposes. The simplest method is to tie the strobe to a PIA control line and look for a change in the appropriate bit of the PIA Control register.

2) Finding the center of the time interval during which the data is stable. We would prefer to determine the value of the data at the center of the pulse rather than at the edges, where the data may be changing. Finding the center requires a delay of one-half of a transmission interval (bit time) after the edge. Sampling the data at the center also means that small timing errors have little effect on the accuracy of the reception.

3) Recognizing a special starting code. This is easy if the code is a single bit or if we have some timing information. The procedure is more complex if the code is long and could start at any time. Shifting will be necessary to determine where the transmitter is starting its bits, characters, or messages (this is often called a search for the correct "framing").

4) Sampling the data several times. This reduces the probability of receiving data incorrectly from noisy lines. Majority logic (such as best 3 out of 5 or 5 out of 8) can be used to decide on the actual data value.

Reception is, of course, much more difficult than transmission, since the peripheral controls the reception and the computer must interpret timing information generated by the peripheral. In transmission, the computer provides the proper timing and formatting for a specific peripheral.

CONTROL AND STATUS INFORMATION

Peripherals may require or provide other information besides data and timing. We refer to other information transmitted by the computer as "control information"; it may select modes of operation, start or stop processes, clock registers, enable buffers, choose formats or protocols, provide operator displays, count operations, or identify the type and priority of the operation. We refer to other information transmitted by the peripheral as "status information"; it may indicate the mode of operation, the readiness of devices, the presence of error conditions, the format of protocol in use, and other states or conditions.

The computer handles control and status information just like data. This information seldom changes, even though actual data may be transferred at a high rate. The control or status information may be single bits, digits, words, or multiple words. Often single bits or short fields are combined and handled by a single input or output port.

Combining status and control information into bytes reduces the total number of I/O port addresses required by the peripherals. However, the combination does mean that individual status input bits must be separately interpreted and control output bits must be separately determined. The procedures for isolating status bits and setting or resetting control bits are as follows:

Separating Out Status Bits

Step 1) Read status data from the peripheral

Step 2) Logical AND with a mask (the mask has ones in bit positions that must be examined, and zeros elsewhere)

Step 3) Shift the separated bits to the least significant bit positions

SEPARATING STATUS INFORMATION

Step 3 is unnecessary if the field is a single bit, since the Zero flag will contain the complement of that bit after Step 2 (try it!). A Shift or Load instruction can replace Step 2 if the field is a single bit and occupies the least significant, most significant, or next to most significant bit position. These positions are often reserved for the most frequently used status information. You should try to write the required instruction sequences for the 6800 processor.

Setting and Clearing Control Bits

Step 1) Read prior control information

Step 2) Logical AND with mask to clear bits (mask has zeros in bit positions to be cleared, ones elsewhere)

Step 3) Logically OR with mask to set bits (mask has ones in bit positions to be set, zeros elsewhere)

Step 4) Send new control information to peripheral

COMBINING CONTROL INFORMATION

Here again the procedure is simpler if the field is a single bit and occupies a position at the end of the word.

1) A 3-bit field in bit positions 2 through 4 of a PIA data register is a scaling factor. Place that factor in Accumulator A.

```
*
* READ STATUS DATA FROM INPUT PORT
*
  LDAA    PIADR           READ STATUS DATA
*
* MASK OFF UNWANTED BITS AND SHIFT
*
  ANDA    #%00011100  MASK SCALING FACTOR
  LSRA                    SHIFT TWICE TO NORMALIZE
  LSRA
```

2) Accumulator A contains a 2-bit field that must be placed in bit positions 3 and 4 of a PIA data register.

```
*
* MOVE DATA TO FIELD POSITIONS
*
  ASLA                    SHIFT DATA TO BIT POSITIONS 3 AND 4
  ASLA
  ASLA
  ANDA    #%00011000  CLEAR OUT OTHER BITS
*
* COMBINE NEW FIELD POSITIONS WITH OTHER DATA
*
  ORAA    PIADR           COMBINE NEW DATA WITH OLD
  STAA    PIADR           OUTPUT COMBINED DATA
```

DOCUMENTING STATUS AND CONTROL TRANSFERS

Documentation is a serious problem in handling control and status information. The meanings of status inputs or control outputs are seldom obvious. The programmer should clearly indicate the purposes of input and output operations with comments such as "CHECK IF READER IS ON", "CHOOSE EVEN PARITY OPTION", or "ACTIVATE BIT RATE COUNTER". The Logical and Shift instructions will otherwise be very difficult to remember, understand, or debug.

EXAMPLES

An Unencoded Keyboard

Purpose: Recognize a key closure from an unencoded 3 x 3 keyboard and place the number of the key that was pressed in Accumulator B.

Keyboards are just collections of switches (see Figure 11-18). Small numbers of keys are easiest to handle if each key is attached separately to a bit of an input port. Interfacing the keyboard is then the same as interfacing a set of switches.

MATRIX KEYBOARD

Keyboards with more than eight keys require more than one input port and therefore multibyte operations. This is particularly wasteful if the keys are logically separate, as in a calculator or terminal keyboard where the user will only strike one at a time. The number of input lines required may be reduced by connecting the keys into a matrix, as shown in Figure 11-19. Now each key represents a potential connection between a row and a column. The keyboard matrix requires n + m external lines, where n is the number of rows and m is the number of columns. This compares to n x m external lines if each key is separate. Table 11-10 compares the number of keys required by typical configurations.

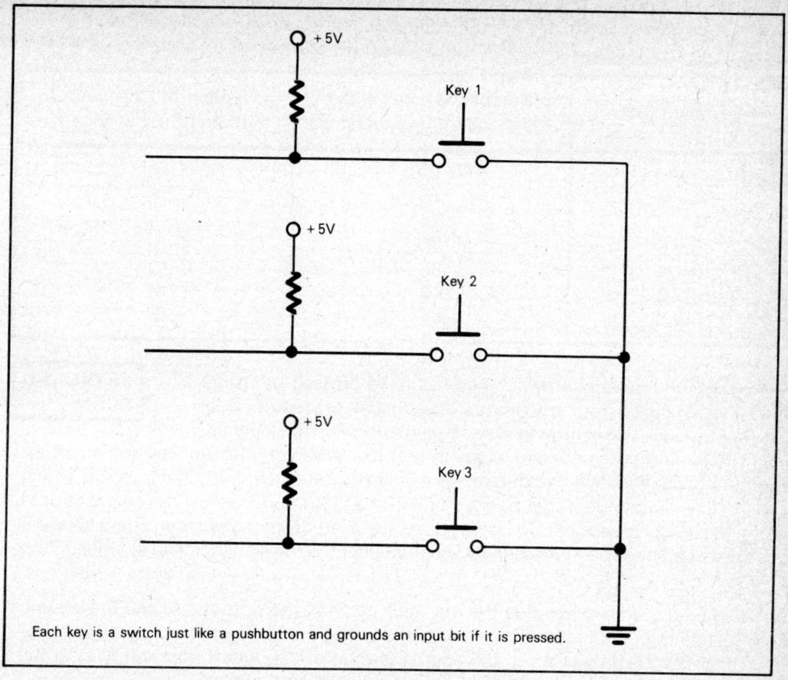

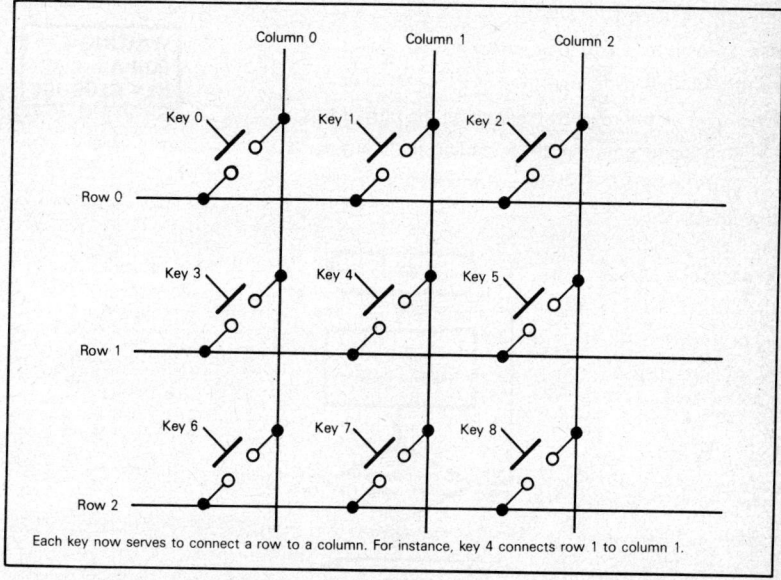

Figure 11-18. A Small Keyboard

Figure 11-19. A Keyboard Matrix

Table 11-10. Comparison Between Independent Connections
and Matrix Connections for Keyboards

Keyboard Size	Number of Lines with Independent Connections	Number of Lines with Matrix Connections
3 x 3	9	6
4 x 4	16	8
4 x 6	24	10
5 x 5	25	10
6 x 6	36	12
6 x 8	48	14
8 x 8	64	16

KEYBOARD SCAN

A program can determine which key has been pressed by using the external lines from the matrix. The usual procedure is a "keyboard scan". We ground Row 0 and examine the column lines. If any lines are grounded, a key in that row has been pressed, causing a row-to-column connection. We can determine which key was pressed by determining which column line is grounded; that is, which bit of the input port is zero. If no column line is grounded, we proceed to Row 1 and repeat the scan. Note that we can check to see if any keys at all have been pressed by grounding all the rows at once and examining the columns.

The keyboard scan requires that the row lines be tied to an output port and the column lines to an input port. Figure 11-20 shows the arrangement. The CPU can ground a particular row by placing a zero in the appropriate bit of the output port and ones in the other bits.

The CPU can determine the state of a particular column by examining the appropriate bit of the input port.

Task 1: Wait for a key to be pressed.

WAITING FOR A KEY CLOSURE

The procedure is as follows:

1) Ground all the rows by clearing all the output bits.
2) Fetch the column inputs by reading the input port.
3) Return to Step 1 if all the column inputs are ones.

Flowchart:

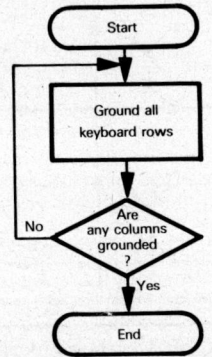

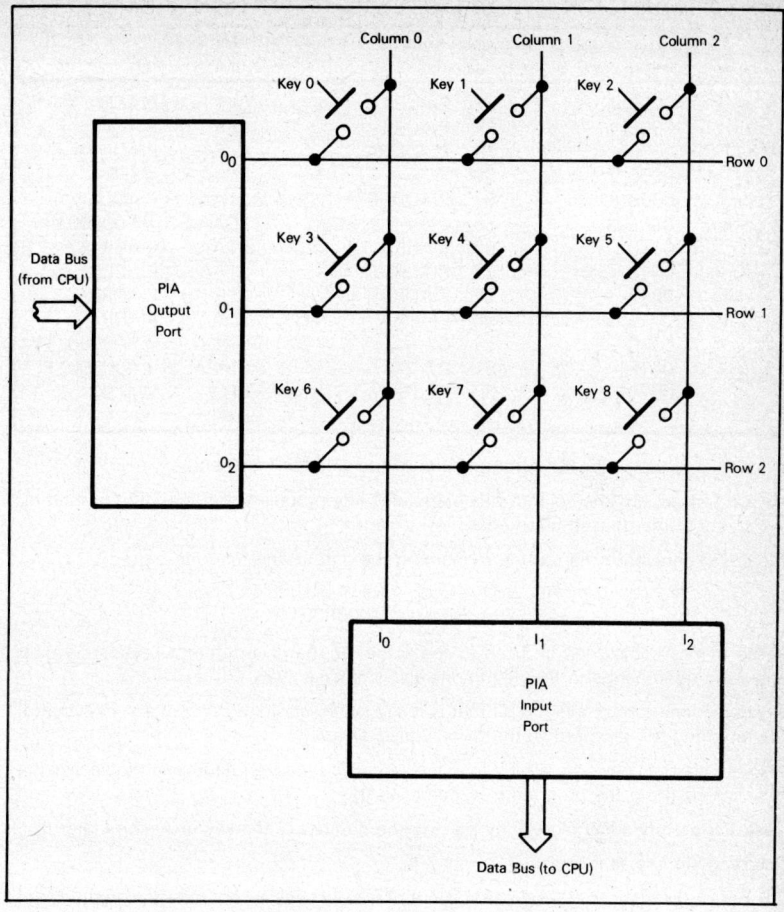

Figure 11-20. I/O Arrangement for a Keyboard Scan

Source Program:

```
         CLR    PIACRA            CLEAR OUT CONTROL REGISTERS
         CLR    PIACRB
         CLR    PIADDRA           MAKE PIA A SIDE INPUTS
         LDAA   #$FF              MAKE PIA B SIDE OUTPUTS
         STAA   PIADDRB
         LDAA   #%00000100        ACCESS DATA REGISTERS
         STAA   PIACRA
         STAA   PIACRB
         CLR    PIADRB            GROUND ALL KEYBOARD ROWS
WAITK    LDAA   PIADRA            GET KEYBOARD COLUMN DATA
         ANDA   #%00000111        MASK COLUMN BITS
         CMPA   #%00000111        ARE ANY COLUMNS GROUNDED?
         BEQ    WAITK             NO, WAIT UNTIL ONE IS
         SWI
```

Object Program:

Memory Address (Hex)	Memory Contents (Hex)		Instruction (Mnemonic)	
0000	7F	PIACRA		CLR	PIACRA
0003	7F	PIACRB		CLR	PIACRB
0006	7F	PIADDRA		CLR	PIADDRA
0009	86	FF		LDAA	#$FF
000B	B7	PIADDRB		STAA	PIADDRB
000E	86	04		LDAA	#%00000100
0010	B7	PIACRA		STAA	PIACRA
0013	B7	PIACRB		STAA	PIACRB
0016	7F	PIADRB		CLR	PIADRB
0019	B6	PIADRA	WAITK	LDAA	PIADRA
001C	84	07		ANDA	#%00000111
001E	81	07		CMPA	#%00000111
0020	27	F7		BEQ	WAITK
0022	3F			SWI	

PIA side B is the keyboard output port and side A is the input port.

Masking off all but the column bits eliminates any problems that could be caused by the states of the unused input lines.

We could generalize the routine by naming the output and masking patterns:

```
ALLGND  EQU   %11111000
ALLOPN  EQU   %00000111
```

These names could then be used in the actual program; a different keyboard would only require a change in the definitions and a re-assembly.

Of course, one side of a PIA is all that is really necessary for a 3 x 3 or 4 x 4 keyboard. Try rewriting the program so that it only uses side A.

You can shorten this program by five bytes by using Indexed addressing to access the PIA. Try rewriting the program to accomplish this.

Task 2: Identify a key closure by placing the number of the key in Accumulator B.

The procedure is as follows:

1) Set key number to -1, keyboard output port to all ones except for a zero in bit 0, and row counter to number of rows.
2) Fetch the column inputs by reading the input port.
3) If any column inputs are zero, proceed to Step 7.
4) Add the number of columns to the key number to reach next row.
5) Update the contents of the output port by shifting the zero bit left one position.
6) Decrement row counter. Go to Step 2 if any rows have not been scanned, otherwise go to Step 9.
7) Add 1 to key number. Shift column inputs right one bit.
8) If Carry = 1, return to Step 7.
9) End of program.

Flowchart:

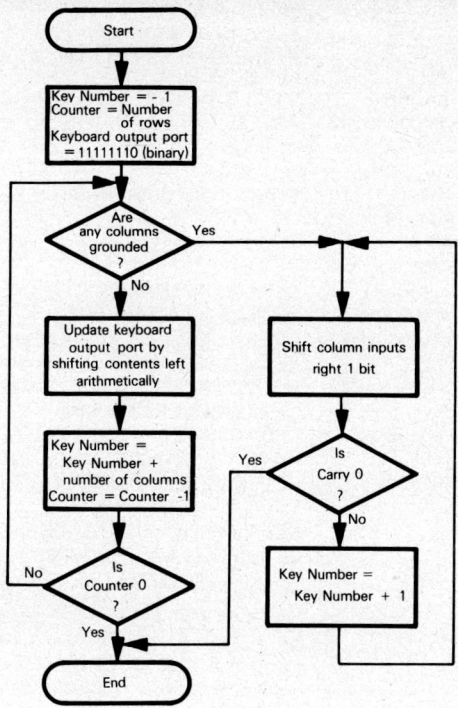

Source Program:

```
        CLR    PIACRA            CLEAR OUT CONTROL REGISTERS
        CLR    PIACRB
        CLR    PIADRA            MAKE PIA A SIDE INPUTS
        LDAB   #$FF              KEY NUMBER = -1
        STAB   PIADRB            MAKE PIA B SIDE OUTPUTS
        LDAA   #%00000100        ACCESS DATA REGISTERS
        STAA   PIACRA
        STAA   PIACRB
        LDAA   #%11111110        START BY GROUNDING ROW ZERO
        STAA   PIADRB
        LDAA   #3                COUNTER = NUMBER OF ROWS
        STAA   $40
FROW    LDAA   PIADRA            GET COLUMN INPUTS
        ANDA   #%00000111        MASK OFF COLUMN BITS
        CMPA   #%00000111        ARE ANY COLUMNS GROUNDED?
        BNE    FCOL              YES, GO DETERMINE WHICH ONE
        ADDB   #3                NO, KEY NUMBER = KEY NUMBER
                                   + NUMBER OF COLUMNS
        ASL    PIADRB            UPDATE SCAN PATTERN FOR NEXT ROW
        DEC    $40               HAVE ALL ROWS BEEN SCANNED?
        BNE    FROW              NO, SCAN NEXT ONE
        SWI
FCOL    INCB                     KEY NUMBER = KEY NUMBER + 1
        LSRA                     IS THIS COLUMN GROUNDED?
        BCS    FCOL              NO, EXAMINE NEXT ONE
        SWI
```

Object Program:

Memory Address (Hex)	Memory Contents (Hex)		Instruction (Mnemonic)	
0000	7F	PIACRA	CLR	PIACRA
0003	7F	PIACRB	CLR	PIACRB
0006	7F	PIADRA	CLR	PIADRA
0009	C6	FF	LDAB	#$FF
000B	F7	PIADRB	STAB	PIADRB
000E	86	04	LDAA	#%00000100
0010	B7	PIACRA	STAA	PIACRA
0013	B7	PIACRB	STAA	PIACRB
0016	86	FE	LDAA	#%11111110
0018	B7	PIADRB	STAA	PIADRB
001B	86	03	LDAA	#3
001D	97	40	STAA	$40
001F	B6	PIADRA FROW	LDAA	PIADRA
0022	84	07	ANDA	#%00000111
0024	81	07	CMPA	#%00000111
0026	26	0B	BNE	FCOL
0028	CB	03	ADDB	#3
002A	78	PIADRB	ASL	PIADRB
002D	7A	0040	DEC	$40
0030	26	ED	BNE	FROW
0032	3F		SWI	
0033	5C	FCOL	INCB	
0034	44		LSRA	
0035	25	FC	BCS	FCOL
0037	3F		SWI	

Each time a row scan fails, we must add the number of columns to the key number so as to move past the present row (try it on the keyboard in Figure 11-20).

This program can be generalized by making the number of rows, the number of columns, and the masking pattern into named parameters with EQU pseudo-operations.

Another alternative is to use the bidirectional capability of the PIA. This technique is described on page 5-8 of the Motorola 6800 Applications Manual.

What is the result of the program if no keys are being pressed? Change the program so that it starts the scan over again in that case.

An Encoded Keyboard

Purpose: Fetch data, when it is available, from an encoded keyboard that provides a strobe along with each data transfer.

An encoded keyboard provides a unique code for each key. It has internal electronics that perform the scanning and identification procedure of the previous example. The tradeoff is between the simpler software required by the encoded keyboard and the lower hardware cost of the unencoded keyboard.

Encoded keyboards may use diode matrices, TTL encoders, or MOS encoders. The codes may be ASCII, EBCDIC, or a custom code. PROMs are often part of the encoding circuitry.

The encoding circuitry may do more than just encode key closures. It may also debounce the keys and handle "rollover", the problem of more than one key being struck at the same time. Common ways of handling rollover include "2-key rollover", whereby two keys (but not more) struck at the same time are resolved into separate closures, and "n-key rollover", whereby any number of keys struck at the same time are resolved into separate closures.

The encoded keyboard also provides a strobe with each data transfer. The strobe identifies a new closure. Figure 11-21 shows the interface between an encoded keyboard and the 6800 microprocessor. The keyboard strobe is latched into bit 7 of the PIA Control register. Bit 1 of the Control register determines which edge of the strobe is recognized by the PIA.

Note that the PIA contains a serial, edge-sensitive latched status port as well as a data port. It also contains an inverter than can be used to handle strobes of either polarity (Control register bit 1 = 0 to recognize a high-to-low transition). The PIA can replace several simple circuit elements. The designer can make corrections by changing the contents of the Control register (in software) rather than by rewiring a breadboard. For example, changing the active edge requires the changing of a single program bit, whereas it might require additional circuit elements and rewiring on a breadboard.

Task: Wait for an active-low strobe on control line CA1 and then place the data from the Data register in Accumulator A.

Note that reading the data from the Data register clears the status bit (this circuitry is part of the 6820 PIA).

Flowchart:

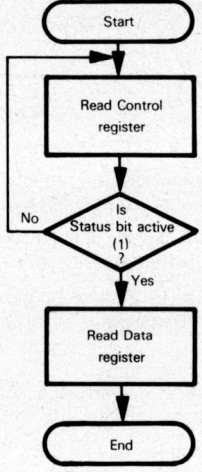

The hardware must hold the control lines in a logic one state while $\overline{\text{RESET}}$ is active to prevent the accidental setting of status flags. An initial read of the Data registers in the startup routine may be used to clear the status flags.[4]

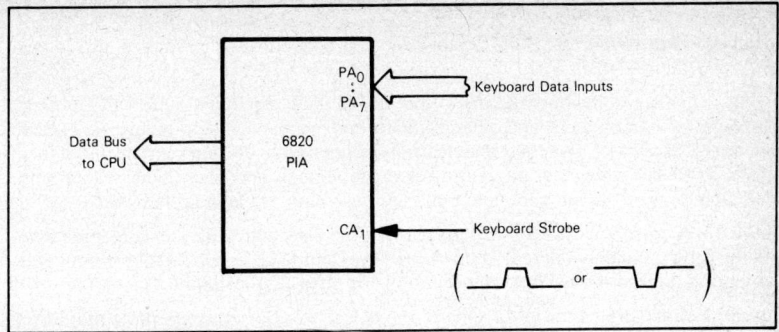

Figure 11-21. I/O Interface for an Encoded Keyboard

Source Program:

```
        CLR     PIACRA          CLEAR OUT CONTROL REGISTER
        CLR     PIADDRA         MAKE DATA LINES INPUTS
        LDAA    #%00000100      ACCESS DATA REGISTER
        STAA    PIACRA
KBWAIT  LDAA    PIACRA          IS THERE NEW KEYBOARD DATA?
        BPL     KBWAIT          NO, WAIT UNTIL THERE IS
        LDAA    PIADRA          YES, FETCH DATA
        SWI
```

Object Program:

Memory Address (Hex)	Memory Contents (Hex)			Instruction (Mnemonic)	
0000	7F	PIACRA		CLR	PIACRA
0003	7F	PIADDRA		CLR	PIADDRA
0006	86	04		LDAA	#%00000100
0008	B7	PIACRA		STAA	PIACRA
000B	B6	PIACRA	KBWAIT	LDAA	PIACRA
000E	2A	FB		BPL	KBWAIT
0010	B6	PIADRA		LDAA	PIADRA
0013	3F			SWI	

To make the status bit react to low-to-high transitions on CA1, you can simply replace LDAA #%00000100 with LDAA #%00000110.

Show that reading the Data register clears the status bit. Hint: Save the contents of the Control register in memory before the instruction LDAA PIADRA is executed. What happens if you replace LDAA with STAA? How about TST, CLR, COM, ADD? Remember that writing into the Data register does not clear the status bit. Nor does writing into the Control register. What happens if you replace LDAA PIADRA with STAA PIACRA?

A Digital-to-Analog Converter

Purpose: Send data to an 8-bit digital-to-analog converter, which has an active-low latch enable.

Digital-to-analog converters produce the continuous signals required by motors, solenoids, relays, actuators, and other electrical and mechanical output devices. Typical converters consist of switches and resistor ladders with the appropriate resistance values. Typically, you must provide a reference voltage and some other digital and analog circuitry, although complete units are becoming available at low cost.[5]

Figure 11-22 describes the 8-bit Signetics NE5018 D/A converter, which contains an on-chip 8-bit parallel data input latch. A low level on the $\overline{LE}$ (Latch Enable) input gates the input data into the latches, where it remains after $\overline{LE}$ goes high.

Figure 11-23 illustrates the interfacing of the device to a 6800 system. Note that the B side of the PIA automatically produces the active-low strobe required to latch the data into the converter; CB2 acts as an Output Ready signal. Remember that CB2 goes low on the Enable pulse following a write operation on the B side Data register, and remains low until the next Enable pulse (see Table 11-5). The Control register bits are:

Bit 5 = 1 to make CB2 an output
Bit 4 = 0 to make CB2 a pulse
Bit 3 = 1 to make CB2 a brief Output Ready strobe

Note that the PIA contains an output latch. The data therefore remains stable during and after the conversion. The converter typically requires only a few microseconds to produce an analog output.

In applications where eight bits of resolution are not enough, 10- to 16-bit converters can be used. Additional port logic is required to pass all the data bits; some converters provide part of this logic.

The PIA serves both as a parallel port and as a serial control port. CB2 is a pulse that lasts one clock cycle after the data is latched into the PIA. This pulse is long enough to meet the requirements (typically 400 ns) of the NE5018 converter.

Task: Send data from memory location 0040 to the converter.

Flowchart:

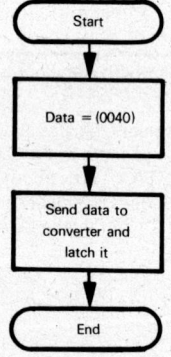

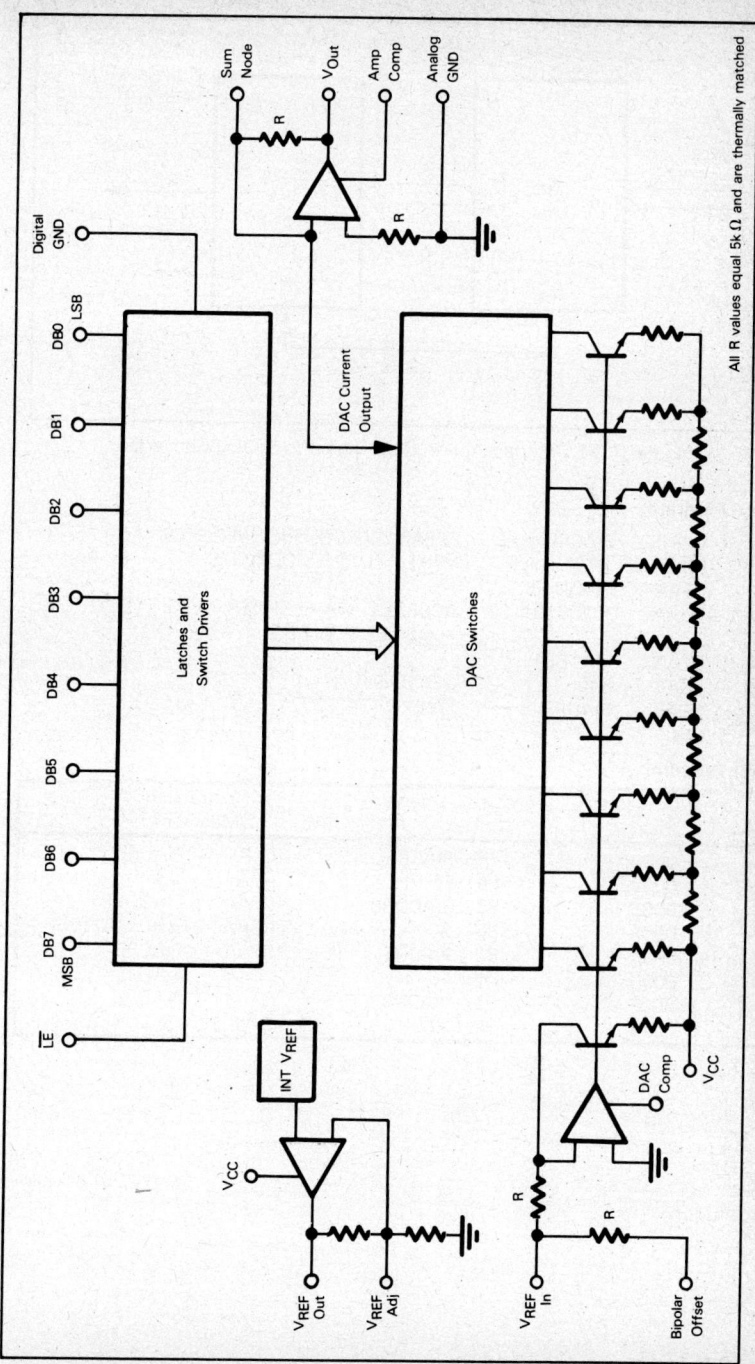

Figure 11-22. Signetics NE5018 D/A Converter

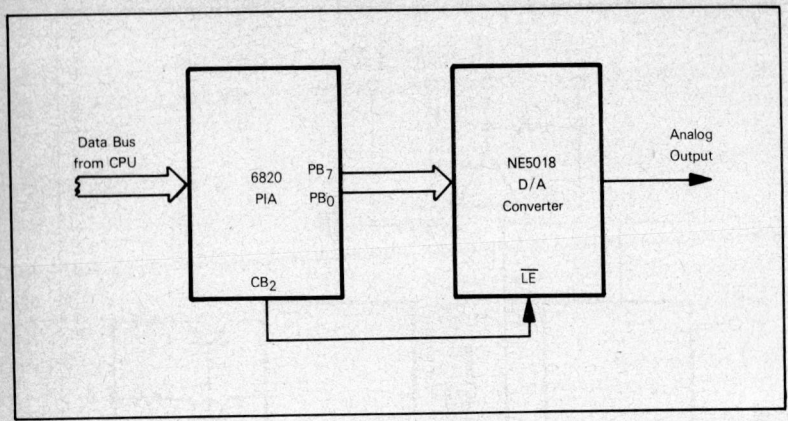

Figure 11-23. Interface for an 8-bit Digital-to-Analog Converter

Source Program:

CLR	PIACRB	CLEAR OUT CONTROL REGISTER
LDAA	#$FF	MAKE ALL LINES OUTPUTS
STAA	PIADDRB	
LDAA	#%00101100	ACCESS DATA REGISTER, MAKE OUTPUT LINE A BRIEF STROBE
STAA	PIACRB	
LDAB	$40	GET DATA
STAB	PIADRB	SEND DATA TO DAC AND LATCH
SWI		

Object Program:

Memory Address (Hex)	Memory Contents (Hex)		Instruction (Mnemonic)	
0000	7F	PIACRB	CLR	PIACRB
0003	86	FF	LDAA	#$FF
0005	B7	PIADDRB	STAA	PIADDRB
0008	86	2C	LDAA	#%00101100
000A	B7	PIACRB	STAA	PIACRB
000D	D6	40	LDAB	$40
000F	F7	PIADRB	STAB	PIADRB
0012	3F		SWI	

We could use the level output from CB2 if the Latch Enable signal were active-high. This pulse would easily meet the length requirements, since it would last for several instruction cycles. The program would then be:

```
CLR    PIACRB          CLEAR OUT CONTROL REGISTER
LDAA   #$FF            MAKE ALL LINES OUTPUTS
STAA   PIADDRB
LDAA   #%00110100      MAKE CB2 A LEVEL
STAA   PIACRB
LDAB   $40             GET DATA
STAB   PIADRB          SEND DATA TO DAC OUTPUT PORT
LDAA   #%00111100      OPEN DAC LATCH (ENABLE HIGH)
STAA   PIACRB
LDAA   #%00110100      LATCH DATA (ENABLE LOW)
STAA   PIADRB
SWI
```

An inverter gate could also provide an active-high strobe. Note how many more instructions are necessary to use the level output.

The CB2 pulse from the 6820 device can serve as a "Byte Out" or other control signal, since writing the data into the port activates it. Note, however, that the pulse is a fairly brief strobe since it only lasts one clock cycle.

Analog-to-Digital Converter

Purpose: Fetch data from an 8-bit analog-to-digital converter which requires an Initiate Conversion pulse to start the conversion process and has a Data Valid line to indicate the completion of the process and the availability of valid data.

Analog-to-digital converters handle the continuous signals produced by various types of sensors and transducers. The converter produces the digital output which the computer requires.

One form of an analog-to-digital converter is the successive-approximation device, which makes a direct 1-bit comparison during each clock cycle. Such converters are fast, but have little noise immunity. Dual slope integrating converters are another form of analog-to-digital converter. These devices take longer but are more resistant to noise. Other techniques, such as the incremental charge balancing technique, are also used.

Analog-to-digital converters usually require some external analog and digital circuitry. Complete units are becoming available at low cost.

Figure 11-24 shows the 8-bit Teledyne Semiconductor 8703 A/D converter. The device contains a result latch and three-state data outputs. A pulse on the Initiate Conversion starts conversion of the analog input; after about two milliseconds the result will go to the output latches and the Data Valid output will indicate this by switching first low and then high. Data is read from the latches by applying a '0' to the $\overline{\text{ENABLE}}$ input.

Figure 11-25 shows the interface for the 6800 processor and the 8703 converter.[6] (See also D. Guzeman, "Marry Your μP to Monolithic A/Ds", Electronic Design, January 18, 1977, pp. 82-86.) CA2 is used to provide the Initiate Conversion pulse (active high). CA1 is used for the Data Valid signal (Data Valid goes from low to high when the conversion has been completed and data is available). Remember that the PIA has no input latch, so either the converter must hold the data or a separate latch will be necessary. The important edge on the Data Valid line is the low-to-high edge, which indicates the completion of the conversion.

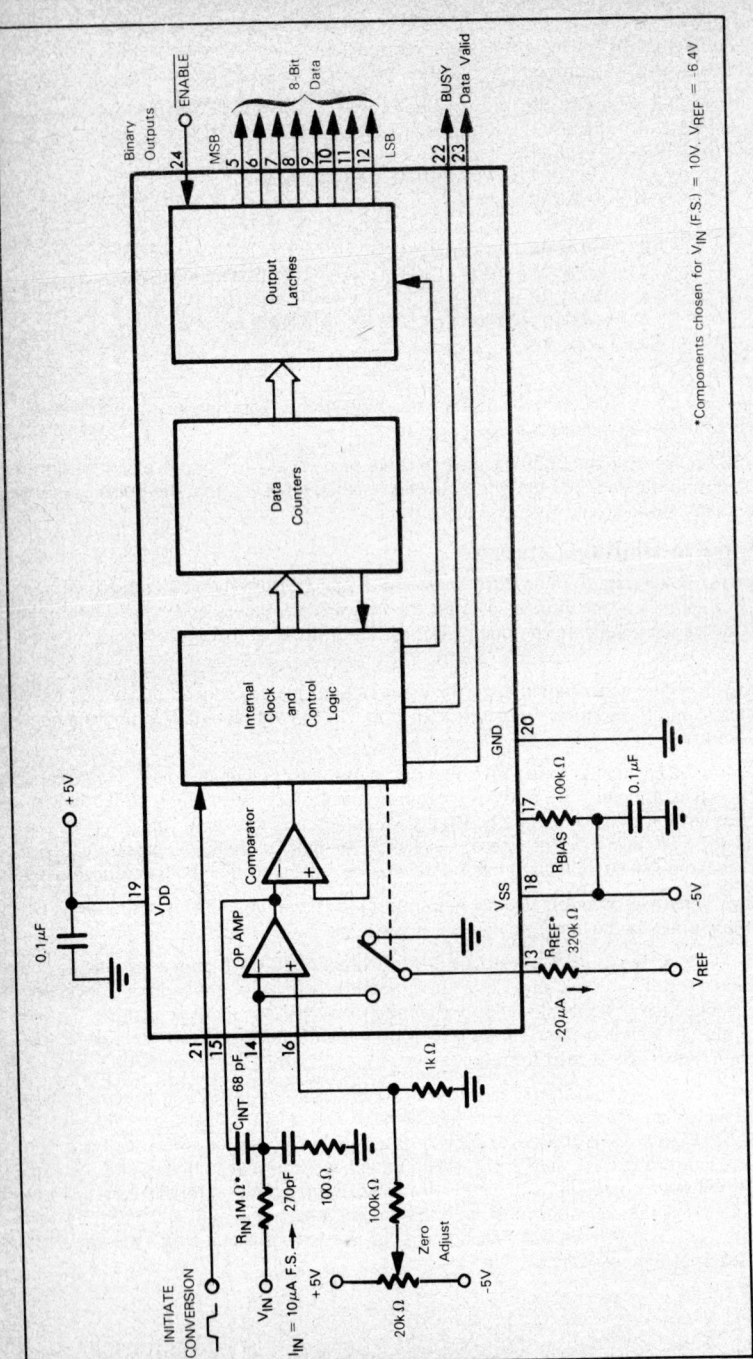

Figure 11-24. Teledyne 8703 A/D Converter

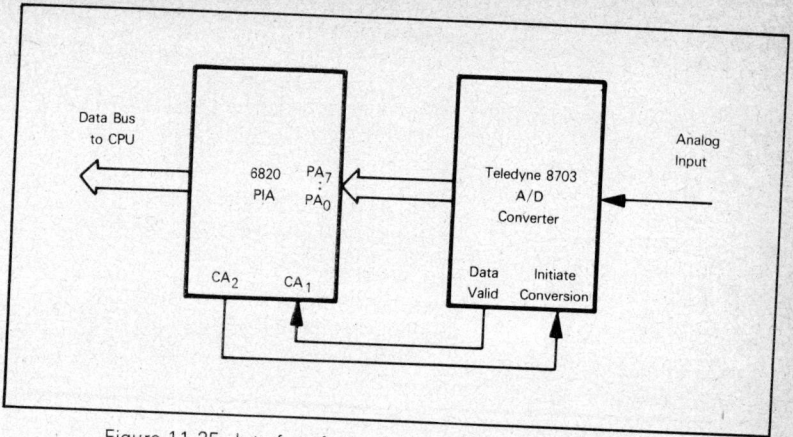

Figure 11-25. Interface for an 8-bit Analog-to-Digital Converter

Task: Start the conversion process, wait for Data Valid to go low and then high, and then read the data and store it in memory location 0040.

Flowchart:

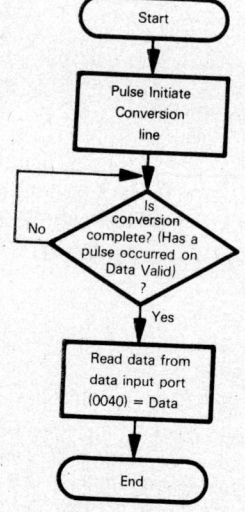

You should include an initial read of the Data register in the startup routine to clear the status flags originally.

Note that here the PIA serves as a parallel data port, a serial status port, and a serial control port.

Source Program:

```
         CLR    PIACRA          CLEAR OUT CONTROL REGISTER
         CLR    PIADDRA         MAKE DATA LINES INPUTS
         LDAA   #%00110110      INITIATE CONVERSION A LEVEL, DATA VALID
                                  ACTIVE LOW-TO-HIGH
         STAA   PIACRA
         LDAB   #%00111110
         STAB   PIACRA          SEND INITIATE CONVERSION HIGH
         STAA   PIACRA          SEND INITIATE CONVERSION LOW
WTBSY    LDAA   PIACRA          IS DATA VALID?
         BPL    WTBSY           NO, WAIT
         LDAA   PIADRA          YES, FETCH DATA FROM CONVERTER
         STAA   $40             SAVE CONVERTER DATA
         SWI
```

Object Program:

Memory Address (Hex)	Memory Contents (Hex)		Instruction (Mnemonic)		
0000	7F	PIACRA		CLR	PIACRA
0003	7F	PIADDRA		CLR	PIADDRA
0006	86	36		LDAA	#%00110110
0008	B7	PIACRA		STAA	PIACRA
000B	C6	3E		LDAB	#%00111110
000D	F7	PIACRA		STAB	PIACRA
0010	B7	PIACRA		STAA	PIACRA
0013	B6	PIACRA	WTBSY	LDAA	PIACRA
0016	2A	FB		BPL	WTBSY
0018	B6	PIADRA		LDAA	PIADRA
001B	97	40		STAA	$40
001D	3F			SWI	

This program would use less memory but more time if the Index register were used to address the PIA. Why would it take more time? Try rewriting the program to use the Index register.

The PIA Control register bits are:

Bit 5 = 1 to make CA2 an output
Bit 4 = 1 to make CA2 a level
Bit 3 = value of level on CA2
Bit 1 = 1 to set bit 7 on a low-to-high transition on the Data Valid line.

Note that Data Valid is high except for about $5\mu s$ before the end of the conversion. It returns to a high level when the conversion is completed and new data is available from the latches. A delay routine of appropriate length (longer than the maximum guaranteed conversion time) could replace the examination of the status bit.

A Teletypewriter (TTY)

Purpose: Transfer data to and from a standard 10-character-per-second serial teletypewriter.

> **TTY INTERFACE**

The common teletypewriter transfers data in an asynchronous serial mode. The procedure is as follows:

1) The line is normally in the one state.
2) A Start bit (zero bit) precedes each character.
3) The character is usually 7-bit ASCII with the least significant bit transmitted first.
4) The most significant bit is a Parity bit, which may be even, odd, or fixed at zero or one.
5) Two stop bits (logic one) follow each character.

> **STANDARD TTY CHARACTER FORMAT**

Figure 11-26 shows the format. Note that each character requires the transmission of eleven bits, of which only seven contain information. Since the data rate is ten characters per second, the bit rate is 10 x 11, or 110 Baud. Each bit therefore has a width of 1/110 of a second, or 9.1 milliseconds. This width is an average; the teletypewriter does not maintain it to any high level of accuracy.

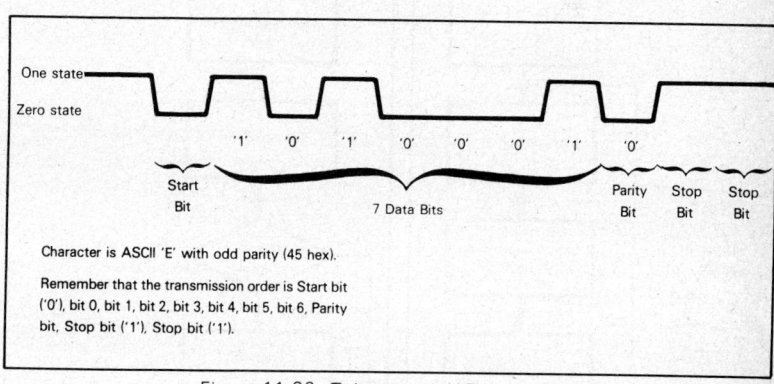

Figure 11-26. Teletypewriter Data Format

For a teletypewriter to communicate properly with a computer, the following procedures are necessary:

Receive (flowcharted in Figure 11-27):

> **TTY RECEIVE MODE**

Step 1) Look for a Start bit (a logic zero) on the data line.
Step 2) Center the reception by waiting one-half bit time, or 4.55 milliseconds.
Step 3) Fetch the data bits, waiting one bit time before each one. Assemble the data bits into a word by first shifting the bit to the Carry and then circularly shifting the data with the Carry. Remember that the least significant bit is received first.
Step 4) Generate the received Parity and check it against the transmitted Parity. If they do not match, indicate a "Parity error".
Step 5) Fetch the Stop bits (waiting one bit time between inputs). If they are not correct (if both Stop bits are not one), indicate a "framing error".

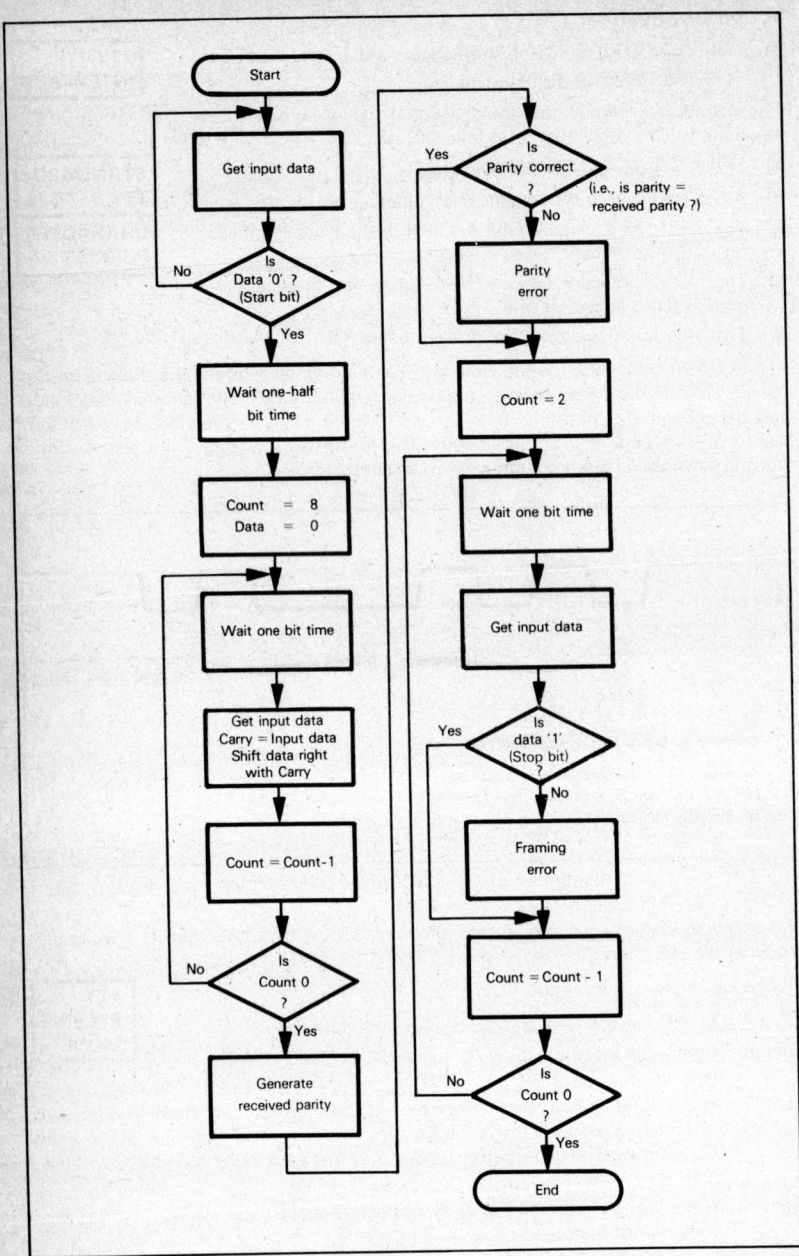

Figure 11-27. Flowchart for Receive Procedure

Task: Fetch data from a teletypewriter through bit 7 of a PIA data port and place the data in memory location 0040. For procedure, see Figure 11-27.

Source Program:

(Assuming that the serial port is bit 7 of the PIA and that no parity or framing is necessary)

TTY RECEIVE PROGRAM

```
            CLR    PIACRA         CLEAR OUT CONTROL REGISTER
            CLR    PIADDRA        MAKE DATA LINES INPUTS
            LDAA   #%00000100     ACCESS DATA REGISTER
            STAA   PIACRA
WAITS       LDAA   PIADRA         IS THERE A START BIT?
            BMI    WAITS          NO, WAIT
            JSR    DLY2           YES, DELAY HALF BIT TIME TO CENTER
            LDAA   #%10000000     COUNT WITH BIT IN MSB
TTYRCV      JSR    DELAY          WAIT 1 BIT TIME
            ROL    PIADRA         GET DATA BIT
            RORA                  ADD TO DATA WORD
            BCC    TTYRCV         CONTINUE IF COUNT BIT NOT IN CARRY
            STAA   $40
            SWI
```

(Delay program)

```
DLY2        LDX    #$0238         COUNT FOR 4.55 MS
            BRA    DLY
DELAY       LDX    #$0470         COUNT FOR 9.1 MS
DLY         DEX
            BNE    DLY
            RTS
```

Remember that bit 0 of the data is received first.

Object Program:

Memory Address (Hex)	Memory Contents (Hex)			Instruction (Mnemonic)	
0000	7F	PIACRA		CLR	PIACRA
0003	7F	PIADDRA		CLR	PIADDRA
0006	86	04		LDAA	#%00000100
0008	B7	PIACRA		STAA	PIACRA
000B	B6	PIADRA	WAITS	LDAA	PIADRA
000E	2B	FB		BMI	WAITS
0010	BD	0030		JSR	DLY2
0013	86	80		LDAA	#%10000000
0015	BD	0035	TTYRCV	JSR	DELAY
0018	79	PIADRA		ROL	PIADRA
001B	46			RORA	
001C	24	F7		BCC	TTYRCV
001E	97	40		STAA	$40
0020	3F			SWI	
0030	CE	0238	DLY2	LDX	#$0238
0033	20	03		BRA	DLY
0035	CE	0470	DELAY	LDX	#$0470
0038	09		DLY	DEX	
0039	26	FD		BNE	DLY
003B	39			RTS	

This program assumes that the Stack can be used for subroutine calls; either the monitor must initialize the Stack Pointer or you will have to initialize the Stack Pointer as shown in Chapter 10.

The constants for the delay routine were calculated just as shown earlier in this chapter. You might try determining them for yourself. The delays do not have to be highly accurate because the reception is centered, the messages are short, the bit rate is low, and the teletypewriter is not highly accurate itself.

How would you extend this program to check for the two Stop bits? They must both be one, or a framing error has occurred.

How would you extend this program to check parity? Hint: clear Accumulator B to start and Exclusive OR the received data with the contents of B after each bit time.

Transmit (flowcharted in Figure 11-28)

TTY TRANSMIT MODE

Step 1) Transmit a Start bit (i.e., a logic one).
Step 2) Transmit the seven data bits, starting with the least significant bit.
Step 3) Generate and transmit the Parity bit.
Step 4) Transmit two Stop bits (i.e., logic ones).

The transmission routine must wait one bit time between each operation.

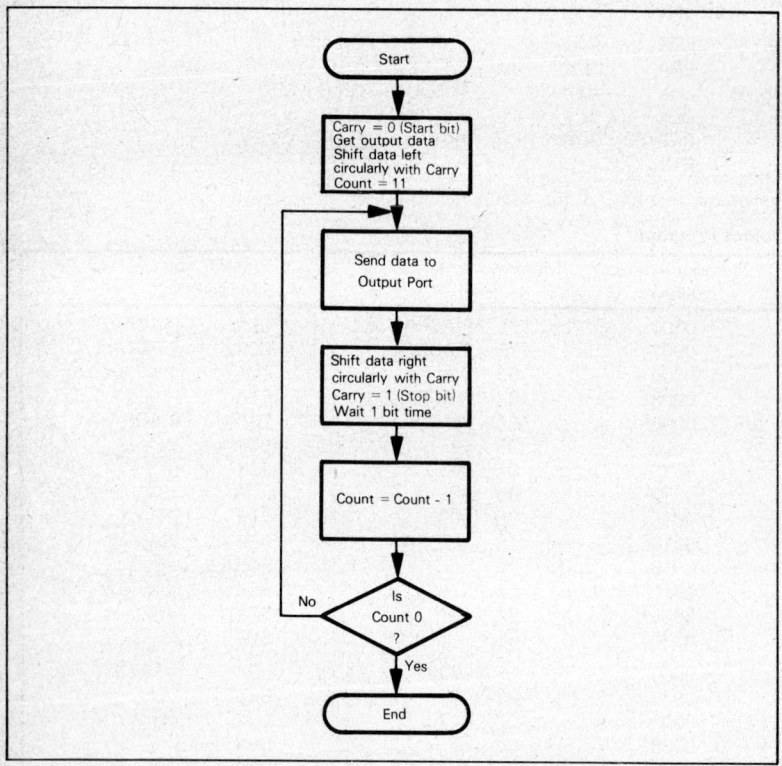

Figure 11-28. Flowchart for Transmit Procedure

Task: Transmit data to a teletypewriter through bit 0 of a PIA data port (see procedure in Figure 11-28). The data is in memory location 0040.

Source Program:

(Assuming that parity need not be generated)

TTY TRANSMIT PROGRAM

	CLR	PIACRA	CLEAR OUT CONTROL REGISTER
	LDAA	#$FF	MAKE DATA LINES OUTPUTS
	STAA	PIADDRA	
	LDAA	#%00000100	ACCESS DATA REGISTER
	STAA	PIACRA	
	LDAA	$40	GET DATA
	LDAB	#11	11 BITS IN CHARACTER
	CLR	PIADRA	SEND START BIT
TTYTX	JSR	DELAY	WAIT 1 BIT TIME
	SEC		STOP BIT = 1
	RORA		GET NEXT BIT OF CHARACTER
	ROL	PIADRA	SEND TO TTY
	DECB		
	BNE	TTYTX	
	SWI		

The DELAY subroutine is the same as before. Remember that bit 0 of the data must be transmitted first.

Object Program:

Memory Address (Hex)	Memory Contents (Hex)			Instruction (Mnemonic)	
0000	7F	PIACRA		CLR	PIACRA
0003	86	FF		LDAA	#$FF
0005	B7	PIADDRA		STAA	PIADDRA
0008	86	04		LDAA	#%00000100
000B	B7	PIACRA		STAA	PIACRA
000D	96	40		LDAA	$40
000F	C6	0B		LDAB	#11
0011	7F	PIADRA		CLR	PIADRA
0014	BD	0030		TTYTX JSR	DELAY
0017	0D			SEC	
0018	46			RORA	
0019	79	PIADRA		ROL	PIADRA
001C	5A			DECB	
001D	26	F5		BNE	TTYTX
001F	3F			SWI	

CLR PIADRA clears all the bits in the Data register and hence generates a Start bit. In actual applications, you will find it necessary to place a one on the teletypewriter line after configuration, since that line should be in the one state when no data are being transmitted.

Each character consists of 11 bits, starting with a Start bit (zero) and ending with two Stop bits (ones).

How would you extend this program to generate parity? Hint: add all the bits together in the least significant position:

```
        CLRA            PARITY = ZERO
        LDAB    $40     GET DATA
CPAR    ABA             ADD NEXT BIT TO PARITY
        LSRB
        BNE     CPAR
```

Why does this procedure work? Try it on some examples. This program generates even parity. How would you generate odd parity?

These procedures are sufficiently common and complex to merit a special LSI device: the UART,[7] or Universal Asynchronous Receiver/Transmitter.   **UART**

The UART will perform the reception procedure and provide the data in parallel form and a Data Ready signal. It will also accept data in parallel form, perform the transmission procedure, and provide a Peripheral Ready signal when it can handle more data. UARTs may have many other features, including:

1) Ability to handle various bit lengths (usually 5 to 8), parity options, and numbers of Stop bits (usually 1, 1-1/2, and 2).

2) Indicators for framing errors, parity errors, and "overrun errors" (failure to read a character before another one is received).

3) RS-232[8] compatibility; i.e., a Request-to-Send (RTS) output signal that indicates the presence of data to communications equipment and a Clear-to-Send (CTS) input signal that indicates, in response to RTS, the readiness of the communications equipment. There may be provisions for other RS-232 signals, such as Received Signal Quality, Data Set Ready, or Data Terminal Ready.

4) Tristate outputs and control compatibility with a microprocessor.

5) Clock options that allow the UART to sample incoming data several times in order to detect false Start bits and other errors.

6) Interrupt facilities and controls.

UARTs act as four parallel ports: an input data port, an output data port, an input status port, and an output control port. The status bits include error indicators as well as Ready flags. The control bits select various options. UARTs are inexpensive ($5 to $50, depending on features) and easy to use.

THE 6850 ASYNCHRONOUS COMMUNICATIONS INTERFACE ADAPTER (ACIA)

The 6850 ACIA, or Asynchronous Communications Interface Adapter (see Figure 11-29), is a UART specifically designed for use in 6800-based microcomputers. It occupies two memory addresses and contains two read-only registers (received data and status) and two write-only registers (transmitted data and control). Tables 11-11 and 11-12 describe the contents of these registers.

ACIA REGISTERS

Note the following special features of the ACIA:

SPECIAL FEATURES OF ACIA

1) Read and write cycles address physically distinct registers. Therefore, you cannot use the ACIA registers as addresses for instructions like Increment, Decrement, or Shift, which involve both read and write cycles.

2) The ACIA Control register cannot be read by the CPU. You will have to save a copy of the Control register in memory if the program needs its value.

3) The ACIA has no Reset input. It can be reset only by placing ones in Control register bits 0 and 1. This procedure (called MASTER RESET) is necessary before the ACIA is used, in order to avoid having a random starting character.

4) The RS-232 signals are all active-low. Request-to-Send (RTS), in particular, should be brought high to make it inactive if it is not in use.

5) The ACIA requires an external clock. Typically 1760 Hz is supplied and the ÷ 16 mode (Control register bit 1 = 0, bit 0 = 1) is used. The ACIA will use the clock to center the reception in order to avoid false Start bits caused by noise on the lines.

6) The Data Ready (receive data register full, or RDRF) flag is bit 0 of the Status register. The Peripheral Ready (transmit data register empty, or TDRE) flag is bit 1 of the Status register.

Task: Receive data from a teletypewriter through an ACIA and place the data in memory location 0040.

Source Program:

```
         LDAA    #%00000011    MASTER RESET ACIA
         STAA    ACIACR
         LDAA    #%01000101    CONFIGURE ACIA FOR TTY WITH ODD PARITY
         STAA    ACIACR
WAITD    LDAA    ACIASR        GET ACIA STATUS
         LSRA                  HAS DATA BEEN RECEIVED?
         BCC     WAITD         NO, WAIT
         LDAA    ACIADR        FETCH DATA
         STAA    $40           AND SAVE IT
         SWI
```

Table 11-11. Definition of ACIA Register Contents

Data Bus Line Number	Buffer Address			
	RS·R/W̅ Transmit Data Register (Write Only)	RS·R/W Receive Data Register (Read Only)	R̅S̅·R/W̅ Control Register (Write Only)	R̅S̅·R/W Status Register (Read Only)
0	Data Bit 0*	Data Bit 0	Counter Divide Select 1 (CR0)	Receive Data Register Full (RDRF)
1	Data Bit 1	Data Bit 1	Counter Divide Select 2 (CR1)	Transmit Data Register Empty (TDRE)
2	Data Bit 2	Data Bit 2	Word Select 1 (CR2)	Data Carrier Detect (D̅C̅D̅)
3	Data Bit 3	Data Bit 3	Word Select 2 (CR3)	Clear-to-Send (C̅T̅S̅)
4	Data Bit 4	Data Bit 4	Word Select 3 (CR4)	Framing Error (FE)
5	Data Bit 5	Data Bit 5	Transmit Control 1 (CR5)	Receiver Overrun (OVRN)
6	Data Bit 6	Data Bit 6	Transmit Control 2 (CR6)	Parity Error (PE)
7	Data Bit 7***	Data Bit 7**	Receive Interrupt Enable (CR7)	Interrupt Request (I̅R̅Q̅)

* Leading bit = LSB = Bit 0
** Data bit will be zero in 7-bit plus parity modes
*** Data bit is "don't care" in 7-bit plus parity modes

Object Program:

Memory Address (Hex)	Memory Contents (Hex)		Instruction (Mnemonic)	
0000	86	03		LDAA #%00000011
0002	B7	ACIACR		STAA ACIACR
0005	86	45		LDAA #%01000101
0007	B7	ACIACR		STAA ACIACR
000A	B6	ACIASR	WAITD	LDAA ACIASR
000D	44			LSRA
000E	24	FA		BCC WAITD
0010	B6	ACIADR		LDAA ACIADR
0013	97	40		STAA $40
0015	3F			SWI

Table 11-12. Meaning of the ACIA Control Register Bits

CR6	CR5	Function
0	0	$\overline{RTS}$ = low, Transmitting Interrupt Disabled
0	1	$\overline{RTS}$ = low, Transmitting Interrupt Enabled
1	0	$\overline{RTS}$ = high, Transmitting Interrupt Disabled
1	1	$\overline{RTS}$ = low, Transmits a Break level on the Transmit Data Output, Transmitting Interrupt Disabled

CR4	CR3	CR2	Function
0	0	0	7 Bits + Even Parity + 2 Stop Bits
0	0	1	7 Bits + Odd Parity + 2 Stop Bits
0	1	0	7 Bits + Even Parity + 1 Stop Bit
0	1	1	7 Bits + Odd Parity + 1 Stop Bit
1	0	0	8 Bits + 2 Stop Bits
1	0	1	8 Bits + 1 Stop Bit
1	1	0	8 Bits + Even Parity + 1 Stop Bit
1	1	1	8 Bits + Odd Parity + 1 Stop Bit

CR1	CR0	Function
0	0	÷ 1
0	1	÷ 16
1	0	÷ 64
1	1	Master Reset

The program must reset the ACIA originally by placing ones in Control register bits 0 and 1. The ACIA does have an internal power-on reset which holds the ACIA in the reset state until Master Reset is applied.

The program configures the ACIA control register as follows:

EXAMPLE OF ACIA CONFIGURATION

Bit 7 = 0 to disable the receiver interrupt

Bit 6 = 1 to make Request-to-Send ($\overline{RTS}$) high (inactive)

Bit 5 = 0 to disable the transmitter interrupt

Bit 4 = 0 for 7-bit words

Bit 3 = 0, Bit 2 = 1 for odd parity with 2 Stop bits

Bit 1 = 0, Bit 0 = 1 for ÷ 16 clock (1760 Hz must be supplied)

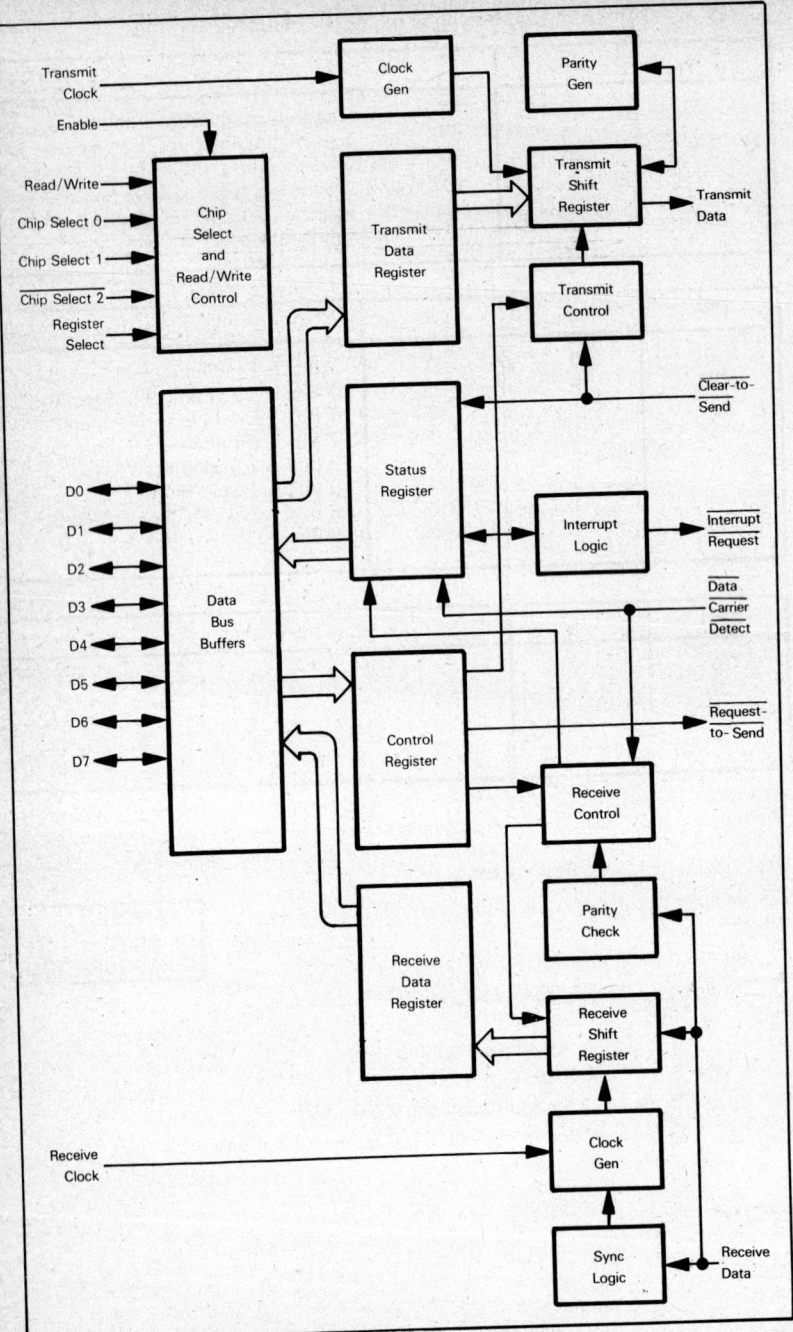

Figure 11-29. Block Diagram of the 6850 ACIA

The received data status bit is Status register bit 0. What would happen if we tried to replace

    LDAA   ACIASR
    LSRA

with the single instruction

    LSR   ACIASR?

Remember that the Status and Control registers share an address but are physically distinct.

Try adding an error checking routine to the program. Set

    (0041) = 0 if no errors occurred
            = 1 if a parity error occurred
              (Status register bit 6 = 1)
            = 2 if an overrun error occurred
              (Status register bit 5 = 1)
            = 3 if a framing error occurred
              (Status register bit 4 = 1)

ADDRESSING AN ACIA

The Index register can be used to help address an ACIA. If the Control and Status register address is loaded into the Index register, the data registers can be referred to with an offset of 1. The changes are:

Old		New (X)=ACIACR	
STAA	ACIACR	STAA	X
LDAA	ACIASR	LDAA	X
LDAA	ACIADR	LDAA	1,X

Task: Send data from memory location 0040 to a teletypewriter through an ACIA.

Source Program:

```
        LDAA  #%00000011   MASTER RESET ACIA
        STAA  ACIACR
        LDAA  #%01000101   CONFIGURE ACIA FOR TTY
                             WITH ODD PARITY
        STAA  ACIACR
        LDAA  #%00000010
WAITR   BITA  ACIASR       IS ACIA READY?
        BEQ   WAITR        NO, WAIT
        LDAA  $40          YES, GET DATA
        STAA  ACIADR       AND TRANSMIT IT
        SWI
```

11-79

Object Program:

Memory Address (Hex)	Memory Contents (Hex)		Instruction (Mnemonic)	
0000	86	03	LDAA	#%00000011
0002	B7	ACIACR	STAA	ACIACR
0005	86	45	LDAA	#%01000101
0007	B7	ACIACR	STAA	ACIACR
000A	86	02	LDAA	#%00000010
000C	B5	ACIASR	WAITR BITA	ACIASR
000F	27	FB	BEQ	WAITR
0011	96	40	LDAA	$40
0013	B7	ACIADR	STAA	ACIADR
0016	3F		SWI	

The transmitter status bit is Status register bit 1. How could you modify the receive program to use the Bit Test instruction?

STANDARD INTERFACES

Other standard interfaces besides the TTY current-loop and RS-232 can also be used to connect peripherals to the microcomputer. Popular ones include:

1) The serial RS449, RS422, and RS423 interfaces.[9]
2) The 8-bit parallel General Purpose Interface Bus, also known as IEEE-488 or Hewlett-Packard Interface Bus (HPIB).[10]
3) The S-100 or Altair/Imsai hobbyist bus.[11] This is also an 8-bit bus.
4) The Intel Multibus.[12] This is another 8-bit bus that can, however, be expanded to handle 16 bits in parallel.

PROBLEMS

1) Separating Closures from an Unencoded Keyboard

Purpose: The program should read entries from an unencoded 3 x 3 keyboard and place them in an array. The number of entries required is in memory location 0040 and the array starts in memory location 0041.

Separate one closure from the next by waiting for the current closure to end. Remember to debounce the keyboard (this can simply be a 1 ms wait).

Sample Problem:

```
              (0040) = 04
              Entries are 7, 2, 2, 4
    Result:   (0041) = 07
              (0042) = 02
              (0043) = 02
              (0044) = 04
```

2) Read a Sentence from an Encoded Keyboard

Purpose: The program should read entries from an ASCII keyboard (7 bits with a zero Parity bit) and place them in an array until it receives an ASCII period (hex 2E). The array starts in memory location 0040. Each entry is marked by a strobe as in the example given under An Encoded Keyboard.

Sample Problem:

Entries are H, E, L, L, O, .

Result: (0040) = 48 H
        (0041) = 45 E
        (0042) = 4C L
        (0043) = 4C L
        (0044) = 4F O
        (0045) = 2E .

3) A Variable Amplitude Square Wave Generator

Purpose: The program should generate a square wave, as shown in the next figure, using a D/A converter. Memory location 0040 contains the scaled amplitude of the wave, memory location 0041 the length of a half cycle in milliseconds, and memory location 0042 the number of cycles.

Assume that a digital output of 80_{16} to the converter results in an analog output of zero volts. In general, a digital output of D results in an analog output of $(D-80)/80 \times -V_{REF}$ volts.

Sample Problem:

    (0040) = A0 (hex)
    (0041) = 04
    (0042) = 03

Result:

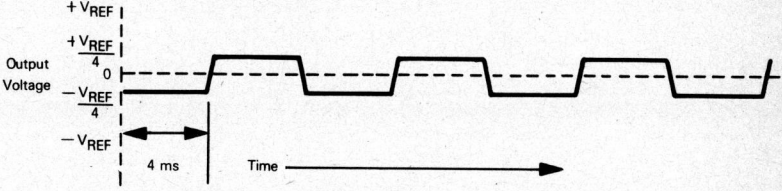

The base voltage is 80_{16} = 0 volts. Full scale is 100_{16} = $-V_{REF}$ volts. So $A0_{16}$ =

$$(A0-80)/80 \times -V_{REF} = -V_{REF}/4$$

The program produces 3 pulses of amplitude $V_{REF}/4$ with a half cycle length of 4 ms.

4) Averaging Analog Readings

Purpose: The program should take four readings from an A/D converter 10 milliseconds apart and place the average in memory location 0040. Assume that the A/D converter takes less than 100 microseconds to convert, so that the conversion time can be ignored.

Sample Problem:

Readings are (hex) 86, 89, 81, 84
Result: (0040) = 85

5) A 30 Character-per-Second Terminal

Purpose: Modify the transmit and receive routines of the example given under A Teletypewriter to handle a 30 cps terminal that transfers ASCII data with one stop bit and even parity. How could you write the routines to handle either terminal depending on a flag bit in memory location 0040; e.g., (0040) = 0 for the 30 cps terminal, (0040) = 1 for the 10 cps terminal?

REFERENCES

[1] Barnes, J., and V. Gregory, "Use Microprocessors to Enhance Performance with Noisy Data", EDN, August 20, 1976, pp. 71-72.

[2] Swanson, R., "Understanding Cyclic Redundancy Codes", Computer Design, November 1975, pp. 93-99.

[3] For the use of a bit-rate generator, see G. Nash, "Microprocessor Software Programs Bit-Rate Generator", EDN, August 20, 1977, pp. 134-137.

[4] J. Gilmore and R. Huntington, "Designing with the 6820 Peripheral Interface Adapter", Electronics, December 23, 1976, pp. 85-86.

[5] See, for example, A. Mrozowski, "Analog Output Chips Shrink A/D Conversion Software", Electronics, June 23, 1977, pp. 130-133.

[6] For more complete descriptions of the use of A/D converters with the 6800 processor, see:
D. Aldridge, "Analog-to-Digital Conversion Techniques with the M6800 Microprocessor System", Motorola Semiconductor Products Application Note AN-757, Motorola, Inc., Phoenix, AZ, 1975.

D. Fullagar et al., "Interfacing Data Converters and Microprocessors", Electronics, December 9, 1976, pp. 81-89.

S. Kelly, "Low-Cost Data Acquisition Systems", Electronic Design, November 22, 1976, pp. 152-157.

[7] For a discussion of UARTs, see P. Rony et al., "The Bugbook IIa", E and L Instruments, Inc., 61 First Street, Derby, CT 06418; or D.G. Larsen et al., "INWAS: Interfacing with Asynchronous Serial Mode", IEEE Transactions on Industrial Electronics and Control Instrumentation, February 1977, pp. 2-12.

[8] You can find introductory descriptions of RS-232 in F.W. Etcheverry, "Binary Serial Interfaces", EDN, April 20, 1976, pp. 40-43; and in G. Pickles, "Who's Afraid of RS-232?, Kilobaud, May 1977, pp. 50-54.

[9] D. Morris, "Revised Data Interface Standards", Electronic Design, September 1, 1977, pp. 138-141.

[10] J.B. Peatman, Microcomputer-Based Design, McGraw-Hill, New York, 1977.
S.C. Baunach, "An Example of an M6800-based GPIB Interface", EDN, September 20, 1977, pp. 125-128.

A more detailed version of this article, complete with program listing and schematics, is available from Tektronix, Inc., Box 500, Beaverton, OR 97077.

[11] D. Denney and J. Broom, "Why Not a Standard 100-Wire Bus Structure?", Computer, October 1976, pp. 57-58.

M.L. Smith, "Build Your Own Interface", Kilobaud, June 1977, pp. 22-28.

[12] T. Rolander, "Intel Multibus Interfacing", Intel Application Note Ap-28, Intel Corporation, Santa Clara, CA, 1977.

Chapter 12
INTERRUPTS

Interrupts are serial inputs that the CPU examines as part of each instruction cycle. These inputs allow the CPU to react to events at the hardware level rather than at the software level through checking status bits (polling). Interrupts generally require more hardware than ordinary (programmed) I/O, but provide a faster and more direct response. You may want to review the discussion of interrupts in Volume I of <u>An Introduction to Microcomputers</u>.

REASONING BEHIND INTERRUPTS

Why use interrupts? Interrupts allow events such as alarms, power failure, the passage of a certain amount of time, and peripherals having data or being ready to accept data to get the immediate attention of the CPU. The programmer does not need to have the CPU check status bits with sequences involving conditional Branch instructions. Nor need the programmer worry about missing events. An interrupt system is like the bell on a telephone -- it rings when a call is received so that you don't have to pick up the receiver occasionally to see if someone is on the line. The CPU can go about its normal business (and get a lot more done). When something happens, the interrupt rouses the CPU and forces it to service the input before resuming normal operations. Of course, this simple description becomes more complicated (just like a telephone switchboard) when there are many interrupts of varying importance and tasks which cannot be interrupted.

CHARACTERISTICS OF INTERRUPT SYSTEMS

The implementation of interrupt systems varies greatly. Among the questions that must be answered to characterize a particular system are:

1) How many interrupt inputs are there?
2) How does the CPU respond to an interrupt?
3) How does the CPU determine the source of an interrupt if the number of sources exceeds the number of inputs?
4) Can the CPU differentiate between important and unimportant interrupts?
5) How and when is the interrupt system enabled and disabled?

There are many different answers to these questions. The aim of all the implementations, however, is to have the CPU respond rapidly to interrupts and resume normal activity afterwards.

The number of interrupt inputs on the CPU chip determines the number of different responses that the CPU can produce without any additional hardware or software. Each input can produce a different internal response. Unfortunately, most microprocessors have a very small number (one or two, typically) of separate interrupt inputs.

The ultimate response of the CPU to an interrupt must be to transfer control to the correct interrupt service routine and to save the current value of the Program Counter. The CPU must therefore execute a Jump-to-Subroutine or Call instruction with the beginning of the interrupt service routine as its address. This action will save the return address in the Stack and transfer control to the interrupt service routine. The amount of external hardware required to produce this response varies greatly. Some CPUs internally generate the instruction and the address; others require external hardware to form them. The CPU can only generate a different instruction or address for each separate input.

POLLING
VECTORING

If the number of interrupting devices exceeds the number of inputs, the CPU will need extra hardware or software to identify the source of the interrupt. In the simplest case, the software can be a polling routine which checks the status of the devices that may be interrupting. The only advantage of such a system over normal polling is that the CPU knows that at least one device is active. The alternative solution is for additional hardware to provide a unique data input (or "vector") for each source. The two alternatives can be mixed; the vectors can identify groups of inputs from which the CPU can identify a particular one by polling.

PRIORITY

An interrupt system which can differentiate between important and unimportant interrupts is called a "priority interrupt system". Internal hardware can provide as many priority levels as there are inputs. External hardware can provide additional levels through the use of a Priority register and comparator. The external hardware does not allow the interrupt to reach the CPU unless its priority is higher than the contents of the Priority register. A priority interrupt system may need a special way to handle low-priority interrupts that may be ignored for long periods of time.

ENABLING AND DISABLING INTERRUPTS

Most interrupt systems can be enabled or disabled. In fact, most CPUs automatically disable interrupts when a RESET is performed (so that the programmer can configure the interrupt system) and on accepting an interrupt (so that the interrupt will not interrupt its own service routine). The programmer may wish to disable interrupts while preparing or processing data, performing a timing loop, or executing a multi-word operation.

NON-MASKABLE INTERRUPT

An interrupt which cannot be disabled (sometimes called a "non-maskable interrupt") may be useful to warn of power failure, an event that obviously must take precedence over all other activities.

DISADVANTAGES OF INTERRUPTS

The advantages of interrupts are obvious, but there are also disadvantages. These include:

1) Interrupt systems may require a large amount of extra hardware.
2) Interrupts still require data transfers under program control through the CPU. There is no speed advantage as there is with DMA.
3) Interrupts are random inputs which make debugging and testing difficult. Errors may occur sporadically, and therefore may be very hard to find (for a discussion of designing with interrupts, see Baldridge, R.L., "Interrupts Add Power, Complexity to µC-System Design", EDN, August 5, 1977, pp. 67-73).
4) Interrupts may involve a large amount of overhead if many registers must be saved and the source must be determined by polling.

6800 INTERRUPT SYSTEM

The 6800's internal response to an interrupt is moderately complex. The interrupt system consists of:

6800 INTERRUPT INPUTS

1) An active-low maskable interrupt ($\overline{IRQ}$) and an active-low non-maskable interrupt ($\overline{NMI}$).
2) An interrupt disable bit I (1 to disable the maskable interrupt), which is bit 4 of the Condition Code register.

2) PIA and ACIA addresses are rarely consecutive or evenly spaced; therefore, separate instructions are necessary to examine each input. Polling routines are therefore difficult to expand. Tables of I/O addresses could be used, but are awkward to handle with a single Index register.

3) Interrupts that are polled first may shut out those that are polled later unless the order of polling is varied. However, the lack of consecutive addresses makes varying the order of polling difficult.

6800 Vectored Interrupt Systems

The problem of polling in 6800-based systems has typically been solved by special methods, unique to a particular application or microcomputer (see, for example, J.D. Logan and P.S. Kreager, "Using a Microprocessor", Computer Design, September 1975, pp. 69-77). The 6828 Priority Interrupt Controller does provide an eight-level vectored interrupt system. This device simply recognizes the addresses FFF8 and FFF9 (see Table 12-1) when they appear on the Address Bus and replaces them with one of the eight vectors. We will not discuss this device or 6800 vectored interrupt systems any further. You can find a description of the 6828 device in Volume II of An Introduction to Microcomputers.

6800 VECTORED INTERRUPTS

EXAMPLES

A Startup Interrupt

Purpose: The computer waits for a PIA interrupt to occur before starting actual operations.

Many systems remain inactive until the operator actually starts them or a DATA READY signal is received. On RESET, such systems must initialize the Stack Pointer, enable the startup interrupt, and execute a WAI instruction. Remember that RESET disables the processor interrupt as well as all the PIA interrupts. In the flowchart, the decision as to whether startup is active is made in hardware (i.e., by the CPU examining the interrupt input internally) rather than in software.

Flowchart:

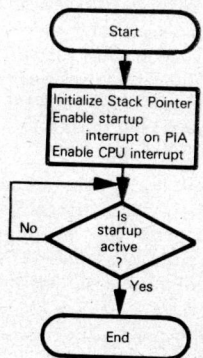

Source Program:

Main Program:

```
        SEI                     DISABLE INTERRUPT
        STS     $3E             SAVE MONITOR STACK POINTER
        LDS     #$58            INITIALIZE USER STACK POINTER
        LDAA    #%00000101
        STAA    PIACRA
        CLI                     ENABLE CPU INTERRUPT
        WAI                     AND WAIT
```

Interrupt Service Routine:

```
        ORG     INTRP
        LDAA    PIADRA          CLEAR INTERRUPT
        LDS     $3E             RESTORE MONITOR STACK POINTER
        SWI
```

Object Program:

Memory Address (Hex)	Memory Contents (Hex)		Instruction (Mnemonic)	
Main Program:				
0000	0F		SEI	
0001	9F	3E	STS	$3E
0003	8E	0058	LDS	#$58
0006	86	05	LDAA	#%00000101
0008	B7	PIACRA	STAA	PIACRA
000B	0E		CLI	
000C	3E		WAI	
Interrupt Service Routine:				
INTRP	B6	PIADRA	LDAA	PIADRA
INTRP+3	9E	3E	LDS	$3E
INTRP+5	3F		SWI	

The exact location of the interrupt service routine varies with the microcomputer. If your microcomputer has no monitor, you can simply place whatever address you want in memory locations FFF8 and FFF9 (or whatever locations respond to those addresses). You must then start the interrupt routine at the address you chose.

INTERRUPTS ON PARTICULAR MICROCOMPUTERS

If your microcomputer has a monitor, the monitor will occupy addresses FFF8 and FFF9. Those addresses will either contain a starting address at which you must place your interrupt service routine, or will contain the starting address of a routine that allows you to choose the starting address of the interrupt service routine. A typical monitor routine would be:

INTERRUPT HANDLING BY MONITORS

```
MONINT  LDX     USRINT   GET USER ADDRESS FOR INTERRUPT
                         SERVICE ROUTINE
        JMP     X        AND JUMP TO IT
```

You must then place the address of your service routine in memory locations USRINT and USRINT+1. Remember that MONINT is an address in the monitor program and its value is in addresses FFF8 and FFF9.

You can include the loading of memory locations USRINT and USRINT+1 in your main program:

```
        LDX     #INTRP  GET STARTING ADDRESS OF SERVICE ROUTINE
        STX     USRINT  STORE IT AT USER ADDRESS
```

These instructions must precede the enabling of the interrupts.

If the example program were actually entered only on $\overline{\text{RESET}}$ the SEI and STS $3E instructions would be unnecessary. Furthermore, the LDS $3E instruction in the service routine would be replaced by LDS #USRSTK.

On some 6800-based microcomputers, you may not be able to use the WAI instruction. This is because, if the PIAs are enabled with VMA, they will not accept interrupts when VMA is inactive (as it is after the execution of WAI). You can overcome the problem by replacing WAI with the endless loop instruction:

```
HERE    BRA     HERE
```

or 20 followed by FE in hexadecimal.

The main program only enables the interrupt from the startup PIA. Note that this interrupt is enabled (by setting bit 0 of the PIA Control register to 1) before the CPU interrupt is enabled (by clearing the I bit). You must also initialize the Stack Pointer before enabling the CPU interrupt (why?).

In this example the values that the 6800 CPU stores in the Stack are not useful. The easiest way to discard them is to restore the starting address of the Stack to the Stack Pointer.

Remember that accepting an interrupt automatically disables the interrupt system. This allows the real startup routine to configure all the PIAs and other interrupt sources before re-enabling the interrupts. Note that you must clear the startup interrupt in the service routine (with the otherwise useless LDAA PIADRA instruction) or else it will interrupt again as soon as the interrupt system is re-enabled.

A Keyboard Interrupt

Purpose: The computer waits for a keyboard interrupt and places the data from the keyboard in memory location 0040.

KEYBOARD INTERRUPT

Sample Problem:

```
        Keyboard data = 06
        Result:  (0040) = 06
```

Flowchart:

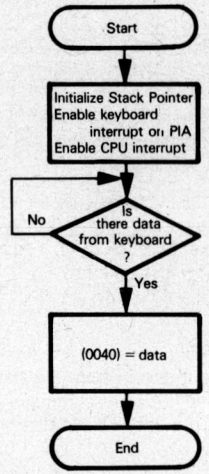

Source Program:

Main Program:

```
        SEI                     DISABLE INTERRUPT
        STS     $3E             SAVE MONITOR STACK POINTER
        LDS     #$58            INITIALIZE USER STACK POINTER
        CLR     PIACRA          CLEAR OUT KEYBOARD PIA
        CLR     PIADRA          MAKE DATA LINES INPUTS
        LDAA    #%00000101      ENABLE KEYBOARD INTERRUPT ON PIA
        STAA    PIACRA
        CLI                     ENABLE CPU INTERRUPT
        WAI                     AND WAIT
```

Interrupt Service Routine:

```
        ORG     INTRP
        LDAA    PIADRA          GET KEYBOARD DATA
        STAA    $40             SAVE KEYBOARD DATA
        LDS     $3E             RESTORE MONITOR STACK POINTER
        SWI
```

Object Program:

Memory Address (Hex)	Memory Contents (Hex)		Instruction (Mnemonic)	
Main Program:				
0000	0F		SEI	
0001	9F	3E	STS	$3E
0003	8E	0058	LDS	#$58
0006	7F	PIACRA	CLR	PIACRA
0009	7F	PIADRA	CLR	PIADRA
000C	86	05	LDAA	#%00000101
000E	B7	PIACRA	STAA	PIACRA
0011	0E		CLI	
0012	3E		WAI	
Interrupt Service Routine:				
INTRP	B6	PIADRA	LDAA	PIADRA
INTRP+3	97	40	STAA	$40
INTRP+5	9E	3E	LDS	$3E
INTRP+7	3F		SWI	

You must configure the PIA completely before enabling the interrupts.

Note that you cannot use the registers to directly pass data from the interrupt service routine to the main program. This is because RTI restores the old values of the registers. For example, if you wanted to wait for a non-zero value from the keyboard, the new program (after configuring the PIA) would be:

```
        CLR    $40         MARKER = 0
        CLI                ENABLE CPU INTERRUPT
WAITNZ  LDAA   $40         IS THERE NON-ZERO DATA FROM KEYBOARD?
        BEQ    WAITNZ      NO, WAIT
        LDS    $3E         RESTORE MONITOR STACK POINTER
        SWI
```

or (in hexadecimal):

Object Program:

Memory Address (Hex)	Memory Contents (Hex)			Instruction (Mnemonic)	
0011	7F	0040		CLR	$40
0014	0E			CLI	
0015	96	40	WAITNZ	LDAA	$40
0017	27	FC		BEQ	WAITNZ
0019	9E	3E		LDS	$3E
001B	3F			SWI	

The only changes in the service routine are an RTI (3B) instead of SWI at the end and the elimination of the LDS $3E instruction.

Note the following features of this program:

1) Memory location 0040 is used to transfer results from the service routine to the program. Why couldn't you use Accumulator A instead? The advantage of the 6800 method is that it allows you free use of the registers during the interrupt service routine. This is important if the registers are being used in the main program.

2) RTI automatically re-enables the CPU interrupt, since it restores the old value of the I bit (which must have been zero -- why?) from the Stack.

3) You must clear memory location 0040 before entering the waiting loop. Does it matter precisely when the program enables the interrupt? Try some alternative orderings.

The interrupt could also cause characters to be entered into a buffer until a carriage return was received. But remember that RTI restores all the registers from the Stack so that changing the registers in the service routine does not change their values in the main program. A possible program would be:

FILLING A BUFFER VIA INTERRUPTS

Source Program:

Main Program:

```
        SEI                     DISABLE INTERRUPT
        STS     $3E             SAVE MONITOR STACK POINTER
        LDS     #$58            INITIALIZE USER STACK POINTER
        CLR     PIACRA          CLEAR OUT KEYBOARD PIA
        CLR     PIADRA          MAKE DATA LINES INPUTS
        LDAA    #%00000101      ENABLE KEYBOARD INTERRUPT ON PIA
        STAA    PIACRA
        LDX     #$43            START KEYBOARD BUFFER POINTER
        STX     $41
        CLR     $40             CLEAR CARRIAGE RETURN FLAG
        CLI                     ENABLE CPU INTERRUPT
WAITCR  TST     $40             WAIT FOR CARRIAGE RETURN
        BEQ     WAITCR
        LDS     #$3E            RESTORE MONITOR STACK POINTER
        SWI
```

Interrupt Service Routine:

```
        ORG     INTRP
        LDAA    PIADRA          GET KEYBOARD DATA
        LDX     $41             GET KEYBOARD BUFFER POINTER
        STAA    X               SAVE KEYBOARD DATA
        INX                     UPDATE BUFFER POINTER
        STX     $41
        CMPA    #CR             IS DATA A CARRIAGE RETURN?
        BNE     ENDINT          NO, END OF ROUTINE
        INC     $40             YES, SET CARRIAGE RETURN FLAG
ENDINT  RTI
```

Memory location 0040 contains a flag that is set when a carriage return character is received. Memory locations 0041 and 0042 contain the keyboard buffer pointer. Memory location 0043 is the starting address of the keyboard buffer. Why can't you leave the keyboard buffer pointer in the Index register and the carriage return flag in Accumulator B?

An alternative is to have the interrupt fill one buffer while the main program uses another. This procedure is called "double buffering", and requires some management to determine which buffer is available and to mark when a buffer becomes empty or full.

DOUBLE BUFFERING

Flowcharts:

Main Program:

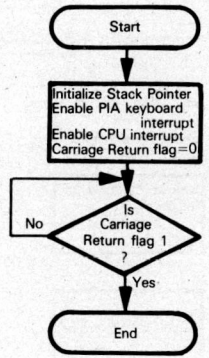

Interrupt Service Routine:

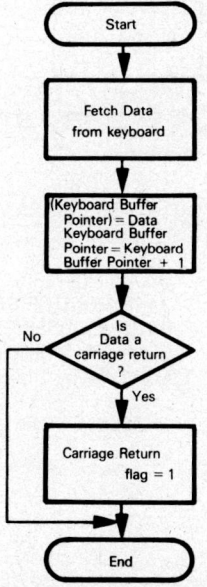

In a real application, the CPU could perform other tasks between interrupts. It could, for instance, edit, move, or transmit a line from one buffer while the interrupt was filling another buffer.

A Printer Interrupt

Purpose: The computer waits for a printer interrupt and sends the data from memory location 0040 to the printer.

Sample Problem:

    (0040) = 51
    Result: Printer receives a 51 (ASCII Q) when it is ready.

Flowchart:

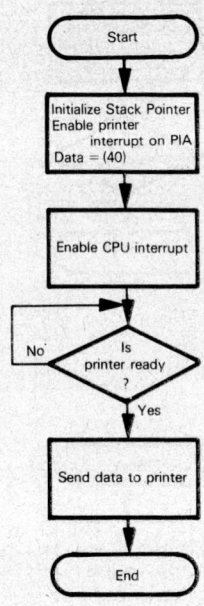

Source Program:

Main Program:

SEI		DISABLE INTERRUPT
STS	$3E	SAVE MONITOR STACK POINTER
LDS	#$58	INITIALIZE USER STACK POINTER
CLR	PIACRB	CLEAR OUT PRINTER PIA
LDAA	#$FF	MAKE DATA LINES OUTPUTS
STAA	PIADRB	
LDAA	#%00000101	ENABLE PRINTER INTERRUPT ON PIA
STAA	PIACRB	
LDAA	$40	GET DATA
CLI		ENABLE CPU INTERRUPT
WAI		AND WAIT

Interrupt Service Routine:

```
        ORG     INTRP
        STAA    PIADRB      SEND DATA TO PRINTER
        LDAA    PIADRB      CLEAR PRINTER INTERRUPT
        LDS     $3E         RESTORE MONITOR STACK POINTER
        SWI
```

Object Program:

Memory Address (Hex)	Memory Contents (Hex)		Instruction (Mnemonic)	
Main Program:				
0000	0F		SEI	
0001	9F	3E	STS	$3E
0003	8E	0058	LDS	#$58
0006	7F	PIACRB	CLR	PIACRB
0009	86	FF	LDAA	#$FF
000B	B7	PIADRB	STAA	PIADRB
000E	86	05	LDAA	#%00000101
0010	B7	PIACRB	STAA	PIACRB
0013	96	40	LDAA	$40
0015	0E		CLI	
0016	3E		WAI	
Interrupt Service Routine:				
INTRP	B7	PIADRB	STAA	PIADRB
INTRP+3	B6	PIADRB	LDAA	PIADRB
INTRP+6	9E	3E	LDS	$3E
INTRP+8	3F		SWI	

You can use the registers to pass data from the main program to the interrupt service routine. Although the 6800 saves all the user registers in the Stack, it does not actually change any values except the I bit (from 0 to 1 -- why?) in the Condition Code register.

In this program you must be careful as to exactly when the interrupts are enabled. If we reversed the order of the CLI and LDAA $40 instructions, an interrupt recognized immediately after CLI would cause an error. What would the service routine send to the printer? This error could be very difficult to spot since it would only have an effect on those rare occasions when the interrupt occurs during the execution of CLI. Such random errors are usually in the interrupt system, since the rest of the program is predictable and repeatable.

Note that the interrupt service routine has a dummy read instruction (LDAA PIADRB) which clears the interrupt. What would happen if this instruction were omitted?

RESET clears the Data register to start. Therefore, the initial value of the output data will be zero.

Remember that you may find it necessary to include a dummy read at the start of the main program to clear an interrupt bit that may have been accidentally set during RESET or otherwise. LDAA or TST can be used as the dummy read instruction.

Here again, you could have the printer continue to interrupt until the CPU transferred an entire line of data ending with a carriage return. A possible main program and service routine would be:

EMPTYING A BUFFER WITH INTERRUPTS

Source Program:

Main Program:

	SEI		DISABLE INTERRUPT
	STS	$3E	SAVE MONITOR STACK POINTER
	LDS	#$58	INITIALIZE USER STACK POINTER
	CLR	PIACRB	CLEAR OUT PRINTER PIA
	LDAA	#$FF	MAKE DATA LINES OUTPUTS
	STAA	PIADRB	
	LDAA	#%00000101	ENABLE PRINTER INTERRUPT ON PIA
	STAA	PIACRB	
	LDX	#$43	START PRINTER BUFFER POINTER
	STX	$41	
	CLR	$40	CLEAR CARRIAGE RETURN FLAG
	CLI		ENABLE CPU INTERRUPT
WAITCR	TST	$40	WAIT UNTIL CARRIAGE RETURN
	BEQ	WAITCR	
	LDS	$3E	
	SWI		

Interrupt Service Routine:

	ORG	INTRP	
	LDX	$41	GET PRINTER BUFFER POINTER
	LDAA	X	GET PRINTER DATA
	STAA	PIADRB	SEND DATA TO PRINTER
	INX		UPDATE BUFFER POINTER
	STX	$41	
	CMPA	#CR	IS DATA A CARRIAGE RETURN?
	BNE	ENDINT	NO, END OF ROUTINE
	INC	$40	YES, SET CARRIAGE RETURN FLAG
ENDINT	RTI		

Again, double buffering could be used to allow I/O and processing to occur at the same time without ever halting the CPU.

A Real-Time Clock Interrupt

Purpose: The computer waits for an interrupt from a real-time clock.

> **REAL-TIME CLOCK**

A real-time clock simply provides a regular series of pulses. The interval between the pulses can be used as a time reference. Real-time clock interrupts can be counted to give any multiple of the basic time interval. A real-time clock can be produced by dividing down the CPU clock, by using a separate timer or a programmable timer like the 6840 device for 6800-based microcomputers, or by using external sources such as the AC line frequency.

Note the tradeoffs involved in determining the frequency of the real-time clock. A high frequency (say 10 kHz) allows the creation of a wide range of time intervals of high accuracy. On the other hand, the overhead involved in counting real-time clock interrupts

> **FREQUENCY OF REAL-TIME CLOCK**

may be considerable, and the counts will quickly exceed the capacity of a single 8-bit register or memory location. The choice of frequency depends on the precision and timing requirements of your application. The clock may, of course, consist partly of hardware; a counter may count high frequency pulses and only interrupt the processor occasionally.

One problem is synchronizing operations with the real-time clock. Clearly, there will be some effect on the precision of the timing interval if the CPU starts the measurement randomly during a clock period, rather than exactly at the beginning. Some ways to synchronize operations are:

SYNCHRONIZATION WITH REAL-TIME CLOCK

1) Start the CPU and clock together. $\overline{\text{RESET}}$ or a startup interrupt can start the clock as well as the CPU.
2) Allow the CPU to start and stop the clock under program control.
3) Use a high-frequency clock so that an error of less than one clock period will be small.
4) Line up the clock (by waiting for an edge or interrupt) before starting the measurement.

A real-time clock interrupt should have very high priority, since the precision of the timing intervals will be affected by any delay in servicing the interrupt. The usual practice is to make the real-time clock the highest priority interrupt except for power failure. The clock interrupt service routine is generally kept extremely short so that it does not interfere with other CPU activities.

PRIORITY OF REAL-TIME CLOCK

a) Wait for Real-Time Clock

Source Program:

Main Program:

```
        SEI                     DISABLE CPU INTERRUPT
        STS     $3E             SAVE MONITOR STACK POINTER
        LDS     #$58            INITIALIZE USER STACK POINTER
        LDAA    #%00000101      ENABLE REAL-TIME CLOCK INTERRUPT
        STAA    PIACRA
        CLI                     ENABLE CPU INTERRUPT
        WAI                     AND WAIT
```

Interrupt Service Routine:

```
        ORG     INTRP
        LDAA    PIADRA          CLEAR REAL-TIME CLOCK INTERRUPT
        LDS     $3E             RESTORE MONITOR STACK POINTER
        SWI
```

Object Program:

Memory Address (Hex)	Memory Contents (Hex)		Instruction (Mnemonic)	
Main Program:				
0000	0F		SEI	
0001	9F	3E	STS	$3E
0003	8E	0058	LDS	#$58
0006	86	05	LDAA	#%00000101
0008	B7	PIACRA	STAA	PIACRA
000B	0E		CLI	
000C	3E		WAI	
Interrupt Service Routine:				
INTRP	B6	PIADRA	LDAA	PIADRA
INTRP+3	9E	3E	LDS	$3E
INTRP+5	3F		SWI	

If bit 1 of the PIA Control register is 0, the interrupt will occur on the high-to-low (trailing) clock edge. If that bit is 1, the interrupt will occur on the low-to-high (leading) clock edge.

The dummy read (LDAA PIADRA) in the service routine is necessary to clear the clock interrupt.

b) Wait for 10 Real-Time Clock Interrupts

Source Program:

Main Program:

```
        SEI                     DISABLE CPU INTERRUPT
        STS     $3E             SAVE MONITOR STACK POINTER
        LDS     #$58            INITIALIZE USER STACK POINTER
        LDAA    #%00000101      ENABLE REAL-TIME CLOCK PIA INTERRUPT
        STAA    PIACRA
        CLR     $40             CLEAR REAL-TIME CLOCK COUNTER
        LDAA    #10             DESIRED COUNT IS 10
        CLI                     ENABLE CPU INTERRUPT
WTCNT   CMPA    $40             HAS CLOCK COUNTER REACHED 10?
        BNE     WTCNT           NO, WAIT
        LDS     $3E             RESTORE MONITOR STACK POINTER
        SWI
```

Interrupt Service Routine:

```
        ORG     INTRP
        LDAA    PIADRA          CLEAR REAL-TIME CLOCK INTERRUPT
        INC     $40             INCREMENT REAL-TIME CLOCK COUNTER
        RTI
```

Object Program:

Memory Address (Hex)	Memory Contents (Hex)		Instruction (Mnemonic)	
Main Program:				
0000	0F		SEI	
0001	9F	3E	STS	$3E
0003	8E	0058	LDS	#$58
0006	86	05	LDAA	#%00000101
0008	B7	PIACRA	STAA	PIACRA
000B	7F	0040	CLR	$40
000E	86	0A	LDAA	#10
0010	0E		CLI	
0011	91	40	WTCNT CMPA	$40
0013	26	FC	BNE	WTCNT
0015	9E	3E	LDS	$3E
0017	3F		SWI	
Interrupt Service Routine:				
INTRP	B6	PIADRA	LDAA	PIADRA
INTRP+3	7C	0040	INC	$40
INTRP+6	3B		RTI	

Note that you cannot transfer data back to the main program in the registers (e.g., you could not use Accumulator A as a counter instead of memory location 0040).

The 6846 combination chip (ROM-I/O-timer) has a 16-bit programmable interval timer-counter that can be used to perform a variety of timing functions.

A real-time clock interrupt routine may maintain real time in several memory locations. For example, the following routine uses addresses 0040 through 0043 as follows:

MAINTAINING REAL TIME

    0040 - hundredths of seconds
    0041 - seconds
    0042 - minutes
    0043 - hours

Flowchart:

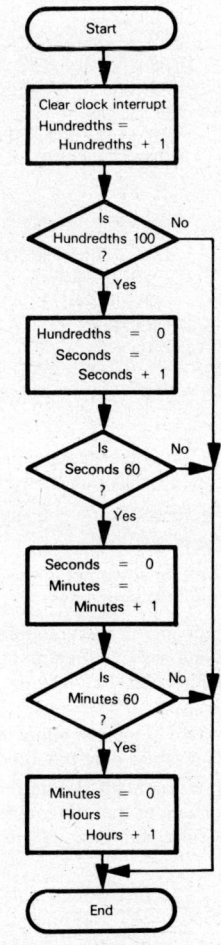

We assume that the routine is triggered by a 100 Hz clock.

Source Program:

```
        ORG     INTRP
        LDAA    PIADRA      CLEAR CLOCK INTERRUPT
        LDX     #$40
        INC     X           UPDATE HUNDREDTHS OF SECONDS
        LDAA    #100        IS THERE A CARRY TO SECONDS?
        CMPA    X
        BNE     ENDINT      NO, DONE
        CLR     X           YES, MAKE HUNDREDTHS ZERO
        INC     1,X         UPDATE SECONDS TO MINUTES
        LDAA    #60         IS THERE A CARRY?
        CMPA    1,X
        BNE     ENDINT      NO, DONE
        CLR     1,X         YES, MAKE SECONDS ZERO
        INC     2,X         UPDATE MINUTES TO HOURS
        CMPA    2,X         IS THERE A CARRY?
        BNE     ENDINT      NO, DONE
        CLR     2,X         YES, MAKE MINUTES ZERO
        INC     3,X         UPDATE HOURS
ENDINT  RTI
```

Now a wait of 300 ms could be produced in the main program with the routine:

```
        LDAA    $40         GET CURRENT REAL TIME
        ADDA    #30         DESIRED TIME IS 30 COUNTS (HUNDREDTHS
                               OF SECONDS LATER)
        CMPA    #100        MOD 100
        BCS     WAIT30
        SUBA    #100
WAIT30  CMPA    $40         WAIT UNTIL DESIRED TIME
        BNE     WAIT30
```

Of course, the program could perform other tasks and only check the elapsed time occasionally. How would you produce a delay of 7 seconds? 3 minutes?

Sometimes you may want to keep time in ASCII or decimal digits. How would you revise the last program to handle these alternatives?

You can disable the clock interrupt (or any other interrupt) when it is no longer needed in any of the following ways:

DISABLING INTERRUPTS

1) By executing an SEI instruction in the main program. This disables the entire interrupt system. An SEI instruction in the service routine has no effect, since RTI restores the old I bit. Actually, the interrupt is disabled during the service routine anyway.

2) By clearing bit 0 of the PIA Control register either during the service routine or during the main program. This disables only the interrupt from one side of one PIA.

3) By setting the interrupt bit in the Stack during the service routine. The following program will do the job (remember that the interrupt bit is bit 4 of the Condition Code register and that the Condition Code register is the top entry in the Stack -- see Figure 12-2):

```
        PULA                GET CONDITION CODE REGISTER
        ORAA    #%00010000  SET INTERRUPT BIT
        PSHA                RETURN CONDITION CODE REGISTER TO
                               STACK
```

RTI will then cause a return to the main program with the entire interrupt system disabled.

More generally, you can change any of the register values in the Stack easily by using the TSX instruction to move the address of the first occupied Stack location to the Index register. Now the registers can be accessed with indexed offsets as follows:

CHANGING REGISTER VALUES IN STACK

Condition Code register	0,X
Accumulator B	1,X
Accumulator A	2,X
8 MSBs of Index register	3,X
8 LSBs of Index register	4,X
8 MSBs of Program Counter	5,X
8 LSBs of Program Counter	6,X

For example, the following program will make the returned value of Accumulator A one larger than the original value:

```
TSX              ACCESS STACK
INC   2,X        ADD 1 TO 'A' VALUE
```

A Teletypewriter Interrupt

Purpose: The computer waits for data to be received from a teletypewriter and stores the data in memory location 0040.

1) Using an ACIA

   (7-bit characters with odd parity and two stop bits).

ACIA INTERRUPT ROUTINE

Source Program:

```
SEI                        DISABLE CPU INTERRUPT
STS    $3E                 SAVE MONITOR STACK POINTER
LDS    #$58                INITIALIZE USER STACK POINTER
LDAA   #%00000011          MASTER RESET ACIA
STAA   ACIACR
LDAA   #%11000101          ENABLE ACIA INTERRUPT
STAA   ACIACR
CLI                        ENABLE CPU INTERRUPT
WAI                        AND WAIT
ORG    INTRP
LDAA   ACIADR              GET DATA FROM ACIA
STAA   $40                 AND SAVE IT
LDS    $3E                 RESTORE MONITOR STACK POINTER
SWI
```

Object Program:

Memory Address (Hex)	Memory Contents (Hex)		Instruction (Mnemonic)	
Main Program:				
0000	0F		SEI	
0001	9F	3E	STS	$3E
0003	8E	0058	LDS	#$58
0006	86	03	LDAA	#%00000101
0008	B7	ACIACR	STAA	ACIACR
000B	86	C5	LDAA	#%11000101
000D	B7	ACIACR	STAA	ACIACR
0010	0E		CLI	
0011	3E		WAI	
Interrupt Service Routine:				
INTRP	B6	ACIADR	LDAA	ACIADR
INTRP+3	97	40	STAA	$40
INTRP+5	9E	3E	LDS	$3E
INTRP+7	3F		SWI	

Remember that the ACIA has no RESET input, so a MASTER RESET (making Control register bits 0 and 1 both '1') is necessary before the ACIA is used. The ACIA Control register configuration is:

> Bit 7 = 1 to enable the receive interrupt
>
> Bit 6 = 0, Bit 5 = 1 to disable the transmitter interrupt and make $\overline{RTS}$ high (inactive)
>
> Bit 4 = 0, Bit 3 = 0, Bit 2 = 1 to select 7-bit data with odd parity and two stop bits
>
> Bit 1 = 0, Bit 0 = 1 for ÷ 16 clock (1760 Hz)

To determine if a particular ACIA is the source of an interrupt, the CPU must examine the interrupt request bit, bit 7 of the Status register. The program must examine the Receive Data Register Full bit (Status register bit 0) and the Transmitter Data Register Empty bit (Status register bit 1) to differentiate between receive and transmit interrupts.

Either reading the Receive Data register or writing into the Transmit Data register clears the ACIA interrupt request bit.

2) Using a PIA

   (Received data tied to both data bit 7 and to control line 1 of the PIA).

START BIT INTERRUPT

Source Program:

Main Program:

SEI		DISABLE CPU INTERRUPT
STS	#3E	SAVE MONITOR STACK POINTER
LDS	#$58	INITIALIZE USER STACK POINTER
CLR	PIACRA	CLEAR OUT CONTROL REGISTER
CLR	PIADRA	MAKE DATA LINES INPUTS
LDAA	#%00000101	ENABLE TTY PIA INTERRUPT
STAA	PIACRA	
CLI		ENABLE CPU INTERRUPT
WAI		AND WAIT
JSR	TTYRCV	FETCH DATA FROM TTY
LDS	$3E	RESTORE MONITOR STACK POINTER
SWI		

Interrupt Service Routine:

ORG	INTRP	
LDAA	PIADRA	CLEAR START BIT INTERRUPT
LDAA	#%00000100	DISABLE TTY PIA INTERRUPT
STAA	PIACRA	
RTI		

Object Program:

Memory Address (Hex)	Memory Contents (Hex)		Instruction (Mnemonic)	
Main Program:				
0000	0F		SEI	
0001	9F	3E	STS	$3E
0003	8E	0058	LDS	#$58
0006	7F	PIACRA	CLR	PIACRA
0009	7F	PIADRA	CLR	PIADRA
000C	86	05	LDAA	#%00000101
000E	B7	PIACRA	STAA	PIACRA
0011	0E		CLI	
0012	3E		WAI	
0013	BD	TTYRCV	JSR	TTYRCV
0016	9E	3E	LDS	$3E
0018	3F		SWI	
Interrupt Service Routine:				
INTRP	B6	PIADRA	LDAA	PIADRA
INTRP+3	86	04	LDAA	#%00000100
INTRP+5	B7	PIACRA	STAA	PIACRA
INTRP+8	3B		RTI	

Subroutine TTYRCV is the teletypewriter receive routine shown in the previous chapter.

The edge used to cause the interrupt is very important here. The transition from the normal '1' state to the '0' state must cause the interrupt, since this transition identifies the start of the transmission. The '0' to '1' transition will not occur until a non-zero data bit is received.

The service routine must disable the PIA interrupt, since otherwise each '1' to '0' transition in the character will cause an interrupt. Note that the ignored transitions will be cleared when the data bits are read. Of course, you must re-enable the PIA interrupt after the entire character has been read.

MORE GENERAL SERVICE ROUTINES

More general service routines that are part of a complete interrupt-driven system must handle the following tasks:

TASKS FOR GENERAL SERVICE ROUTINES

1) Saving any needed data in the Stack so that the interrupted program can be correctly resumed. Remember that the 6800 automatically saves all registers and flags.

    Note that the 6800 PSH instructions transfer the contents of an Accumulator to the Stack.

2) Establishing the priority of the interrupt, perhaps by writing the priority into an external register.

    The rest of the interrupt system can then be re-enabled. Remember that in order to restore the old priority correctly, you must save it in the Stack along with the other status. A copy of the current priority must be saved in RAM if the external register is write-only.

3) Restoring the old priority and other data before returning to the interrupted program.

The service routine should be transparent as far as the interrupted program is concerned (i.e., it should have no incidental effects).

Any standard subroutines that are used by an interrupt service routine must be re-entrant. If some subroutines cannot be made re-entrant, the interrupt service routine must have separate versions to use.

For some real-life examples of designing 6800-based systems with interrupts, see:

Baunach, S.C., "An Example of an M6800-based GPIB Interface", EDN, September 20, 1977, pp. 125-128.

Cannon, L.E., and P.S. Kreager, "Using a Microprocessor: a Real-Life Application. Part 2 - Software", Computer Design, October 1975, pp. 81-89.

Fullager, D., et al., "Interfacing Data Converters and Microprocessors", Electronics, December 8, 1976, pp. 81-89.

Hill, S.A. "Multiprocess Control Interface Makes Remote μP Command Possible", EDN, February 5, 1976, pp. 87-89.

Holderby, W.S., "Designing a Microprocessor-based Terminal for Factory Data Collection", Computer Design, March 1977, pp. 81-88.

Lange, A., "OPTACON Interface Permits the Blind to 'Read' Digital Instruments", EDN, February 5, 1976, pp. 84-86.

Logan, J.D., and P.S. Kreager, "Using a Microprocessor: a Real-Life Application. Part 1 - Hardware", Computer Design, September 1975, pp. 69-77.

Moore, A., and M. Eidson, "Printer Control", Application Note available from Motorola Semiconductor Products, Phoenix, AZ.

PROBLEMS
1) A Test Interrupt
Purpose: The computer waits for a PIA interrupt to occur, then executes the endless loop instruction

        HERE   BRA   HERE

until the next interrupt occurs.

2) A Keyboard Interrupt
Purpose: The computer waits for a 4-digit entry from a keyboard and places the digits in memory locations 0042 through 0045 (first one received in 0042). Each digit entry causes an interrupt. The fourth entry should also result in the disabling of the keyboard interrupt.

Sample Problem:

    Keyboard data = 04, 06, 01, 07
    Result: (0042) = 04
            (0043) = 06
            (0044) = 01
            (0045) = 07

3) A Printer Interrupt
Purpose: The computer sends four characters from memory locations 0042 through 0045 (starting with 0042) to the printer. Each character is requested by an interrupt. The fourth transfer also disables the printer interrupt.

4) A Real-Time Clock Interrupt
Purpose: The computer clears memory location 0040 initially and then complements memory location 0040 each time the real-time clock interrupt occurs. How would you change the program so that it complements memory loation 0040 after every ten interrupts? How would you change the program so that it leaves memory location 0040 at zero for ten clock periods, FF (hex) for five clock periods, and so on continuously? You may want to use a display rather than memory location 0040 so that it will be easier to see.

5) A Teletypewriter Interrupt
Purpose: The computer receives data from an interrupting ACIA and stores the characters in a buffer starting in memory location 0042. The process continues until the computer receives a carriage return (0D hex). Assume that the characters are 7-bit ASCII with odd parity. How would you change your program to use a PIA? Assume that subroutine TTYRCV is available, as in the example. Include the carriage return as the final character in the buffer.

Chapter 13
PROBLEM DEFINITION AND PROGRAM DESIGN

THE TASKS OF SOFTWARE DEVELOPMENT

In the previous chapters, we have concentrated on the writing of short programs in assembly language. While this is an important topic, it is only a small part of the total problem of software development. Although writing assembly language programs seems like a major task to the newcomer, it soon becomes relatively simple. By now, you should be familiar with most of the standard methods for programming in assembly language on the 6800 microprocessor. The next four chapters will describe how to formulate tasks as programs and how to put short programs together to form a working system.

Software development consists of many stages. Figure 13-1 is a flowchart of the software development process. Its stages are:

STAGES OF SOFTWARE DEVELOPMENT

- Problem definition
- Program design
- Coding
- Debugging
- Testing
- Documentation
- Maintenance and redesign

Each of these stages is important in the construction of a working system. Note that coding, the writing of programs in a form that the computer understands, is only one of seven stages.

In fact, coding is usually the easiest stage to define and perform. The rules for writing computer programs are easy to learn. They vary somewhat from computer to computer, but the basic techniques remain the same. Few software projects run into trouble because of coding; indeed, coding is not the most significant part of software development. Experts estimate that a programmer can write one to ten fully debugged and documented statements per day. Clearly, the mere coding of one to ten statements is hardly a full day's effort. On most software projects, coding occupies less than 25% of the programmer's time.

RELATIVE IMPORTANCE OF CODING

Measuring progress in the other stages is difficult. You can say that half of the program has been written, but you can hardly say that half of the errors have been removed or half of the problem has been defined. Timetables for such stages as program design, debugging, and testing are difficult to produce. Many days or weeks of effort may result in no clear progress. Furthermore, an incomplete job in one stage may result in tremendous problems later. For example, poor problem definition or program design can make debugging and testing very difficult. Time saved in one stage may be spent many times over in later stages.

MEASURING PROGRESS IN STAGES

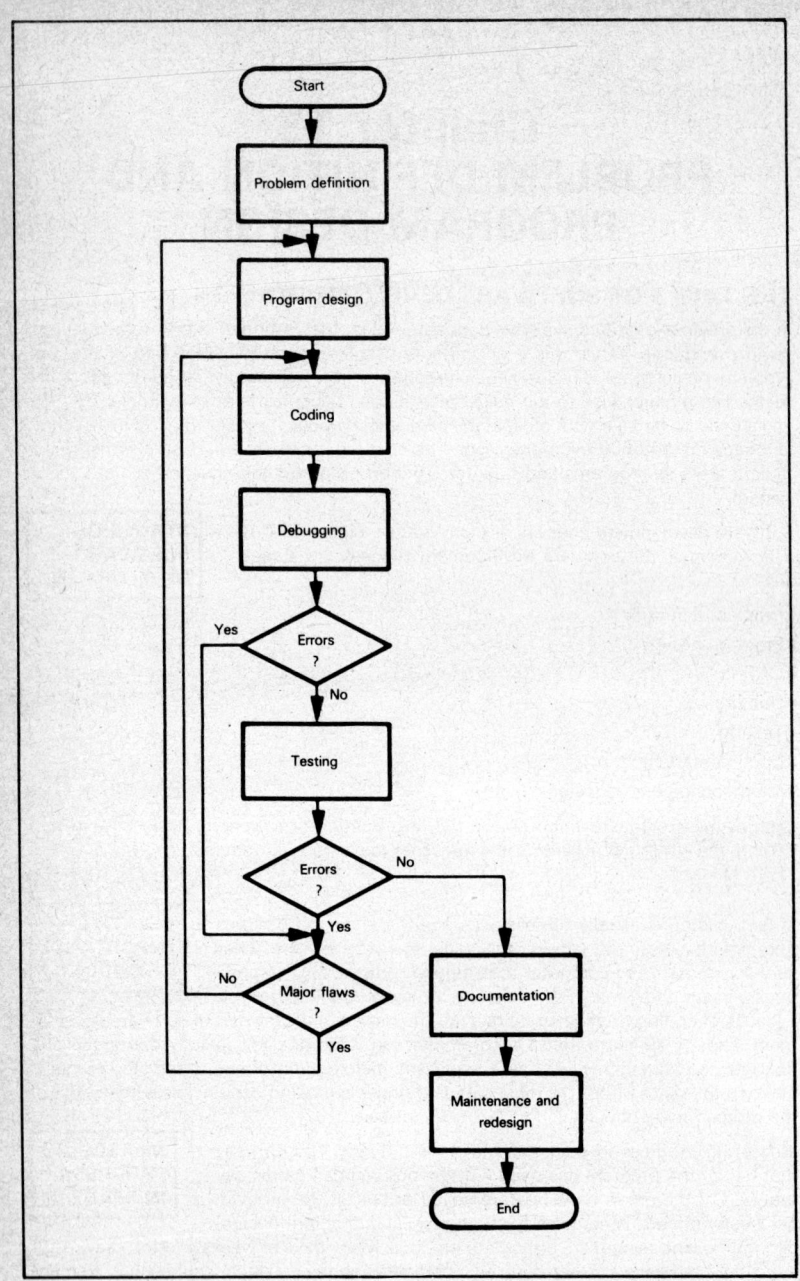

Figure 13-1. Flowchart of Software Development

DEFINITION OF THE STAGES

Problem definition is the formulation of the task in terms of the requirements it places on the computer. For example, what is necessary to make a computer control a tool, run a series of electrical tests, or handle communications between a central controller and a remote instrument? Problem definition requires that you determine the forms and rates of inputs and outputs, the amount and speed of processing that is needed, and the types of possible errors and their handling. Problem definition takes a vaguely defined idea of building a computer-controlled system and defines the tasks and requirements for the computer.

PROBLEM DEFINITION

Program design is the outline of the computer program which will perform the tasks that have been defined. In the design stage, the tasks are described in a way that can easily be converted into a program. Among the useful techniques in this stage are flowcharting, structured programming, modular programming and top-down design.

PROGRAM DESIGN

Coding is the writing of the program in a form that the computer can either directly understand or translate. The form may be machine language, assembly language or a high-level language.

CODING

Debugging, also called program verification, is making the program do what the design specified that it would do. In this stage, you use such tools as breakpoints, traces, simulators, logic analyzers and in-circuit emulators. The end of the debugging stage is hard to define, since you never know when you have found the last error.

DEBUGGING

Testing, also referred to as program validation, is ensuring that the program performs the overall system tasks correctly. The designer uses simulators, exercisers and various statistical techniques to get some measure of the program's performance.

TESTING

Documentation is the description of the program in the proper form for users and maintenance personnel. Documentation also allows the designer to develop a program library so that subsequent tasks will be far simpler. Flowcharts, comments, memory maps and library forms are some of the tools used in documentation.

DOCUMENTATION

Maintenance and redesign are the servicing, improvement and extension of the program. Clearly, the designer must be ready to handle field problems in computer-based equipment. Special diagnostic modes or programs and other maintenance tools may be required. Upgrading or extension of the program may be necessary to meet new requirements or handle new tasks.

MAINTENANCE AND REDESIGN

The rest of this chapter will consider only the problem definition and program design stages. Chapter 14 will discuss debugging and testing, and Chapter 15 will discuss documentation, extension and redesign. We will bring all the stages together in some simple systems examples in Chapter 16.

PROBLEM DEFINITION

Typical microprocessor tasks require a lot of definition. For example, what must a program do to control a scale, a cash register or a signal generator? Clearly, we have a long way to go just to define the tasks involved.

DEFINING THE INPUTS

How do we start the definition? The obvious place to begin is with the inputs. We should begin by listing all the inputs that the computer may receive in this application.

Examples of inputs are:
- Data blocks from transmission lines
- Status words from peripherals
- Data from A/D converters

Then, we may ask the following questions about each input: **FACTORS IN INPUT**

1) What is its form; i.e., what signals will the computer actually receive?
2) When is the input available and how does the processor know it is available? Does the processor have to request the input with a strobe signal? Does the input provide its own clock?
3) How long is it available?
4) How often does it change, and how does the processor know that it has changed?
5) Does the input consist of a sequence or block of data? Is the order important?
6) What should be done if the data contains errors? These may include transmission errors, incorrect data, sequencing errors, extra data, etc.
7) Is the input related to other inputs or outputs?

DEFINING THE OUTPUTS

The next step to define is the output. We must list all the outputs that the computer must produce. Examples of outputs include:

- Data blocks to transmission lines
- Control words to peripherals
- Data to D/A converters

Then, we may ask the following questions about each output:

1) What is its form; i.e., what signals must the computer produce?
2) When must it be available, and how does the peripheral know it is available?
3) How long must it be available?
4) How often must it change, and how does the peripheral know that it has changed?
5) Is there a sequence of outputs? Is the order important?
6) What should be done to avoid transmission errors or to sense and recover from peripheral failures?
7) How is the output related to other inputs and outputs?

PROCESSING SECTION

Between the reading of input data and the sending of output results is the processing section. Here we must determine exactly how the computer must process the input data. The questions are:

1) What is the basic procedure (algorithm) for transforming input data into output results? **FACTORS IN PROCESSING**
2) What time constraints exist? These may include data rates, delay times, the time constants of input and output devices, etc.
3) What memory constraints exist? Do we have limits on the amount of program memory or data memory, or on the size of buffers?
4) What standard programs or tables must be used? What are their requirements?
5) What special cases exist, and how should the program handle them?
6) How accurate must the results be?

ERROR HANDLING

An important factor in many applications is the handling of errors. Clearly, the designer must make provisions for recovering from common errors and for diagnosing malfunctions. Among the questions that the designer must ask at the definition stage are:

1) What errors could occur?
2) Which errors are most likely? If a person operates the system, human error is the most common. Following human errors, communications or transmission errors are more common than mechanical, electrical, mathematical or processor errors.
3) Which errors will not be immediately obvious to the system? A special problem is the occurrence of errors that the system or operator may not recognize as incorrect.
4) How can the system recover from errors with a minimum loss of time and data, and yet be aware that an error has occurred?
5) Which errors or malfunctions cause the same system behavior? How can these errors or malfunctions be distinguished for diagnostic purposes?
6) Which errors involve special system procedures? For example, do parity errors require retransmission of data?

> ERROR CONSIDERATIONS

Another question is: How can the field technician systematically find the source of malfunctions without being an expert? Built-in test programs (see, for example, V.P. Srini, "Fault Diagnosis of Microprocessor Systems", Computer, January 1977, pp. 60-65), special diagnostics or signature analysis can help. For a description of signature analysis, see G. Gordon and H. Nadig, "Hexadecimal Signatures Identify Trouble-spots in Microprocessor Systems", Electronics, March 3, 1977, pp. 89-96. There is also an Application Note (#222) entitled "A Designer's Guide to Signature Analysis" available from Hewlett-Packard.

HUMAN FACTORS

Many microprocessor-based systems involve human interaction. Human factors must be considered throughout the development process for such systems. Among the questions that the designer must ask are:

> OPERATOR INTERACTION

1) What input procedures are most natural for the human operator?
2) Can the operator easily determine how to begin, continue and end the input operation?
3) How is the operator informed of procedural errors and equipment malfunctions?
4) What errors is the operator most likely to make?
5) How does the operator know that data has been entered correctly?
6) Are displays in a form that the operator can easily read and understand?
7) Is the response of the system adequate for the operator?
8) Is the system easy for the operator to use?
9) Are there guiding features for an inexperienced operator?
10) Are there shortcuts and reasonable options for the experienced operator?
11) Can the operator always determine or reset the state of the system after interruptions or distractions?

Building a system for people to use is difficult. The microprocessor can make the system more powerful, more flexible and more responsive. However, the designer still must add the human touches that can greatly increase the usefulness and attractiveness of the system and the productivity of the human operator.

EXAMPLES
Response to a Switch

Figure 13-2 shows a simple system in which the input is from a single SPST switch and the output is to a single LED display. In response to a switch closure, the processor turns the display on for one second. This system should be easy to define.

DEFINING SWITCH AND LIGHT SYSTEM

Let us first examine the input and answer each of the questions previously presented:

SWITCH AND LIGHT INPUT

1) The input is a single bit which may be either '0' (switch closed) or '1' (switch open).
2) The input is always available and need not be requested.
3) The input is available for at least several milliseconds after the closure.
4) The input will seldom change more than once every few seconds. The processor only has to handle the bounce in the switch. The processor must monitor the switch to determine when it is closed.
5) There is no sequence of inputs.
6) The obvious input errors are switch failure, failure in the input circuitry, and the operator attempting to close the switch again before a sufficient amount of time has elapsed. We will discuss the handling of these errors later.
7) The input does not depend on any other inputs or outputs.

The next requirement in defining the system is to examine the output. The answers to our questions are:

SWITCH AND LIGHT OUTPUTS

1) The output is a single bit which is '0' to turn the display on, '1' to turn it off.
2) There are no time constraints on the output. The peripheral does not need to be informed of the availability of data.
3) If the display is an LED, the data need only be available for a few milliseconds at a pulse rate of about 100 times per second. The observer will see a continuously lit display.
4) The data must change (go off) after one second.
5) There is no sequence of outputs.
6) The possible output errors are display failure and failure in the output circuitry.
7) The output depends only on the switch input and time.

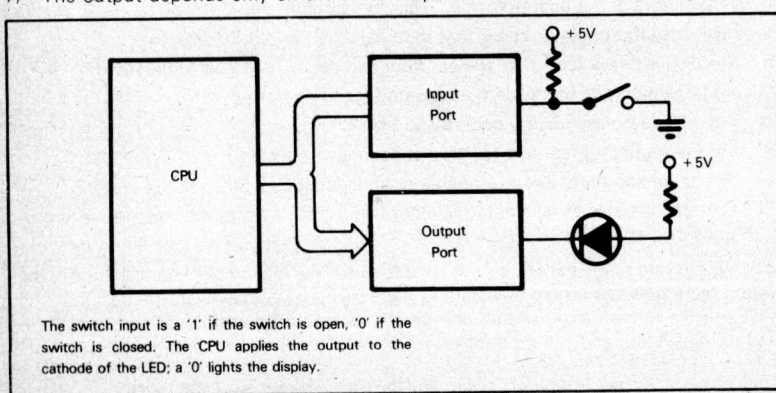

The switch input is a '1' if the switch is open, '0' if the switch is closed. The CPU applies the output to the cathode of the LED; a '0' lights the display.

Figure 13-2. The Switch and Light System

The processing section is extremely simple. As soon as the switch input becomes a logic '0', the CPU turns the light on (a logic '0') for one second. No time or memory constraints exist.

Let us now look at the possible errors and malfunctions. These are:

> **SWITCH AND LIGHT ERROR HANDLING**

1) Another switch closure before one second has elapsed.
2) Switch failure.
3) Display failure.
4) Computer failure.

Surely the first error is the most likely. The simplest solution is for the processor to ignore switch closures until one second has elapsed. This brief unresponsive period will hardly be noticeable to the human operator. Furthermore, ignoring the switch during this period means that no debouncing circuitry or software is necessary, since the system will not react to the bounce anyway.

Clearly, the last three failures can produce unpredictable results. The display may stay on, stay off or change state randomly. Some possible ways to isolate the failures would be:

1) Lamp-test hardware to check the display; i.e., a button that turns the light on independently of the processor.
2) A direct connection to the switch to check its operation.
3) A diagnostic program that exercises the input and output circuits.

If both the display and switch are working, the computer is at fault. A field technician with proper equipment can determine the cause of the failure.

A Switch-Based Memory Loader

Figure 13-3 shows a system which allows the user to enter data into any memory location in a microcomputer. One input port, DPORT, reads data from eight toggle switches. The other input port, CPORT, is used to read control information. There

> **DEFINING A SWITCH-BASED MEMORY LOADER**

are three momentary switches: High Address, Low Address and Data. The output is the value of the last completed entry from the data switches; eight LEDs are used for the display.

The system will also, of course, require various resistors, buffers and drivers.

We shall first examine the inputs. The characteristics of the switches are the same as in the previous example; however, here there is a distinct sequence of inputs, as follows:

1) The operator must set the data switches according to the eight most significant bits of an address, then
2) press the High Address button. The high address bits will appear on the lights, and the program will interpret the data as the high byte of the address.
3) Then the operator must set the data switches with the value of the least significant byte of the address and
4) press the Low Address button. The low address bits will appear on the lights, and the program will consider the data to be the low byte of the address.
5) Finally, the operator must set the desired data into the data switches and
6) press the Data button. The display will now show the data, and the program stores the data in memory at the previously entered address.

The operator may repeat the process to enter an entire program. Clearly, even in this simplified situation, we will have many possible sequences to consider. How do we cope with erroneous sequences and make the system easy to use?

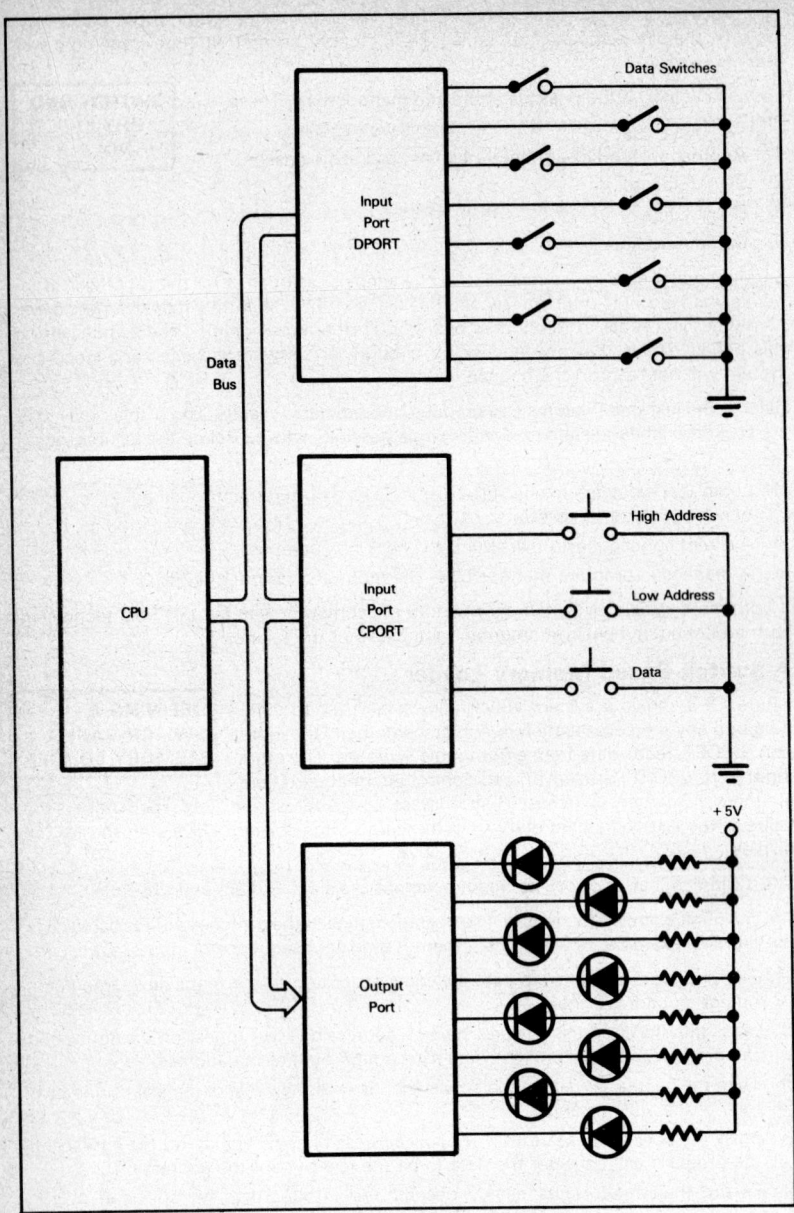

Figure 13-3. The Switch-Based Memory Loader

Output is no problem. After each input, the program sends to the displays the complement (since the displays are active-low) of the input bits. The output data remains the same until the next input operation

The processing section remains quite simple. There are not time or memory constraints. The program can debounce the switches by waiting for a few milliseconds, and must provide complemented data to the displays.

The most likely errors are operator mistakes. These include:

MEMORY LOADER ERROR HANDLING

1) Incorrect entries.
2) Incorrect order.
3) Incomplete entries; for example, forgetting the data.

The system must be able to handle these problems in a reasonable way, since they are certain to occur in actual operation.

The designer must also consider the effects of equipment failure. Just as before, the possible difficulties are:

1) Switch failure.
2) Display failure.
3) Computer failure.

In this system, however, we must pay more attention to how these failures affect the system. A computer failure will presumably cause very unusual behavior by the system, and will be easy to detect. A display failure may not be immediately noticeable; here a Lamp Test feature will allow the operator to check the operation. Note that we would like to test each LED separately, in order to diagnose the case in which output lines are shorted together. In addition, the operator may not immediately detect switch failure; however, the operator should soon notice it and establish which switch is faulty by a process of elimination.

Let us look at some of the possible operator errors. Typical errors will be:

OPERATOR ERROR CORRECTION IN MEMORY LOADER

1) Erroneous data.
2) Wrong order of entries or switches.
3) Trying to go on to the next entry without completing the current one.

The operator will presumably notice erroneous data as soon as it appears on the displays. What is a viable recovery procedure for the operator? Some of the options are:

1) The operator must complete the entry procedure; i.e., enter Low Address and Data if the error occurs in the High Address. Clearly, this procedure is wasteful and would only serve to annoy the operator.

2) The operator may restart the entry process by returning to the high address entry steps. This solution is useful if the error was in the High Address, but forces the operator to re-enter earlier data if the error was in the Low Address or Data stage.

3) The operator may enter any part of the sequence at any time simply by setting the Data switches with the desired data and pressing the corresponding button. This procedure allows the operator to make corrections at any point in the sequence.

This type of procedure should always be preferred over one that does not allow immediate error correction, has a variety of concluding steps, or enters data into the system without allowing the operator a final check. Any added complication in hardware or software will be justified in increased operator efficiency. You should always prefer to let the microcomputer do the tedious work and recognize arbitrary sequences; it never gets tired and never forgets what was in the operating manual.

A further helpful feature would be status lights that would define the meaning of the display. Three status lights, marked "High Address", "Low Address" and "Data", would let the operator know what had been entered without having to remember which button was pressed. The processor would have to monitor the sequence, but the added complication in software would simplify the operator's tasks. Clearly, three separate sets of displays plus the ability to examine a memory location would be even more helpful to the operator.

We should note that, although we have emphasized human interaction, machine or system interaction has many of the same characteristics. The microprocessor should do the work. If complicating the microprocessor's task makes error recovery simple and the causes of failure obvious, the entire system will work better and be easier to maintain. Note that you should not leave consideration of system use and maintenance until the end of the software development process; instead, you should include it right in the problem definition stage.

A Verification Terminal

Figure 13-4 is a block diagram of a simple credit-verification terminal. One input port derives data from a keyboard (see Figure 13-5); the other input port accepts verification data from a transmission line. One output port sends data to a set of displays (see Figure 13-6); another sends the credit card number to the central computer. A third output port turns on one light whenever the terminal is ready to accept an inquiry, and another light when the operator sends the information. The "Busy" light turns off when the response returns. Clearly, the input and output of data will be more complex than in the previous case, although the processing is still fairly simple.

DEFINING A VERIFICATION TERMINAL

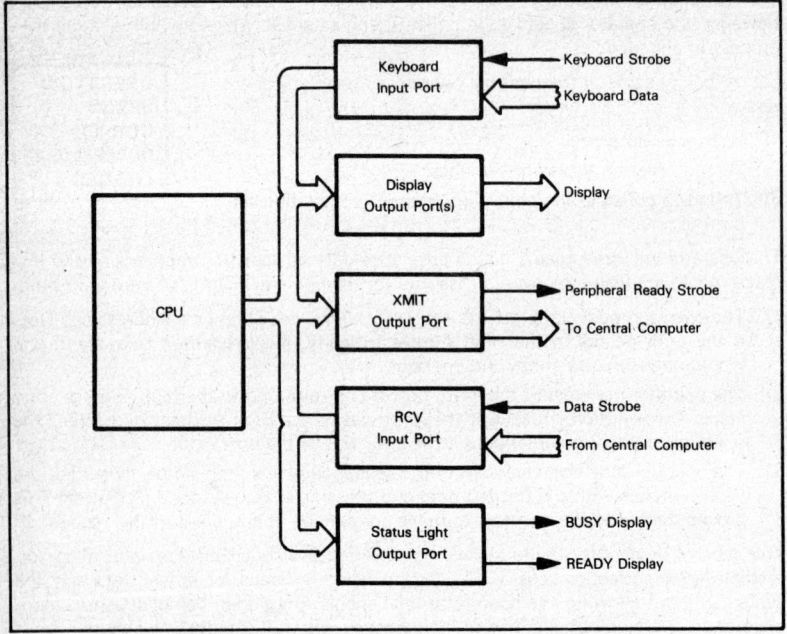

Figure 13-4. Block Diagram of a Verification Terminal

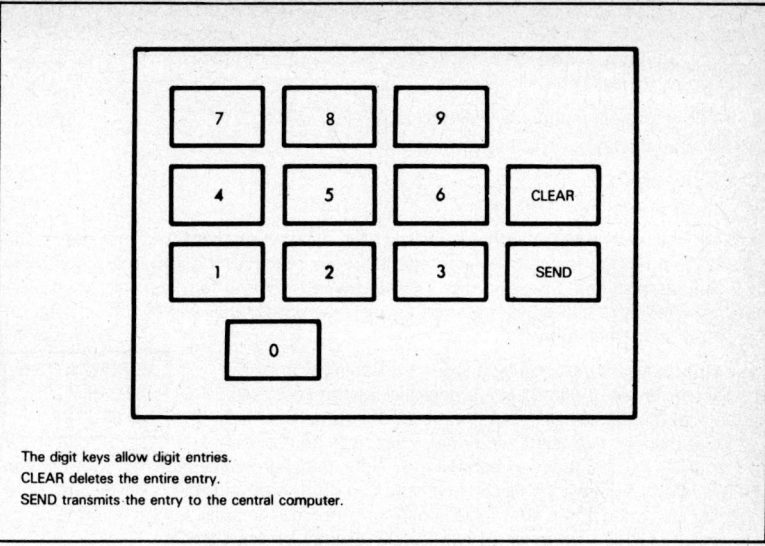

Figure 13-5. Verification Terminal Keyboard

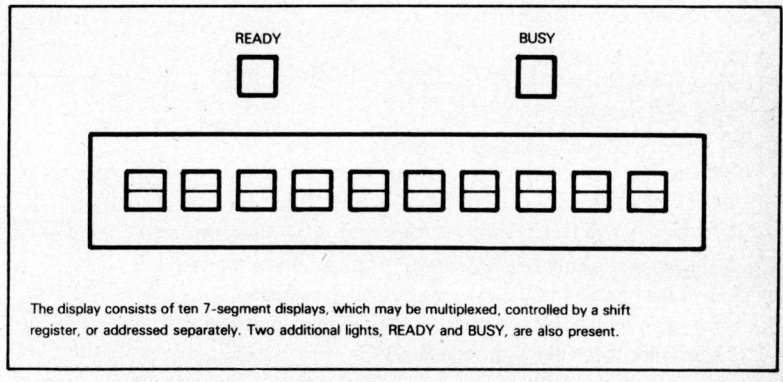

Figure 13-6. Verification Terminal Display

Additional displays may be useful to emphasize the meaning of the response. Many terminals use a green light for "Yes", a red light for "No", and a yellow light for "Consult Store Manager". Note that these lights will still have to be clearly marked with their meanings to handle the situation in which the operator is color-blind.

VERIFICATION TERMINAL INPUTS

Let us first look at the keyboard input. This is, of course, different from the switch input since the CPU must have some way of distinguishing new data. We will assume that each key closure provides a unique hexadecimal code (we can code all the keys into one digit since there are 12 keys) and a strobe. The program will have to recognize the strobe and fetch the hexadecimal number that identifies the key. There is a time constraint, since the program cannot miss any data or strobes. The constraint is not serious, since keyboard entries will be at least several milliseconds apart.

The transmission input similarly consists of a series of characters, each identified by a strobe (perhaps from a UART). The program will have to recognize each strobe and fetch the character. The data being sent across the transmission lines is usually organized into messages. A possible message format is:

1) Introductory characters, or header.
2) Terminal destination address.
3) Coded yes or no.
4) Ending characters, or trailer.

The terminal will check the header, read the destination address, and see if the message is intended for it. If the message is for the terminal, the terminal accepts the data. The address could be (and often is) hard-wired into the terminal so that the terminal only receives messages intended for it. This approach simplifies the software at the cost of some flexibility.

VERIFICATION TERMINAL OUTPUTS

The output is also more complex than in the earlier examples. If the displays are multiplexed, the processor must not only send the data to the display port but must also direct the data to a particular display. We will need either a separate control port or a counter and decoder to handle this. Note that hardware blanking controls can blank leading zeros as long as the first digit in a multi-digit number is never zero. Software can also handle this task. Time constraints include the pulse length and frequency required to produce an apparent continuous display for the operator.

The communications output will consist of a series of characters with a particular format. The program will also have to consider the time required between characters. A possible format for the output message is:

1) Header.
2) Terminal address.
3) Credit card number.
4) Trailer.

A central communications computer may be used to poll the terminals, checking for data ready to be sent.

The processing in this system involves many new tasks, such as:

1) Identifying the control keys by number and performing the proper actions.
2) Adding the header and trailer to the outgoing message.
3) Recognizing the header and trailer in the returning message.
4) Checking the incoming terminal address.

VERIFICATION TERMINAL ERROR HANDLING

Note that none of the tasks involve any complex arithmetic or any serious time or memory constraints.

The number of possible errors in this system is, of course, much larger than in the earlier examples. Let us first consider the possible operator errors. These include:

1) Entering the credit card number incorrectly.
2) Trying to send an incomplete credit card number.
3) Trying to send another number while the central computer is processing one.
4) Clearing non-existent entries.

Some of these errors can be easily handled by correctly structuring the program. For example, the program should not accept the Send key until the credit card number has been completely entered, and it should ignore any additional keyboard entries until the response comes back from the central computer. Note that the operator will know that the entry has not been sent, since the Busy light will not go on. The operator will also know when the keyboard has been locked out (the program is ignoring keyboard entries), since entries will not appear on the display and the Ready light will be off.

Incorrect entries are an obvious problem. If the operator recognizes an error, he or she can use the Clear key to make corrections. The operator would probably find it more convenient to have two Clear keys, one which cleared the most recent key and one which cleared the entire entry. This would allow both for the situation in which the operator recognizes the error immediately and for the situation in which the operator recognizes the error relatively late in the procedure. The operator should be able to correct errors immediately and have to repeat as few keys as possible. The operator will, however, make a certain number of errors without recognizing them. Most credit card numbers include a self-checking digit; the terminal could check the number before permitting it to be sent to the central computer. This step would save the central computer from wasting precious processing time checking the number.

CORRECTING KEYBOARD ERRORS

This requires, however, that the terminal have some way of informing the operator of the error, perhaps by flashing one of the displays or by providing some other special indicator that the operator is sure to notice.

Still another problem is how the operator knows that an entry has been lost or processed incorrectly. Some terminals simply unlock after a maximum time delay. The operator notes that the Busy light has gone off without an answer being received. The operator is then expected to try the entry again. After one or two retries, the operator should report the failure to supervisory personnel.

Many equipment failures are also possible. Besides the displays, keyboard and processor, there now exist the problems of communications errors or failures and central computer failures.

The data transmission will probably have to include error checking and correcting procedures. Some possibilities are:

1) Parity provides an error detection facility but no correction mechanism. The receiver will need some way of requesting re-transmission, and the sender will have to save a copy of the data until proper reception is acknowledged. Parity is, however, very simple to implement.

CORRECTING TRANSMISSION ERRORS

2) Short messages may use more elaborate schemes. For example, the yes/no response to the terminal could be coded so as to provide error detection and correction capability.

3) An acknowledgment and a limited number of retries could trigger an indicator that would inform the operator of a communications failure (inability to transfer a message without errors) or central computer failure (no response at all to the message within a certain period of time). Such a scheme, along with the Lamp Test, would allow fairly simple failure diagnosis.

A communications or central computer failure indicator should also "unlock" the terminal; i.e., allow it to accept another entry. This is necessary if the terminal will not accept entries while a verification is in progress. The terminal may also unlock after a certain maximum time delay. Certain entries could be reserved for diagnostics; i.e., certain credit card numbers could be used to check the internal operation of the terminal and test the displays.

REVIEW OF PROBLEM DEFINITION

Problem definition is as important a part of software development as it is of any other engineering task. Note that it does not require any programming or knowledge of the computer; rather, it is based on an understanding of the system and sound engineering judgment. Microprocessors can offer flexibility which the designer can use to provide a range of features which were not previously available.

Problem definition is independent of any particular computer, computer language or development system. It should, however, provide guidelines as to what type or speed of computer the application will require, and what kind of hardware/software trade-offs the designer can make. The problem definition stage is in fact independent of whether or not a computer is used at all, although a knowledge of the capabilities of the computer can help the designer in suggesting possible implementations of procedures.

PROGRAM DESIGN

Program design is the stage in which the problem definition is formulated as a program. If the program is small and simple, this stage may involve little more than the writing of a one-page flowchart. If the program is larger or more complex, the designer should consider more elaborate methods.

We will discuss flowcharting, modular programming, structured programming and top-down design. We will try to indicate the reasoning behind these methods, and their advantages and disadvantages. We will not, however, advocate any particular method, since there is no evidence that one method is always superior to all others. You should remember that the goal is to produce a good working system, not to follow religiously the tenets of one methodology or another.

All the methodologies do, however, have some obvious principles in common. Many of these are the same principles that apply to any kind of design, such as:

BASIC PRINCIPLES OF PROGRAM DESIGN

1) Proceed in small steps. Do not try to do too much at one time.
2) Divide large jobs into small, logically separate tasks. Make the sub-tasks as independent of one another as possible, so that they can be tested separately and so that changes can be made in one without affecting the others.
3) Keep the flow of control as simple as possible so as to make it easier to find errors.
4) Use pictorial or graphic descriptions as much as possible. They are easier to visualize than word descriptions. This is the great advantage of flowcharts.
5) Emphasize clarity and simplicity at first. You can improve performance (if necessary) once the system is working.
6) Proceed in a thorough and systematic manner. Use checklists and standard procedures.
7) Do not tempt fate. Either do not use methods that you are not sure of, or use them very carefully. Watch for situations that might cause confusion, and clarify them as soon as possible.
8) Keep in mind that the system must be debugged, tested and maintained. Plan for these later stages.
9) Use simple and consistent terminology and methods. Repetitiveness is no fault in program design, nor is complexity a virtue.
10) Have your design completely formulated before you start coding. Resist the temptation to start writing down instructions; it makes no more sense than making parts lists or laying out circuit boards before you know exactly what will be in the system.
11) Be particularly careful of factors that may change. Make the implementation of likely changes as simple as possible.

FLOWCHARTING

Flowcharting is certainly the best-known of all program design methods. Programming textbooks describe how programmers first write complete flowcharts and then start writing the actual program. In fact, few programmers have ever worked this way, and flowcharting has often been more of a joke or a nuisance to programmers than a design method. We will try to describe both the advantages and disadvantages of flowcharts, and show the place of this technique in program design.

ADVANTAGES OF FLOWCHARTING

The basic advantage of the flowchart is that it is a pictorial representation. People find such representations much more meaningful than written descriptions. The designer can visualize the whole system and see the relationships of the various parts. Logical errors and inconsistencies often stand out instead of being hidden in a printed page. At its best, the flowchart is a picture of the entire system.

Some of the more specific advantages of flowcharts are:

1) Standard symbols exist (see Figure 13-7) so that flowcharting forms are widely recognized.
2) Flowcharts can be understood by someone without a programming background.
3) Flowcharts can be used to divide the entire project into sub-tasks. The flowchart can then be examined to measure overall progress.
4) Flowcharts show the sequence of operations and can therefore aid in locating the source of errors.
5) Flowcharting is a technique widely used in other areas besides programming.

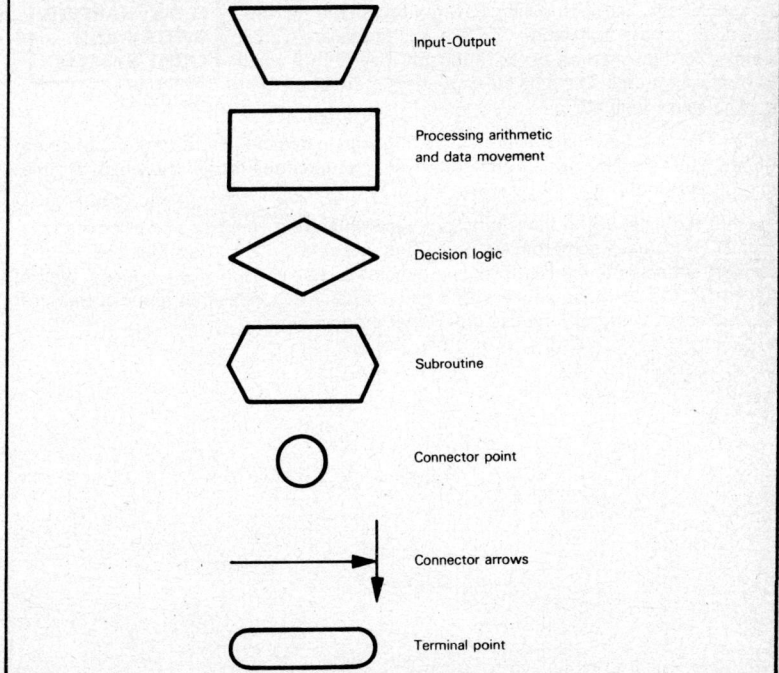

Figure 13-7. Standard Flow Diagram Symbols

These advantages are all important. There is no question that flowcharting will continue to be an important design technique. But we should stop and look at some of the disadvantages of flowcharting as a program design method, e.g.:

DISADVANTAGES OF FLOWCHARTING

1) Flowcharts are difficult to design, draw or change in all except the simplest situations.
2) There is no easy way to debug or test a flowchart.
3) Flowcharts tend to become cluttered. Designers find it difficult to balance between the amount of detail needed to make the flowchart useful and the amount which makes the flowchart little better than a program listing.
4) Flowcharts only show the program organization. They do not show the organization of the data or the structure of the input/output modules.
5) Flowcharts do not help with hardware or timing problems or give hints as to where these problems might occur.

Thus, flowcharting is a helpful technique which you should not try to extend too far. Flowcharts are useful as program documentation, since they have standard forms and are comprehensible to non-programmers. As a design tool, however, flowcharts cannot provide much more than a starting outline; the programmer cannot debug a detailed flowchart and the flowchart is often more difficult to design than the program itself.

EXAMPLES

Response to a Switch

This simple task, in which a single switch turns on a light for one second, is easy to flowchart. In fact, such tasks are typical examples for flowcharting books, although they form a small part of most systems. The data structure here is so simple that it can be safely ignored.

FLOWCHARTING SWITCH AND LIGHT SYSTEM

Figure 13-8 is the flowchart. There is little difficulty in deciding on the amount of detail required. The flowchart gives a straightforward picture of the procedure, which anyone could understand.

Note that the most useful flowcharts may ignore program variables and ask questions directly. Of course, compromises are often necessary here. Two versions of the flowchart are sometimes helpful — one general version in layman's language, which will be useful to non-programmers, and one programmer's version in terms of the program variables, which will be useful to other programmers.

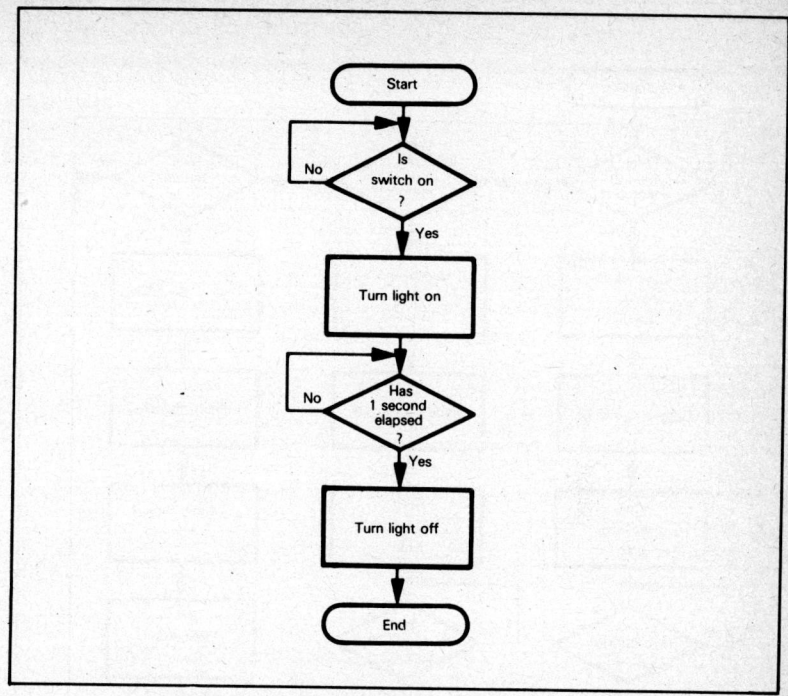

Figure 13-8. Flowchart of One-Second Response to a Switch

The Switch-Based Memory Loader

This system (refer to Figure 13-3) is considerably more complex than the previous example, and involves many more decisions. The flowchart (see Figure 13-9) is more difficult to write and not as straightforward as the previous example. In this example, we run into the problem that there is no way to debug or test the flowchart.

FLOWCHARTING THE SWITCH-BASED MEMORY LOADER

The flowchart in Figure 13-9 includes the improvements we suggested as part of the problem definition. Clearly, this flowchart is beginning to get cluttered and lose its advantages over a written description. Adding other features which define the meaning of the entry with status lights and allow the operator to check entries after completion would make the flowchart even more complex. Writing the complete flowchart from scratch could quickly become a formidable task. However, once the program has been written, the flowchart is useful as documentation.

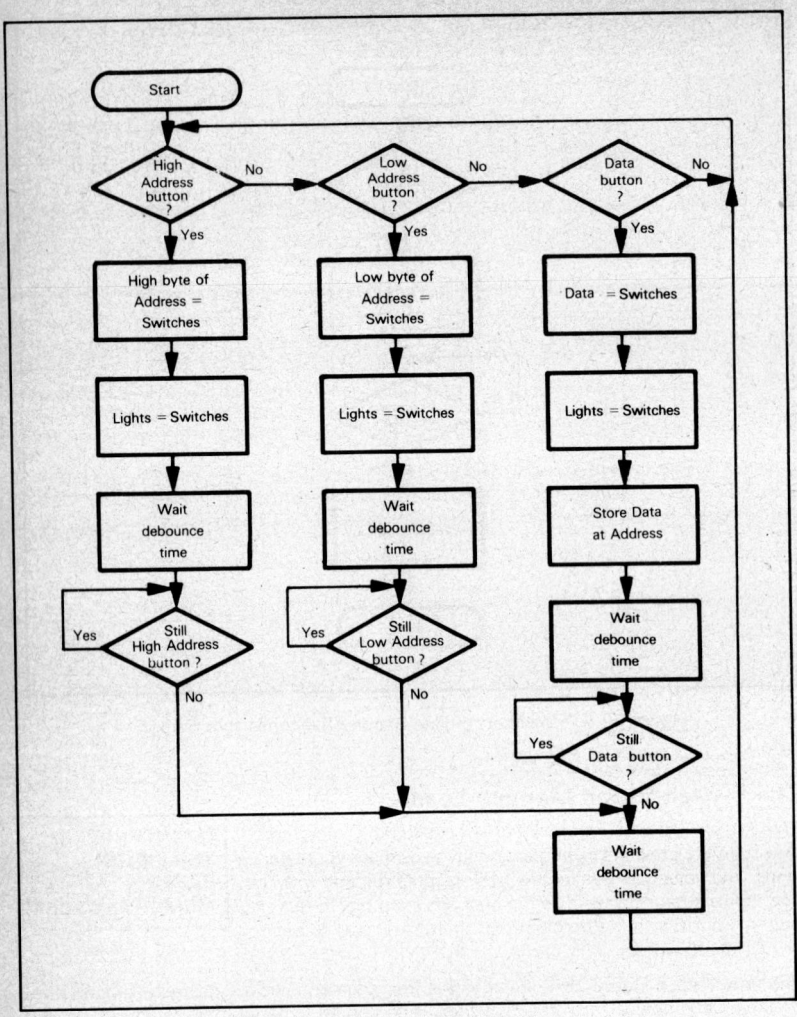

Figure 13-9. Flowchart of Switch-Based Memory Loader

The Credit-Verification Terminal

In this application (see Figures 13-4 through 13-6), the flowchart will be even more complex than in the switch-based memory loader case. Here, the best idea is to flowchart sections separately so that the flowcharts remain manageable. However, the presence of data structures (as in the multi-digit display and the messages) will make the gap between flowchart and program much larger.

FLOWCHARTING THE CREDIT VERIFICATION

FLOWCHARTING SECTIONS

Let us look at some of the sections. Figure 13-10 shows the keyboard entry process for the digit keys. The program must fetch the data after each strobe and place the digit in the display array if there is room for it. If there are already ten digits in the array, the program simply ignores the entry.

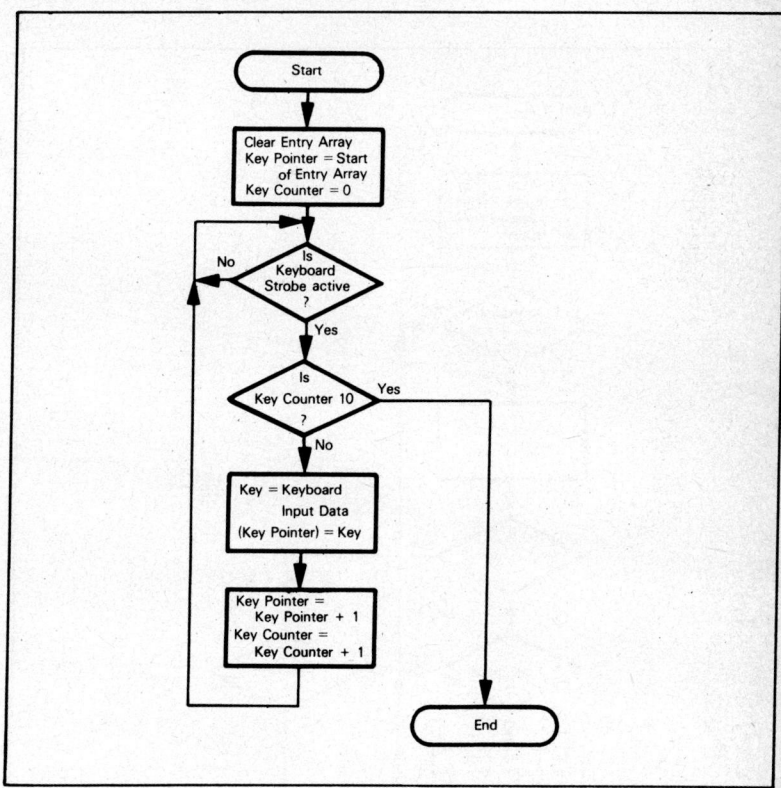

Figure 13-10. Flowchart of Keyboard Entry Process

The actual program will have to handle the displays at the same time. Note that either software or hardware must de-activate the keyboard strobe after the processor reads a digit.

Figure 13-11 adds the Send key. This key, of course, is optional. The terminal could just send the data as soon as the operator enters a complete number. However, that procedure would not give the operator a chance to check the entire entry. The flowchart with the Send key is more complex because there are two alternatives:

1) If the operator has not entered ten digits, the program must ignore the Send key and place any other key in the entry.
2) If the operator has entered ten digits, the program must respond to the Send key by transferring control to the Send routine, and ignore all other keys.

Note that the flowchart has become much more difficult to organize and to follow. There is also no obvious way to check the flowchart.

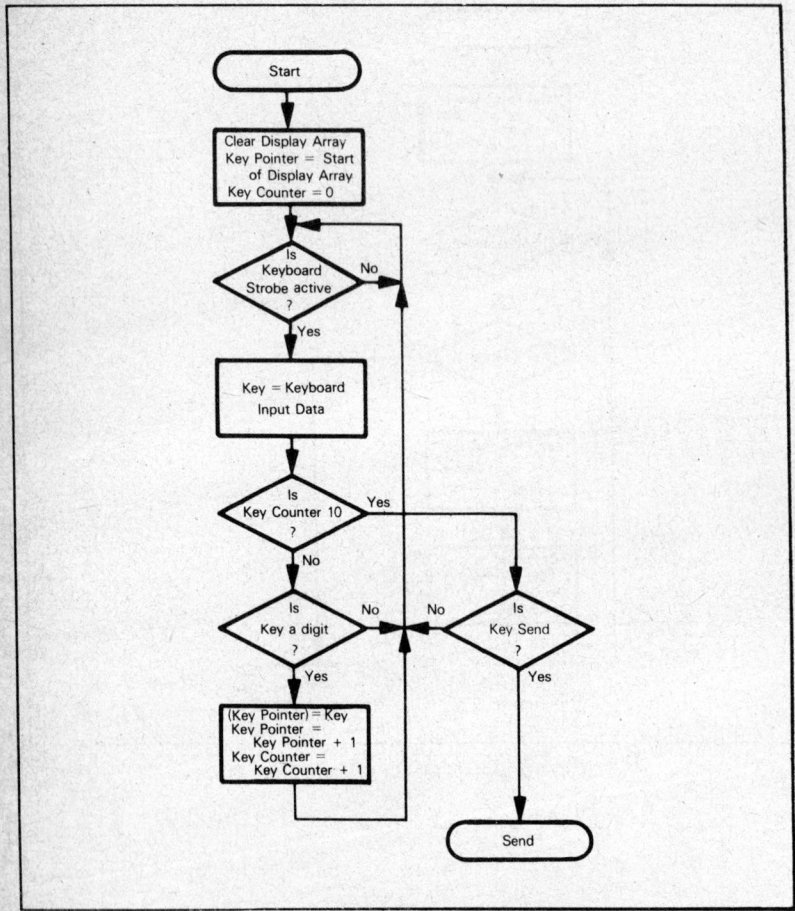

Figure 13-11. Flowchart of Keyboard Entry Process with Send Key

Figure 13-12 shows the flowchart of the keyboard entry process with all the function keys. In this example, the flow of control is by no means simple. Clearly, some written description is necessary. The organization and layout of complex flowcharts requires careful planning. We have followed the process of adding features to the flowchart one at a time, but this still results in a large amount of redrawing. Again we should remember that, throughout the keyboard entry process, the program must also refresh the displays if they are multiplexed and not controlled by shift registers or other hardware.

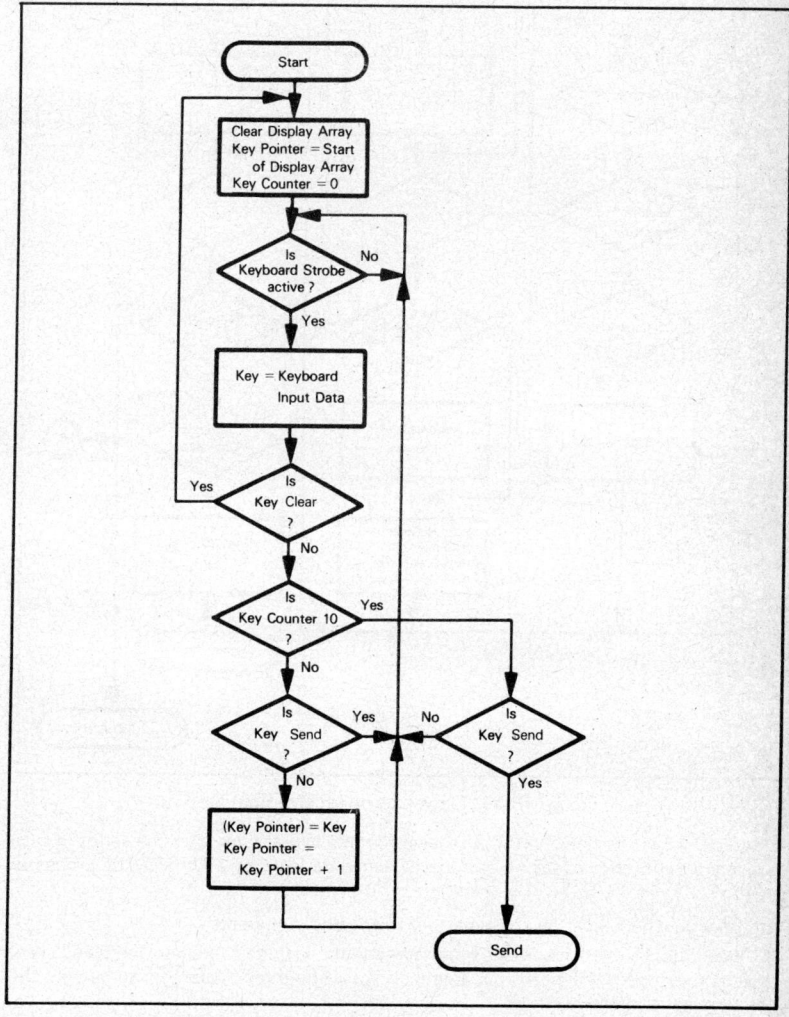

Figure 13-12. Flowchart of Keyboard Entry Process with Function Keys

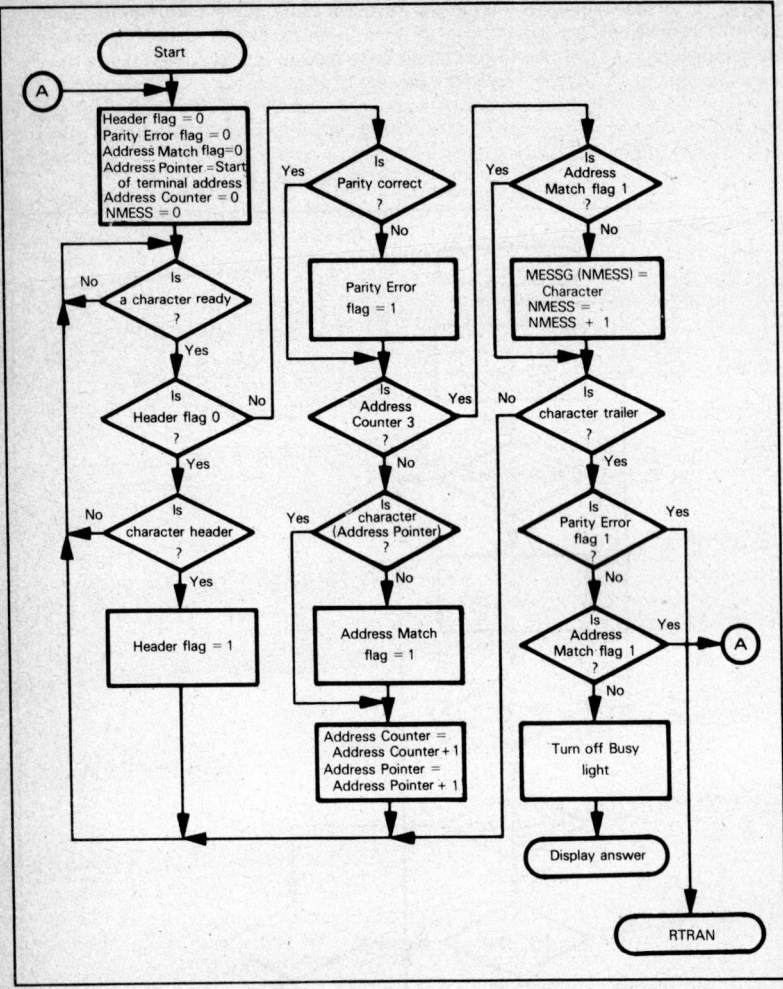

Figure 13-13. Flowchart of Receive Routine

Figure 13-13 is the flowchart of a receive routine. We assume that the serial/parallel conversion and error checking is done in hardware (e.g., by a UART). The processor must:

1) Look for the header (we assume that it is a single character).
2) Read the destination address (we assume that it is three characters long) and see if the message is meant for this terminal; i.e., if the three characters agree with the terminal address.
3) Wait for the trailer character.
4) If the message is meant for the terminal, turn off the Busy light and go to Display Answer routine.
5) In the event of any errors, request re-transmission by going to RTRAN routine.

This routine involves a large number of decisions, and the flowchart is neither simple nor obvious.

Clearly, we have come a long way from the simple flowchart (Figure 13-8) of the first example. A complete set of flowcharts for the transaction terminal would be a major task. It would consist of several inter-related charts with complex logic, and would require a large amount of effort. Such an effort would be just as difficult as writing a preliminary program, and not as useful, since you could not check it on the computer.

MODULAR PROGRAMMING

Once programs become large and complex, flowcharting is no longer a satisfactory design tool. However, the problem definition and the flowchart can give you some idea as to how to divide the program into reasonable sub-tasks. The division of the entire program into sub-tasks or modules is called "modular programming". Clearly, most of the programs we presented in earlier chapters would typically be modules in a large system program. The problems that the designer faces in modular programming are how to divide the program into modules and how to put the modules together.

The advantages of modular programming are obvious: **ADVANTAGES OF MODULAR PROGRAMMING**

1) A single module is easier to write, debug and test than an entire program.

2) A module is likely to be useful in many places and in other programs, particularly if it is reasonably general and performs a common task. You can build up a library of standard modules.

3) Modular programming allows the programmer to divide tasks and use previously written programs.

4) Changes can be incorporated into one module rather than into the entire system.

5) Errors can often be isolated and then attributed to a single module.

6) Modular programming gives an idea of how much progress has been made and how much of the work is left.

The idea of modular programming is such an obvious one that its disadvantages are often ignored. These include: **DISADVANTAGES OF MODULAR PROGRAMMING**

1) Fitting the modules together can be a major problem, particularly if different people write the modules.

2) Modules require very careful documentation, since they may affect other parts of the program, such as data structures used by all the modules.

3) Testing and debugging modules separately is difficult, since other modules may produce the data used by the module being debugged and still other modules may use the results. You may have to write special programs (called "drivers") just to produce sample data and test the programs. These drivers require extra programming effort which adds nothing to the total system.

4) Programs may be very difficult to modularize in any reasonable way. If you modularize the program poorly, integration will be very difficult, since almost all errors and the resulting changes will involve several modules.

5) Modular programs often require extra time and memory, since the separate modules may repeat functions.

Therefore, while modular programming is certainly an improvement over simply trying to write the entire program from scratch, it does have some disadvantages as well.

Important considerations include restricting the amount of information shared by modules, limiting design decisions that are subject to change to a single module and restricting the access of one module to another. D.L. Pamas (see the References) has been a leader in the area of modular programming.

EXAMPLES
Response to a Switch

This simple program can be divided into two modules:

Module 1 waits for the switch to be turned on and turns the light on in response.

Module 2 provides the one-second delay.

> MODULARIZING THE SWITCH AND LIGHT SYSTEM

Module 1 is likely to be specific to the system, since it will depend on how the switch and light are attached. Module 2 will be generally useful, since many tasks require delays. Clearly, it would be advantageous to have a standard delay module which could provide delays of varying lengths. The module will require careful documentation so that you will know how to specify the length of the delay, how to call the module, and what registers and memory locations the module affects.

A general version of Module 1 would be far less useful, since it would have to deal with different types and connections of switches and lights.

You would probably find it simpler to write a module for a particular configuration of switches and lights rather than try to use a standard routine. Note the difference between this situation and Module 2.

The Switch-Based Memory Loader

The switch-based memory loader is difficult to modularize, since all the programming tasks depend on the hardware configuration and the tasks are so simple that modules hardly seem worthwhile. The flowchart in Figure 13-9 suggests that one module might be the one that waits for the operator to press one of the three pushbuttons.

> MODULARIZING THE SWITCH-BASED MEMORY LOADER

Some other modules might be:

1) A delay module that provides the delay required to debounce the switches.
2) A switch and display module that reads the data from the switches and sends it to the displays.
3) A Lamp Test module.

Highly system-dependent modules such as the last two are unlikely to be generally useful. This example is not one in which modular programming offers great advantages.

The Verification Terminal

The verification terminal, on the other hand, lends itself very well to modular programming. The entire system can easily be divided into three main modules:

> MODULARIZING THE VERIFICATION TERMINAL

1) Keyboard and display module.
2) Data transmission module.
3) Data reception module.

A general keyboard and display module could handle many keyboard- and display-based systems. the sub-modules would perform such tasks as:

1) Recognizing a new keyboard entry and fetching the data.
2) Clearing the array in response to a Clear key.
3) Entering digits into storage.
4) Looking for the terminator or Send key.
5) Displaying the digits.

Although the key interpretations and the number of digits will vary, the basic entry, data storage and data display processes will be the same for many programs. Such function keys as Clear would also be standard. Clearly, the designer must consider which modules will be useful in other applications, and pay careful attention to those modules.

The data transmission module could also be divided into such sub-modules as:

1) Adding the header character.
2) Transmitting characters as the output line can handle them.
3) Generating delay times between bits or characters.
4) Adding the trailer character.
5) Checking for transmission failures; i.e., no acknowledgment or inability to transmit without errors.

The data reception module could include sub-modules which:

1) Look for the header character.
2) Check the message destination address against the terminal address.
3) Store and interpret the message.
4) Look for the trailer character.
5) Generate bit or character delays.

REVIEW OF MODULAR PROGRAMMING

Modular programming can be very helpful if you abide by the following rules:

RULES FOR MODULAR PROGRAMMING

1) Use modules of 20 to 50 lines. Shorter modules are usually a waste of time, while longer modules are seldom general and may be difficult to integrate.
2) Try to make modules reasonably general. Differentiate between common features like ASCII code or asynchronous transmission formats, which will be the same for many applications and key identifications, and number of displays or number of characters in a message, which are likely to be unique to a particular application. Make the changing of the latter parameters simple. Major changes like different character codes should be handled by separate modules.
3) Take extra time on modules like delays, display handlers, keyboard handlers, etc., which will be useful in other projects or in many different places in the present program.
4) Try to keep modules as distinct and logically separate as possible.
5) Do not try to modularize simple tasks where rewriting the entire task may be easier than assembling or modifying the module.

Note here how important it is that each design decision (such as the bit rate, message format, or error-checking procedure) be implemented in only one module. A change in any of these decisions will then only require changes to that single module.

INFORMATION-HIDING PRINCIPLE

The other modules should be written so that they are totally unaware of the values chosen or the methods used in the implementing module. An important concept here is Pamas' "information-hiding principle", whereby modules only share information that is absolutely essential to getting the task done. Other information is hidden within a single module.

STRUCTURED PROGRAMMING

How do you keep modules distinct and stop them from interacting with one another? How do you write a program which has a clear sequence of operations so that you can isolate and correct errors? One answer is to use the methods known as "structured programming", whereby each part of the program consists of elements from a limited set of structures and each structure has a single entry and a single exit.

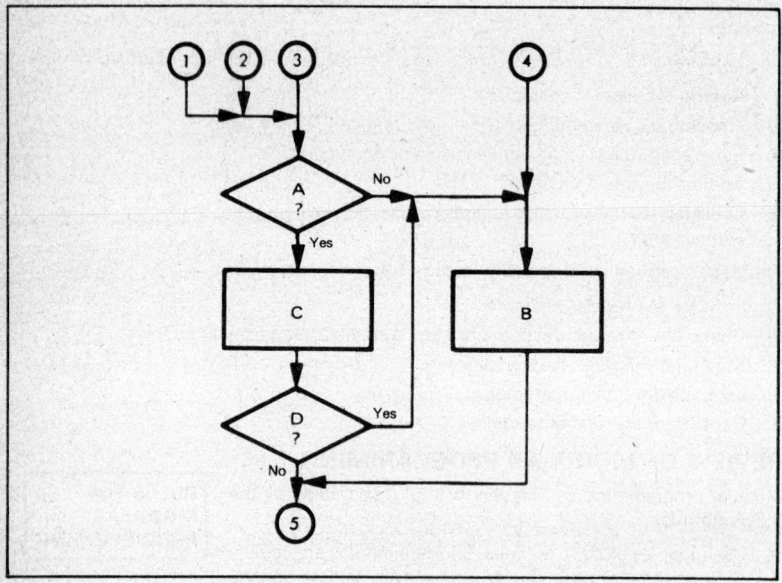

Figure 13-14. Flowchart of an Unstructured Program

Figure 13-14 shows a flowchart of an unstructured program. If an error occurs in Module B, we have five possible sources for that error. Not only must we check each possible sequence, but we also have to make sure that any changes made to correct the error do not affect any of the other sequences. The usual result is that debugging the program becomes like trying to hang on to an octopus. Every time you think the situation is under control, there is another loose tentacle somewhere.

The answer to this problem is to establish a clear sequence of operations so that you can isolate errors. Such a clear sequence uses single-entry, single-exit modules. The basic modules that are needed are:

BASIC STRUCTURES OF STRUCTURED PROGRAMMING

1) An ordinary sequence; i.e., a linear structure in which statements or structures are executed consecutively. In the sequence:
   P1
   P2
   P3

   the computer executes P1 first, P2 second and P3 third. P1, P2 and P3 may be single instructions or entire programs.

2) A conditional structure.

The common one is "if A then P1 else P2", where A is a condition and P1 and P2 are programs. The computer executes P1 if A is true, and P2 if A is false. Figure 13-15 shows the logic of this structure. Note that the structure has a single entry and a single exit; there is no way to enter or leave P1 or P2 other than through the structure.

3) A loop structure.

The common loop structure is "do P while A", where A is a condition and P is a program. The computer checks A and executes P if A is true. This structure (see Figure 13-16) also has a single entry and a single exit. Note that the computer will not execute P at all if A is originally false, since the value of A is checked before the execution of P.

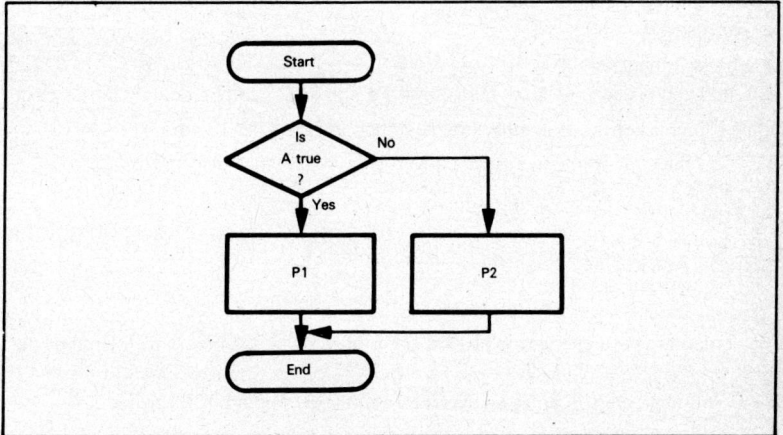

Figure 13-15. Flowchart of the If-Then-Else Structure

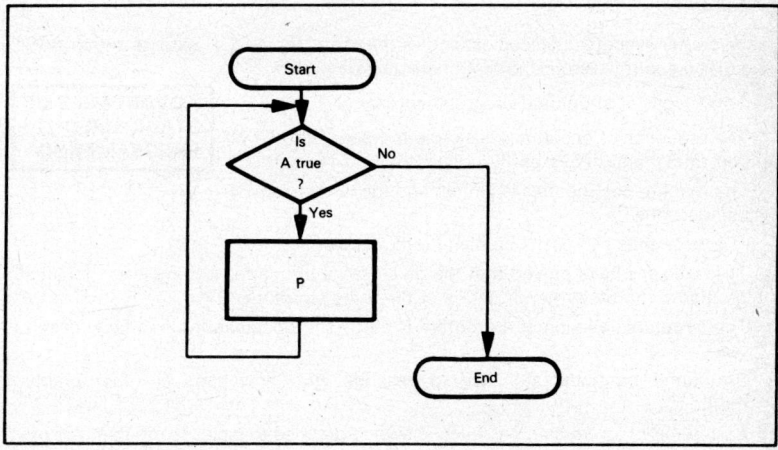

Figure 13-16. Flowchart of the Do-While Structure

Note the following features of structured programming:

1) Only the three basic structures are permitted.
2) Structures may be nested to any level of complexity so that any program can, in turn, contain any of the structures.
3) Each structure has a single entry and a single exit.

Some examples of the conditional structure illustrated in Figure 13-15 are:

EXAMPLES OF STRUCTURES

1) P2 included:
   if $X \geq 0$ then NPOS = NPOS+1
       else NNEG = NNEG+1

Both P1 and P2 are single statements.

2) P2 omitted:
   if $X \neq 0$ then Y = 1/X

Here no action is taken if A $(X \neq 0)$ is false. P2 and "else" can be omitted in this case.

Some examples of the loop structure illustrated in Figure 13-16 are:

1) Form the sum of integers from 1 to N.
   I = 0
   SUM = 0
   do while I < N
       I = I+1
       SUM = SUM+I
   end

The computer executes the loop as long as I < N. If N = 0, the program within the "do-while" is not executed at all.

2) Count characters in an array SENTENCE until you find an ASCII period.
   NCHAR = 0
   do while SENTENCE (NCHAR) $\neq$ PERIOD
       NCHAR = NCHAR+1
   end

The computer executes the loop as long as the character in SENTENCE is not an ASCII period. The count is zero if the first character is a period.

The advantages of structured programming are:

ADVANTAGES OF STRUCTURED PROGRAMMING

1) The sequence of operations is simple to trace. This allows you to test and debug easily.
2) The number of structures is limited and the terminology is standardized.
3) The structures can easily be made into modules.
4) Theoreticians have proved that the given set of structures is complete; that is, all programs can be written in terms of the three structures.
5) The structured version of a program is partly self-documenting and fairly easy to read.
6) Structured programs are easy to describe with flowcharts or other graphic methods.
7) Structured programming has been shown in practice to increase programmer productivity.

Structured programming basically forces much more discipline on the programmer than does modular programming. The result is more systematic and better-organized programs.

The disadvantages of structured programming are:

> **DISADVANTAGES OF STRUCTURED PROGRAMMING**

1) Only a few high-level languages (e.g., PL/M, PASCAL) will directly accept the structures. The programmer therefore has to go through an extra translation stage to convert the structures to assembly language code. The structured version of the program, however, is often useful as documentation.
2) Structured programs often execute slower and use more memory than unstructured programs.
3) Limiting the structures to the three basic forms makes some tasks very awkward to perform. The completeness of the structures only means that all programs can be implemented with them; it does not mean that a given program can be implemented efficiently or conveniently.
4) The standard structures are often quite confusing; e.g., nested "if-then-else" structures may be very difficult to read since there may be no clear indication of where the ones inside end. A series of nested "do-while" loops can also be difficult to read.
5) Structured programs only consider the sequence of program operations, not the flow of data. Therefore, the structures may handle data awkwardly.
6) Few programmers are accustomed to structured programming. Many find the standard structures awkward and restrictive.

We are neither advocating nor discouraging the use of structured programming. It is one way of systematizing program design. In general, it is most useful in the following situations:

> **WHEN TO USE STRUCTURED PROGRAMMING**

1) Larger programs, perhaps exceeding 1000 instructions.
2) Applications in which memory usage is not critical.
3) Low-volume applications where software development costs, particularly testing and debugging, are important factors.
4) Applications that do not involve complex data structures.
5) Applications involving string manipulation, process control or other algorithms, rather than simple bit manipulations.
6) Applications where a high-level language is being used.

In the future we expect the cost of memory to decrease, the average size of microprocessor programs to increase, and the cost of software development to increase. Therefore, methods like structured programming, which decrease software development costs for larger programs but use more memory, will become more valuable.

EXAMPLES

Response to a Switch

The structured version of this example is:

> **STRUCTURED PROGRAMMING IN THE SWITCH AND LIGHT SYSTEM**

```
SWITCH = OFF
do while SWITCH = OFF
   READ SWITCH
end
LIGHT = ON
DELAY 1
LIGHT = OFF
```

ON and OFF must have the proper definitions for the switch and light. We assume that DELAY is a module that provides a delay given by its parameter in seconds.

A statement in a structured program may actually be a subroutine. However, in order to conform to the rules of structured programming, the subroutine cannot have any exits other than the one that returns control to the main program.

Since "do-while" checks the condition before executing the loop, we set the variable SWITCH to OFF before starting. The structured program is straightforward, readable, and easy to check by hand. However, it would probably require somewhat more memory than an unstructured program, which would not have to initialize SWITCH and could combine the reading and checking procedures.

The Switch-Based Memory Loader

The switch-based memory loader is a more complex structured programming problem. We may implement the flowchart of Figure 13-9 as follows (an * indicates a comment):

STRUCTURED PROGRAMMING FOR THE SWITCH-BASED MEMORY LOADER

```
*
*INITIALIZE VARIABLES
*
HIADDRESS = 0
LOADDRESS = 0
*
*THIS PROGRAM USES A DO-WHILE CONSTRUCT WITH NO CONDITION
*(CALLED SIMPLY DO-FOREVER). THEREFORE, THE SYSTEM CONTINUALLY
*EXECUTES THE PROGRAM CONTAINED IN THIS DO-WHILE LOOP.
*
do forever
*
*TEST FOR HIADDRESS BUTTON; PERFORM THE REQUIRED PROCESSING
*IF IT IS ON.
*
  if HIADDRBUTTON = 1 then begin
    HIADDRESS = SWITCHES
    LIGHTS = SWITCHES
    DELAY (DEBOUNCETIME)
    do while HIADDRBUTTON = 1
      DELAY (DEBOUNCETIME)
    end
  end
*
*TEST FOR LOADDRESS BUTTON; PERFORM LOW ADDRESS PROCESSING
*IF IT IS ON.
*
  if LOADDRBUTTON = 1 then begin
    LOADDRESS = SWITCHES
    LIGHTS = SWITCHES
    DELAY (DEBOUNCETIME)
    do while LOADDRBUTTON = 1
      DELAY (DEBOUNCETIME)
    end
  end
```

* *TEST FOR DATABUTTON, AND STORE DATA INTO MEMORY
* *IF IT IS ON
*
```
  if DATABUTTON = 1 then begin
    DATA = SWITCHES
    LIGHTS = SWITCHES
    (HIADDRESSLOADDRESS) = DATA
    DELAY (DEBOUNCETIME)
    do while DATABUTTON = 1
      DELAY (DEBOUNCETIME)
    end
  end
```
*
*THE ABOVE END TERMINATES THE
* do forever LOOP.
*

Structured programs are not easy to write, but they can give a great deal of insight into the overall program logic. You can check the logic of the structured program by hand before writing any actual code.

The Credit-Verification Terminal

Let us look at the keyboard entry for the transaction terminal. We will assume that the display array is ENTRY, the keyboard strobe is KEYSTROBE, and the keyboard data is KEYIN. The structured program without the function keys is:

STRUCTURED PROGRAM FOR THE CREDIT-VERIFICATION TERMINAL

STRUCTURED KEYBOARD ROUTINE

NKEYS = 10
*
*CLEAR ENTRY TO START
*
```
  do while NKEYS > 0
    NKEYS = NKEYS - 1
    ENTRY(NKEYS) = 0
  end
```

*FETCH A COMPLETE ENTRY FROM KEYBOARD
*
```
  do while NKEYS < 10
    if KEYSTROBE = ACTIVE then begin
      KEYSTROBE = INACTIVE
      ENTRY(NKEYS) = KEYIN
      NKEYS = NKEYS+1
    end
  end
```

Adding the SEND key means that the program must ignore extra digits after it has a complete entry, and must ignore the SEND key until it has a complete entry. The structured program is:

NKEYS = 10
*
*CLEAR ENTRY TO START
*
```
  do while NKEYS > 0
    NKEYS = NKEYS - 1
    ENTRY(NKEYS) = 0
  end
```

```
*
*WAIT FOR COMPLETE ENTRY FOLLOWED BY SEND KEY

  do while KEY ≠ SEND OR NKEYS ≠ 10
    if KEYSTROBE = ACTIVE then begin
      KEYSTROBE = INACTIVE
      KEY = KEYIN
*
*SAVE DIGIT IF ENTRY NOT ALREADY COMPLETE
*
      if NKEYS ≠ 10 AND KEY ≠ SEND then begin
        ENTRY(NKEYS) = KEY
        NKEYS = NKEYS+1
      end
    end
  end
```

Note the following features of this structured program:

1) The second if-then is nested within the first one since keys are only entered after a strobe is recognized. If the second if-then were on the same level as the first, a single key could fill the entry, since its value would be entered into the array during each iteration of the do-while loop.
2) KEY need not be defined initially, since NKEY is set to zero as part of the clearing of the entry.

Adding the CLEAR key allows the program to clear the entry originally by simulating the pressing of CLEAR; i.e., by setting NKEYS to 10 and KEY to CLEAR before starting. The structured program must also only clear digits which have previously been filled. The new structured program is:

```
*
*SIMULATE COMPLETE CLEARING
*
NKEYS = 10
KEY = CLEAR
*
*WAIT FOR COMPLETE ENTRY AND SEND KEY
*
do while  KEY ≠ SEND OR NKEYS ≠ 10
*
*CLEAR WHOLE ENTRY IF CLEAR KEY STRUCK
*
  if KEY = CLEAR then begin
    KEY = 0
    do while NKEYS > 0
      NKEYS = NKEYS - 1
      ENTRY(NKEYS) = 0
    end
  end
```

*
*GET DIGIT IF ENTRY INCOMPLETE
*
  if KEYSTROBE = ACTIVE then begin
    KEYSTROBE = INACTIVE
    KEY = KEYIN
    if KEY < 10 AND NKEYS ≠ 10 then begin
      ENTRY(NKEYS) = KEY
      NKEYS = NKEYS+1
    end
  end
end

Note that the program resets KEY to zero after clearing the array, so that the operation is not repeated.

We can similarly build a structured program for the receive routine. An initial program could just look for the header and trailer characters. We will assume that RSTB is the indicator that a character is ready. The structured program is:

STRUCTURED RECEIVE ROUTINE

*
*CLEAR HEADER FLAG TO START
*
HFLAG = 0
*
*WAIT FOR HEADER AND TRAILER
*
do while HFLAG = 0 OR CHAR ≠ TRAILER
*
*GET CHARACTER IF READY, LOOK FOR HEADER
*
  if RSTB = ACTIVE then begin
    RSTB = INACTIVE
    CHAR = INPUT
    if CHAR = HEADER then
      HFLAG = 1
  end

Now we can add the section that checks the message address against the three digits in TERMINAL ADDRESS (TERMADDR). If any of the corresponding digits are not equal, the ADDRESS MATCH flag (ADDRMATCH) is set to 1.

```
*CLEAR HEADER FLAG, ADDRESS MATCH FLAG, ADDRESS COUNTER TO START
*
HFLAG = 0
ADDRMATCH = 0
ADDRCTR = 0
*
*WAIT FOR HEADER, DESTINATION ADDRESS AND TRAILER
*
do while HFLAG = 0 OR CHAR ≠ TRAILER OR ADDRCTR ≠ 3

   *GET CHARACTER IF READY
   *
     if RSTB = ACTIVE then begin
        RSTB = INACTIVE
        CHAR = INPUT
     end
   *
   *CHECK FOR TERMINAL ADDRESS AND HEADER
   *
     if HFLAG = 1 AND ADDRCTR ≠ 3 then
        if CHAR ≠ TERMADDR(ADDRCTR) then begin
        ADDRMATCH = 1
        ADDRCTR = ADDRCTR+1
     if CHAR = HEADER then HFLAG = 1
end
```

The program must now wait for a header, a three-digit identification code, and a trailer. You must be careful of what happens during the iteration when the program finds the header, and of what happens if an erroneous identification code character is the same as the trailer.

A further addition can store the message in MESSG. NMESS is the number of characters in the message; if it is not zero at the end, the program knows that the terminal has received a valid message. We have not tried to minimize the logic expressions in this program.

```
*CLEAR FLAGS, COUNTERS TO START
*
HFLAG = 0
ADDRMATCH = 0
ADDRCTR = 0
NMESS = 0
*
*WAIT FOR HEADER, DESTINATION ADDRESS AND TRAILER
*
do while HFLAG = 0 OR CHAR ≠ TRAILER OR ADDRCTR ≠ 3

   *GET CHARACTER IF READY
   *
     if RSTB = ACTIVE then begin
        RSTB = INACTIVE
        CHAR = INPUT
     end
```

* *READ MESSAGE IF DESTINATION ADDRESS = TERMINAL ADDRESS
*
  if HFLAG = 1 AND ADDRCTR = 3 then
    if ADDRMATCH = 0 AND CHAR ≠ TRAILER then begin
      MESSG(NMESS) = CHAR
      NMESS = NMESS+1
  end
*
*CHECK FOR TERMINAL ADDRESS
*
  if HFLAG = 1 AND ADDRCTR ≠ 3 then
    if CHAR ≠ TERMADDR(ADDRCTR) then begin
    ADDRMATCH = 1
    ADDRCTR = ADDRCTR+1
*
*LOOK FOR HEADER
*
  if CHAR = HEADER then HFLAG = 1
end

The program only checks for the identification code if it found a header during a previous iteration. It only accepts the message if it has previously found a header and a complete, matching destination address. The program must work properly during the iterations when it finds the header, the trailer and the last digit of the destination address. It must not try to match the header with the terminal address or place the trailer or the final digit of the destination address in the message. You might try adding the rest of the logic from the flowchart (Figure 13-13) to the structured program. Note that the order of operations is often critical. You must be sure that the program does not complete one phase and start the next one during the same iteration.

REVIEW OF STRUCTURED PROGRAMMING

Structured programming brings discipline to program design. It forces you to limit the types of structures you use and the sequence of operations. It provides single-entrance, single-exit structures which you can check for logical accuracy. Structured programming often makes the designer aware of inconsistencies or possible combinations of inputs. Structured programming is not a cure-all, but it does bring some order into a process that can be chaotic. The structured program should also aid in debugging, testing and documentation.

Structured programming is not simple. The programmer must not only define the problem adequately, but must also work through the logic carefully. This is tedious and difficult, but it can result in a clearly written, working program.

TERMINATORS FOR STRUCTURES

The particular structures we have presented are not ideal and are often awkward. In addition, it can be difficult to distinguish where one structure ends and another begins, particularly if they are nested. Theorists may provide better structures in the future, or designers may wish to add some of their own. Some kind of terminator for each structure seems necessary, since indenting does not always clarify the situation. "End" is a logical terminator for the "do-while" loop. There is no obvious terminator, however, for the "if-then-else" statement; some theorists have suggested "endif" or "fi" ("if" backwards), but these are both awkward and do not contribute to the readability of the program.

We suggest the following rules for applying structured programming:

RULES FOR STRUCTURED PROGRAMMING

1) Begin by writing a basic flowchart to help define the logic of the program.
2) Start with the "if-then-else" and "do-while" constructs. They are known to be a complete set, i.e., any program can be written in terms of these structures.
3) Indent each level a few spaces from the previous level, so that you will know which statements belong where.
4) Use terminators for each structure; e.g., "end" for the "do-while" and "endif" or "fi" for the "if-then-else". The terminators plus the indentation should make the program reasonably clear.
5) Emphasize simplicity and readability. Leave lots of spaces, use meaningful names, and make expressions as clear as possible. Do not try to minimize the logic at the cost of clarity.
6) Comment the program in an organized manner.
7) Check the logic. Try all the extreme cases or special conditions and a few sample cases. Any logical errors you find at this level will not return to plague you later.

TOP-DOWN DESIGN

The remaining problem is how to check and integrate modules or structures. Certainly we want to divide a large task into sub-tasks. But how do we check the sub-tasks in isolation and put them together? The standard procedure, called "bottom-up design", requires extra work in testing and debugging and leaves the entire integration task to the end. What we need is a method that will allow testing and debugging to occur in the actual program environment and will subdivide the system integration into a series of modular tasks.

BOTTOM-UP DESIGN

This method is "top-down design". Here we start by writing the overall supervisor program. We replace the undefined sub-programs by program "stubs", temporary programs which may either record the entry, provide the answer to a selected test problem, or do nothing. We then test the supervisor program to see that its logic is correct.

TOP-DOWN DESIGN METHODS

PROGRAM STUBS

We proceed by expanding the stubs. Each stub will often contain sub-tasks, which we will temporarily represent as stubs. This process of expansion, debugging and testing continues until all the stubs are replaced by working programs. Note that testing and integration occur at each level, rather than all at the end. No special driver or data generation programs are necessary. We get a clear idea of exactly where we are in the design. Top-down design assumes modular programming, and is compatible with structured programming as well.

EXPANDING PROGRAM STUBS

ADVANTAGES OF TOP-DOWN DESIGN

The disadvantages of top-down design are:

1) The overall design may not mesh well with system hardware.
2) It may not take good advantage of existing software.
3) A suitable stub may be difficult to write, particularly if the same stub must work correctly in several different places.
4) Top-down design may not result in generally useful modules.
5) Errors at the top level can have catastrophic effects, whereas errors in bottom-up design are usually limited to a particular module.

DISADVANTAGES OF TOP-DOWN DESIGN

In large programming projects, top-down design has been shown to greatly improve programmer productivity. However, almost all of these projects have used some bottom-up design in cases where the top-down method would have resulted in a large amount of extra work.

Top-down design is a useful tool that should not be followed to extremes. It provides the same discipline for system testing and integration that structured programming provides for module design. The method, however, has more general applicability since it does not really assume the use of programmed logic. However, top-down design may not result in the most efficient implementation.

EXAMPLES
Response to a Switch

The first structured programming example actually demonstrates top-down design as well. The program was:

> TOP-DOWN DESIGN OF SWITCH AND LIGHT SYSTEM

```
SWITCH = OFF
do while SWITCH = OFF
   READ SWITCH
end
LIGHT = ON
DELAY 1
LIGHT = OFF
```

Almost all of these statements are really stubs, since none of them is fully defined. For example, what does READ SWITCH mean? If the switch were one bit of input port SPORT, it really means

```
SWITCH = SPORT AND SMASK
```

where SMASK has a '1' bit in the appropriate position.

Similarly, DELAY 1 actually means (if the processor itself provides the delay):

```
REG = COUNT
do while REG ≠ 0
   REG = REG - 1
end
```

COUNT is the appropriate number to provide a one-second delay. The expanded version of the program is:

```
SWITCH = 0
do while SWITCH = 0
   SWITCH = SPORT AND MASK
end
LIGHT = ON
REG = COUNT
do while REG ≠ 0
   REG = REG - 1
end
LIGHT = NOT (LIGHT)
```

Certainly this program is more explicit, and could more easily be translated into actual instructions or statements.

The Switch-Based Memory Loader

This example is more complex than the first example, so that we must proceed more systematically. Here again, the structured program really contains stubs.

> **TOP-DOWN DESIGN OF SWITCH-BASED MEMORY LOADER**

For example, if the HIGH ADDRESS button is one bit of input port CPORT, "if HIADDRBUTTON = 1" really means:

1) Input from CPORT.
2) Complement.
3) Logical AND with HAMASK;

where HAMASK has a '1' in the appropriate bit position and '0s' elsewhere. Similarly, the condition "if DATABUTTON = 1" really means:

1) Input from CPORT.
2) Complement.
3) Logical AND with DAMASK.

So, the initial stubs could just assign values to the buttons, e.g.,

    HIADDRBUTTON = 0
    LOADDRBUTTON = 0
    DATABUTTON = 0

A run of the supervisor program should show that it takes the implied "else" path through the "if-then-else" structures, and never reads the switches. Similarly, if the stub were

    HIADDRBUTTON = 1

the supervisor program should stay in the "do while HIADDRBUTTON = 1" loop waiting for the button to be released. These simple runs check the overall logic.

Now we can start expanding each stub and seeing if the expansion produces a reasonable overall result. Note how debugging and testing proceed in a straightforward and modular manner. We expand the HIADDRBUTTON = 1 stub to

    READ CPORT
    HIADDRBUTTON = NOT (CPORT) AND HAMASK

The program should wait for the HIGH ADDRESS button to be closed. The program should then display the values of the switches on the lights. This run checks for the proper response to the HIGH ADDRESS button.

We then expand the LOW ADDRESS button module to

    READ CPORT
    HIADDRBUTTON = NOT (CPORT) AND LAMASK

With the LOW ADDRESS button in the closed position, the program should display the values of the switches on the lights. This run checks for the proper response to the LOW ADDRESS button.

Similarly, we can expand the DATA button module and check for the proper response to that button. The entire program will then have been tested in a systematic manner.

When all the stubs have been expanded, the coding, debugging and testing stages will all be complete. Of course, we must know exactly what results each stub should produce. However, many logical errors will become obvious at each level without any further expansion.

The Transaction Terminal

This example, of course, will have more levels of detail. We could start with the following program (see Figure 13-17 for a flowchart):

TOP-DOWN DESIGN OF VERIFICATION TERMINAL

```
KEYBOARD
ACK = 0
do while ACK = 0
   TRANSMIT
   RECEIVE
   end
DISPLAY
```

Here KEYBOARD, TRANSMIT, RECEIVE and DISPLAY are program stubs which will be expanded later. KEYBOARD, for example, could simply place a ten-digit verified number in the appropriate buffer.

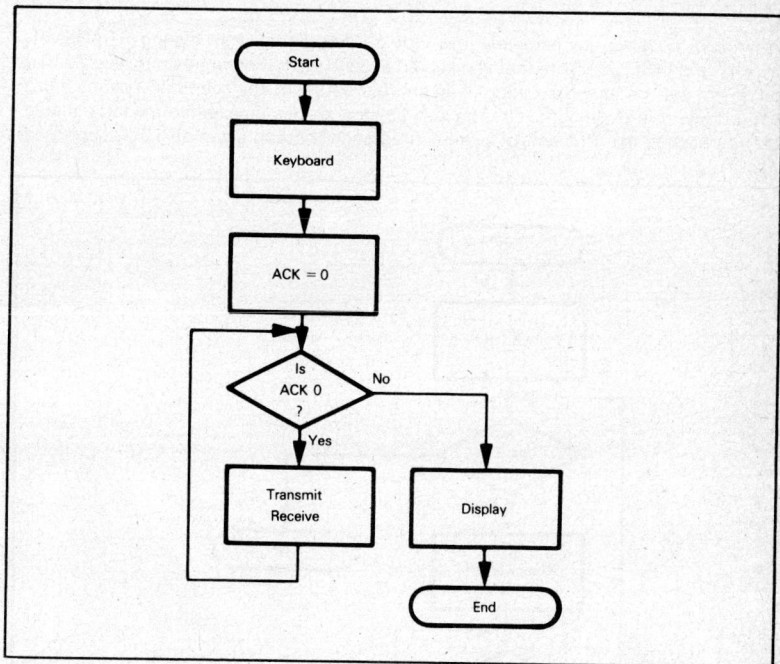

Figure 13-17. Initial Flowchart for Transaction Terminal

The next stage of expansion could produce the following program for KEYBOARD (see Figure 13-18):

EXPANDING THE KEYBOARD ROUTINE

```
VER = 0
do while VER = 0
  COMPLETE = 0
  do while COMPLETE = 0
    KEYIN
    KEYDS
  end
  VERIFY
end
```

Here VER = 0 means that an entry has not been verified; COMPLETE = 0 means that the entry is incomplete. KEYIN and KEYDS are the keyboard input and display routines respectively. VERIFY checks the entry. A possible stub for KEYIN would simply place a random entry (from a random number table or generator) in the buffer and set COMPLETE to 1.

We would continue by similarly expanding, debugging and testing TRANSMIT, RECEIVE and DISPLAY. Note that you should expand each program by one level so that you do not perform the integration of an entire program at any one time. You must use your judgment in defining levels. Too small a step wastes time, while too large a step gets you back to the problems of system integration that top-down design is supposed to solve.

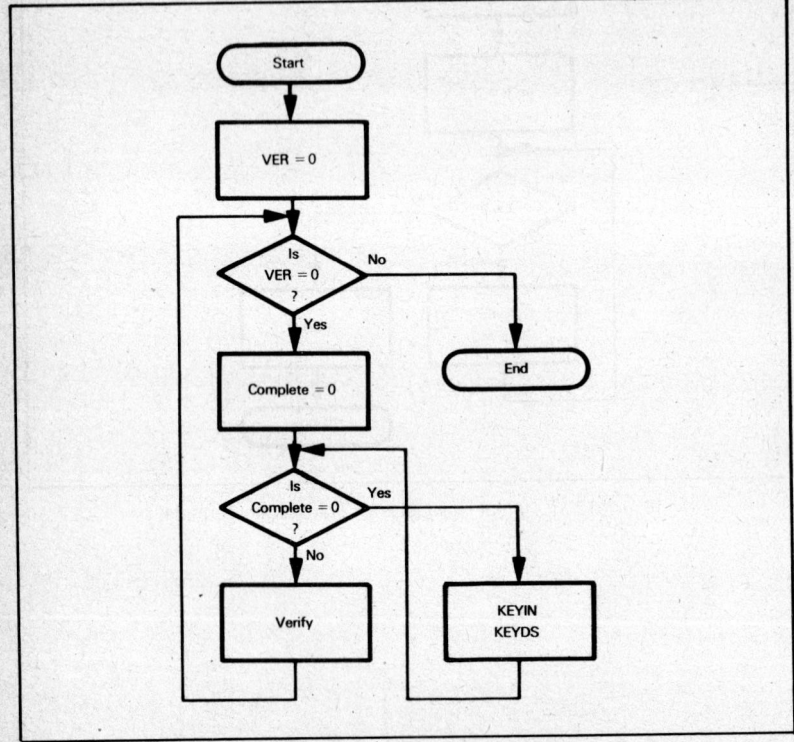

Figure 13-18. Flowchart for Expanded KEYBOARD Routine

REVIEW OF TOP-DOWN DESIGN

Top-down design brings discipline to the testing and integration phases of program design. It provides a systematic method for expanding a flowchart or problem definition to the level required to actually write a program. Together with structured programming, it forms a complete set of design techniques.

Like structured programming, top-down design is not simple. The designer must have defined the problem carefully and must work systematically through each level. Here again the methodology may seem tedious, but the payoff can be substantial if the designer really follows the rules.

We recommend the following approach to top-down design:

> **FORMAT FOR TOP-DOWN DESIGN**

1) Start with a basic flowchart.
2) Make the stubs as complete and as separate as possible.
3) Define precisely all the possible outcomes from each stub and select a test set.
4) Check each level carefully and systematically.
5) Use the structures from structured programming.
6) Expand each stub by one level. Do not try to do too much in one step.
7) Watch carefully for common tasks and data structures.
8) Test and debug after each stub expansion. Do not try to do an entire level at a time.
9) Be aware of what the hardware can do. Do not hesitate to stop and do a little bottom-up design where that seems necessary.

REVIEW OF PROBLEM DEFINITION AND PROGRAM DESIGN

You should note that we have spent an entire chapter without mentioning any specific microprocessor or assembly language, and without writing a single line of actual code. Hopefully, though, you now know a lot more about the examples than you would have if we had just asked you to write the programs at the start. Although we often think of the writing of computer instructions as a key part of software development, it is actually one of the easiest stages.

Once you have written a few programs, the coding stage will become simple. You will soon learn the instruction set, recognize which instructions are really useful, and remember the common sequences that make up the largest part of most programs. You will then find that many of the other stages of software development remain difficult and have few clear rules.

We have suggested here some ways to systematize the important early stages. In the problem definition stage, you must define all the characteristics of the system — its inputs, outputs, processing, time and memory constraints, and error handling. You must particularly consider how the system will interact with the larger system of which it is a part, and whether that larger system includes electrical equipment, mechanical equipment or a human operator. You must start at this stage to consider how to make the system easy to use and maintain.

In the program design stage, several techniques can help you to systematically specify and document the logic of your program. Modular programming forces you to divide the total program into small, distinct modules. Structured programming provides a systematic way of defining the logic of those modules, while top-down design is a systematic method for integrating and testing them. Of course, no one can compel you to follow all of these techniques; they are, in fact, guidelines more than anything else. But they do provide a unified approach to the definition and design stages, and you should consider them a basis on which to develop your own approach.

REFERENCES

1. Hughes, J.L. and J.I. Michtom, A Structured Approach to Programming, Prentice-Hall, Englewood Cliffs, N.J., 1977.
2. Ulrickson, R.W., "Software Modules are the Building Blocks", Electronic Design, February 1, 1977, pp. 62-66.
3. Ulrickson, R.W., "Solve Software Problems Step-by-Step", Electronic Design, January 18, 1977, pp. 54-58.
4. Yourdon, E.U., Techniques of Program Structure and Design, Prentice-Hall, Englewood Cliffs, N.J., 1975.
5. Parnas, D.L., "On the Criteria to be Used in Decomposing Systems into Modules", Communications of the ACM, December 1972, pp. 1053-1058.
6. Parnas, D.L., "A Technique for Software Module Specifications with Examples", Communications of the ACM, May 1972, pp. 330-336.
7. Wirth, N., Systematic Programming: An Introduction, Prentice-Hall, Englewood Cliffs, N.J., 1973.

Chapter 14
DEBUGGING AND TESTING

As we noted at the beginning of the previous chapter, debugging and testing are among the most time-consuming stages of software development. Even though such methods as modular programming, structured programming, and top-down design can simplify programs and reduce the frequency of errors, debugging and testing still are difficult because they are so poorly defined. The selection of an adequate set of test data is seldom a clear or scientific process. Finding errors sometimes seems like a game of "pin the tail on the donkey", except that the donkey is moving and the programmer must position the tail by remote control. Surely, few tasks are as frustrating as debugging programs.

This chapter will first describe the tools available to aid in debugging. It will then discuss basic debugging procedures, describe the common types of errors, and present some examples of program debugging. The last sections will describe how to select test data and test programs.

We will not do much more than describe the purposes of most of the debugging tools. There is very little standardization in this area, and not enough space to discuss all the devices and programs that are currently available. The examples should give you some idea of the uses, advantages, and limitations of particular hardware or software aids.

SIMPLE DEBUGGING TOOLS

The simplest debugging tools available are:

- A single-step facility
- A breakpoint facility
- A Register Dump program (or utility)
- A Memory Dump program

The single-step facility allows you to execute the program one clock cycle at a time. Only some 6800-based microcomputers have this facility, since the circuitry is fairly complex. Of course,

SINGLE-STEP

the only things that you will be able to see when the computer executes a single-step are the states of the output lines that you are monitoring. The most important lines are:

- Data Bus
- Address Bus
- VMA and READ/WRITE signals

If you monitor these lines (either in hardware or in software), you will be able to see the progression of addresses, instructions, and data as the program executes. You will be able to tell what kind of operations the CPU is performing. This information will be sufficient to inform you of such errors as incorrect Jump instructions, omitted or incorrect addresses, erroneous operation codes, or incorrect data values. However, you cannot see the contents of registers and flags without some additional debugging facility or a special sequence of instructions. Many of the operations of the program cannot be checked immediately.

LIMITATIONS OF SINGLE-STEP MODE

There are many errors that a single-step mode cannot help you to find. These include timing errors and errors in the interrupt or DMA systems. Furthermore, the single-step mode is very slow, typically executing a program at less than one millionth of the speed of the processor itself. Therefore, to single-step through one second of real processor time would take more than ten days. The single-step mode is only useful to check the logic of short instruction sequences.

BREAKPOINT

A breakpoint is a place at which the program will automatically halt or wait so that the user can examine the current status of the system. The program will usually not start again until the operator clears the breakpoint. The breakpoint allows you to check or pass through an entire section of a program. Thus, to see if an initialization routine is correct, you can place a breakpoint at the end of it and run the program. You can then check memory locations and registers to see if the entire section is correct. However, note that if the section is not correct you'll still have to pin down the error, either with earlier breakpoints or with a single-step mode.

Breakpoints complement the single-step mode. You can use breakpoints either to localize the error or to pass through sections that you know are correct. You can then do the detailed debugging in the single-step mode. Note that breakpoints do not affect program timing; they can therefore be used to check input/output and interrupts.

SWI AS A BREAKPOINT

Breakpoints often use part or all of the microprocessor interrupt system. The 6800 has a special Software Interrupt instruction that can act as a breakpoint. If you are not already using the maskable interrupt (IRQ) and the non-maskable interrupt (NMI) in your program, you can use those vectors as externally controlled breakpoints. Table 14-1 gives the destination addresses for the various vectors. Chapter 12 describes the vectors in more detail. The breakpoint routine can print register and memory contents, or just wait (by executing a conditional jump dependent on a switch input) until the user allows the computer to proceed. But, remember that the interrupts (including SWI) use the Stack and Stack Pointer to store the return address and register contents. Figure 14-1 shows a routine in which SWI results in an endless loop. The programmer would have to clear this breakpoint with a Reset or Interrupt signal.

A more powerful facility could allow the user to enter an address to which the processor would transfer control. Another possibility would be a return dependent on a switch, i.e.

```
          ORG     $FFFA       SOFTWARE INTERRUPT BREAKPOINT
BRKPT     TST     PIADRA      WAIT FOR SWITCH TO CLOSE
          BPL     BRKPT
          RTI     PIA
```

Of course, other PIA data or control lines could also be used. Remember that RTI automatically re-enables the interrupts. If the interrupt comes from a PIA, an instruction will have to read the corresponding data register and clear the interrupt status bit.

Table 14-1. 6800 Interrupt Vectors

Input	Vector Addresses (Hex)
IRQ	FFF8, FFF9
SWI	FFFA, FFFB
NMI	FFFC, FFFD
RESET	FFFE, FFFF

```
            ORG     $FFFA           SOFTWARE INTERRUPT BREAKPOINT
    BRKPT   BRA     BRKPT           WAIT IN PLACE
```

Figure 14-1. A Simple Breakpoint Routine

A register dump facility on a microcomputer is a program that lists the contents of all the CPU registers. This information is usually not directly obtainable. The following routine will print the con-

REGISTER DUMP

tents of all the registers on the system printer, if we assume that PRNT prints the contents of Accumulator A as two hexadecimal digits. Figure 14-2 is a flowchart of the program and Figure 14-3 shows a typical result. This program assumes that an interrupt or SWI has stored all the registers in the Stack.

```
*
* USE STACK POINTER AS STARTING ADDRESS
*
        LDAB    #7              NUMBER OF BYTES = 7
        TSX                     GET START OF REGISTER STORAGE
*
* PRINT CONTENTS OF REGISTERS
* ORDER IS CONDITION CODES, B, A, X (HIGH), X (LOW), PC (HIGH), PC (LOW)
*
PRN1    LDAA    X               GET A BYTE FROM STACK
        JSR     PRNT            AND PRINT IT
        INX
        DECB
        BNE     PRN1
*
* PRINT STACK POINTER — HIGH, LOW
*
        DEX
        STX     TEMP            MOVE STACK POINTER TO MEMORY
        LDAA    TEMP            PRINT MSBS OF POINTER
        JSR     PRNT
        LDAA    TEMP+1          PRINT LSBS OF POINTER
        JSR     PRNT
        RTI
```

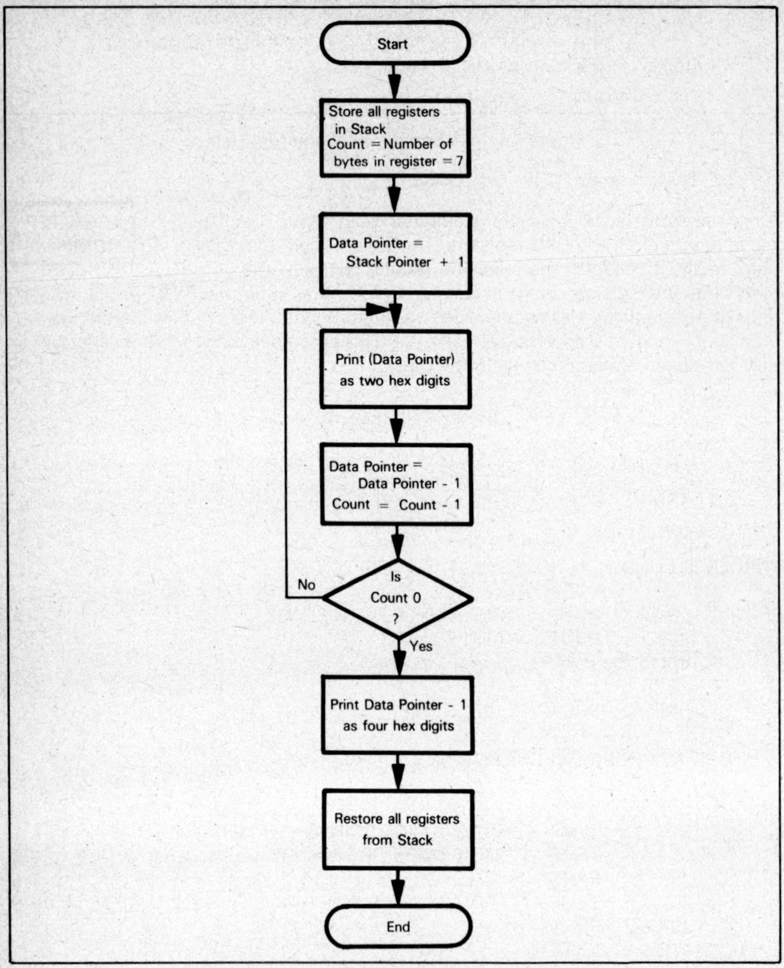

Figure 14-2. Flowchart of Register Dump Program

D8	(CCR)
05	(B)
03	(A)
27	(IXH)
1F	(IXL)
C5	(PCH)
06	(PCL)
01	(SPH)
70	(SPL)

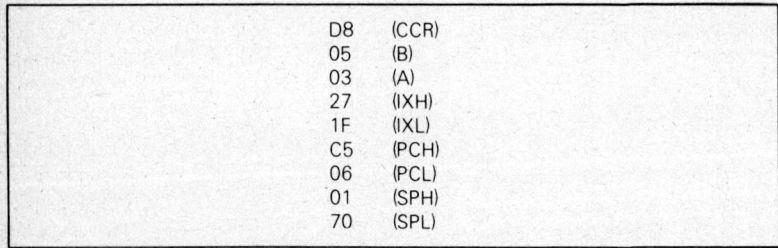

Figure 14-3. Results of a Typical Register Dump (6800)

A memory dump is a program that lists the contents of memory on an output device (such as a printer). This is a much more efficient way to examine data arrays or entire programs than just looking at single locations. However, very large memory dumps are not useful (except to supply scrap paper) because of the sheer mass of information that they produce. They may also take a long time to execute on a slow printer. Small dumps may, however, provide the programmer with a reasonable amount of information that can be examined as a unit. Relationships such as regular repetitions of data patterns or offsets of entire arrays may become obvious.

MEMORY DUMP

A general dump is often rather difficult to write. The programmer should be careful of the following situations:

1) The size of the memory area exceeds 256 bytes, so that a single 8-bit counter will not suffice.
2) The ending location is an address smaller than the starting location. This should be treated as an error, since the user would seldom want to print the entire memory contents in an unusual order.

Since the speed of the memory dump is usually dependent on the speed of the output device, the efficiency of the routine seldom matters. The following program will reject cases where the starting address is larger than the ending address, and will handle blocks of any length. We assume that the starting address is in the Index register and the ending address is in memory locations LASTAD and LASTAD+1.

```
*
* LOOK FOR END BEFORE START
*
        STX     STRTAD      SAVE STARTING ADDRESS
        LDAA    STRTAD
        CMPA    LASTAD      IS STARTING ADDRESS ABOVE ENDING?
        BHI     DONE        YES, THROUGH
        BNE     DUMP        OKAY IF STARTING ADDRESS BELOW
        LDAA    STRTAD+1    IF MSBS EQUAL, LOOK AT LSBS
        CMPA    LASTAD+1
        BHI     DONE        THROUGH IF STARTING ADDRESS LARGER
*
* PRINT CONTENTS OF 1 LOCATION
*
DUMP    LDAA    X           GET A LOCATION
        JSR     PRNT        AND PRINT IT
        CPX     LASTAD      ENDING ADDRESS REACHED?
        BEQ     DONE        YES, QUIT
        INX
        BRA     DUMP
DONE    SWI
```

Remember that the CPX instruction sets Z if and only if the two 16-bit numbers are equal. However, CPX does not affect C at all, and determines N only from the subtraction of the most significant bytes.

1000	23	1F	60	54	37	28	3E	00
1008	6E	42	38	17	59	44	98	37
1010	47	36	23	81	E1	FF	FF	5A
1018	34	ED	BC	AF	FE	FF	27	02

Figure 14-4. Results of a Typical Memory Dump

Figure 14-4 shows the output from a dump of memory locations 1000 to 101F.

This routine correctly handles the case in which the starting and ending locations are the same. The user will have to interpret the results carefully if the dump area includes the Stack, since the dump subroutine itself uses the Stack. PRNT may also change memory locations.

MORE ADVANCED DEBUGGING TOOLS

The more advanced debugging tools that are most widely used are:

- Simulator programs to check software
- Logic analyzers to check signals and timing

Many variations of both these tools exist, and we shall only discuss the standard features.

The simulator is the computerized equivalent of the pencil-and-paper computer. It is a computer program that goes through the operating cycle of another computer, keeping track of the contents of all the registers, flags, and memory locations. We could, of course, do this by hand, but it would require a large amount of effort and close attention to the exact effects of each instruction. The simulator program never gets tired or confused, forgets an instruction or register, or runs out of paper.

Most simulators are large FORTRAN programs. They can be purchased or used on the time-sharing services. The 6800 simulator is available in several versions from different sources.

Typical simulator features are:

1) A breakpoint facility. Usually, breakpoints can be set after a particular number of cycles have been executed, when a memory location or one of a set of memory locations is referenced, when the contents of a location or one of a set of locations are altered, or on other conditions.

2) Register and memory dump facilities that can display the values of memory locations, registers, and I/O ports.

3) A trace facility that will print the contents of particular registers or memory locations whenever the program changes or uses them.

4) A load facility that allows you to set values initially or change them during the simulation.

Some simulators can also simulate input/output, interrupts, and even DMA.

The simulator has many advantages:

1) It can provide a complete description of the status of the computer, since the simulator program is not restricted by pin limitations or other physical problems.

2) It can provide breakpoints, dumps, traces, and other facilities, without using any part of the processor's memory space or control system. These facilities will therefore not interfere with the user program.

3) Programs, starting points, and other conditions are easy to change.

4) All the facilities of a large computer, including peripherals and software, are available to the microprocessor designer.

On the other hand, the simulator is limited by its software base and its separation from the real microcomputer. The major limitations are:

1) The simulator cannot help with timing problems, since it operates far more slowly than real time and does not re-create actual hardware or interfaces.

2) The simulator cannot fully re-create the input/output system.

3) The simulator is usually quite slow. Reproducing one second of actual processor time may require hours of computer time. Using the simulator can be quite expensive.

The simulator represents the software side of debugging; it has the typical advantages and limitations of a wholly software-based approach. The simulator can provide insight into program logic and other software problems, but cannot help with timing, I/O, and other hardware problems.

The logic or microprocessor analyzer is the hardware solution to debugging. Basically, the analyzer is the parallel digital version of the standard oscilloscope. The analyzer displays information in binary, hexadecimal or mnemonic form on a CRT, and has a variety of triggering events, thresholds, and inputs. Most analyzers also have a memory so that they can display the past contents of the busses.

LOGIC ANALYZER

The standard procedure is to set a triggering event, such as the occurrence of a particular address on the Address Bus or instruction on the Data Bus. For example, one might trigger the analyzer if the microcomputer tries to store data in a particular address or execute an input or output instruction. One may then look at the sequence of events that preceded the breakpoint. Common problems you can find in this way include short noise spikes (or glitches), incorrect signal sequences, overlapping wave-forms, and other timing or signaling errors. Of course, a software simulator could not be used to diagnose those errors any more than a logic analyzer could conveniently be used to find errors in program logic.

Logic analyzers vary in many respects. Some of these are:

IMPORTANT FEATURES OF LOGIC ANALYZERS

1) Number of input lines. At least 24 are necessary to monitor an 8-bit Data Bus and a 16-bit Address Bus. Still more are necessary for control signals, clocks, and other important inputs.
2) Amount of memory. Each previous state that is saved will occupy several bytes.
3) Maximum frequency. It must be several MHz to handle the fastest processors.
4) Minimum signal width (important for catching glitches).
5) Type and number of triggering events allowed. Important features are pre- and post-trigger delays; these allow the user to display events occurring before or after the trigger event.
6) Methods of connecting to the microcomputer. This may require a rather complex interface.
7) Number of display channels.
8) Binary, hexadecimal or mnemonic displays.
9) Display formats.
10) Signal hold time requirements.
11) Probe capacitance.
12) Single or dual thresholds.

All of these factors are important in comparing different logic and microprocessor analyzers, since these instruments are new and unstandardized. A tremendous variety of products is already available, and this variety will become even greater in the future.

Logic analyzers, of course, are only necessary for systems with complex timing. Simple applications with low-speed peripherals have few hardware problems that a designer cannot handle with a standard oscilloscope. For more information about logic analyzers, see

R.L. Down, "Understanding Logic Analyzers", Computer Design, June 1977, pp. 188-191

W.A. Farnbach, "Bring up Your μP", Electronic Design, July 10, 1976, pp. 80-85

B. Farly, "Logic Analyzers Aren't All Alike", Electronic Design, Feb. 1, 1978, pp. 70-76

K. Pines, "What Do Logic Analyzers Do?", Digital Design, September 1977, pp. 55-77

N.A. Robin, "The Logic Analyzer: A Computer Troubleshooting Tool", Computer Design, March 1976, pp. 89-96

S. Runyon, "Focus on Logic and μP Analyzers", Electronic Design, February 1, 1977, pp. 40-50

A. Santoni, "The Latest Logic Analyzers Offer More Functions and Less Cost", Electronic Design, Feb. 1, 1978, pp. 26-32

DEBUGGING WITH CHECKLISTS

The designer cannot possibly check an entire program by hand; however, there are certain trouble spots that the designer can easily check. You can use systematic hand-checking to find a large number of errors without resorting to any debugging tools.

The question is where to place the effort. The answer is on points that can be handled with either a yes-no answer or with a simple arithmetic calculation. Do not try to do complex arithmetic, follow all the flags, or try every conceivable case. Limit your hand checking to matters that can be settled easily. Leave the complex problems to be solved with the aid of the various debugging tools. But proceed systematically; build your checklist and make sure that the program performs the basic operations correctly.

> **WHAT TO INCLUDE IN CHECKLIST**

The first step is to compare the flowchart or structured program with the actual code. Make sure that everything that appears in one also appears in the other. A simple checklist will do the job. It is easy to completely omit a branch or a processing section.

Next concentrate on the program loops. Make sure that all registers and memory locations used inside the loops have been initialized before they are used. This is a common source of errors; once again, a simple checklist will suffice.

Now look at each conditional branch. Select a sample case that should produce a branch and one that should not; try both of them. Is the branch correct or reversed? If the branch involves checking whether a number is above or below a threshold, try the equality case. Does the correct branch occur? Make sure that your choice is consistent with the problem definition.

Look at the loops as a whole. Try the first and last iterations by hand; these are often troublesome special cases. What happens if the number of iterations is zero; i.e., there is no data or the table has no elements? Does the program fall through correctly? Programs often will perform one iteration unnecessarily, or, even worse, decrement counters past zero before checking them.

Check off everything down to the last statement. Don't assume (hopefully) that the first error is the only one in the program. Hand checking will allow you to get the maximum benefit from debugging runs, since you will get rid of many simple errors ahead of time.

A quick review of the hand checking questions:

> **HAND CHECKING QUESTIONS**

1) Is every element of the program design in the program (and vice versa for documentation purposes)?
2) Are all registers and memory locations used inside loops initialized before they are used?

3) Are all conditional branches correct?
4) Do all loops start and end properly?
5) Are equality cases handled correctly?
6) Are trivial cases handled correctly?

LOOKING FOR ERRORS

Of course, despite all these precautions (or if you skip over some of them), programs often still don't work. The designer is left with the problem of how to find the mistakes. The hand checklist provides a starting place if you didn't use it earlier; some of the errors that you may not have eliminated are:

COMMON ERRORS

1) Failure to initialize variables such as counters, pointers, sums, etc. Do not assume that registers, memory locations, or flags necessarily contain zero before they are used.

2) Inverting a conditional jump, such as using Branch on Carry Set when you mean Branch on Carry Clear. Remember the effects of a comparison or subtraction (A is the contents of the Accumulator, M the contents of the register or memory location).

Zero = 1 if A = M
     = 0 if A ≠ M
Carry = 1 if A < M
      = 0 if A ≥ M

Note particularly that Carry = 0 if A = M (the equality case). So, Branch on Carry Set means jump if A < M and Branch on Carry Clear means jump if A ≥ M. If you want the equality case on the other side, use Branch if Higher (BHI) or Branch on Lower or Same (BLS). For example, if you want a jump if A ≥ 10, use

CMPA #10
BCC ADDR

If, on the other hand, you want a jump if A < 10, use

CMPA #10
BHI ADDR

3) Updating the counters and pointers in the wrong place or not at all. Be sure that there are no paths through a loop which either skip or repeat the updating instructions.

4) Failure to fall through correctly in trivial cases such as no data in a buffer, no tests to be run, or no entries in a transaction. Don't assume that such cases will never occur unless the program has specifically eliminated them.

Other problems to watch for are:

5) Reversing the order of operands.

Remember, for example, that TAB moves A to B, not the other way around.

6) Changing condition flags before you use them.

Remember that LDAA, LDX, LDS, INC, and DEC affect all the flags except the Carry, while INX and DEX affect the Zero flag. Remember also that RTI and TAP change all the flags.

7) Confusing the Index register and the indexed memory location.

Remember that CLR X clears the memory location addressed by the Index register, not the Index register itself. Note the difference between INC X and INX; the former adds 1 to the contents of an 8-bit memory location (address in X) while the latter adds 1 to the contents of the 16-bit Index register.

8) Confusing values and addresses.

    Remember that LDX #$1000 loads X with the number 1000 (hex), while LDX $1000 loads X with the contents of memory locations 1000 and 1001. A similar distinction applies to LDAA COUNT and LDAA #COUNT.

9) Accidentally re-initializing a register or memory location.

    Make sure that no Jump instructions transfer control back to initialization statements.

10) Confusing numbers and addresses.

    Remember that the ASCII and EBCDIC representations of digits differ from the digits themselves. For example, ASCII 7 is hex 37, whereas hex 07 is the ASCII Bell character.

11) Confusing binary and decimal numbers.

    Remember that the BCD representation of a number is different from its binary representation. For example, BCD 36 is binary 54 (try it).

12) Reversing the order in subtraction. Be careful also with other operations (like division) that do not commute.

    Remember that SUB and CMP produce A-M, not M-A.

13) Ignoring the effects of subroutines and macros.

    Don't assume that calls to subroutines or references to macros don't change flags, registers, or memory locations. Be sure of exactly what effects they have. Note that it is very important to document these effects.

14) Using the Shift instructions improperly.

    Remember the precise effects of ASR, ASL, LSR, ROL, and ROR. They are 1-bit shifts that affect all the flags. ASL and LSR both clear the empty bit. ASR preserves the sign bit (i.e., extends it). ROR and ROL are circular shifts that include the Carry. Remember that all the flags are affected, even if these instructions are applied to the data in a memory location.

15) Counting the length of an array incorrectly.

    Remember that there are five (not four) memory locations included in addresses 0100 through 0104, inclusive.

16) Confusing 8- and 16-bit registers.

    The Accumulators and Condition Code register are eight bits long, while the Index register, Stack Pointer, and Program Counter are 16 bits long. You cannot transfer the contents of an Accumulator to the Index register, or vice versa.

17) Forgetting that 16-bit numbers occupy two memory locations.

    LDX $40 loads the Index register from memory locations 0040 and 0041. Similarly, STS $50 stores the contents of the Stack Pointer in memory locations 0050 and 0051. Note that CPX, LDS, LDX, STS, and STX all can use 8-bit direct addresses on page zero, even though they are 16-bit operations.

18) Confusing the Stack and the Stack Pointer.

    DES, INS, LDS, and STS affect the Stack Pointer, not the contents of the Stack. PSH and PUL transfer data to or from the Stack. Remember that JSR, BSR, RTS, RTI, and SWI also use the Stack. Remember also that you must initialize the Stack Pointer before calling any subroutines or allowing any interrupts.

19) Changing a register or memory location before using it.

    Remember that LDA, STA, LDX, STX, etc. change the contents of the destination (but not the source).

20) Forgetting to transfer control past sections of the program that should not be executed in particular situations.

    Remember that the computer will proceed sequentially through the program memory unless specifically ordered to do otherwise.

Interrupt-driven programs are particularly difficult to debug, since errors may occur randomly. If, for example, the program enables the interrupts a few instructions too early, an error will only occur if an interrupt is received while the program is executing those few instructions. In fact, you can usually assume that randomly occurring errors are caused by the interrupt system (see W.J. Weller, Assembly Level Programming for Small Computers, Lexington Books). Typical errors in interrupt-driven programs are:

DEBUGGING INTERRUPT-DRIVEN PROGRAMS

1) Forgetting to re-enable interrupts after accepting one and servicing it.

   The processor disables the interrupt system automatically on Reset, on executing SWI, or on accepting an interrupt. Be sure that no possible sequences fail to re-enable the interrupt.

2) Forgetting that RTI will automatically re-enable the interrupts unless you set the I bit in the Stack.

3) Enabling interrupts before establishing all the necessary conditions such as priority, flags, etc.

   A checklist can aid here.

4) Leaving results in registers and destroying them in the restoration process. Remember that RTI restores all the registers from the Stack.

5) Forgetting that the interrupts leave all the register contents in the Stack, whether you use them or not.

   You may have to re-initialize or update the Stack Pointer.

6) Forgetting to clear a PIA interrupt by reading the Data register even if no reading is actually necessary.

7) Not disabling the interrupt during multi-word transfers or instruction sequences.

Hopefully these lists will at least give you some idea of where to look. Unfortunately, even the most systematic debugging can still leave some truly puzzling problems.

Debugging Example 1: Decimal to Seven-Segment Conversion

The program converts a decimal number in memory location 0040 to a seven-segment code in memory location 0041. It blanks the display if memory location 0040 does not contain a decimal number.

DEBUGGING A CODE CONVERSION PROGRAM

Initial Program (from flowchart in Figure 14-5):

```
          LDAA    $40              GET DATA
          CMPA    #9               IS DATA GREATER THAN 9?
          BCS     DONE             YES, DONE
          LDX     SSEG             GET ADDRESS OF SEVEN-SEGMENT TABLE
          LDAA    X                GET ELEMENT FROM TABLE
DONE      STAA    $41              SAVE SEVEN-SEGMENT CODE
          SWI
SSEG      FCB     $3F,$06,$5B,$4F,$66
          FCB     $6D,$7D,$07,$4D,$6F
```

Using the checklist procedure, we were able to find the following errors:

1) The block that cleared Result had been omitted.
2) The conditional branch was incorrect.

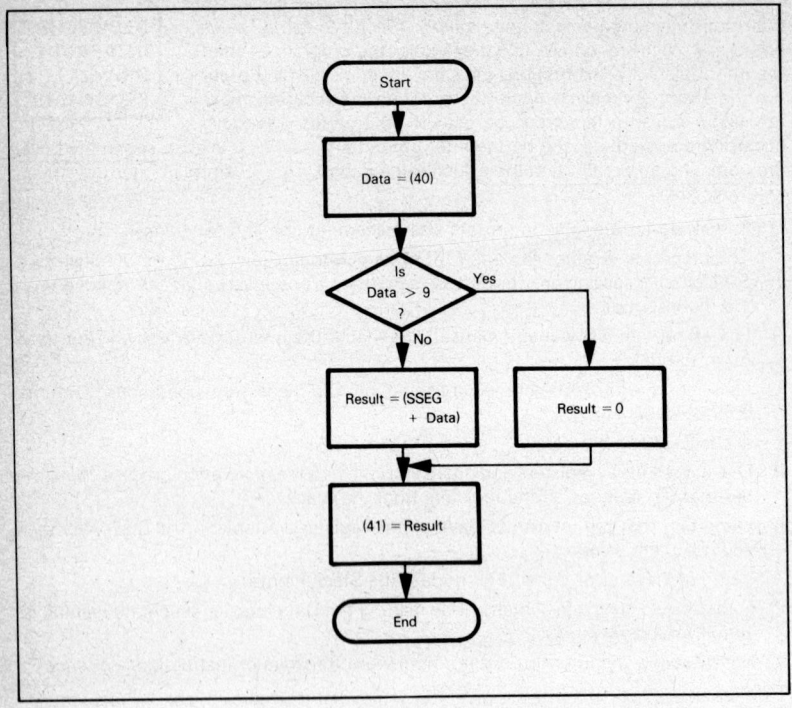

Figure 14-5. Flowchart of Decimal to Seven-Segment Conversion

For example, if the data is zero, CMPA #9 sets the Carry, since 0 < 9. However, the jump on the opposite condition, i.e., BCC DONE, still does not produce the correct result. Now the program handles the equality case incorrectly, since, if the data is 9, CMPA #9 clears the Carry and causes a jump. The correct version is

```
            CMPA    #9          IS DATA GREATER THAN 9?
            BHI     DONE        YES, DONE
```

Second Program:

```
            CLRB                GET BLANK CODE FOR DISPLAY
            LDAA    $40         GET DATA
            CMPA    #9          IS DATA GREATER THAN 9?
            BHI     DONE        YES, DONE
            LDX     SSEG        GET ADDRESS OF SEVEN-SEGMENT TABLE
            LDAA    X           GET ELEMENT FROM TABLE
DONE        STAA    $41         SAVE SEVEN-SEGMENT CODE
            SWI
SSEG        FCB     $3F,$06,$4B,$4F,$66
            FCB     $6D,$7D,$07,$7D,$6F
```

This version was hand checked successfully.

Since the program was simple, the next stage was to single-step through it with real data. The data selected for the trials was:

```
0            (the smallest number)
9            (the largest number)
10           (a border case)
6B   (hex)   (random)
```

The first trial was with zero in location 0040. The program proceeded with no apparent errors until it tried to execute the LDAA X instruction. The contents of the Address Bus during the data fetch were 3F06, an address that did not even exist in the system. Clearly, something had gone wrong.

It was now time for some more hand checking. Since we knew that BHI was correct, the error was clearly subsequent to that instruction but before LDAA X. The hand check showed that LDX SSEG placed 3F06 in the Index register. Clearly, we want the address SSEG, not its contents. The addressing should be immediate rather than direct. But we still have to add SSEG and the data in Accumulator A. This requires some manipulation, as we have seen earlier in Chapters 4, 7, and 9. The corrected version is:

Third Program:

```
            CLRB                GET BLANK CODE FOR DISPLAY
            LDAA     $40        GET DATA
            CMPA     #9         IS DATA GREATER THAN 9?
            BHI      DONE       YES, DONE
            STAA                TEMPX+1
USE DATA IN OFFSET ADDRESS
            LDAA     #SSEGU     GET MSBS OF TABLE ADDRESS
            STAA     TEMPX
            LDX      TEMPX      GET OFFSET ADDRESS
            LDAA     SSEGL,X    GET ELEMENT FROM TABLE
DONE        STAA     $41        SAVE SEVEN-SEGMENT CODE
            SWI
TEMPX       RMB      2
SSEG        FCB      $3F,$06,$5B,$4F,$66
            FCB      $6D,$7D,$07,$7D,$6F
SSEGU       EQU      SSEG/256
SSEGE       EQU      SSEGU*256
SSEGL       EQU      SSEG-SSEGE
```

This program produced the following results:

Data	Result
00	3F
09	6F
0A	0A
6B	6B

The program was not clearing the result if the data was invalid; i.e., greater than 9. The program never used the blank code in Accumulator B. Since the program was simple, it could be tested for all the decimal digits. The results were:

Data	Result
0	3F
1	06
2	5B
3	4F
4	66
5	6D
6	7D
7	07
8	7D
9	6F

Note that the result for number 8 is wrong — it should be 7F. Since everything else is correct, the error is almost surely in the table. In fact, entry 8 in the table had been miscopied.

The final program is:

*
* DECIMAL TO SEVEN-SEGMENT CONVERSION
*

```
        CLRB              GET BLANK CODE FOR DISPLAY
        LDAA    $40       GET DATA
        CMPA    #9        IS DATA GREATER THAN 9?
        BHI     DONE      YES, DONE
        STAA    TEMPX+1   USE DATA IN OFFSET ADDRESS
        LDAA    #SSEGU    GET MSBS OF TABLE ADDRESS
        STAA    TEMPX     GET OFFSET ADDRESS
        LDAB    SSEGL,X   GET ELEMENT FROM TABLE
DONE    STAB    $41       SAVE SEVEN-SEGMENT CODE
        SWI
TEMPX   RMB     2
SSEG    FCB     $3F,$06,$5B,$4F,$66
        FCB     $6D,$7D,$07,$7F,$6F
SSEGU   EQU     SSEG/256
SSEGE   EQU     SSEGU*256
SSEGL   EQU     SSEG-SSEGE
```

The errors encountered in this program are typical of the ones that 6800 assembly language programmers should anticipate. They include:

- Failing to initialize variables
- Inverting conditional branches
- Branching incorrectly in the equality case
- Confusing immediate and direct addressing, i.e., data and addresses
- Forgetting the distinction between 8-bit data and 16-bit addresses
- Branching to the wrong place, so that one path through the program is incorrect
- Copying lists of numbers incorrectly

Note that straightforward instructions like ADD, SUB, JMP, etc. seldom produce any problems.

Debugging Example 2: Sort into Decreasing Order

DEBUGGING A SORT PROGRAM

The program sorts an array of unsigned 8-bit binary numbers into decreasing order. The array begins in memory location 0042 and its length is in memory location 0041.

Initial Program (from flowchart in Figure 14-6):

```
            LDAA    #1          INTERCHANGE FLAG = 1
            STAA    $40
            LDAA    $41         COUNT = LENGTH OF ARRAY
            LDX     #$42        POINT TO START OF ARRAY
PASS        LDAB    X           GET AN ELEMENT
            CMPB    1,X         IS PAIR IN CORRECT ORDER?
            BCS     COUNT       YES, NO INTERCHANGE NECESSARY
            STAB    1,X         NO, INTERCHANGE PAIR
COUNT       DECA                IS PASS COMPLETE?
            BNE     PASS        NO, CONTINUE PASS
            TST     $40         YES, IS INTERCHANGE FLAG ZERO?
            BNE     PASS        NO, MAKE ANOTHER PASS
            SWI
```

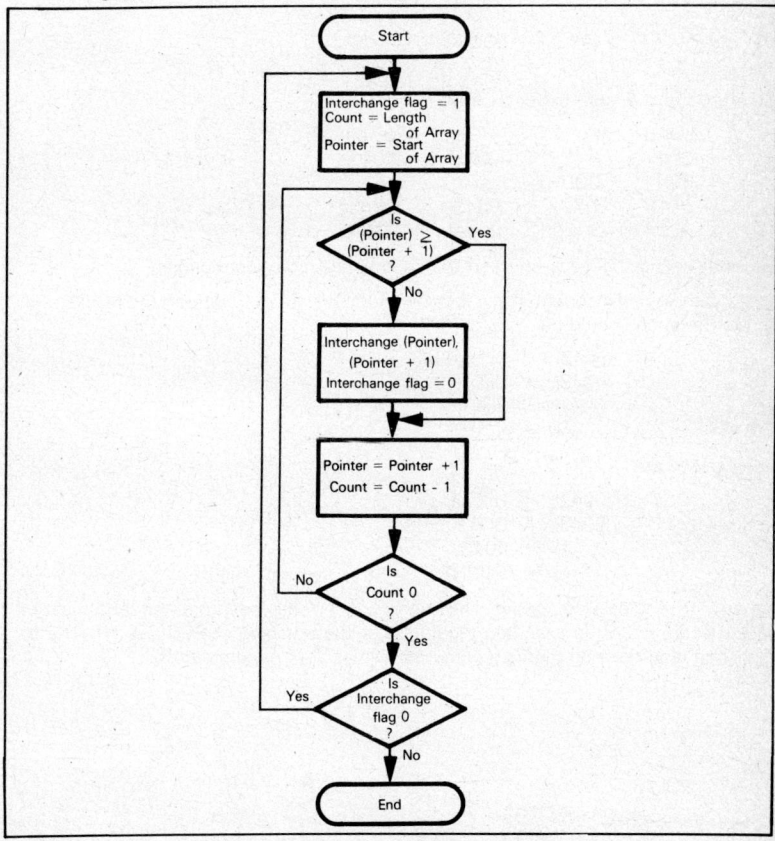

Figure 14-6. Flowchart of Sort Program

The hand check shows that all the blocks in the flowchart have been implemented in the program and that all the registers have been initialized. The conditional branches must be examined carefully. The instruction BCS COUNT must force a branch if the new value is less than or equal to the old value. Note that the equality case must not result in an interchange, since this will create an endless loop with the two equal elements being switched back and forth.

Try an example.

$$(0041) = 30$$
$$(0042) = 37$$

CMPB 1,X results in the calculation of 30-37. The Carry is set to 1. This example should result in an interchange, but does not. BCC COUNT will provide the proper branch in this case. If the two numbers are equal, the comparison will clear the Carry and BCC COUNT is again correct.

How about BNE PASS at the end of the program? If there are any elements out of order, the contents of memory location 0040 will be zero, so the branch is wrong. It should be BEQ PASS.

Now try the first time through. The initialization results in the following:

$$(B) = 1$$
$$(A) = COUNT$$
$$(X) = 0042$$

The effects of the loop instructions are:

```
LDAB    X           (B) = (0042)
CMPB    X           (0042) = (0043)
BCC     COUNT
STAB    1,X         (0043) = (0042)
DECA                (A) = COUNT - 1
```

Note that we have already checked the conditional Jump instructions.

Clearly the logic is incorrect. If the first two numbers are out of order, the results after the first iteration should be:

$$(0042) = OLD\ (0043)$$
$$(0043) = OLD\ (0042)$$
$$(X) = 0043$$
$$(A) = COUNT - 1$$

Instead, they are:

$$(0042) = Unchanged$$
$$(0043) = OLD\ (0042)$$
$$(X) = 0042$$
$$(A) = COUNT - 1$$

The error in X is easy to correct. The instruction INX has been omitted, and must be placed where it will be executed regardless of the outcome of BCC COUNT. The interchange requires a bit more care and the use of both Accumulators:

```
PSHA
LDAA    1,X
STAB    1,X
STAA    X
PULA
```

An interchange always requires a temporary location in which one number can be stored while the other one is being transferred. The Stack is used here for temporary storage.

All of these changes require a new copy of the program:

```
        LDAA    #1              INTERCHANGE FLAG
        STAA    $40
        LDAA    $41             COUNT = LENGTH OF ARRAY
        LDX     #$42            POINT TO START OF ARRAY
PASS    LDAB    X               GET AN ELEMENT
        CMPB    1,X             IS PAIR IN CORRECT ORDER?
        BCC     COUNT           YES, NO INTERCHANGE NECESSARY
        PSHA                    NO, INTERCHANGE ELEMENTS
        LDAA    1,X
        STAB    1,X
        STAA    X
        PULA
COUNT   INX
        DECA                    IS PASS COMPLETE?
        BNE     PASS            NO, CONTINUE PASS
        TST     $40             IS INTERCHANGE FLAG ZERO?
        BEQ     PASS            YES, MAKE ANOTHER PASS
        SWI
```

How about the last iteration? Let's say that there are three elements:

$$(0041) = 03$$
$$(0042) = 02$$
$$(0043) = 04$$
$$(0044) = 06$$

Each time through, the program increments X by 1. So, at the start of the third iteration,

$$(X) = 0042 + 2 = 0044$$

The effects of the loop instructions are:

```
        LDAB    X               (B)    = (0044)
        CMPB    1,X             (0044) = (0043)
```

This is incorrect; the program has tried to move beyond the end of the data. The previous iteration should, in fact, have been the last one, since the number of pairs is one less than the number of elements. The correction is to reduce the number of iterations by 1; i.e., place DECA after LDAA $41.

How about the trivial cases? What happens if the array contains no elements at all, or only one element? The answer is that the program does not work correctly, and may change a whole block of data improperly without any warning (try it!). The corrections to handle the trivial cases are simple but essential; the cost is only a few memory locations to avoid problems that could be very difficult to find later. The new program is:

```
        LDAA    #1              INTERCHANGE FLAG = 1
        STAA    $40
        LDAA    $41             GET LENGTH OF ARRAY
        CMPA    #1              IS THERE MORE THAN ONE ELEMENT?
        BLS     DONE            NO, NO ACTION NECESSARY
        DECA                    NUMBER OF PAIRS = LENGTH - 1
        LDX     #$42            POINT TO START OF ARRAY
```

```
PASS    LDAB    X           GET AN ELEMENT
        CMPB    1,X         IS PAIR IN CORRECT ORDER?
        BCC     COUNT       YES, NO INTERCHANGE NECESSARY
        PSHA                NO, INTERCHANGE ELEMENTS
        LDAA    1,X
        STAB    1,X
        STAA    X
        PULA
COUNT   INX
        DECA                IS PASS COMPLETE?
        BNE     PASS        NO, CONTINUE PASS
        TST     $40         IS INTERCHANGE FLAG ZERO?
        BEQ     PASS        YES, MAKE ANOTHER PASS
DONE    SWI
```

Now it's time to check the program on the computer or on the simulator. A simple set of data is:

(0041) = 02
(0042) = 00
(0043) = 01

This set consists of two elements in the wrong order. The program should take two passes. The first pass should rearrange the elements, producing:

(0042) = 01
(0043) = 00
(0040) = 00

The second pass should complete the operation and produce:

(0040) = 01

This program is rather long for single-stepping, so we'll use breakpoints instead. Each breakpoint will halt the computer and print the contents of all the registers. The breakpoints will come:

1) After LDX #$42 to check the initial conditions.
2) After CMPB 1,X to check the comparison.
3) After PULA to check the interchange.
4) After TST $40 to check the completion of a pass through the array.

The contents of the registers after the first breakpoint were:

Register	Contents
CC	F0
B	00
A	01
X	0042

These are all correct, so the program calculated the initial conditions correctly in this case.

The results at the second breakpoint were:

Register	Contents
CC	F9
B	00
A	01
X	0042

These results are also correct.

The results at the third breakpoint were:

Register	Contents
CC	F1
B	00
A	01
X	0042

Checking memory showed:

(0040) = 01
(0042) = 01
(0043) = 00

The results at the fourth breakpoint were:

Register	Contents
CC	F0
B	00
A	01
X	0043
(0040)	01

Here, memory location 0040 is not correct; its value should be zero to indicate that an interchange occurred. In fact, a look at the program shows that no instruction ever changes memory location 0040 to mark the occurrence of an interchange. The correction is to place the instruction CLR $40 after BCC COUNT.

Now the procedure is to load memory location 0040 with the correct value and continue. The second iteration of the second breakpoint gives:

Register	Contents
CC	F9
B	00
A	01
X	0043

Clearly, the program has proceeded incorrectly without re-initializing the registers (particularly the Index register). The conditional jump that depends on the interchange flag should transfer control all the way back to the start of the program, not to the label PASS.

The final version of the program is:

```
SORT    LDAA    #1              INTERCHANGE FLAG = 1
        STAA    $40
        LDAA    $41             GET LENGTH OF ARRAY
        CMPA    #1              IS THERE MORE THAN ONE ELEMENT?
        BLS     DONE            NO, NO ACTION NECESSARY
        DECA                    NUMBER OF PAIRS = LENGTH - 1
        LDX     #$42            POINT TO START OF ARRAY
PASS    LDAB    X               GET AN ELEMENT
        CMPB    1,X             IS PAIR IN CORRECT ORDER?
        BCC     COUNT           YES, NO INTERCHANGE NECESSARY
        CLR     $40             NO, INTERCHANGE FLAG = 0
        PSHA                    INTERCHANGE ELEMENTS
        LDAA    1,X
        STAB    1,X
        STAA    X
        PULA
```

```
COUNT   INX
        DECA                IS PASS COMPLETE?
        BNE     PASS        NO, CONTINUE PASS
        TST     $40         IS INTERCHANGE FLAG ZERO?
        BEQ     SORT        YES, MAKE ANOTHER PASS
        SWI
```

Clearly we cannot check all the possible input values for this program. Two other simple sets of data for debugging purposes are:

1) Two equal elements
   - (0041) = 02
   - (0042) = 00
   - (0043) = 00

2) Two elements already in decreasing order
   - (0041) = 02
   - (0042) = 01
   - (0043) = 00

INTRODUCTION TO TESTING

Program testing is closely related to program debugging. Surely some of the test cases will be the same as the test data used for debugging, such as:

USING TEST CASES FROM DEBUGGING

- Trivial cases such as no data or a single element
- Special cases that the program singles out for some reason
- Simple examples that exercise particular parts of the program

In the case of the decimal to seven-segment conversion program, these cases cover all the possible situations. The test data consists of:

- The numbers 0 through 9
- The boundary case 10
- The random case 6B

The program does not distinguish any other cases. Here debugging and testing are virtually the same.

In the sorting program, the problem is more difficult. The number of elements could range from 0 to 255, and each of the elements could lie anywhere in that range. The number of possible cases is therefore enormous. Furthermore, the program is moderately complex. How do we select test data that will give us a degree of confidence in that program? Here testing requires some design decisions. The testing problem is particularly difficult if the program depends on sequences of real-time data. How do we select the data, generate it, and present it to the microcomputer in a realistic manner?

Most of the tools mentioned earlier for debugging are helpful in testing also. Logic or microprocessor analyzers can help check the hardware; simulators can help check the software. Other tools can also be of assistance; e.g.,

TESTING AIDS

1) I/O simulations that can simulate a variety of devices from a single input and a single output device.
2) In-circuit emulators that allow you to attach the prototype to a development system or control panel and test it.
3) ROM simulators that have the flexibility of a RAM but the timing of the particular ROM or PROM that will be used in the final system.

4) Real-time operating systems that can provide inputs or interrupts at specific times (or perhaps randomly) and mark the occurrence of outputs. Real-time breakpoints and traces may also be included.
5) Emulations (often on micro-programmable computers) that may provide real-time execution speed and programmable I/O.

See, for example, H.R. Burris, "Time-Scaled Emulations of the 8080 Microprocessor", Proceedings of the 1977 National Computer Conference, pp. 937-946.

6) Interfaces that allow another computer to control the I/O system and test the microcomputer program.
7) Testing programs that check each branch in a program for logical errors.
8) Test generation programs that can generate random data or other distributions.

Formal testing theorems exist, but they are usually applicable only to very short programs.

You must be careful that the test equipment does not invalidate the test by modifying the environment. Often, test equipment may buffer, latch, or condition input and output signals. The actual system may not do this, and may therefore behave quite differently.

Furthermore, extra software in the test environment may use some of the memory space or part of the interrupt system. It may also provide error recovery and other features that will not exist in the final system. A software test bed must be just as realistic as a hardware test bed, since software failure can be just as critical as hardware failure.

Emulations and simulations are, of course, never precise. They are usually adequate for checking logic, but can seldom help test the interface or the timing. On the other hand, real-time test equipment does not provide much of an overview of the program logic and may affect the interfacing and timing.

SELECTING TEST DATA

Very few real programs can be checked for all cases. The designer must choose a sample set that in some sense describes the entire range of possibilities.

Testing should, of course, be part of the total development procedure. Top-down design and structured programming provide for testing as part of the design. This is called structured testing. (See D.A. Walsh, "Structured Testing", Datamation, July 1977, pp. 111-118.) Each module within a structured program should be checked separately. Testing, as well as coding, should be modular, structured, and top-down.

STRUCTURED TESTING

But that leaves the question of selecting test data for a module. The designer must first list all special cases that a program recognizes. These may include:

TESTING SPECIAL CASES

- Trivial cases
- Equality cases
- Special situations

The test data should include all of these.

You must next identify each class of data that statements within the program may distinguish. These may include:

FORMING CLASSES OF DATA

- Positive or negative numbers
- Numbers above or below a particular threshold
- Data that does or does not include a particular sequence or character
- Data that is or is not present at a particular time

If the modules are short, the total number of classes should still be small even though each division is multiplicative; i.e., two two-way divisions result in four data classes.

You must now separate the classes according to whether the program produces a different result for each entry in the class (as in a table) or produces the same result for each entry (such as a warning that a parameter is above a threshold). In the discrete case, one may include each element if the total number is small or sample if the number is large. The sample should include all boundary cases and at least one case selected randomly. Random number tables are available in books, and random number generators are part of most computer facilities.

SELECTING DATA FROM CLASSES

You must be careful of distinctions that may not be obvious. For example, the 6800 will regard an 8-bit unsigned number greater than 127 as negative; you must consider this when using the Jump instructions BPL and BMI. You must also watch for instructions that do not affect flags, overflow in signed arithmetic, and the distinctions between address-length (16-bit) quantities and data-length (8-bit) quantities.

Testing Example 1: Sort Program

The special cases here are obvious:

TESTING A SORT PROGRAM

- No elements in the array
- One element, magnitude may be selected randomly

The other special case to be considered is one in which elements are equal.

There may be some problem here with signs and data length. Note that the array itself must contain fewer than 256 elements. The use of the instruction CLR $40 rather than DEC $40 to clear the interchange flag means that there will be no difficulty if the number of elements or interchanges exceeds 128.

We could check the effects of sign by picking half the regular test cases with numbers of elements between 128 and 255 and half between 2 and 127. All magnitudes should be chosen randomly so as to avoid unconscious bias as much as possible.

Testing Example 2: Self-Checking Numbers (see Chapter 8)

Here we will presume that a prior validity check has ensured that the number has the right length and consists of valid digits. Since the program makes no other distinctions, test data should be selected randomly. Here a random number table or random number generator will prove ideal; the range of the random numbers is 0 to 9.

TESTING AN ARITHMETIC PROGRAM

TESTING PRECAUTIONS

The designer can simplify the testing stage by designing programs sensibly. You should use the following rules:

RULES FOR TESTING

1) Try to eliminate trivial cases as early as possible without introducing unnecessary distinctions.
2) Minimize the number of special cases. Each special case means additional testing and debugging time.

3) Consider performing validity or error checks on the data prior to processing.
4) Be careful of inadvertent and unnecessary distinctions, particularly in handling signed numbers or using operations that refer to signed numbers.
5) Check boundary cases by hand. These are often a source of errors. Be sure that the problem definition specifies what is to happen in these cases.
6) Make the program as general as reasonably possible. Each distinction and separate routine increases the required testing.
7) Divide the program and design the modules so that testing can proceed in steps in conjunction with the other stages of software development.

CONCLUSIONS

Debugging and testing are the stepchildren of the software development process. Most projects leave far too little time for them and most textbooks neglect them. But designers and managers often find that these stages are the most expensive and time-consuming. Progress may be very difficult to measure or produce. Debugging and testing microprocessor software is particularly difficult because the powerful hardware and software tools that can be used on larger computers are seldom available for microcomputers.

The designer should plan debugging and testing carefully. We recommend the following procedure:

1) Try to write programs that can easily be debugged and tested. Modular programming, structured programming, and top-down design are useful techniques.
2) Prepare a debugging and testing plan as part of the program design. Decide early what data you must generate and what equipment you will need.
3) Debug and test each module as part of the top-down design process.
4) Debug each module's logic systematically. Use checklists, breakpoints, and the single-step mode. If the program logic is complex, consider using the software simulator.
5) Check each module's timing systematically if this is a problem. An oscilloscope can solve many problems if you plan the test properly. If the timing is complex, consider using a logic or microprocessor analyzer.
6) Be sure that the test data is a representative sample. Watch for any classes of data that the program may distinguish. Include all special and trivial cases.
7) If the program handles each element differently or the number of cases is large, select the test data randomly.
8) Record all test results as part of the documentation. If problems occur, you will not have to repeat test cases that have already been checked.

Chapter 15
DOCUMENTATION AND REDESIGN

The actual working program is not the only requirement of software development. Adequate documentation is also an important part of a software product. Not only does documentation help the designer in the testing and debugging stages, it is also essential for later use and extension of the program. A poorly documented program will be difficult to maintain, re-use, or extend.

Occasionally, the first version of a program uses too much memory or executes too slowly. The designer must then consider ways to improve the program. This stage is called redesign, and requires that you concentrate on the parts of the program that can yield the most improvement.

SELF-DOCUMENTING PROGRAMS

Although no program is ever completely self-documenting, some of the rules that we mentioned earlier can help. These include:

RULES FOR SELF-DOCUMENTING PROGRAMS

- Clear, simple structure with as few transfers of control (jumps) as possible
- Use of meaningful names and labels
- Use of names for I/O devices, parameters, numerical factors, etc.
- Emphasis on simplicity rather than on minor savings in memory usage, execution time, or typing

For example, the following program sends a string of characters to a teletypewriter:

```
        LDAB    $40
        LDX     #$1000
W       LDAA    X
        STAA    $8008
        JSR     XXX
        INX
        DECB
        BNE     W
        SWI
```

Even without comments we can improve the program, as follows:

```
COUNT   EQU     $40
MESSG   EQU     $1000
TTYPIA  EQU     $8008
        LDAB    COUNT
        LDX     #MESSG
OUTCH   LDAA    X
        STAA    TTYPIA
        JSR     BITDLY
        INX
        DECB
        BNE     OUTCH
        SWI
```

Surely this program is easier to understand than the earlier version. Even without further documentation, you could probably guess at the function of the program and the meanings of most of the variables. Other documentation techniques cannot substitute for self-documentation.

Some further notes on choosing names:

CHOOSING USEFUL NAMES

1) Use the obvious name when it is available, like TTY or CRT for output devices, START or RESET for addresses, DELAY or SORT for subroutines, COUNT or LENGTH for data.
2) Avoid acronyms like S16BA for SORT 16-BIT ARRAY. These seldom mean anything to anybody.
3) Use full words or close to full words when possible, like DONE, PRINT, SEND, etc.
4) Keep the names as distinct as possible.

COMMENTS

The most obvious form of additional documentation is the comment. However, very few programs (including most of those in books) have really effective comments. You should consider the following guidelines for good comments.

COMMENTING GUIDELINES

1) Don't repeat the meaning of the instruction code. Rather, explain the purpose of the instruction in the program. Comments like

    DECB   B = B-1

add nothing to documentation. Rather, use

    DECB   LINE NUMBER = LINE NUMBER-1

Remember that you know what the operation codes mean and anyone else can look them up in the manual. The important point is to explain what task the program is performing.

2) Make the comments as clear as possible. Do not use abbreviations or acronyms unless they are well-known (like ASCII, PIA, or UART) or standard (like no for number, ms for millisecond, etc.). Avoid comments like

    DECB   LN = LN-1
              or
    DECB   DEC. LN BY 1

The extra typing simply is not all that expensive.

3) Comment every important or obscure point. Be particularly careful to mark operations that may not have obvious functions, such as

    ANDA   #%00100000   TAPE READER BIT OFF
                         or
    LDAA   GCODL,X   INDEX GRAY CODE TABLE

Clearly, I/O operations often require extensive comments. If you're not exactly sure of what an instruction does, or if you have to think about it, add a clarifying comment. The comment will save you time later and will be helpful in documentation.

4) Don't comment the obvious. A comment on each line simply makes it difficult to find the important points. Standard sequences like

```
        INX
        DECB
        BNE     SRCH
```

need not be marked unless you're doing something special. One comment will often suffice for several lines, as in

```
        LSRA                    GET MOST SIGNIFICANT DIGIT
        LSRA
        LSRA
        LSRA

        LDAA    $40             EXCHANGE MOST SIGNIFICANT...
        LDAB    $41             AND LEAST SIGNIFICANT BYTES
        STAA    $41
        STAB    $40
```

5) Place comments on the lines to which they refer or at the start of a sequence.
6) Keep your comments up-to-date. If you change the program, change the comments.
7) Use standard forms and terms in commenting. Don't worry about repetitiveness. Varied names for the same things are confusing, even if the variations are just COUNT and COUNTER, START and BEGIN, DISPLAY and LEDS, or PANEL and SWITCHES.

    There's no real gain in not being consistent. The variations may seem obvious to you now, but may not be clear later; others will get confused from the very beginning.

8) Make comments brief. Leave a complete explanation to the documentation. Otherwise, he program gets lost in the comments and you may have a hard time even finding it.
9) Keep improving your comments. If you come to one that you can't read or understand, take the time to change it. If you find that the listing is getting crowded, add some blank lines. The comments won't improve themselves; in fact, they'll just seem to become worse as you leave the task behind and forget exactly what you did.

Remember, comments are important. Good ones will save you time and effort. Put some work into comments and try to make them as effective as possible.

Commenting Example 1: Multiple-Precision Addition

COMMENTING EXAMPLES

The basic program is:

```
        LDAB    $40
        LDX     #$41
        CLC
ADDW    LDAA    X
        ADCA    $10,X
        STAA    X
        INX
        DECB
        BNE     ADDW
        SWI
```

First, comment the important points. These are typically initializations, data fetches, and processing operations. Don't bother with standard sequences like updating pointers and counters. Remember that names are clearer than numbers, so use them freely.

The new version of the program is:

```
LENG    EQU     $40
NUMB1   EQU     $41
N2OFF   EQU     $10
        LDAB    LENG        COUNT=LENGTH OF NUMBERS
        LDX     #NUMB1      START AT LSBS OF NUMBERS
        CLC
ADDW    LDAA    X           GET 8 BITS OF 1ST NUMBER
        ADCA    N2OFF,X     ADD 8 BITS OF 2ND NUMBER
        STAA    X           STORE SUM IN 1ST NUMBER
        INX
        DECB
        BNE     ADDW
        SWI
```

QUESTIONS FOR COMMENTING

Second, look for any instructions that might not have obvious functions and mark them. Here, the purpose of CLC is to clear the Carry the first time through.

Third, ask yourself whether the comments tell you what you would need to know if you wanted to use the program, e.g.:

1) Where is the program entered? Are there alternative entry points?
2) What parameters are necessary? How and in what form must they be supplied?
3) What operations does the program perform?
4) From where does it get the data?
5) Where does it store the results?
6) What special cases does it consider?
7) What does the program do about errors?
8) How does it exit?

Some of the questions may not be relevant to a particular program and some of the answers may be obvious. Make sure that you won't have to sit down and dissect the program to figure out what the answers are. Remember that too much explanation is just dead wood that you will have to clear out of the way. Is there anything that you would add to or subtract from this listing? If so, go ahead — you are the one who has to feel that the commenting is adequate and reasonable.

```
LENG    EQU     $40
NUMB1   EQU     $41
N2OFF   EQU     $10
        LDAB    LENG        COUNT=LENGTH OF NUMBERS
        LDX     #NUMB1      START AT LSBS OF NUMBERS
        CLC                 CLEAR CARRY FOR LSBS
ADDW    LDAA    X           GET 8 BITS OF 1ST NUMBER
        ADCA    N2OFF,X     ADD 8 BITS OF 2ND NUMBER
        STAA    X           STORE SUM IN 1ST NUMBER
        INX
        DECB
        BNE     ADDW
        SWI
```

Commenting Example 2: Teletypewriter Output

The basic program is:

```
        LDAA    $40
        ASLA
        LDAB    #11
TBIT    STAA    $8008
        JSR     BITD
        RORA
        SEC
        DECB
        BNE     TBIT
        SWI
```

Commenting the important points and adding names gives:

```
NBITS   EQU     11          NUMBER OF BITS IN CHARACTER
TDATA   EQU     $40         TRANSMITTED DATA
TTYPIA  EQU     $8008
        LDAA    $DATA       GET DATA
        ASLA                START BIT = 0
        LDAB    #NBITS      COUNT = NUMBER OF BITS IN CHARACTER
TBIT    STAA    TTYPIA      SEND BIT TO TTY
        JSR     BITD        WAIT 1 BIT TIME
        RORA                GET NEXT BIT
        SEC                 STOP BIT = 1
        DECB
        BNE     TBIT
        SWI
```

Note how easily we could change this program so that it would transfer a whole string of data, starting at the address in locations DPTR and DPTR+1 and ending with an "03" (ASCII ETX) character. Furthermore, let us make the terminal a 30 cps device with one stop bit (we will have to change BITD). Try making the changes before looking at the listing.

```
DPTR    EQU     $40         START OF OUTPUT BUFFER
ENDCH   EQU     3           ENDING CHARACTER = ETX
NBITS   EQU     10          NUMBER OF BITS PER CHARACTER
TRMPIA  EQU     $8008
        LDX     DPTR        GET STARTING ADDRESS
TCHAR   LDAA    X           GET A CHARACTER
        CMPA    #ENDCH      IS IT ENDING CHARACTER?
        BEQ     DONE        YES, DONE
        ASLA
        LDAB    #NBITS      COUNT = NUMBER OF BITS
TBIT    STAA    TRMPIA      SEND BIT TO TTY
        JSR     BITD        WAIT 1 BIT TIME
        RORA                GET NEXT BIT
        SEC                 STOP BIT = 1
        DECB
        BNE     TBIT
        INX
        BRA     TCHAR
DONE    SWI
```

Good comments can make it easy for you to change a program to meet new requirements. For example, try changing the last program so that it:
- Starts each message with ASCII STX (02 hex) followed by a three-digit identification code stored in memory locations 0030 through 0032
- Adds no start or stop bits
- Waits 1 ms between bits
- Transmits 40 characters, starting with the one located at the address in DPTR and DPTR+1
- Ends each message with two consecutive ASCII ETXs (03 hex)

FLOWCHARTS AS DOCUMENTATION

We have already described the use of flowcharts as a design tool in Chapter 13. Flowcharts are also useful in documentation, particularly if:

| HINTS FOR USING FLOWCHARTS |

- They are not so detailed as to be unreadable
- Their decision points are clearly explained and marked
- They include all branches
- They correspond to the actual program listings

Flowcharts are helpful if they give you an overall picture of the program. They are not helpful if they are just as difficult to read as an ordinary listing.

STRUCTURED PROGRAMS AS DOCUMENTATION

Structured programs (see Chapter 13) can also serve as part of the documentation if:
- You describe the purpose of each section in the comments
- You make it clear which statements are included in each conditional or loop structure by using indentation and ending markers
- You make the total structure as simple as possible
- You use a consistent, well-defined language

The structured program can help you to check the logic or to improve it. Furthermore, since the structured program is machine-independent, it can also aid you in implementing the same task on another computer.

MEMORY MAPS

A memory map is simply a list of all the memory assignments in a program. The map allows you to determine the amount of memory needed, the locations of data or subroutines, and the parts of memory not allocated. The map is a handy reference for finding storage locations and entry points and for dividing memory between different routines or programmers. The map will also give you easy access to data and subroutines if you need them in later extensions or in maintenance. Sometimes a graphical map is more helpful than a listing.

A typical map would be:

| TYPICAL MEMORY MAP |

Program Memory

Address	Routine	Purpose
E000-E1FF	INTRPT	INTERRUPT SERVICE ROUTINE FOR KEYBOARD
E200-E240	BRKPT	SOFTWARE INTERRUPT ROUTINE
E241-E250	DELAY	DELAY PROGRAM
E251-E270	DSPLY	DISPLAY CONTROL PROGRAM
E271-E3F7	MAIN	MAIN PROGRAM
E3F8-E3FF		INTERRUPT AND RESET VECTORS

Data Memory

0	NKEYS	NUMBER OF KEYS
1- 2	KPTR	KEYBOARD BUFFER POINTER
3-20	TEMP	TEMPORARY STORAGE
21-60	KBFR	KEYBOARD BUFFER
61-70	DBFR	DISPLAY BUFFER
71-7F	STACK	RAM STACK

The map may also list additional entry points and include a specific description of the unused parts of memory.

PARAMETER AND DEFINITION LISTS

Parameter and definition lists at the start of the program and each subroutine make understanding and changing the program far simpler. The following rules can help:

1) Separate RAM locations, I/O units, parameters, definitions, and memory system constants.

2) Arrange lists alphabetically when possible, with a description of each entry.

RULES FOR DEFINITION LISTS

3) Give each parameter that might change a name and include it in the lists. Such parameters may include timing constants, inputs or codes corresponding to particular keys or functions, control or masking patterns, starting or ending characters, thresholds, etc.

4) Make the memory system constants into a separate list. These constants will include Reset and interrupt service addresses, the starting address of the program, RAM areas, Stack areas, etc.

5) Give each port used by an I/O device a name, even though devices may share ports in the current system. The separation will make expansion or reconfiguration much simpler.

A typical list of definitions is:

TYPICAL DEFINITION LIST

```
* MEMORY SYSTEM CONSTANTS
*
RESET    EQU    $E300    RESET ADDRESS
INTRP    EQU    $E200    INTERRUPT ENTRY
RAMST    EQU    0        START OF DATA STORAGE
STPTR    EQU    $017F    START OF STACK
*
* I/O UNITS
*
DSPLY    EQU    $8006    OUTPUT PIA FOR DISPLAYS
KBDIN    EQU    $8004    INPUT PIA FOR KEYBOARD
KBDOT    EQU    $8006    OUTPUT PIA FOR KEYBOARD
TTYPIA   EQU    $8008    TTY DATA PORT
*
* RAM MEMORY
*
NKEYS    RMB    1        NUMBER OF KEYS
KPTR     RMB    2        KEYBOARD BUFFER POINTER
KBFR     RMB    $40      KEYBOARD INPUT BUFFER
DBFR     RMB    $10      DISPLAY DATA BUFFER
TEMP     RMB    $14      TEMPORARY STORAGE
*
```

* PARAMETERS

GOKEY	EQU	10	IDENTIFICATION OF "GO" KEY
MSCNT	EQU	$7C	COUNT FOR 1 MS DELAY
OPEN	EQU	$0F	PATTERN FOR OPEN KEYS
TBOUNC	EQU	2	DEBOUNCE TIME IN MS
TPULS	EQU	1	PULSE LENGTH FOR DISPLAYS

* DEFINITIONS

ALL1	EQU	$FF	ALL ONES PATTERN
STCON	EQU	$08	START CONVERSION PULSE

Of course, the RAM entries will usually not be in alphabetical order, since the designer must order these so as to minimize the number of address changes required in the program.

LIBRARY ROUTINES

Standard documentation of subroutines will allow you to build up a library of useful programs. The idea is to make these programs as easily accessible as possible. A standard format will allow you or anyone else to see at a glance what the program does. The best procedure is to make up a standard form and use it consistently. Save these programs in a well-organized manner (for example, according to processor, language, and type of program), and you will soon have a useful set. But remember that, without organization and proper documentation, using the library may be more difficult than rewriting the program from scratch. Debugging a system requires a precise understanding of all the effects of each subroutine.

Among the information that you will need in the standard form is:

STANDARD PROGRAM LIBRARY FORMS

- Purpose of the program
- Processor used
- Language used
- Parameters required and how they are passed to the subroutine
- Results produced and how they are passed to the main program
- Number of bytes of memory used
- Number of clock cycles required. This number may be an average or a typical figure, or it may vary widely. Actual execution time will, of course, depend on the processor clock rate.
- Registers affected
- Flags affected
- A typical example
- Error handling
- Special cases
- Documented program listing

If the program is complex, the standard library form should also include a general flowchart or a structured program. As we have mentioned before, a library program is most likely to be useful if it performs a single distinct function in a reasonably general manner.